P9-DCY-923

The
LOST
GIRLS

By the same author

Fiction
Great Eastern Land
Real Life
English Settlement
After Bathing at Baxter's: Stories
Trespass
The Comedy Man
Kept: A Victorian Mystery
Ask Alice
At the Chime of a City Clock
Derby Day
Secondhand Daylight
The Windsor Faction
From the Heart (Amazon Kindle Single)
Wrote for Luck: Stories
Rock and Roll is Life

Non-fiction
A Vain Conceit: British Fiction in the '80s
Other People: Portraits from the Nineties (with Marcus Berkmann)
After the War: The Novel and England Since 1945
Thackeray
Orwell: The Life
On the Corinthian Spirit: The Decline of Amateurism in Sport
Bright Young People: The Rise and Fall of a Generation 1918–1940
What You Didn't Miss: A Book of Literary Parodies
The Prose Factory: Literary Life in England Since 1918
The New Book of Snobs

The
LOST
GIRLS

LOVE & LITERATURE IN
WARTIME LONDON

D.J. TAYLOR

PEGASUS BOOKS
NEW YORK LONDON

THE LOST GIRLS

Pegasus Books, Ltd.
148 West 37th Street, 13th Floor
New York, NY 10018

First Pegasus Books hardcover edition February 2020

Typeset in Garamond Pro by SX Composing DTP, Rayleigh, Essex

ISBN: 978-1-64313-315-7

10 9 8 7 6 5 4 3 2 1

Printed in the United States of America
Distributed by W. W. Norton & Company

For Nicky Loutit

. . . adventurous young women who flitted around London, alighting briefly here and there, and making the best of any random perch on which they happened to descend . . . They were not lost in the Victorian meaning of the term; often they had highly respectable families, with whom they sometimes corresponded; nor was their private behaviour always notably promiscuous. What distinguished them – and used to touch my heart – was their air of waywardness and loneliness. They were courageous, too, and seemed perfectly capable of existing without any thought for past or future.

Peter Quennell's definition of the Lost Girls,
The Wanton Chase (1980)

. . . an empty and destructive girl, mischievous but never lethal on any big scale.

Edmund Wilson on Barbara, *The Fifties* (1985)

. . . she had a look of someone always struggling to go beyond herself – to escape from her social class, the convent where she was educated, into some pagan aesthete world of artists and literary geniuses who could save her.

Stephen Spender on Sonia, *New Selected Journals* (2012)

On Friday I lunched with Christopher and Camilla and dined with Cyril Connolly. His mistress loves me still.

Evelyn Waugh on Lys, *The Letters of Evelyn Waugh* (1980)

. . . a wayward beauty who had been the Egeria to many remarkable men, some of whom she wed.

George Weidenfeld on Janetta, *Remembering My Good Friends: An Autobiography* (1995)

Contents

Part Two

A Note on Names

One mark of the Lost Girls' complex emotional lives is the number of surnames they managed to accumulate. Lys was, successively, Lys Dunlap, Lys Lubbock, Lys Connolly (by deed poll) and Lys Koch. Barbara began life as Barbara Skelton before re-emerging as Barbara Connolly, Barbara Weidenfeld and, ultimately, Barbara Jackson. Sonia was born Sonia Brownell, became Sonia Orwell (very occasionally Sonia Blair) and was briefly known as Sonia Pitt-Rivers. Janetta was at various times addressed as Janetta Woolley, Janetta Slater, Janetta Sinclair-Loutit (by deed poll), Janetta Kee, Janetta Jackson and, finally, as Janetta Parladé, strictly speaking the Marquesa de Apezteguia. To avoid confusion, I have tended to refer to them simply as 'Lys', 'Barbara', 'Sonia' and 'Janetta'.

Monetary Values

For a rough estimate of their contemporary worth, the sums of money mentioned here need, depending on the year involved, to be multiplied by a factor of between 50 and 60. Thus Janetta's £10 monthly allowance from her mother in 1939 would be bring in something over £600 in 2019. The fee for a 3000-word short story published in *Horizon* (6 guineas) in the early 1940s would be around £300. Janetta's wedding present from her father (£50) when she married Hugh Slater would be the equivalent of £2750.

The Cast in September 1939

Lys, aged twenty-one. Clerical worker and part-time model. Known for her exceptional beauty. Married to Ian Lubbock, an aspiring actor.

Janetta, aged seventeen. Recently left her mother's house in the south of France and eloped to Geneva with a much older man.

Barbara, aged twenty-three. Model and *poule de luxe*. Currently living at an address in Kinnerton Street, Mayfair, and at her cottage (the 'Cot') in Hastingleigh, Kent.

Sonia, aged twenty-one. Nicknamed 'the Euston Road Venus'. Involved in a relationship with the (married) artist William Coldstream.

Glur (Joyce Warwick-Evans), aged twenty-two. Former model. Married to the writer and part-time advertising man Peter Quennell.

Angela, aged twenty-seven. Janetta's half-sister. Known for her erratic behaviour. Currently married to the society columnist Patrick Balfour.

Diana, aged twenty-four. Daughter of the proprietor of a printing firm. Involved in a relationship with Cyril Connolly.

Joan, aged twenty-seven. Daughter of Viscount Eyres-Monsell, former First Lord of the Admiralty. Recently married to the journalist John Rayner. Photographer. Friend of Cyril Connolly.

'Anna Kavan' (the pseudonym of Helen Emily Woods), aged thirty-eight. Writer. About to publish her ground-breaking novel, *Asylum Piece*. Travelling abroad, possibly in America.

Cyril Connolly, aged thirty-six. Critic and man of letters. Author of a novel, *The Rock Pool* (1936) and a work of non-fiction, *Enemies of Promise* (1938). Married to Jean Bakewell, an American heiress. Film critic of *Time and Tide*.

George Orwell (pseudonym of Eric Blair), aged thirty-six. Spanish Civil War veteran. Author of four novels, the most recent, *Coming Up for Air*, published in August 1939. Married to Eileen O'Shaughnessy and running a small grocer's shop in Wallington, Hertfordshire.

Evelyn Waugh, aged thirty-five. Novelist and travel writer. Author of – among other novels – *Decline and Fall* (1928), *Vile Bodies* (1930) and *A Handful of Dust* (1934).

Nancy Mitford, aged thirty-four. Eldest of the five daughters of Lord and Lady Redesdale. Author of three novels, including *Highland Fling* (1931). Friend of Waugh and Connolly.

Lucian Freud, aged sixteen. Grandson of Sigmund Freud. Studying at the East Anglian School of Art and Drawing at Dedham, Essex.

Peter Quennell, aged thirty-four. Poet, critic and advertising copywriter. Currently married to his third wife, Glur. Friend of Connolly.

Peter Watson, aged thirty-one. Son of Sir George Watson Bt, margarine millionaire. Art collector and philanthropist.

Feliks Topolski, aged thirty-two. Artist. Of Polish origin, but resident in Britain since 1935. Illustrator of plays by George Bernard Shaw.

Kenneth Sinclair-Loutit, aged twenty-six. Doctor. Spanish Civil War veteran. Married to Thora Silverstone.

Stephen Spender, aged thirty. Poet and critic. Author of *Forward from Liberalism* (1937). Recently divorced from his first wife, Inez Pearn. Member of the Communist Party. Friend of Connolly and Watson.

Brian Howard, aged thirty-four. Dandy, aesthete and former Bright Young Person. Author of a book of poems, *God Save the King* (1931). Currently living in the south of France.

Frances, aged thirty-nine, and Ralph Partridge, aged forty-five. Second-generation members of the Bloomsbury Group. Living at Ham Spray, Wiltshire, formerly the home of Lytton Strachey. Friends of Janetta.

Julian Maclaren-Ross, aged twenty-seven. Author and former vacuum-cleaner salesman. Known for his erratic behaviour. Living in near destitution in Bognor Regis.

Robert Kee, aged nineteen. Studying at Magdalen College, Oxford.

Farouk bin Faud, aged nineteen. King of Egypt.

Introduction:
An Evening in Bedford Square

What, in short, was the point of Connolly? Why did people put up
with frequent moroseness, gloom, open hostility? Why, if he were
about in the neighbourhood, did I always take steps to get hold
of him? The question is hard to answer. The fact remains that I
did . . .

Anthony Powell, *Infants of the Spring* (1976)

It is just past seven o'clock on a rainy evening in the early part of
September 1942 and twilight is falling over the Bloomsbury
pavements. Here in the fourth year of war, Bedford Square is not
looking its best. The railings from the vast private garden in its centre
have been taken away, supposedly to be made into Spitfires, and half-
a-dozen allotments have risen to displace the lawn on the northernmost
side. Over on the western quadrant comes direct evidence of armed
conflict: a bomb crater dating back to the early part of the Blitz and
still not filled in, and several piles of rubble, so ancient now that there
are knots of wild flowers growing out of the bare earth. Two or three
of the houses are derelict, with boarded-up windows and notices
tacked to the front doors advising alternative arrangements for post.
The air-raid wardens are on the prowl – there is a wardens' post over

1

on the corner of Gower Street – and all over the square the soft light gleaming from the frontages is being extinguished as the blackout curtains go up.

Reaching the square's north-eastern corner, on her way down Gower Street from the Underground station at Euston Square, Naomi stops to take her bearings. She is less than familiar with this part of the capital, or indeed with any part of it beyond the square mile or so around London Wall, where she works as a copy-typist for a firm of veneer and inlay importers. She is a tall, nervous-looking, red-haired girl in her very early twenties, and rather nonplussed at the prospect of the social experience that lies before her. Nevertheless, in the pocket of her Aquascutum mackintosh is a gilt-edged invitation card on which has been printed the words MR CYRIL CONNOLLY: HORIZON: AT HOME, the day's date and an address, and Naomi is determined to put it to good use. Truth to tell, Naomi is not quite sure why she has come in search of the flat in Bedford Square, where Mr Cyril Connolly is at home, rather than going back to her parents' house in Shepperton. George, an apprentice compositor for the printing firm that Mr Connolly employs, and the source of the invitation, had said it would be a lark and that afterwards they could go and have supper at a Lyons. But now George has gone down with influenza, leaving Naomi to make the journey on her own.

Why is she here? Despite hailing from Shepperton, where such things as literary parties are unheard of, and working for the veneer and inlay importers at London Wall, Naomi, always keen on 'reading' and adventurous in her tastes, has heard of Cyril Connolly. There has been mention of him at the book circle she attends on Tuesday evenings above a shop in the high street. She has seen yellow-jacketed copies of *Horizon*, the literary magazine he conducts, at the railway station bookstalls next to the piles of *Lilliput*, *Picture Post* and the *Strand Magazine*. And in Shepperton public library she discovered a book he had written about the snares and pitfalls that lay in wait for young writers – snares and pitfalls that did not seem so very terrible to Naomi, who had been educated at the local secondary school and secretarial college, but were doubtless much worse when, like Mr Connolly, you had been to Eton and Balliol College, Oxford. The one photograph she has ever seen of him showed a fat, jowly man with a receding hairline and an oddly grumpy expression. All the same, Naomi is prepared to concede that over him, and his magazine, and his invitation card, and the tall houses of Bedford Square looming beneath the darkening sky, hangs an undeniable scent of glamour.

Number 49 Bedford Square, on one of whose upper floors Mr Connolly and *Horizon* are at home, is on the southern side. There are one or two people disappearing through its front door, a faint noise of conversation borne on the breeze. Suddenly, all the conviction with which Naomi stepped off the Underground train at Euston Square and marched down Gower Street with her face angled against the rain dwindles away to nothing. This, after all, is Bloomsbury, rumour of whose depravities and moral laxness has carried even as far as Shepperton, and here she is, wearing an Aquascutum mackintosh, a calf-length floral skirt and a pair of the housemaid's shoes that her mother thinks 'sensible' for daily use, carrying a bottle of red Algerian wine that turned out to be the only vintage procurable at the shop next to the Underground station, and with strict instructions from her mother to be home by ten. For a moment her courage fails her – in that flat there will be girls with half-crown accents and dresses that stop at the knee, of the kind she sometimes sees coming out of the Piccadilly restaurants, not to mention Mr Connolly and his clever friends; she will be exposed and ridiculed for having the cheek to infiltrate this citadel of culture when she should have been at home in Shepperton eating warmed-up shepherd's pie and listening to *It's That Man Again* on the radio. Then, for some reason, her sense of resolve renews itself and she crosses the road, skips past the skidding army lorry that threatens to swallow her up, climbs the stairs and arrives, rather flushed and short of breath, in the open doorway.

Curiously, there is no one here except a formidably good-looking girl a year or two older than herself with a high-pitched voice and a Veronica Lake hairdo who shakes her hand and relieves her of the Algerian red. 'It's awfully kind of you to come bearing gifts,' she says, waving her hand at an occasional table just inside the door, 'but we've rather a lot already.' And sure enough the table is crammed with what, even to Naomi's amateur eye, can be identified as expensive bottles of claret and burgundy of a kind no longer available in shops. Naomi tries to explain about George and his influenza and the transferred invitation, but suddenly a tall, wavy-haired man in a grey suit and what looks like a Charvet tie has materialised between them, put one hand on the other girl's shoulder and demanded of her in a high, stuttering voice: 'My dear, who is this y-young person? She looks as if she should s-s-scarcely be allowed out. We shall have her p-p-parents accusing Cyril of spiriting her away for *immoral purposes*, and then where shall we be?' Naomi is ready to shrink back in terror at this apparition, but the girl merely gives him an affectionate shove that sends him faltering back into the flat. 'You mustn't mind Brian,' she says. 'He's a sweetie really, but he's just been stood up by his boyfriend and that always puts him in a mood. Now do come in and hang up your things.'

Obediently, Naomi attaches her mackintosh to one of the pegs in the hallway and proceeds in the direction of the noise. This is coming from a large, elegant space, which her mother would probably call a parlour but which she has an idea is more properly defined as a drawing room. Here music is playing from a gramophone and twenty or thirty people are talking at the tops of their voices. Cigarette smoke hangs in dense clouds above their heads. Another girl hands her a glass of wine and she realises that the fear instilled in her by the sight of Brian, who is what her father would call a nancy boy, has been replaced by simple curiosity. Looking round the room she sees that Connolly is standing with one elbow on a mantelpiece strewn with invitation cards, talking to a tall man with a toothbrush moustache who resembles an elongated version of Charlie Chaplin. With his bow tie, his tweed jacket and a pair of flannels that are starting to go at the knee, Connolly, she thinks, looks like a teacher in a film set in a boys' private school. The women, oddly enough, are not as she imagined them. Several of them, for example, are wearing trousers, and at least one – tray of drinks in hand, and long, untamed hair falling into her eyes – is walking around the room without her shoes on. She notices that they talk to each other in drawling voices and have a habit of laughing at things that do not immediately seem funny. None of them – this is to be expected, she knows – takes the slightest interest in her.

There are other guests flooding into the room now. A short, fat person in a bowler hat who looks already as if he has had too much to drink. A lean, blue-suited man with a quiff of blond forelock who says something to Connolly and is crossly rebuked. Beyond them, a sulky-looking woman with poodle-cut hair done up in kirby grips stands in the doorway for a moment, stares furiously around her for a second as if she hates the room and everyone in it and herself for being dragged into its devitalising orbit, and then disappears.

Still, Naomi realises, no one has spoken to her or so much as noticed the fact of her existence. The feeling that she has wandered into a play whose script has been made available to everyone except herself is about to become embarrassing, when one of the women handing round drinks decides to take pity on her. Her name, she volunteers, is Liza; she works part-time in the *Horizon* office, which is not here in Bedford Square but around the corner in Lansdowne Terrace, and she is happy to explain who the people in the room are and their connection to Connolly. For example, the man with the stammer who terrified her in the doorway is called Brian Howard and, although one of Connolly's oldest friends, rather a 'scamp'. The elongated version of Charlie Chaplin is George Orwell, a frequent contributor to the magazine, whose work Connolly and 'Peter', the magazine's proprietor, revere. The man with the unruly hair is Peter Quennell, who lodges in the attic, and Barbara, she of the poodle-cut and the furious stare who declined to come into the room, is the girl who lives with him there, and of whom Connolly strongly disapproves. And Naomi wonders what her father, who is puritanically minded, would make of parties fuelled by what is presumably black-market claret, attended by 'scamps' in Charvet ties who have been stood up by their boyfriends and men who live with their girls in the room upstairs.

Liza proves unexpectedly talkative: Naomi suspects that she is pleased to have an audience. And so she chatters on – rather, Naomi thinks, like a tour-guide escorting a group of visitors around a museum. The man in the tropical coat with the swordstick clasped beneath his arm is a writer called Maclaren-Ross, whom Connolly admires but thinks is too often liable to cause trouble. The sharp-faced boy is Lucian, one of the magazine's artistic discoveries, of whose grandfather – and here Liza gives a little laugh – Naomi may have heard. Naomi hasn't. Neither, to her chagrin, has she heard of the fat man in the bowler hat, who is called Evelyn Waugh and apparently 'terribly famous'. But queerly enough – or perhaps not so queerly, female solidarity being what it is – it is the women to whom her eye invariably returns. None of them, she deduces, is much older than she is herself. There are three in particular: the one who welcomed her at the door – clearly in charge of the proceedings, she thinks, as she keeps coming in to survey the room and make sure that people's glasses are filled – the one with the helmet of brown hair that half covers her face, and a third girl, plumper than the others and slightly more conventionally dressed, who is having a loud argument with the boy named Lucian about something called significant form. Liza explains that the first girl – Connolly's lady-friend, it turns out, although still apparently married to a man called Ian – is called Lys Lubbock, pronounced 'Lease', that the one talking to Lucian is Sonia Brownell – sometimes jokingly referred to as the

'Euston Road Venus' – and the one with bare, brown feet is Janetta (her surname for some reason currently in doubt), and that all of them are so devoted to Connolly that they have been known to bring him their ration books. And Naomi wonders why this dumpy, middle-aged man, who reminds her of the churchwarden bringing round the collection plate on Sunday mornings, should inspire such regard among a group of women who, she decides, really ought to be seated in restaurants overlooking the Pacific Ocean with Ronald Colman and Gregory Peck.

'There's gin in the other room if you want some,' says Liza, who clearly intends to make an evening of it, but Naomi shakes her head, for the glass and a half of red wine she has drunk has gone to her head, the clock on the wall above the mantelpiece a foot or two beyond Connolly's head is showing ten to nine, and it is a long way back to Shepperton. Unhooking her mackintosh – which in her absence has acquired a streak of cigarette ash running down one of the arms – from its peg, she sees that Lys is standing in the doorway, arms crossed over her chest, examining Connolly with a look of unfeigned admiration, like a mother watching a small child take its first tottering steps across a carpet.

Outside the rain has stopped and the square is black as pitch: a wind has got up and is crazing the tops of the trees in the wild garden. The ARP wardens have all gone away. She reaches the small semi-detached house in Shepperton at three minutes past ten, to be soundly scolded by her mother, told that George is feeling better and has telephoned to ask after her, and sent upstairs with a cup of cocoa to the bedroom she shares with her younger sister. Gladys, who is seventeen and works in a munitions factory, is already in bed with her face shiny with cold cream and her hair done up in curl-papers. 'Did you have a nice time?' she asks – a bit sleepily – as Naomi (who has almost resolved to buy herself a pair of trousers, whatever her mother may say) steps out of her shoes and divests herself of the calf-length floral skirt. 'Very interesting,' Naomi says, with the memory of Connolly, Lys, Brian and the others rampaging through her head. 'Not really your kind of thing, though.'

None of this happened. Naomi, George, Gladys, the semi-detached house at Shepperton – none of them exists. Neither, as described, does the party at 49 Bedford Square on that damp September night in 1942. On the other hand, something very like it with most of the same personnel took place dozens of times in the 1940s, and while there is no absolute proof that Orwell, Waugh, Quennell, Lucian Freud, Dylan Thomas (another *Horizon* habitué) and Julian Maclaren-Ross ever stood together on Connolly's drawing-room carpet in Bedford Square, there is every chance that they did. Connolly, it scarcely needs saying, was a convivial man, who enjoyed having his friends around him and spent much of his time blurring the distinction between his personal and professional life. And so the history of *Horizon* is as much about parties and luncheons, drinks at the Ritz Bar and the Café Royal, as it is about earnest editorial conferences and words being put on paper. But although long stretches of it are concerned with his habits, achievements and influence, this is not a book about Cyril Connolly. Rather, it is a study of the women who formed a substantial part of his circle during the Second World War and the years that followed it, the women who fizzed in his slipstream, the women whom at various times he employed, fell in love with and very often schemed to marry, and over whom he cast a spell so prodigious that when he died, over three decades later, they came in relays to sorrow over his hospital bed.

A study of the *women*. Plenty of books have been written about Connolly in the four-and-a-half decades since his death: two full-length biographies, histories of *Horizon*, editions of his journals and his journalism, to add to the reissues of his one indisputable master-piece, *Enemies of Promise*. Only Evelyn Waugh and George Orwell, among his immediate contemporaries, have done better. Much less attention has been paid to Barbara, Lys, Sonia, Janetta and the other girls who during the 1940s and in varying degrees after it were the handmaidens at his court. There are obvious reasons for this. Connolly was at the centre of the world that sustained him. *Horizon* was his creation, his project, his personal mission, a vehicle for writers who, with certain exceptions, were cut from his own cloth, which is to say men of the same age and the same social and intellectual background. Of the ninety or so contributors brought together in *The Golden Horizon* (1953), the anthology in which Connolly celebrated the best of the magazine's ten-year crop, exactly seven were women. He was, in terms of the rarefied landscape through which he moved, a titanic figure, to be flattered, deferred to and appeased: a target for ridicule and spiteful gossip, perhaps, but also a grand literary panjandrum in a world where grand literary panjandrums mattered. Evelyn Waugh, to take an obvious example of the deeply ambiguous terms on which it was possible to live with Connolly, might have spent twenty years exchanging injurious tittle-tattle about him with Nancy Mitford, but no one was more conscious than Waugh of the debt he owed him or the respect with which he ought to be treated.

Much of the literary history of the 1940s, consequently, consists of watching Connolly in action: gliding from party to party, from romantic conquest to romantic conquest, from high profile commission to high profile commission. It is easy enough, in the course of this grand *promenade*, to miss the women, but they are always there: arranging Connolly's life for him, doing his chores, typing his letters, opening his mail, conciliating his whims and occasionally risking his serious displeasure by striking out on paths of their own. What gives Barbara, Lys, Sonia, Janetta and the others their fascination is, on the one hand, the pungency of their individual personalities – they were strong-minded, intelligent women who for the most part lived their lives as they chose – and, on the other, the things they represent. From one angle they are a way into a certain kind of war-era bohemian life in which glamour and sophistication and something very close to poverty are inextricably combined, where the dinner at the fashionable restaurant gives way to the sleepless night in the unheated bedsitting room, where boyfriend *a* is a peer of the realm while boyfriend *b* is a penniless painter. A world, more to the point, of recklessness and unreliable contraception, where love affairs have a habit of ending in the abortionist's clinic. From another, they exemplify a unique moment in twentieth-century British social history in which a tiny group of upper-middle-class young women broke free from the restrictions of their upbringing and achieved a degree of personal freedom that would have been unknown to the generation before them. Naturally these liberties came at a cost, and personal fulfilment and public success were very often accompanied by deeply felt private hurt.

All these journeys – individual and communal – were given greater potency by the fact that they took place in wartime and were pursued – sometimes literally – to an accompaniment of falling bombs and the slither of telegrams falling through the letterbox. 'For the undamaged survivors, the 1940s were a magical period', a woman at large in wartime London once affectionately recalled, but again the survival came at a cost; sometimes the damage could take years to declare itself. If there is another factor that unites Lys, Barbara, Sonia, Janetta and their friends it is the sense of personal trauma: of promising relationships cut short by circumstance; of lives not falling into the comfortable grooves that the people living them anticipated; of freedom, self-reliance and self-determination, but also vulnerability, isolation, pain and loss. Peter Quennell, who christened them 'the lost girls', admired their courage and their tenacity while at the same time noting their detachment and the intensely precarious nature of their lives.

And then there is the question of milieu, background and association. Outwardly conventional upper-middle-class young women the majority of the Lost Girls may have been, but their trajectories reach out to encompass vast stretches of mid-century experience.

The last decades of the Raj; the late thirties art world; *haute couture*; second-generation Bloomsbury; wartime Cairo; left-wing politics – in each of these very different worlds, their modishly shod feet left an indelible print. Finally, there are the careers they fashion after the wartime world of *Horizon*, Connolly's parties and bomb-cratered streets is over. In time, the Lost Girls will go on to write and appear in novels, have affairs with dukes, feature in celebrity divorce cases and – in the case of Sonia – marry one of the most celebrated writers of the whole twentieth century.

For the moment all this lies in the future. But its origins can be found here in the Bedford Square drawing room in the early years of the Second World War, as the plumes of cigarette smoke rise to the ceiling, the black-market wine is brought out from its hiding place, Connolly's contributors carouse and, from their various vantage points – from brocaded sofas or high-backed chairs or treading barefoot across the carpet – the Lost Girls look on.

Part One

1.

The Wanton Chase

To be a young man these days. What wouldn't I give for that! Think of the time they have. No chaperones; bachelor girls with flats and latchkeys. People say that the modern girl knows how to look after herself. I fancy that's just what she does know . . .

Alec Waugh, *"Sir," She Said* (1930)

Of all the phantom party-goers assembled in Cyril Connolly's Bedford Square drawing room on that September evening in 1942, the guest most familiar with Lost Girl routines was Peter Quennell. Even at this early stage, with the third year of the war only just complete, Quennell could have happily taken on the task of compiling a full-scale gazetteer of their haunts, homes and affiliations. It was not merely that, in the shape of his third wife Glur, he was precariously married to one Lost Girl, or that, in the form of Connolly's fellow-lodger Barbara Skelton, he was in hot pursuit of another. It was simply that the life he led – vagrant, rootless, opportunistic – was almost expressly designed to place him in their company. The territory he stalked – the room in someone's flat, the early evening drink in the Ritz Bar, the Bloomsbury party – was theirs, and most of his complicated social existence was spent in a world which they themselves inhabited. Several of Connolly's biographers have noted his role as a kind of one-man introduction service, guiding his friend into the orbit of women he would later live with, marry or fruitlessly pursue. It was Quennell, after all, who had introduced Connolly to Lys, just as a month or two later he had introduced him to Barbara. Both encounters would turn out to have a serious impact on Connolly's ever more convoluted emotional life.

Even more significant was Quennell's practical experience of what a relationship with a Lost Girl could be like when the chips were down. The letters he exchanged with Barbara around the time they moved into the Bedford Square attic can make melancholy reading. 'I have been hoping I might get a letter from you,' runs a desperate entreaty from sometime in early 1942. 'Naturally I don't deserve one, but it would have been nice.' An earlier note conveys all the pained displeasure of the prospectively abandoned. 'WHAT's this about going to the country and never wanting to see me again?' And then there is the letter sent from Quennell's desk at the Ministry of Economic Warfare on New Year's Day 1943, addressed to 'Skeltie darling' and acknowledging the dismal truth that 'Writing to you is like masturbation – it produces a feeling of relief but ultimately does no good. Up to a point I can enjoy myself without you, but – *why* I don't quite know – you have become a part (tho' often an uncomfortable part) of my life, & (in spite of all my good resolutions) I find myself missing you . . .' If it was hell to live with Barbara, who was quite capable of throwing the kitchen crockery about when roused, then not living with her could be even worse. Quennell's romantic life in the early 1940s is, consequently, hedged about with deep unease, the awareness that what he wanted made him miserable barbed by a lurking suspicion that not having it would make him more miserable still.

Forty years later, in one of the volumes of discreet and gentlemanly memoirs with which he beguiled his old age – books so discreet and gentlemanly that much of the female cast appears under pseudonyms – Quennell sat down to conceptualise the tiny part of the wartime

demographic he had spent so much of his time observing four decades before. The Lost Girls, he decided, were 'adventurous young
women who flitted around London, alighting briefly here and there,
and making the best of any random perch on which they happened
to descend'. Almost immediately, though, there were distinctions to
be drawn. Quennell's wandering female tribe were not 'lost' in the
Victorian sense of the word – that is, seduced, abandoned and thrown
out of doors by outraged parents. Most of them, he concedes, came
from highly respectable families with whom they kept intermittently
in touch and from whom they could solicit funds when the going got
tough. Neither, at least in the context of the notoriously rackety
1940s, were their private lives particularly dissipated. 'What distinguished them – and used to touch my heart – was their air of
waywardness and loneliness.' They were 'courageous', Quennell
thought, living in the moment, 'perfectly capable of existing without
any thought for past or future'.

Of all the accounts of Lys, Barbara, Sonia, Janetta and their
satellites, this is the one that comes closest to establishing what they
were really like, the air that they carried around with them, the
shimmer of the personalities on display, and the curious sense of
detachment that attends their progress through the drawing rooms
and basements of wartime Bloomsbury. In her portrait of Sonia,
Hilary Spurling suggests of the women who helped out at *Horizon*,
answered Cyril's letters and hovered over his engagement diary that
'all of them were in some sense sports from the upper-middle-class
typing pool, freelancing energetically between the constraints of
school and marriage'. But this, you suspect, is to domesticate them,
to impose a degree of social homogeneity that did not in the end
exist, and to ignore some of the factors that both gave them their
individual sheen and brought them together as a distinctive social
unit. The Second World War drew thousands of young women to
London to work in government offices or factories, to live in hostels
or furnished flats, spend their leisure hours in pubs and cheap

restaurants and chase an existence that their mothers' generation would have thought inconceivable. The novels of the 1940s are full of them – pale, brightly lipsticked Sheila in Monica Dickens's *The Fancy* (1943), say, who escapes the confines of her Home Counties upbringing for a job in munitions and an affair with a married man. But Sheila, for all her determination to carve out a life of her own, is not a Lost Girl. Theirs was a far more exclusive status, in which a whole host of factors, ranging from looks to social connection, combined to produce a figure who is more or less unique.

What were a Lost Girl's defining characteristics? How, at a distance of nearly eighty years, can we identify her and separate her from the crowd? One obvious factor was her date of birth. Most Lost Girls tend to have born at around the time of the First World War. Angela Culme-Seymour (b. 1912) was one of the more senior members; Janetta (b. 1921) the most junior. Another factor was her startling – at times almost outrageous – beauty. '*Mais que tu as devenue belle*,' one of Sonia's early boyfriends is supposed to have told her. A man briefly entangled with Barbara in the 1950s noted that 'to catch her eye was more or less to enter into a conspiracy'. The normally dispassionate Frances Partridge thought that Janetta had 'the most beautiful female body I have ever seen'.

These attractions were difficult to keep under wraps. The Lost Girl's portrait appeared in *Vogue*. She modelled dresses for celebrated couturiers such as Schiaparelli or Norman Hartnell. She appeared in fashion magazines endorsing hand and face cream. To beauty could be added, for the most part, high intelligence, which had, by and large, little formal grounding. Although there were brief appearances at art schools and technical colleges, no Lost Girl seems to have attended a university or indeed stayed in education much beyond her mid-teens, and such learning as she acquired tended to be picked up on the hoof: a friend recalled Sonia gambolling around Connolly like a Labrador puppy as they walked down a street together, rapturously absorbing each new pronouncement that he let fall. For all her sulks and sarcasm, Barbara was remembered as, deep down, possessing an odd streak of seriousness, a half-buried intellectual twist that allowed her to combine a relish for causing trouble for its own sake with a genuine shyness, uncertainty and eagerness to learn.

In most cases these deficiencies were down to a fractured and oppressive family life that the majority of Lost Girls spent their adolescence scheming to escape. If only Lys was a bona-fide orphan, then the others tended to be the product of one-parent families in difficult circumstances, in some cases sent prematurely into the world by relatives with whom they had dramatically fallen out. Barbara left home to live in a YWCA hostel at the tender age of fifteen. The newly liberated Janetta could be found lodging in a room on the upper floor of a house owned by her brother-in-law and attending Chelsea Polytechnic. Standards of parental responsibility were not high. Angela remembered her mother telling her when she was in her mid-teens that 'From now on you must be free to do anything you want.' What sort of thing? her daughter innocently wondered. 'Well, when you're older, you must have lovers. You're so pretty you should have heaps of them.'

None of this was calculated to encourage a settled existence or a hankering for conventional life. Freedom and the lack of parental constraint gave the Lost Girls a welcome sense of independence, but it also made them vulnerable, pliable, easy prey for less than scrupulous older men. Outward self-confidence very often disguised a deep-rooted naivety, an inability to judge the people they knocked up against or the codes by which they operated. Asked why, at the age of seventeen, she had allowed herself to be seduced by a man old enough to be her father, Janetta is supposed to have answered that she assumed it was 'what one did'.

But there was another vital point of connection that marked out the Lost Girl hurrying across the Bloomsbury square or being stood lunch by some rapt admirer at the Café Royal from the thousands of other young women at large in wartime London. This was the kind of man with whom she associated, might live with or, in exceptional circumstances, marry. The social catchment area from which Lost Girls drew their significant others was by no means extensive. Although there were occasional interludes with men met in government offices, or rich admirers who might fall into the category of 'sugar daddy', the Lost Girl's boyfriend tended to be a writer, an artist or at any rate a man who existed on the fringe of these interconnected worlds. So comparatively restricted was the talent pool, that they were very often the same men. At least three of the principal Lost Girls had affairs with Arthur Koestler. All four are thought at some point in their careers to have shared a bed with Lucian Freud. Two of them married the millionaire physicist Derek Jackson.

Freud, still in his teens when he began his lady-killing progress, was very much an exception to the standard protocols of Lost Girl romance. Most Lost Girls came from homes whose male parents were either absent, surrogate or disliked. If it overstates the case to suggest that Barbara, Lys, Sonia and their friends were in search of father figures to fill the emotional gaps that had yawned through their childhoods, then it is a fact that most Lost Girls' boyfriends were ten or even fifteen years older than their companions at the Ritz Bar or the Café Royal. Naturally, much of this imbalance was down to demographics, specifically the absence from their social or professional circles of young men: the Lost Girl, after all, tended to take possession of her London bedsit at a time when most of her male contemporaries were still at school or university. But there is still a sense of their looking upwards, wanting to acquire knowledge and expertise from practised operators in the generation above. An added complication was that nearly all of these came with baggage – abandoned wives, former mistresses who might make trouble, pending divorce cases, children needing financial support. None of this made for an easy ride.

As for the attitude that they brought to these relationships, pragmatism, often extending to an outright fatalism – the sense of things being done because it was expected they should happen – abounded. There was a general feeling that the present should be grasped at, while the future could take care of itself. The Bloomsbury diarist Frances Partridge recalled Janetta noting of her first wedding that it was 'an unimportant ceremony, and will remain so until I want a divorce'. Impulsive, affectionate and at times dangerously alluring, the Lost Girl could sometimes be spoilt, unpredictable and uncomfortably farouche. The records of her progress through wartime bohemia are crammed with split-second desertions, lightning throwings-over, affections transferred from one man to another at the drop of a Cartier cigarette case. It was Barbara, reproached by one of her boyfriends for the rows, suspicion and ill-feeling that characterised their relationship, who replied, without apparent irony, 'I *like* things to be difficult.'

Most social historians, handed evidence of a group of young people behaving in an unusual way, tend to diagnose the emergence of a youth cult. With the Lost Girls, this kind of categorisation would be a mistake. As well as being numerically insignificant, they were also narrowly exclusive. Even if it could be proved to exist, the club they were a part of was distinguished not by its membership rules or admission fees but by much less tangible prescriptions of dress, style and demeanour. Unlike most youth cults they did not propagandise their activities, and the publicity they attracted came long after the world they diffidently ornamented had ceased to function. All the same, it is impossible to follow Barbara's impulsive trail through the South Kensington bedsits for very long without suspecting that, in however extreme a form, she is a manifestation of a sociological process that had been going on for upwards of sixty years: the process by which young women from middle- and upper-class families began to break away from the circumstances of their upbringing, go out into the world and forge some kind of life for themselves – a life, more to the point, that could be lived on their own terms and among companions of their own choosing.

Anxieties about the greater freedom allowed to young women and the increasing licentiousness of their behaviour had been a subject of public debate on both sides of the Atlantic since at least the mid-Victorian era. In fact, the first use of term 'Lost Girls' dates from as far back as 1889, when a Mrs J. G. Fraser wrote an article in an American magazine called the *Congregationalist* entitled 'Our Lost Girls: A Mother Sadly Regrets that She Can Not Have the Training of Her Daughter' and lamenting the fact that modern adolescents seemed more interested in exchanging visits with their friends than the solace of family life. In Mrs Fraser's bewildered wake, the lexicon of aberrant teenage behaviour steadily expanded its range. 'Flappers', 'bachelor girls' and their American cousins the 'bachelorettes', 'New Women', 'the Modern Girl' – each of these new-fangled social categorisations seemed to offer a kind of moral quicksand on which the unwary turn-of-the-century young woman was ripe to founder. The culprit, most conservative commentators agreed, was modernity itself: the economic developments that encouraged young women to seek employment rather than sitting at home; the movement for women's education; the blandishments of a burgeoning world of popular entertainment that valued theatre and cinema above what were increasingly seen as the quaint consolations of the familial hearth.

Nearly all these social groupings were so broadly defined as to call most of the judgements that could be made about the women who reposed in them seriously into question. 'Flapper' had originally been a late Victorian term for an underage prostitute. By the early 1900s it had become generalised to the point of vagueness. In Ian Hay's best-selling Edwardian novel *Pip: A Romance of Youth* (1907), for example, a 'flapper' is simply a gawky teenage girl not yet launched into society, frivolous, inexperienced and highly impressionable. Thus, young Miss Elsie Innes, introduced to its hero a few months before she has put her hair up, is described as being 'in the last stages of what slangy young men call "flapperdom"'. Later, at a cricketing house party, one of the guests is 'a solitary "flapper" of fifteen, who, untrammelled as yet by fear of Mrs Grundy, was having the time of her life with the two callowest members of the Eleven'. In much the same way, W. N. P. Barbellion's *The Journal of a Disappointed Man* (1919) has a diary entry from 1908 recording a beach-side encounter with 'a pretty flapper in a pink sunbonnet'. Come the post-war era, the definition had grown broader still, to the point where almost any woman under the age of thirty who went to parties or led a vaguely pleasurable life could be drawn into its catchment area. A *Punch* cartoon from the early 1930s, for example, shows a 'very young flapper' exulting in the atmosphere of a room where several young people are frenziedly dancing the Charleston, while a 'mature ditto' advises that she 'should have seen the cocktail parties of the dear old Twenties'.

None of this, clearly, has much to do with Barbara, Sonia and their friends. The 'Bachelor Girl', on the other hand, who turns up in English fiction at about the time of the Great War, offers a much sharper twist on the ancestral thread. Voluable, hard-headed and independent-minded, the heroine of Leonard Merrick's short story 'The Tale that Wouldn't Do' (1918) is characterised as 'an extraordinarily nice girl, with seventeen faces. She changes them while she talks . . . If she didn't laugh at orange blossoms, you might approve her.' As well as disapproving of marriage, loathing her more domestically minded opposite number the 'Chiffon Girl', and believing that she can live on equal non-sexual terms with male 'chums', the Bachelor Girl has marked bohemian tendencies ('I was a kid,' she nonchalantly explains, 'about nineteen – just beginning to paint.') For her, the ideal life consists of freedom from parental constraints, drawing lessons in Parisian art schools and the chance to wear slightly unusual clothes.

Nothing, of course, is quite so relative as emancipation: to the girls of the 1940s magazine office the degree of freedom obtained by their Edwardian predecessors would have seemed scarcely worth the having. Nonetheless, however limited the concessions they may have won from disapproving parents, their very existence was enough to remind the people who observed them in action just how much the world was changing. Musing on the early life of T. S. Eliot's first wife Vivienne Haigh-Wood (b. 1888), for example, Anthony Powell immediately marked her down as 'one of those slightly (only very slightly) "liberated" girls, mildly highbrow, of immediately pre-first war period'. As a small boy – Powell was born in 1905 – he could actually remember having witnessed some of them at large in Edwardian society and 'the great to-do made about their drinking and smoking. The fact that, even as a child, one was aware of the slight difference they represented.'

If the newly emancipated middle-class girl had begun to make her presence felt in the drawing rooms of the pre-1914 era, then the Great War propelled her out into the world at large. Urgently in demand to nurse wounded soldiers, staff canteens or otherwise assist the war effort, hundreds of thousands of young women who would previously have filled in the time between school and marriage with low-grade clerical work found themselves living away from home in conditions which even the most vigilant parent would have been hard pressed to supervise. As a disillusioned paterfamilias in Alec Waugh's *"Sir," She Said* (1930) grimly puts it:

'Forty years ago a father had the running of his daughter's life. To-day she runs her own. You haven't got to find eligible young men for her. It's she who'll find ineligible ones for you. We used to talk about the latchkey as being the symbol of emancipation. It isn't now. It's a cheque-book that's the symbol. As soon as a girl's got a banking account she's free, and most of them have it. It's the war that did it. The war telescoped events. A process that should have taken fifty years got compressed into a third of a decade. Parental authority had to go when girls were W.A.A.C.S. and W.R.E.N.S. working at canteens, in camps, driving lorries, keeping their own hours. You couldn't keep any control over their acquaintances then. You just didn't know what they were doing. When the war was over they weren't going to give up that freedom.'

Tracking the adventures of two sisters named Julia and Melanie Terance around post-war London, Waugh's novel might be described as a study of the consequences of female emancipation. Twenty-something Julia works in a Mayfair dress shop and inhabits her own flat. Late teenage Melanie, though still living at home, enjoys an independent lifestyle, which consists of overspending her allowance, gadding about in restaurants and nightclubs, and coming home at three o'clock in the morning. As for their romantic entanglements, the elder sister is secretly conducting an affair with a married man, while the younger, over whose apparent indiscretions Julia dutifully frets, marries a highly suitable American after a whirlwind romance. Over both their heads hangs the warning of the double standard, which allows men to amuse themselves while ostracising women thought to have behaved badly, and the misery of their mother, who sadly concludes that 'The modern daughter ran her own life . . . Nor was there any real, compensating comradeship. Girls did not want mothers who would be mistaken for their sisters.'

Julia and Melanie are not Lost Girls. However liberated they may seem to a disapproving older generation, their ambitions are only a slight variation on existing arrangements. At bottom, all they really want is true love and a conventional upper-middle-class marriage: the life their mother leads but with just a little more glamour and shine, a little more personal fulfilment and self-determination. Neither do they suffer from the unsettled domestic background, with its unremitting catalogue of deaths, desertions and problematic second marriages that was the Great War's legacy to post-war family life and which sent many a genuine Lost Girl on her way. Consider, for example, the early career of Lady Violet Pakenham, whose father, the 5th Earl of Longford, died at Gallipoli when she was three. The sixth child of a seven-strong brood, Lady Violet was brought up with her younger sister Julia according to the prescriptions of her mother's Victorian girlhood. But in the era of jazz, nightclubs and freak parties, motherly vigilance could only go so far. If an annual allowance of £400, courtesy of a paternal trust fund, brought her daughter a measure of independence, then the discovery that Lady Longford was terminally ill could only widen the gap. By her early twenties, Violet had solved the problem of parental disapproval by continuing to live at home but assuming that her mother's prohibitions had no bearing on the rackety social life that she now began to pursue.

Freed from parental shackles, the twenty-one-year-old girl set about sampling London nightlife. While there were invitations to debutante dances and hunt balls, in keeping with her status as an earl's daughter, there were also excursions to Soho clubs and bottle parties given by people with whom earls' daughters rarely came into contact. There was a memorable evening around this time when she and her current boyfriend pooled invites to see how many entertainments they could attend by dawn: the total came to eleven. By day Lady Violet might be found at such upmarket retreats as the Savoy Grill or the Berkeley Hotel, but her after-hours haunts – the Bag O'Nails, say, or the notorious '43 in Gerrard Street – were unrepentantly louche. A thinly disguised version of the latter is, after all, the setting for Sebastian Flyte and Charles Ryder's drunken night out in Evelyn Waugh's *Brideshead Revisited* (1945). Meanwhile, relatives looked disbelievingly on. Her elder sister Mary, an art student in whose studio Violet had posed naked, remarked that 'she went to nightclubs and bars and seemed to have done anything she chose'. By 1933, with her mother dead, she was living at the family home in Rutland Gate with two of her sisters, entirely free from adult supervision. None of this makes Lady Violet a Lost Girl, or even a prototypical version of one: within a year she was safely married to Anthony Powell. On the other hand, the circumstances of her early life are a classic Lost Girl's breeding ground. They were also, at least in the context of recent English social life, highly unusual. From the nude modelling to the small-hours visits to Gerrard Street or even the term spent at LSE, hardly any of the activities to which she applied herself would have been permitted a woman of her upbringing before 1914.

Neither would most of the high jinks embraced by the members of the one inter-era youth cult with which the Lost Girls had some definite connection. These were the Bright Young People, the pleasure-seeking gang of blue-blooded socialites and arts-world bohemians whose well-publicised entertainments and 'stunt parties' made them a fixture of newspaper gossip columns in the late 1920s. Certainly, there were one or two Bright Young Women whose exploits exceeded anything that Barbara managed to carry off. Elizabeth Ponsonby, daughter of Arthur Ponsonby, Labour leader of the House of Lords, the model for 'The Hon. Agatha Runcible' in *Vile Bodies* and the despair of her highly respectable parents, featured as a principal witness at the inquest of a man who had driven his car off the road while being hotly pursued by one of her former boyfriends. Brenda Dean Paul, 'the society drug addict', appeared at Marlborough Street Magistrates' Court in November 1931 to answer seven charges of offences against the Dangerous Drugs Act, was bound over for three years and, having absconded to France, ended up in Holloway prison.

At the same time, the links between the Bright Young People and the *Horizon* circle were more than those of faint behavioural resemblance. Connolly himself had operated on the group's highbrow fringe, selling snippets of gossip to magazine editors and being snapped at fancy dress parties. In the aftermath of the 'Mozart Party' held at the Burlington Arcade in April 1930, when half-a-dozen exquisites in period costume escaped into Piccadilly, and were photographed alongside some bewildered workmen pretending to dig up the pavement with a pneumatic drill, he can be seen in wig and knee breeches quizzing the spectacle through a lorgnette. Patrick Balfour, too, was a paid-up Bright Young Person, and, as the *Daily Sketch*'s 'Mr Gossip', a key figure in metropolitan social life of the late

1920s, while Brian Howard was burlesqued into the scene-swelling Johnnie Hoop of Waugh's *Vile Bodies*, who spends his time designing outsize party invitations. ('These had two columns of close print: in one was a list of all the things that Johnnie hated, and in the other all the things he thought he liked.')

The Bright Young Women went about their daily lives in a blizzard of media attention. Brenda's autobiography was serialised in the *News of the World*; her French trip was marked by newspaper posters proclaiming BRENDA'S LATEST ESCAPADE. Elizabeth's wedding to a suitor named Dennis Pelly in March 1929 attracted lavish press coverage. The long-suffering Lady Redesdale, mother of the Mitford sisters, is supposed to have remarked that if she saw a headline that began PEER'S DAUGHTER IN . . . she knew, instinctively, that one of her children was involved. All this worked its effect, on the one hand alerting newspaper readers to the fact that there existed a group of well-bred and well-connected young women who seemed to have cut themselves off from the supervising forces that had previously regulated female lives, and on the other encouraging their awareness of similar behaviour in less exalted social circles. By the late 1930s, consequently, the Lost Girl – although she was never referred to as such – had become a recognisable 'type', particularly in upmarket fiction, whose cast list frequently includes a girl in her late teens thrown mysteriously on her own resources, parentless or at any rate detached from the family home, staying with relatives not entirely confident of their ability to deal with her, or living in hotels or boarding houses, and doing more or less as she likes.

Elizabeth Bowen's *The Death of the Heart* (1938), for example, has a starring role for sixteen-year-old Portia, an orphan who returns to London after her father's death to live with her much older half-brother Thomas, a product of the old man's first marriage. Her new life is lived out mostly in the company of Thomas and his wife Anna, a somewhat fastidious man of letters named St Quentin and brisk, brash family friend, twenty-something Eddie, and its uncertainty lies in her difficulty of comprehending what the people she comes into contact with are 'like'. Taking everyone she meets at face value, rarely suspecting that their inner lives may differ from what appears on the surface, Portia, who at sixteen is 'losing her childish majesty', is eventually plunged into crisis. Bowen, you deduce, is captivated by Portia, of whom it is most commonly said that she is a 'sweet kid', wants to establish what makes her tick and why she behaves in the way she does.

The fault, it soon becomes clear, lies in her upbringing, to which Bowen devotes many a fascinated paragraph. Portia's father and his second family turn out to have spent most of their time as shabby-genteel continental tourists. As Portia remembers it: 'When we took flats, they were in people's villas. Mother liked that, in case something should happen. But lately we lived in hotels . . . But mother and I got fond of it, in a way. We used to make up stories about the people at dinner, and it was fun to watch people come and go.' Set down in holiday resorts before the fashionable crowds have arrived ('when the funicular was not working yet') her adolescence is a matter of 'skidding about in an out-of-season nowhere of railway stations and rocks, filing off wet third-class decks of lake steamers, choking over the bones of *loups de mer*, giggling into eiderdowns that smelled of the person-before-last'. All this can seem uncomfortably close to the early lives of some genuine Lost Girls, as are some of the manifest deficiencies of Portia's education. Sent to a private tutor's establishment in Cavendish Square, which offers 'classes for delicate girls, girls who did not do well at school, girls putting in time before they went abroad, girls who were not to go abroad at all', she is described as being 'unused to learning. She had not learnt that one must learn.'

If Portia is essentially passive, ripe to be imposed upon and embarrassed (as when Eddie, assuming the role of boyfriend, decides to interrupt her stay at the seaside with Anna's old governess), then Jill, in Julian Maclaren-Ross's 'Five Finger Exercises' (1942) seems a much more forceful proposition. For its time, a surprisingly explicit account of a painter's seduction of a teenage girl in a hotel on the Sussex coast, the story rests, once again, on its heroine's oddity, her complete detachment from most of the constraints of contemporary life. Thirty-year-old Jocelyn, coming upon her unexpectedly in the hotel lounge, immediately senses her naivety, but also her matter-of-fact willingness to be taken advantage of. Cross-examination reveals that she has run away from school ('I just got tired of it') to live in London and work in a department store. Don't her parents object, Jocelyn wonders. 'They don't know where I am.' Declaring herself bored by respectable people ('they're too dull') and intrigued by the details of his professional life ('I suppose you paint women in the nude'), Jill consents to be taken upstairs ('She did not know much about kissing but she improved a little as the afternoon wore on'). What really animates her, once the deed has been accomplished, is Jocelyn's promise to paint her portrait.

Most of Maclaren-Ross's fiction is narrowly autobiographical. There is no reason to suppose that 'Five Finger Exercises' is any different. And as Lost Girl studies go, he has strong claims to be regarded as one of its founding fathers. His short story 'A Bit of a Smash in Madras' was one of *Horizon*'s early discoveries, and he left a striking portrait of Connolly as editor, lounging indolently around the office at Lansdowne Terrace in school-masterish tweed jacket and baggy flannels ('one had the impression that he should have been eating grapes, but at the same time his half-closed eyes missed nothing'), discovered at his table at the Café Royal with a bulging leather satchel and a pile of galley proofs unfurled on his knee. In Anthony Powell's *Books Do Furnish a Room* (1971), set in the arctic winter of 1946–7, Maclaren-Ross features as the end-of-tether literary man 'X. Trapnel', writing parodies and book reviews for a magazine called *Fission*, dealing with its highly efficient editorial assistant Ada Leintwardine (Sonia) and falling calamitously in love with the man-eating Pamela Widmerpool (a projection of Barbara) who, as a parting gesture when their relationship breaks down, throws the manuscript of his unpublished novel into the Regent's Park Canal.

All of which brings us back to the one person capable of uniting the Lost Girls into a single point of focus. For nearly every road in this narrative, it is fair to say, leads back to Cyril Connolly who, at various times in his life, was married to Barbara, engaged in a nine-year (but far from exclusive) relationship with Lys, regarded Janetta as his 'muse' and was thought to have matrimonial designs on Sonia while also conducting affairs with women such as Joan Eyres-Monsell and Diana Witherby who were part of the *Horizon* circle. Four and a half decades after his death, it is difficult to convey the sheer fascination with which Connolly was regarded by the people who knew him in the years before and after the Second World War. Part of it, naturally, was down to his outstanding intellectual gifts. He was one of the most forceful literary critics of the mid-twentieth century, and as such a decisive influence on the generation of writers who followed in his wake: 'Sir', a deferential Philip Larkin is supposed to have said when they met at Auden's funeral, 'you formed me.' Far more, though, took in the pull of his personality and the paralysing mystique he had created for himself – a mystique that the people closest to him were expected enthusiastically to propagandise and share.

To know Connolly was, instantly, to be a part of his schemes, a subscriber not merely to *Horizon* but to all kinds of additional plots and subterfuges, whose participants were often wholly ignorant of the roles they were expected to play. One testimony to Connolly's significance in the literary world of the 1940s – several other worlds that extended beyond it, if it comes to that – is the large numbers of memorial notices he attracted. Nearly every literary man or woman born in the first thirty years of the twentieth century left some account of their dealings with 'Boots', as his *convives* christened him, in testimony to Virginia Woolf's complaint about 'that smartiboots Connolly'. Not all this reminiscence is favourable. Some of Connolly's old friends have mixed feelings. (Stephen Spender, while praising the 'person of exceptional intelligence and sensibility' on display in Clive Fisher's 1995 biography, 'can only see the Cyril who exploited me, as he did many other people'.) Others think his influence largely injurious. But none of them is in any doubt of his significance to the worlds through which he moved or to the people who were caught up in his self-aggrandising wake.

In the territory of personal relations, the Connolly mystique was, at heart, a matter of constructing patterns, fashioning a kind of emotional maze at whose endlessly conflicted centre lurked the tantalising figure of Cyril himself. The ever-charitable Spender believed that the things that were notorious about him (notably 'his having love-affairs with two or three women at a time') were not so much cynical or heartless but the result of straightforward solipsism, the egotistical firework displays of 'someone who had formed a psychological theory about himself and considered that everyone concerned with him should agree that he had to perform this, even if doing so was sacrificial to them.' '[Q]uick under the fat, disloyal, an admirable destroyer. A great taker of quiet notes,' his old friend Alan Pryce-Jones decided. 'Easily wounded, unforgiving, dislikeable, delightful.' As to what Connolly wanted, whether in the sensual realm or anywhere else, the short answer is power. If so, it was power of a relatively subtle sort, in which friends and lovers were expected to circulate around him and indulge his habit of playing them off against each another while affecting not to mind the dizzying levels of capriciousness and obstinacy that were periodically on display.

Curiously, none of this seemed to affect the esteem in which he was held, or the loyalty – sometimes amounting to unfeigned devotion – he regularly attracted in his acolytes. Spender, again, lunching with Diana Witherby shortly before Connolly's death, noted that 'She was very loving about him but told me it was true he was cruel – punishing – to women. She said the worst thing she found when she had her affair with him was that he not only deceived her, but that he liked doing so – took pleasure in telling lies.' And yet Diana, as she acknowledged, continued to be besotted by Connolly, tracked his career, looked on enviously as he pursued other women in locations where she herself could no longer follow. 'I was terribly jealous of him being in Paris,' she told Janetta, long after their affair had come to an end, while experiencing 'a strange feeling that it should be me he writes to there. Dog in the manger? Or rather bitch in the manger – Yes, but we had a lot of Paris together.'

All this raises the question of why so many women put up with Cyril, tolerated his self-absorption and the peculiarities of a moral code that in the early years of the war allowed him to remark, without obvious irony, that 'I shall never believe in women again. I have been perfectly faithful to two women for two years, and now both of them have been unfaithful to me.' The answer lay less in any physical attractions he might have possessed – these were negligible – but in his superabundant charm. Give him a sympathetic companion, Quennell proposed, 'ideally a sympathetic young woman', and suddenly he was a different person. 'The alert face appeared to absorb his jowls; his spider-eyes would dance with fun and malice.' 'Most lovely company,' one of them remembered. 'He always seemed to have an original, delightful new approach to something which made it worth your while being there and listening.' If a first meeting with Connolly sometimes left only the impression of a titanic egotist aflame with condescension then long-term exposure to his conversational style usually steered his account firmly back into credit. 'Pretentious and rude', the novelist Anna Kavan briskly declared, only to revise her opinion to 'really a nice guy under that super-intellectual façade'.

To a bright but undereducated girl with literary or artistic ambitions, this kind of attention was worth having, and the fact that, as one of his biographers notes, he 'enjoyed creating romantic complications in his life' and positively luxuriated in the guilt and unhappiness they brought, was very often a price worth paying for the uncertainty of your position. Equally enticing was the unshakeable evidence of his status, the file of celebrated writers who beat a path to his door, the aspiring youngsters who craved his company, his absolute conviction that posterity would judge him (and by implication those around him) quite as seriously as he judged himself. Spender remembered flying with him once to Brussels and watching, intrigued, as his companion took out a little notebook and scratched out an offending sentence. Connolly explained that he was erasing an unkind remark about a woman they both knew. Should the plane crash and the diary be recovered, he did not want it to be remembered as his last earthly comment.

Guilt. Deception. Boredom. Lofty ideals and promise unfulfilled. All these were Connolly's stock in trade, part of a coruscating personal myth that, carefully burnished up throughout his adult life, went back to the world of his far from promising upbringing. For a man who spent much of his career on the fringes of the *beau monde*, enjoyed hobnobbing with duchesses and regarded the Ritz Hotel as his second home, his background was notably obscure. His father Matthew ('British soldier, conchologist, stamp collector, expert on pedigree racehorses and lover of the culinary arts', as a scientific database once put it) was an officer in the King's Own Yorkshire Light Infantry, who spent his long retirement living in a hotel that adjoined the Natural History Museum, the better to pursue his life-long hobby of collecting snail shells. His son's widely reviewed *Enemies of Promise* (1938) was followed a year later by his own much less well-publicised *A Monographic Survey of South African Non-marine Molluscs*, which took up all of 660 pages of *Annals of the South African Museum*. Well before this date Major Connolly had been deserted by his wife, Maud, who by the 1930s was living in South Africa with her husband's former commanding officer, General Christopher Brooke. Mother-fixated Cyril kept constantly in touch.

Stocky, of medium height and unprepossessing in appearance ('Is that the tug who's been kicked in the face by a mule?' a school contemporary wondered when his name came up), Connolly took a profoundly elegiac view of the world. If the present sometimes threatened to disintegrate beneath his hands, then the past could be endlessly ransacked for bittersweet consolation. One of the formative experiences on which he loved to dwell was the two years spent as a child in Cape Colony. This stirred a lifelong fondness for hot climes and balmy air: his idea of happiness, he once declared, was 'to be writing a tolerably good book and travelling south in the company of someone your conscience permits you to love'. Another was his time at prep school, in this case the notorious intellectual forcing house of St Cyprian's, in Eastbourne, where his contemporaries included George Orwell and Cecil Beaton. Even as a small boy Connolly claimed to be aware of the temperamental differences that separated him from the future author of *Nineteen Eighty-Four*: he was a stage rebel, he deduced; Orwell a real one. But it was Eton, to which he proceeded on a scholarship in 1917, that played the most crucial part in establishing the kind of person that he imagined himself to be. *Enemies of Promise* includes a bravura passage in which, visiting the school with his headmaster to sit the scholarship exam, he lingers on Windsor Bridge listening to two dandified exquisites appraising the technique of a boy in an outrigger passing beneath them. 'Really that man Wilkinson's not at all a bad oar,' one languidly assures the other. To the thirteen-year-old eavesdropper, 'the foppish drawl, the two boys with their hats on the back of their heads, the graceful sculler underneath, seemed the incarnation of elegance and maturity'.

Eton, with its idiosyncratic hierarchies, its studied out-of-dateness and its approval of individualism and wit, might have been made for Connolly. Whereas Orwell, in his four-and-a-half years on the premises, frankly idled, scraped into the Sixth Form at the late age of eighteen and left to pursue what was seen as a second-rate career in the Burma Police, Connolly, after a sticky start, carved out a niche for himself as a court jester and talented trifler, the boy who succeeds without conscious effort, whose hard work takes place offstage and whose affectations are always backed up by a dazzling catalogue of formal achievement. 'Early laurels weigh like lead', the mature Connolly once pronounced. His own teenage triumphs included a Brackenbury scholarship to Balliol College, Oxford, and his election to the Eton Society, 'Pop', a self-elected cadre of senior boys who more or less ruled the school. Keenly aware that most of the candidates were sporting aristocrats, Connolly never lost an opportunity to show his gratitude to Teddy (later Lord) Jessel, the boy who had helped him on his way. A friend who watched them reconnoitre each other in the 1960s thought it 'the funniest thing I've ever seen, because it was as if they were back at Eton, with Cyril nervously deferring: "Do you think this champagne is all right, Teddy?" I was absolutely riveted because I'd never seen him in that position before.'

If Oxford, where Connolly trod water and played only a subsidiary role in the activities of the 'Brideshead Generation' of Waugh, Harold Acton and Brian Howard, would be remembered as a 'three-year daydream' culminating in a third-class degree, then there were still numbers of well-placed helpers anxious to recognise his talent and steer him in towards the high-powered employments that might suit his cosmopolitan tastes. His old Balliol tutor Francis Urquhart commended 'a man of unusual ability'. John Buchan and Henry Newbolt, two of the grandest literary eminences of the day, were induced to read a sample of his correspondence and declared it 'very vivid and interesting'. The American man of letters Logan Pearsall Smith took him on as confidential secretary, allowed him a salary of £8 a week whether he turned up or not and went so far as to pay off his creditors. By 1927 he was freelancing for the *New Statesman* – Pearsall Smith weighed in with a handy introduction to the literary editor – making his first big splash with a long, opinionated critique of the seven-volume *Collected Works of Laurence Sterne* before settling down to a regular fortnightly column reviewing the novels of the day. He was a coming young man, and the journalism he produced in the late 1920s was carefully designed to bolster the image he had devised for himself: at once satirical and disrespectful, informed and inquisitive, concerned – especially when discussing run-of-the-mill middlebrow novels – to tease out some of the social implications of the world that flows beneath their surface. 'Almost the only novel-reviewer in England who does not make me sick', Orwell declared.

Meanwhile, another part of the Connolly myth was shifting into view, a grand psychological edifice that occasionally threatened to displace the self-absorbed reflections on whether one had succeeded or failed and whether success was worth the having in the first place. This was the question of his emotional life. Like several members of the Brideshead Generation – Evelyn Waugh and John Betjeman, for example – he began as an enthusiastic homosexual before switching to girls in his mid-twenties. By 1929 he had taken up with an eighteen-year-old American named Jean Bakewell, a Baltimore heiress so comfortably placed that when Connolly visited her family home he was startled to find that it contained more bathrooms, bedrooms and cars than people. A year later, with a £1000 a year allowance from Jean's parents to sustain them, the newly married couple could be found inhabiting a rented house in the hills between Toulon and Marseilles, and embracing a lifestyle predicated on the ideal of 'living for beauty'. Back in London they rented a spacious flat in the King's Road, Chelsea, where, when not entertaining his friends, Connolly worked desultorily at a novel. *The Rock Pool* (1936), about the (non) activities of a group of wealthy expatriates filling in time in the south of France, was thought too shocking for British publication and had to be brought out by Jack Kahane's Obelisk Press in Paris.

Was this 'living for beauty'? Connolly – always a realist when the professional chips were down – had his doubts. Although *Enemies of Promise*, the book in which he managed to convert the neuroses and insecurities that governed his life into a paying proposition, was a success ('the best book of criticism since the war', Auden pronounced), he was darkly aware that he might not be making the most of his gifts. Here another essential ingredient of the Connolly myth declared itself: an eternal suspicion that the grass was greener on the other side of the fence; the thought that the position you had so carefully built up for yourself was, when closely inspected, doing you more harm than good. Jean might have given him the lifestyle he craved, but could it be that it was ruining him artistically? Might not the idleness and dependency that stopped him writing a succession of masterpieces be cured by a less sybaritic existence? And might not that existence have, necessarily, to be conducted in Jean's absence? Late in 1937, with these arguments marauding through his conscious-ness, he fell in love with Diana Witherby – twelve years his junior and preparing to study at the Chelsea School of Art – and embarked on a relationship in which, as ever with Connolly, huge amounts of cake were had and eaten too. The next eighteen months passed in a welter of uncertainty and recrimination. Diana, appreciating the seriousness of the situation in which she had plunged herself, urged him to go back to his wife. Jean, exerting pressure of a more material kind, closed up the King's Road flat, whose lease had expired, packed her bags and left for Paris. The husband who had wanted to live for beauty was abandoned to a Sloane Square hotel. By the spring of 1939, he was effectively homeless, spending much of his time at Cassis, a downmarket resort on the Bouches-du-Rhône, with a float-ing population of writers and painters.

Who was to blame for this impasse? Connolly, being Connolly, seems to have assumed that all three parties in the transaction were at fault. If he had been unfaithful to his wife, then both wife and mistress were guilty of failing to understand his complex emotional needs. On the one hand, Jean ought to come back to him. On the other, she ought to acknowledge how difficult it was for him to give up his current way of life. Or as he put it in a letter from July 1939, 'If I gave up [Diana] I should feel you had bullied me, unless there were many things you would also give up.'

Meanwhile, the news from beyond the Sloane Square window

was becoming steadily more alarming. Europe was preparing for war; Connolly, able-bodied and still in his mid-thirties, wondered uneasily what the authorities might have in store for him. It could not be any worse than the hackwork that was currently paying his hotel bills: there was a particularly chastening week, in the summer of 1939, when, in his capacity as the *New Statesman*'s film critic, he was reduced to reviewing *Tarzan Finds a Son*. Trapped between two women, unable or perhaps only unwilling to decide where his destiny lay, his professional life in tatters, the wider world about to erupt in conflict, he was self-evidently a man at a crossroads. It was against this unpromising backdrop that *Horizon*, one of the greatest literary magazines of the twentieth century, was born.

2.

'The Little Girl Who Makes Everyone's Heart Beat Faster'

Cyril liked cool girls in a warm climate.

Michael Wishart, *High Diver* (1977)

Stephen Spender's diaries are full of leisurely re-imaginings of the friends he had made in the course of his long and eventful life. In January 1981, forty years and more since they first came across each other, he found himself unexpectedly thinking of Janetta. Spender remembered meeting her in 1938, when she turned up in London 'wearing a trousered suit in dark velvet and carrying a shepherd's crook'. Dark blonde, slender and enigmatic, her unusual costume giving her a faintly androgynous air, she was, he thought, 'a dream person'. That night Spender lay awake thinking of her – 'fantasizing, as they say, because I was still married to Inez [his first wife] and I did not think of having anything to do with her'. A year later they ran into each other again, had dinner and walked in the twilight along Oxford Street as far as Selfridges department store before saying their goodbyes. From the vantage point of his eighth decade, Spender was conscious of a golden opportunity gone missing. He 'would have asked her to go home with him', he recorded, had not timidity stayed his hand. But there was something else – faint, intangible, but decisive – holding him back. 'She was still very attractive,' he decided, 'but she had become the Janetta I've known ever since: not the girl-boy shepherd-shepherdess, but the mysterious elusive woman she's been ever since.' Spender died in 1995, by which time he and Janetta had known each other for nearly sixty years, but all the evidence suggests that, of all his many meetings with her, none was quite so memorable as the first.

If Spender's raptures over the sight of a teenage girl in a trouser suit armed with a shepherd's crook can seem slightly exaggerated, then this, it should straightaway be said, was the effect that Janetta tended to have on people. No literary or artistic bohemian of either sex who chanced upon her in her mid-century heyday seems either to have forgotten the experience or to have been anything other than transfixed by her company. Frances Partridge's diary from May 1945 records her old friend David Garnett coming back from a party where he had met 'an amazingly, almost embarrassingly beautiful girl, who turned out to be Janetta'. The Bloomsbury man of letters Gerald Brenan, to whom she was introduced at the age of fourteen, promptly informed Frances's husband Ralph that 'she sets my heart on fire'. The artist Feliks Topolski, no slouch when it came to judging feminine beauty, declared himself 'bemused' by her 'sublimity'. To Patrick Leigh Fermor, she was 'beautiful in a way that grows, rather than bursts out on one'. Even in old age the compliments kept coming: 'very attractive and tall, and this wonderful bone structure, not wearing make-up', a woman who encountered her in her eighties recalled, 'you've got to be very beautiful to get away with *that*'.

Comparisons with her contemporaries – most of them, inevitably, made by men – are instructive. Lys, everyone agreed, resembled the fashion plate she once had been. Sonia, with her pink-and-white complexion and her tendency to plumpness, looked like a Renoir painting. Much of Barbara's allure hinged on her ability to arrange her clothing in ways that, as one ex-boyfriend put it, made her 'appear more naked'. With Janetta, the effect of her presence in a room, or in front of a camera, is less straightforward. The photographs of her that survive from the 1930s and 1940s – many of them taken by Frances Partridge – convey not so much a formal record of her beauty as a terrific sense of something burrowing away beneath its surface. In one she broods furiously out of a tangle of tied-back hair. In another, she hunches over what looks like a recorder as the writer Eddie Sackville-West and the Partridges' infant son Burgo look on. (Frances captioned this portrait 'Music, Poetry and Innocence'.) In scarcely any of them can she be seen to smile.

There was little in Janetta's early life to hint at the bohemian worlds through which she was later to wander. For all the memory of a long-dead aunt with artistic leanings who had exhibited at the Paris Salon, the Woolleys were soldiers and clergymen and – a fact that became sharply apparent in the years after her birth – casualties of the First World War. Her mother, Jan, had originally been married to a regular army officer and South Africa veteran named George Culme-Seymour. There were two children, Mark and Angela. After Culme-Seymour's death on the Western Front in the spring of 1915, his widow, then living in Tedworth Square, Chelsea, consoled herself with the frequent visits of his younger comrade, Captain Geoffrey Woolley. 'Young, good-looking and unsophisticated', according to his much more worldly stepdaughter, Captain Woolley came, as he discreetly put it, 'to entertain the hope that we should marry when the war was over'. Sanctioned by the bride's father-in-law, who confessed that he had always yearned for such an outcome, the wedding took place in June 1918, after which the family decamped to Oxford, where Geoffrey studied for the priesthood, and then to Rugby School where he took up a teaching post. Although two more children followed in quick succession – Rollo in 1920, Janetta on New Year's Eve 1921 – Jan later told her elder daughter that she knew the marriage had been a mistake a week into the honeymoon.

As befitted his lack of sophistication, Captain Woolley was a modest man, candidly acknowledging that, on joining the army in 1914, he 'had no high ideas of my own fitness or prowess because I really combined a strong sense of duty with a timid nature'. Despite these shortcomings he won a Homeric Victoria Cross when, after a disastrous attack on a fortified hill three miles south-east of Ypres, finding himself stranded in a bomb crater, he managed to bring the surviving soldiers under his command safely home. What he came to think of his wife, his family and especially his daughter may be inferred from his autobiography. *Sometimes a Soldier* (1963) is a supremely odd book, and its oddity lies in the author's reluctance to say anything about the people who were closest to him at crucial stages in his life. The career of pious good works and dutiful self-sacrifice – the chaplaincy of Harrow, respectful attendance on the Duke of York's scheme to bring public school boys and their working-class equivalents together on summer camps – winds diligently on, but once the story reaches the 1920s there are only half-a-dozen incidental references to Jan, and Janetta, extraordinarily, is not mentioned by name.

What had gone wrong? What had happened to separate the Revd Woolley, as he now was, from Jan and Janetta? The answer seems to have lain in Jan's determination to break free of some of the constraints of her highly conventional upper-middle-class existence. There were frequent trips abroad, plausibly explained away as a consequence of her undeniably bad health, but the root cause of the breach was a straightforward distaste for the life that Geoffrey expected her to lead. Meeting wife and daughter for the first time in the 1930s Frances Partridge noted how they seemed to have turned their backs on conventional family arrangements. As for Janetta, who professed to find her father 'bogus', the explanation lay in her undisguised contempt for religious belief. When Geoffrey came to preach at Downe House in Berkshire, where she had been sent to board, this hostility led to her being banned from attending the service. What seems never to have been more than a patchy education came to a temporary halt in 1936 when her mother decided that the pair of them should live together in southern Spain. Janetta's ambition here in her early teens looks as if it was inspired by Robert Louis Stevenson's *Travels with a Donkey in the Cévennes*: 'I knew my mother had taken out an insurance policy that would give me £300 when I was 21, and I thought I was going to buy a donkey and walk across Europe.'

If Jan and Janetta itched to meet less conventional people, then Torremolinos, where they rented a house in the early spring, was the place to find them. The coast around Málaga had not yet been built up, and the fishing villages were full of English visitors come to paint and write. As well as being 'charming and tiny', Torremolinos, Janetta remembered, contained at least half-a-dozen expatriates, with not a tourist in sight. The migrant population included the Bloomsbury literary man Gerald Brenan, who lived with his wife Gamel at nearby Churriana. Gerald already knew Angela and her brother Mark; when Angela arrived in the area with her husband Johnny Churchill, the Brenans were introduced to her mother and half-sister. By the time the Partridges arrived in Málaga for a brief stay in early April 1936, Gerald – always keen on young girls – had fallen under Janetta's spell. She was, he fondly assured Ralph, 'a little girl who makes everyone's heart beat faster'. Frances and Ralph were similarly beguiled. Frances's diary for 12 April notes that they 'walked to Torremolinos . . . Tea with Mrs Woolley and Janetta.' An afternoon's conversation was enough to reveal the family's situation: Jan determined to spend her time out of England; her children finding their father old-fashioned and repressive. Jan the Partridges liked (it was a measure of Mrs Woolley's emancipation from her previous life that Ralph shortly afterwards had an affair with her), but Janetta they found captivating. Already the roots of Frances's lifelong obsession with her younger friend were firmly in place.

But the Woolleys' Spanish idyll was short-lived. On 16 July the army mutinied in Morocco; two days later the rising spread to the mainland and much of Andalusia fell to Franco's Nationalists.

Brenan, visiting Málaga on the morning of 18 July, saw soldiers marching down the main street on their way to proclaim martial law. There were workmen massing in the side-streets and the sound of gunfire. After an attempt by the Nationalists to seize the municipal buildings had been fought off, working-class Republicans swarmed into the town, setting fire to the houses of the bourgeoisie. Thinking that his daughter Miranda would be better off in England, and supposing that Jan and Janetta would be on their way home as soon as possible, Brenan made his way to Torremolinos. Here he discovered that the Woolleys, too, had been caught in the city as it went up in flames and were lucky to escape. Happily by this time the outside world had begun to take an interest in the plight of Málaga's British community. *The Times* offered daily bulletins, informing its readers on 19 July that the 'principal danger spot' was Andalusia 'as it is there that the insurgents stand the best chance of uniting their forces'. By the following day there was talk of a destroyer setting out from Gibraltar 'to help in the evacuation of British subjects in the event of necessity'.

The Governor of Gibraltar, Charles Harington, had a particular reason for ensuring that the Woolleys were swiftly conveyed to safety: he was a distant connection of Jan's. It would be very tempting to regard the rescue operation that followed as a grandiloquent personal gesture backed by the resources of empire. As Janetta put it: 'My mother was apparently a sort of relation of the Governor and he sent a destroyer to collect us.' On the other hand, Harington was a fanatical right-winger and Franco-ite – official bulletins from the Rock had already begun to refer to the elected Republican government as 'Reds' – determined to do his duty to the British population of southern Spain as quickly and conspicuously as possible. On 25 July *The Times* reported that a navy vessel was 'proceeding to Malaga to evacuate 60 British subjects there'. By this time the situation on the ground was serious. The Brenans' house had been searched by an anarchist patrol. When the destroyer arrived off Torremolinos the 'very smart motor boat' despatched to take off the expatriate community was refused permission to land by left-wing activists. In the end, the Woolleys were allowed to take a bus to Málaga. Here, in the company of twenty or so other British passport holders, they were finally allowed to depart.

Back in England, Jan and Janetta soon gravitated to the Partridges' Wiltshire fastness of Ham Spray. A photograph from around this time shows Frances cutting Janetta's hair in a makeshift barber's chair set up on the lawn. Jan, Janetta and Rollo were there at Christmas 1936, after which Jan decided to return to warmer climes. Taking an apartment near Marseilles, she re-installed Janetta, now turned fifteen, at Downe House senior school. The depth of the Partridges' emotional involvement in her life may be gauged from Frances's engagement book, which is sprinkled with information about Janetta's movements and school arrangements. Increasingly, Ham Spray became her base, where she passed her half-terms and holidays in the company of what amounted to surrogate parents. When the summer came and she went to visit her mother, Ralph spent the best part of a week fetching her back.

The roots of this devotion are not easily explained. The Partridges, as Frances's voluminous diaries attest, were shrewd, sophisticated people, great practitioners of Bloomsbury scepticism, frequently unimpressed by the company who came their way, subjecting them – at any rate on paper – to minute interrogations of motive and comprehension and sometimes not liking what they discovered. Janetta, on the other hand, seems to have won their sympathy almost at a stroke, a combination of interest and affection that produced what Frances's biographer calls 'a quasi-parental love for a beautiful, strong-minded girl on the threshold of adulthood'. Brenan, who had also relocated to England with his family, looked longingly on. Wanting to stay at Ham Spray at Christmas 1938 but finding it once again tenanted by Jan and her family, he wrote to tell Frances that he envied her 'the lovely Janetta'.

Gradually Janetta, whom the Partridges now christened 'Wolfie' or 'Wolfers', was moving closer to the social circles occupied by Cyril Connolly and his friends. Her education came to an abrupt end in the summer of 1937 when she persuaded her mother to remove her from Downe House ('a very silly decision,' she later recalled. 'I was very ignorant and [the] school had been very good to me'). Opting to enrol at Chelsea Polytechnic with the aim of studying art, she was soon installed in the house in Warwick Avenue occupied by her half-sister Angela, now married to Patrick Balfour. Sustained by Balfour's job as a gossip-columnist, the couple led an extensive social life, and their teenaged lodger ('half fascinated and half angry') was frequently invited down from her roost in the attic to mingle with their guests. The fact that some of these new associates had aspirations that went well beyond friendship was probably brought home to her by an episode that took place early in the New Year of 1939.

Once again, Christmas had been spent at Ham Spray, where Janetta had celebrated her seventeenth birthday. Three weeks later she, the Partridges and another couple, Heywood Hill (proprietor of the bookshop in Curzon Street) and his wife Anne, were booked to travel to St Gervais in the French Alps for a skiing holiday. A few days before they were due to leave, the normally indefatigable Frances fell ill. Giddy and nauseous, she encouraged husband and friends to leave without her on the assumption that a few days' rest would see her right and allow her to join them later.

There is a suspicion that Ralph had been less than sympathetic. 'My sweetest love,' entreated a missive penned en route, 'I have been so beastly and disagreeable to you – do try to forgive me . . . as I'm going I shall try to enjoy myself.' Janetta added a plaintive codicil: 'Ralph is pink and miserable looking and I do feel it's so awful for you being left there . . . Ralph's in despair and I'm ready to burst into tears.' Over the next few days consoling letters sped back and forth between St Gervais and Ham Spray. The local doctor was doing his best, Frances told her husband. Burgo, the Partridges' three-year-old son, was building a snowman, and Ralph and Janetta must have fun. 'I am so glad you have Wolfers to keep you company,' she declared, 'because no-one could be better.' Not to be outdone, Ralph wrote back assuring her how much he missed her. 'I am not cut out to go away from your side,' he gallantly deposed, 'without you I'm quite lost and hopelessly discouraged.' Not long after this, thinking herself recovered, Frances set off for Paddington through the late January snow, only to find that her dizziness had worsened to the point that she could scarcely stand. She wrote a long letter to Ralph ('Please darling do not be disappointed and do not not not <u>think</u> of coming home. Just keep on enjoying yourself with sweet Wolfers') and returned to Ham Spray, Burgo and the nanny.

For a further week telegrams and letters went back and forth across the Channel: news (from Ralph) of Janetta's prowess on the slopes; Ham Spray gossip (from Frances); talk of Jenny, a refugee from Austria and Ralph's mistress, who, in the grand Bloomsbury tradition of tolerance and *laissez-faire*, Frances charitably indulged and seems even to have given financial support. 'I sent Jenny her cheque yesterday, pretending I could scarcely write,' she explained early in February. 'Oh my, wouldn't she have thought it a chance for her to come in my place?' Jenny, she continued, was 'rather down on Janetta, who she obviously resents as her successor'. It was meant as a joke, but beneath the guilelessness lies a hint that Frances had begun to fret herself over what Ralph – a dedicated ladies' man – might be up to with sweet Wolfers.

Curiously, at this point the tone of Ralph's letters, formerly cheery and informative, began to change. 'I don't really get on well with her,' he complained of his teenage accomplice. 'She's such a child and not a real companion . . . selfish, cross and vain, redeemed by occasional flashes of real sensitiveness and sweetness.' What he omitted to add was that one night at the hotel he had appeared without warning in Janetta's room, flung himself on top of her, burst into tears and declared his love. Janetta, deeply distressed by the sight of a married

49

man twenty-seven years her senior making a spectacle of himself, told him to leave. Within a day or two he had returned to England, pre-empting his arrival with a long and agonised letter to Frances admitting that 'If I'd stayed another week W and I would either not have been on speaking terms or lovers, so it's a good thing from that angle too that I'm leaving. She's rather a cock-teaser and I would have been worked up to reprisals.'

Bloomsbury sangfroid being what it was, Janetta's reappearance at Ham Spray ten days later passed without comment. But there were bigger fish about to swim into Janetta's orbit. Angela had introduced her to Connolly sometime in 1937. Impressed by his personality ('glorious', she remembered) and flattered by the interest he took in her, she happily agreed to a proposal that came her way early in the summer of 1939. Janetta, after visiting Jan in Brittany, wanted to travel on to her mother's bolthole in Cassis. Connolly, no stranger to Cassis or its amenities (Diana had stayed with him there), offered to escort her. All the romantic scenery that filled any stage on which Connolly made one of his assignations was quickly shifted into place. They would be Verlaine and Rimbaud, he proposed, roaming together through the French countryside, and what had originally been conceived as a direct journey from Brittany to Marseilles was swiftly transformed into a kind of magical quest, taking in the parts of France where he had always felt most at home and to whose mythological enchantments he had always responded: Tulle in the north, Rodez in the east, Tonneins in the west, southwards beyond Toulouse . . .

There are several mementoes of this trip, accomplished in a grey Armstrong Siddeley brought from Paris and extending, as Connolly the ever-knowledgeable tour guide got properly into his stride, over several weeks. One is his correspondence with Jean who, apprised of the journey, professed tolerant amusement. 'Darling is le cap Naio fun?' she enquired in mid-May, assuming him to have already arrived at Cassis. 'Who are you staying with, [Diana] or Miss JW? I am glad you have found somebody else who can read maps?' Janetta, Connolly explained, was 'a very sweet and passionate traveller' who suited the 'second adolescence' on which he had now embarked. Another is *The Unquiet Grave* (1944), which re-imagines the tour in a series of densely elegiac fragments:

> For an angora pullover, for a red scarf, for a beret and some brown shoes I am bleeding to death; my heart is as dry as a kidney.

> Peeling off the kilometres to the tune of 'Blue Skies', sizzling down the long black reaches of Nationale Sept, the plane trees going sha-sha-sha through the open window, the windscreen yellowing with crushed midges, she with the Michelin beside me, a handkerchief binding her hair.

> Back-streets of Cannes: tuberoses in the window, the book-shop over the railway bridge which we comb for memoirs and detective stories while the cushions of the car deflate in the afternoon sun . . . torn maps, the wet bathing dress wrapped in a towel . . .

Most of Connolly's friends, on reading this highly emotional travelogue, assumed that its principal focus was his wife ('he sees . . . Jean as the golden past of peaches and beaches and lemurs', Evelyn Waugh noted in his diary.) But it was Janetta on whom Connolly bestowed a presentation copy complete with handwritten corrections and marginalia.

There is no hint in *The Unquiet Grave* that Connolly was absorbed in any topic other than the moment, the scenery and his teenage companion, or that the atmosphere was anything less than idyllic. In fact, the trip was sometimes fraught with tension. There was a particularly difficult moment in the hotel at Vannes, when Connolly, as Janetta put it, 'took it for granted that he could share my bed'. Overawed by the attentions of a man twice her age, sympathetic to her would-be seducer's emotional predicament ('he was very in love + preoccupied by 2 other ladies'), and not wanting to hurt his feelings, she gave in.

There were further difficulties when they reached Tulle. At this time, all foreign nationals resident in France for more than thirty days required a permit. Janetta had come without one. Connolly advised her to apply at the town hall and went off to make some of his regular telephone calls. By this point a gendarme, his suspicions alerted by the sight of a very young Englishwoman, oddly dressed (Janetta's travelling costume consisted of a corduroy suit with a French army cloak and walking stick), unchaperoned and in the company of an older man, decided to intervene. Janetta was detained. Asked where she had been, and where her mother was, she amused herself by replying that she didn't live anywhere and hadn't got a home. When he came to find her, Connolly was arrested on grounds of abducting a minor. In the event these difficulties were smoothed over by way of a telephone call to the British consul in nearby Bordeaux, but Connolly, who had a history of nervous encounters with vigilant authority, was badly rattled: in the days that followed he would barely allow Janetta to get out of the car and instructed her to 'look older'.

There were at least two other summer trips with Connolly through the French countryside, one of them undertaken with Peter Quennell and his wife Glur. To Quennell, this was a 'calamitous holiday'. Deeply preoccupied with 'a new love . . . a very young girl', Connolly was also anxious about Jean, continually phoning the Paris hotel in which she was staying and growing yet more nervous when she failed to answer. There was a minor disaster when Janetta, helping the others to tie their bags to the roof of the car, hitched the spotted red handkerchief which contained her clothes to the bumper and then forgot to retrieve it. By the time she remembered, twenty or thirty miles along the road, all that remained was 'a wreath of dusty shreds'. Her passport was run to earth at the roadside, but there was no sign of her leather wallet. Left in the town of St-Affrique in Aveyron, while she and Connolly turned back to see what might be lying on the asphalt behind them, Quennell and Glur found themselves pacing 'torrid and narrow streets', eyed by suspicious locals who took offence at the skimpiness of Glur's shorts. In the end, they were attacked by a mob of stone-throwing children and had to take refuge in a church.

What did the seventeen-year-old girl make of these excursions? An account of them written over sixty years later convicts Mrs Quennell of unpunctuality and applying too much lipstick, her husband of a lack of sympathy over the lost handkerchief and Cyril of taking too much interest in the local cuisine. There was a particularly disillusioning moment when, as he greedily attacked a plate of strawberries, she found herself revolted by the sight of the juice trickling down his white, hairy fingers: 'I didn't love C,' she reflected, '+ I wondered what I was doing.' But these were minor drawbacks. In general, Janetta was enchanted by his company, admired the countryside through which they passed and relished the information he imparted about France and its culture as the Armstrong Siddeley sped south. By the time he decided to return to London, all the elements for a life-long friendship were firmly in place: 'an extremely nice relationship,' she remembered, 'which just went on always.'

Meanwhile, there were other relationships crashing into gear. At Cassis, Janetta had been introduced to a man named Hugh Slater – christened Humphrey Richard Hugh and known both as 'Humphrey' and 'Hugh' – currently ensconced in the town's bohemian quarter with a painter called Elizabeth. Then in his mid-thirties, a Spanish Civil War veteran and aspiring writer who had risen to the rank of Chief of Operations for the Marxist International Brigades, Slater, like Janetta, was a creature of impulse. Shortly after her return to her mother's house, he decided that he was in love with her. Janetta, trying to reconstruct the events that followed long years later, suspected that she had behaved badly. ('Apparently when he was wondering whether he could leave Elizabeth I had said if you've got any guts you could. Which seems to me an appalling way to talk.') Nonetheless, leave Elizabeth he did. Supported by Jan ('I'm so glad yr with Hugh,' runs a letter from early September, 'I love him'), the couple fled to nearby Toulon, where Slater busied himself writing 'letters to friends explaining how he'd run off with someone of just 17'. Funds were low. Sitting on the post office steps hoping for money to arrive, Janetta was startled to receive a packet from the gendarmerie returning the leather wallet that had fallen out of her bundle on the road to St-Affrique.

Janetta's account of this fugitive love affair has an odd, impressionistic quality: bright fragments of detail gleaming through the shadow of a world preparing for war: taking a bus to Geneva; realising that the short, stocky woman in front of them in the queue for the museum was Gertrude Stein; buying a Dutch cap at a chemist's shop. She was supremely happy, Janetta thought, 'living with someone as fond of me as H was'. An existence devoid of plans, aims or commitments had been suddenly exchanged for one of emotional and intellectual ferment. Some of Janetta's contemporaries might have been bored by a daily round that seems largely to have involved Hugh 'talking, telling me what to read, telling me about politics, about the civil war, about writers & writing & painting'. But the seventeen-year-old girl was aware that this didacticism played an important part in her emotional response: 'It all really interested me & it contributed enormously to discovering that I loved him.'

But amid the intoxicating scents of Hegel and Marx and the difference between 'early revolutionary communism & the useless unintelligent narrow political commissars', there were practical realities at hand. War was drawing closer. Slater, who had spent a month in jail in Perpignan on his way to Spain, was on a police list. They returned to England via Dieppe, where the hotel proprietors looked askance at the Woolworth's curtain ring on Janetta's wedding finger, and made for the Partridges. Here, in a foretaste of many other Ham Spray evaluations, Janetta discovered that 'R & F didn't really like H. & their manner to me was different.' Happily Frances's loyalty to her young protégée remained undimmed. When Janetta discovered she was pregnant, it was she who arranged the abortion and settled the bill. At the nursing home a courteous elderly doctor, who, Frances had warned her, looked like a frog, asked her if she really wanted to go through with it. Yes indeed, Janetta assured him. She was quite certain.

By the end of June 1939, Connolly was back in London. Janetta's involvement with him had come at a crucial juncture in his life. War was looming, his future was uncertain, and the crisis in his emotional affairs showed no sign of letting up. What was he to do? However great his obsession with Diana, he was still capable of writing a long letter to Jean – now returned to Paris – affirming his belief in marriage. The only obstacles preventing their reunion were his pride and her sloth, he even-handedly informed her. Four days later, on 24 July, came a second letter swearing that he loved her as much as ever. This was followed, a few weeks after that, by Connolly himself, half-anxious and yet half-optimistic, conscious, as the lights went out across continental Europe, that his private and professional lives were being slowly drawn together in a single point of focus and that the person capable of solving the dilemma in which he and to a certain extent Jean had lost themselves was one of their mutual friends. This was the arts-world impresario Peter Watson, in whose slipstream Connolly found himself caught up for at least the next ten years.

However discreetly and unobtrusively pursued – he had a horror of personal publicity – Watson's trail runs through vast areas of the upper-bohemian world of the mid-twentieth century. Much of this had to do with his money – even by the standards of the relatively untaxed 1930s he was a fabulously wealthy man – but far more of it seems to have stemmed from both his charm and his unabashed fondness for the good life. Spender, who became a close friend, remembered him as 'one of those rich people who without seeming at all dependent on his wealth . . . manages to get the utmost in the way of pleasure and beauty out of riches'. Women adored him ('Really wonderful,' Janetta recalled, 'kind and glamorous'), an attraction that was in some ways sharpened by his obvious homosexuality. Robbed of any sexual element, the compliments he paid his female friends and the shrewd advice he gave them could be taken at face value. Five years younger than Connolly, tall, slim and saturnine, he was the second son of Sir George Watson, a self-made baronet whose fortune came from a chain of retail dairies. Six months before his death in 1930, the margarine millionaire had established a seven-figure trust fund whose interest allowed Peter an annual income in the region of £50,000.

All this, naturally, made Watson a figure of absorbing interest to his friends. Expensive cars transported him around London and his continental watering holes. Cecil Beaton, who loved him unrequitedly for many years, wrote solicitous letters. There was a Paris apartment in the rue du Bac stuffed with modernist paintings by Braque, Klee and Miró and, or so it seemed to fascinated onlookers, an enticing atmosphere of heightened sensibility and *luxe*. The Connollys had first met him in 1937 at the Austrian mountain resort of Kitzbühel. By Christmas the following year they had progressed to staying at the rue du Bac. Watson, it goes without saying, was Connolly's kind of man, and for reasons in which self-interest contended with a genuine admiration for his new friend's tastes and ambitions. One part of Connolly undoubtedly thought that Watson was exactly the sort of patron who might underwrite his literary schemes, but another part instinctively responded to the reserve and sophistication he brought to his dealings with the world. A third part, here in the late summer of 1939, was narrowly concerned by what he imagined to be Watson's malign influence on Jean. The two, together with Watson's boyfriend Denham Fouts, had seen a great deal of each other in Paris and Connolly feared that in any discussion of their marital disagreements, Watson inclined more to her side than his.

To the problem of what Watson might be saying to Jean could be added the problem of what Connolly wanted to say to Watson. The idea of starting a literary magazine had long absorbed him. 'Favourite daydream' runs a note from as far back as 1934, 'edit a monthly magazine . . . No advertisements. Harmless title, deleterious contents.' As to why a promising young critic should want to set up as an editor, an explanation lies in the absolute centrality of magazine publishing to the literary life of the 1930s. From the stratospheric redoubts of Eliot's *New Criterion* to the middlebrow readership attracted by popular papers such as *John O'London's Weekly*, literary culture was to a very large extent conducted through the pages of weekly and monthly journals: small circulation, maybe – but with an influence that went far beyond their meagre readerships. From Connolly's angle, the editorship of a literary monthly would bring enormous advantages: power, influence, social connections and almost limitless opportunities for nest-feathering.

Nothing had come of the original project, but here in 1939 the omens looked more promising. Several of the era's highbrow magazines, among them Eliot's *Criterion* and Geoffrey Grigson's *New Verse*, had recently shut up shop: there was a small but promising gap in the market. If Watson could be persuaded to put up the money, Connolly reasoned, he might even see a return on his investment. An exchange of letters, in which Watson apologised for any misunderstandings about Jean, was followed by a lunch in Paris on the last day of August where Connolly set out his stall. Despite the fervour of Connolly's advocacy, Watson was unconvinced. Irrespective of the scheme's merits, he knew enough about Connolly – Connolly's idleness, Connolly's unreliability – to wonder whether he might make an effective editor.

All three parties to the transaction – husband, wife and potential sponsor – woke up the next morning to discover that Germany had invaded Poland: Europe was effectively at war. Within a week all three were back in England. Jean went off to stay with friends in Yorkshire. Connolly, for whom the attractions of editing a literary magazine had been increased by the realisation that it might count as war work, decided to renew his suit. Meeting Watson at a party at Elizabeth Bowen's in the last week of September, he took up the conversation that had lapsed nearly a month before in the Parisian pavement café. On this occasion Watson agreed. Time, it turned out, was of the essence. There were already rumours of other war-time literary magazines gestating in Bloomsbury parlours and publishers' offices: Evelyn Waugh, Osbert Sitwell and David Cecil were trying to raise the backing for a monthly to be called 'Duration'. As September gave way to October, at exactly the same time as Lord Gort's British Expeditionary Force began to establish itself in northern France, editor and publisher set to work. Watson, still worrying about Connolly's ability to manage the arrangements on his own, engaged Spender as associate editor and began to investigate some of the duties that the proprietorship of a monthly magazine would entail. Cyril, being Cyril, decided to take a short but invigorating holiday.

There were several reasons why Connolly – in excellent spirits, friends remembered, now that his immediate future had been settled – was looking forward to his early autumn trip to the north Devon coast opposite Lundy Island. One was that Diana had agreed to accompany him. Another, possibly even the reason for his choice of destination, was that Janetta and Hugh were staying in the area. A third was the chance it offered to brood on the possibilities offered by Watson's as yet unquantified largesse. Certainly, the new venture – as yet unnamed – obsessed him. Janetta, whom he visited, remembered 'talking for hours' about the magazine. Who would write for it? Who would work for it? What line, if any, would it take on the war? Who would design its cover? Who would print it? The autumn afternoons grew shorter; the winds blew in from the Bristol Channel; two hundred miles away in London Watson and his associate editor shook hands on the use of Spender's flat as an office; but in the room on the Devon coast the teenage girl and the jowly thirty-six-year-old chattered on: the midwives at *Horizon*'s beginning.

3.

When the Going was Good:
Lys, Connolly and *Horizon* 1939–45

Cyril, Hog Watson and many another lefty are avoiding military service by dint of being editors of a magazine ... which is a reserved occupation. Isn't it brilliant?

Nancy Mitford, letter to Violet Hammersley, 26 December 1940,
Love from Nancy (1993)

Nothing seems to toughen me. People will always fall in love with me because I am sweet and unselfish, only to use me for their own ends and trample upon me.

Lys, letter to Cyril Connolly, early 1950

One evening in the early summer of 1939, three months before Neville Chamberlain's declaration of war on Nazi Germany, a young man called Gavin Ewart was making his way along the western edge of Piccadilly. An aspiring poet, two years down from Cambridge, Ewart was filling in time with secretarial work while he plotted his assault on the citadels of literary London. He was also involved in a relationship with an immensely beautiful girl, two years younger than himself, named Lys Dunlap. Usually Ewart's route home by way of the bus stop at Hyde Park Corner passed without incident.

Now, as he traversed the railings of Green Park, something unusual happened. A sharp-faced boy in his late teens stepped out of the shadows and began to follow him along the pavement, yelling abuse as he went. 'Gavin Ewart is a terrible person,' he kept repeating, 'Gavin Ewart is a terrible person.'

What made the encounter even stranger, Ewart decided, was that he knew who the boy was – a fledgling painter called Lucian Freud whom he had met not long before at the Lansdowne Terrace flat of their mutual friend, Stephen Spender. Why should Freud want to hurl insults at him? What had he done to offend him? But all the way along the western side of Piccadilly the chant continued, like a mantra – 'Gavin Ewart is a terrible person. Gavin Ewart is a terrible person.' The experience was so disquieting that it stuck in Ewart's head for half-a-century, haunted his creative imagination and eventually re-emerged as poetry. In 'Freud', which recasts this tense five minutes or so in some chopped up lines of irregular blank verse, Ewart recalls his bewilderment, his inability to deflect the attack or ask the younger man what he was doing.

> . . . I cowered. I wasn't used to such attacks,
> I'd done nothing whatsoever to deserve such attacks,
> I was innocent and unsophisticated. What could
> > I answer?
> I now realize I should have stopped walking, and
> > made an answer
> Was he drunk, or on drugs – or was it a fugue?
> Is that sort of thing what the shrinks call a fugue?

Without stating the fact in so many words, the next few stanzas offer an explanation for why Lucian Freud should have stalked Ewart home down Piccadilly that evening in summer 1939. Shortly afterwards, Ewart's relationship with Lys came to an end. Not long afterwards, she married a man named Ian Lubbock, met when the two of them were briefly working at the Dorchester Hotel. Ewart never saw Freud again.

But I heard about him, later that year, from
                    Ian Lubbock
when he had married Lys. My girlfriend. Next,
                    Mrs Lubbock.
In 1939, I would guess. He came home one day, he
                    told me,
and found *Lys in bed with Freud* – that's what he told
                    me.
He didn't seem worried; it was like a piece of gossip.

Ewart's final judgement hangs slightly out of reach, but it is tempting to attribute Freud's outburst in Piccadilly to simple jealousy: he wanted Lys to himself. The young painter's pursuit of this gorgeous, and only intermittently attainable girl continued for several years. There were attempts to paint Lys's portrait, while a letter from the end of 1940 records his coming to sit next to her while she had dinner at the Ritz Bar – definite proof, Lys thought, that 'he still seems to be on my trail'.

The Dunlaps were from the west coast of America, not exactly pioneer stock but soldiers and adventurers operating on the margin of a country that was taking shape around them and keenly aware of the opportunities it offered to men with ambition and tenacity. Lys's grandfather, General Edward Dunlap (1848–1926), had fought in the Indian Wars and served as Military Governor of the Philippines. Her father Edward (b. 1872), made a fortune in the Alaskan goldrush, married a Welsh schoolteacher named Ida Davies, and relocated to Wyoming, where he became a successful mine owner. Lys, the younger of his two daughters, was born in nearby Butte, Montana, in 1917. By the time that Mr Dunlap died in an automobile smash in Philadelphia in 1932, his wife and children – there was also a son named Michael – had long since returned to Britain. If there was any family money left, it seems not to have crossed the Atlantic. Orphaned in her mid-teens after her mother's early death, Lys, like many another Lost Girl, was forced to fend for herself.

Following a well-worn route into the inter-war era labour force, she trained at Pitman's secretarial college and the London Polytechnic, and took office jobs. Capable, industrious and supremely good-looking, she supplemented her income with part-time modelling. Lee Miller's *Vogue* photograph from 1941 is a stunning portrait in which, cat-like, aloof and with swept-back waved hair, she wears what might almost be a pastiche parlour-maid's outfit, black-sided with white front and bow. By her early twenties, with Ewart cast to one side, she was married to Ian Lubbock, a schoolteacher with theatrical aspirations, and living in a flat in Great Ormond Street. She was also, by virtue of a stint at the advertising agency in Bruton Street, a friend of Peter Quennell. In all kinds of ways, Lys's path through the London of early 1940 was bringing her ever closer to the man with whom she was to spend the next ten years of her life: the fascinating, alluring and increasingly powerful figure of Cyril Connolly.

By the early autumn of 1939, *Horizon* was no longer a bright idea dreamed up on an idle summer's afternoon but a magazine in embryo. On 7 October, the *New Statesman* printed 'The Ivory Shelter', a surprisingly combative essay from a determined non-combatant, in which Connolly ruminated on the war's likely effect on contemporary writing ('the best modern war literature is pacifist and escapist and either ignores the war or condemns it') and, by implication, the aesthetic stance that any publication edited by him in wartime might be expected to adopt in relation to it. A fortnight later Connolly ramped up his attack by composing a circular letter to the *New Statesman*'s subscribers – a natural home for the brand of leftish-leaning scepticism he proposed to lay before the public – asking for support and suggestions. The firm of H. F. and G. Witherby, run by Diana's father, was engaged as printers; Peter Watson signed a formal contract to underwrite 1000 copies of the first four issues at £33 per number, while agreeing an informal arrangement with the newly appointed editor to pay the magazine's staff and the office expenses.

The bustle and excitement of *Horizon*'s foundation, much of it focusing on the lustre of his own personality, suited Connolly. 'An editor frays away his true personality in the banalities of good mixing', he later complained, 'he washes his mind in other people's bathwater, he sacrifices his inner voice to his engagement book', which rather ignores the satisfaction he took in the day-to-day routines of magazine editing, let alone the constant atmosphere of low-level intrigue. And yet, however enthusiastically he flung himself into arrangements for the launch, interviewed potential assistants and petitioned the great and good for contributions, he was grimly aware that the magazine's position – and by implication his own – was still highly precarious. All Peter Watson had legally committed himself to was a payment of £112 to a Holborn printer. If he disliked what he read, or thought that Connolly was exploiting his good nature or lacked the stamina that such an enterprise required, he might easily withdraw his support. There was also a suspicion that, here in a wartime world of falling investment values, the Watson fortune would soon be worth a great deal less. A generous and enlightened sponsor of the arts, Watson was also a prudent man who would have no qualms in pulling out of an agreement if he decided that his financial situation demanded it. Connolly's early letters in search of contributions were correspondingly downbeat. 'I am editing a paper, monthly of a flimsy kind, called Horizon, with Stephen Spender and Peter (W.),' he informed his old friend Alan Pryce-Jones on 19 October. 'I wish you would let us have something for it . . . We pay, though rather gingerly.'

To amplify Connolly's feeling of unease was the fact that his personal life was, once again, in disarray. Two days after the appearance of his *New Statesman* piece, he and Diana had been involved in a traffic accident in Sloane Square when an army lorry had crashed into the side of their taxi. Connolly was unhurt, but Diana emerged from the collision with a broken pelvis and spent the next two-and-a-half months in hospital. All this was sufficiently dramatic to inspire Jean to return to her husband's side. 'The blackout is really formidable,' Evelyn Waugh noted in his diary, '– all the gossip is of traffic casualties – the night watchman of the St James's knocked down the club steps, Cyril Connolly's mistress lamed for life and Cyril obliged to return to his wife.' But there was an unhappy circularity to the Connollys' new domestic arrangements, for they eventually came to roost at 26a Yeoman's Row, Knightsbridge – the same flat in which Connolly and Patrick Balfour had begun their London lives back in 1927. Looking around the familiar décor of 'this Haunted House', making his way home through streets that had long ago echoed to his tread, Connolly could have been forgiven for wondering exactly what he had achieved in the intervening years.

All this meant that *Horizon*'s debut in the first week of December 1939, its Ministry of Information imprimatur supplied by Connolly and Spender's handily placed friend Harold Nicolson, came hedged about with uncertainty. There had been proud talk of encouraging unknown writers, of bankrolling hitherto unheralded promise, of blithely disregarding both the feuds of the past and the inertia of the present, of an effort to 'synthesise the aestheticism of the Twenties and the puritanism of the Thirties' – both subjects on which Connolly was an acknowledged expert – into something better. But when it came to it none of the famous names whose help Connolly had so avidly solicited – E. M. Forster, Virginia Woolf, T. S. Eliot – had managed to produce anything; in their place came such favourites of the middlebrow reading public as W. Somerset Maugham, Hugh

Walpole and J. B. Priestley – exactly the kind of writers that the younger Connolly had made a point of disparaging in his apprentice years. 'Small, trivial, dull. So I think from not reading it,' Virginia Woolf sniffed to her diary.

However unpromising the omens, the magazine was a success: 3500 copies were disposed of the first number and twice as many of the second (for purposes of comparison with 1930s literary magazines, the circulation of the determinedly populist *London Mercury* rarely exceeded 10,000 while the subscription list to Eliot's *New Criterion* never got into four figures). By the time the fourth number appeared in March 1940, Watson was signifying his approval: 'I find the magazine excellent . . .' he informed his editor. 'Please tell me who is George Orwell: his article is *splendid*.'

The piece that had caught Watson's eye was 'Boys' Weeklies'; there were to be many more like it over the next eight years. As for Connolly's achievement, any kind of judgement on *Horizon*'s merits is liable to be clouded by the difficulty of calibrating what was said about it at the time with some of the compliments (and also some of the brickbats) it attracted long after the editorial office had closed its doors. On the one hand, it takes only a glance at the index to the ten bound volumes or *The Golden Horizon* (1953), Connolly's posthumous anthology, to establish the range and precision of Connolly's tastes. Certainly, a literary magazine that managed to bring together such diverse talents as Orwell, Henry Miller, Sacheverell Sitwell and Octavio Paz would be an ornament to any literary era, let alone that of Connolly and Spender. Almost any number taken at random off the shelf has something to be said for it – the issue of June 1948, say, which features a poem by Louis MacNeice, a fragment of Augustus John's autobiography, Lawrence Durrell on the physician Georg Groddeck and the paintings of André Bauchant. 'It is very proper that you should have proud memories of *Horizon*,' Evelyn Waugh assured Connolly from the vantage point of 1961. 'It was the outstanding publication of its decade.'

From another angle, Waugh's encomium was less a tribute to *Horizon*'s influence than an acknowledgement of some of its failings. To Connolly's detractors – and there were always plenty of these – the magazine was not only a projection of his personality but a home for members of his clique, the friends – not all of them conspicuously talented – he had made at Eton and Oxford, or picked up during his 1930s wanderings: the same old people, his critics insisted, and for the most part saying the same old things. As for the commitment to finding new voices, seeking contributions from parts of the demographic where the era's highbrow magazines rarely strayed, then John Lehmann's *New Writing* can sometimes seem much keener on taking risks, much more sympathetic to working-class voices of the calibre of Sid Chaplin and B. L. Coombes, and there is a rather awful symbolism in the fact that when Connolly got round to publishing a piece about working in a coal mine, the author should turn out to be not a genuine proletarian but an Old Etonian whose parents owned the mine.

There is no getting away from these imputations of gentlemanly suavity, and of a series of aesthetic assumptions that were as much social as literary. But this, it might be argued, was the price that had to be paid for allowing Connolly – a man whose literary sensibilities were inextricably bound up with every other part of his life – to become the enterprise's chief pundit and taste broker. And complaints about Connolly's editorial persona, the favours done and the responsibilities evaded, have a habit of ignoring *Horizon*'s prodigious influence on an artistic world that not only flourished in the 1940s but whose reach extended into the decade beyond. If what became known as the 'Herbivore' culture of the 1950s, the world of the BBC Third Programme, the *New Statesman* critic and the Penguin paperback, had a guiding spirit it could be found here in the office at Lansdowne Terrace in the shape of a jowly, cigar-smoking fat man browsing idly through a sheaf of newly submitted poems before stuffing them in a satchel and going off – quite possibly at someone else's expense – to a light luncheon at the Ritz.

Naturally, there were other beneficiaries of *Horizon*'s success. One of them was Connolly himself. If the magazine gave him a platform and a wider range of contacts than he had previously enjoyed, then it also bolstered his personal prestige, opened up all kinds of avenues for him that had hitherto been closed off. To read Frances Partridge's diaries from the 1950s, with their sightings of Connolly at dinner, or on holiday, or discoursing about books, is to appreciate just how very seriously he was taken, even by those who professed themselves sceptical of the seriousness with which he took himself. 'I feel faint resentment at the way everyone lays out the red carpet for Cyril,' Frances recorded at one point, 'just because he seems to expect it.' Nevertheless, she noted that she had exerted herself 'to cook a reasonably good meal and please and flatter him' because everyone else present clearly wanted him to be kept happy. Frances's friend, Julia Strachey, too, can be found complaining about the 'High Priest of Smarty Literature', a lament in which annoyance and envy are inextricably bound up.

None of this would have been possible without *Horizon*, without the grand *obiter dicta* about literature and its value, the lunches at the Ritz, the willing accomplices and, above all, the powerful mystique that rose above Connolly's head like the scent of myrrh from the tomb. A cynic – Mrs Q. D. Leavis, say, who offered some choice remarks about the personal element in his work – would probably assume that Connolly's literary ambitions were indistinguishable from his social aspirations, or rather that the one led naturally to the other, but this would be overstating the case. Anthony Powell, for example, left him out of his list of famous contemporaries (Waugh, Beaton, Betjeman, Quennell) who aimed to cut a figure in 'smart' society, on grounds that he simply could not suborn his temperament to the fashionable world's demands. As Powell puts it, 'Connolly's inability to put up with sustained smart life largely owing to his own cantankerousness, even his intelligence, was to some extent a fact (on the whole doing him credit) that he could not mask such characteristics in himself, notwithstanding fantastic powers of ingratiation, if he desired to exercise them.' Still, the suspicion lingered that he was happiest in the company of the well-born and the highly connected, and one of the funniest jokes ever played on him involved a group of friends out shooting in the north of Scotland parcelling up a dead duck and sending it south with a note that read, 'With love from Lady Mary.'

Here in early 1940, most of this lay in the future. Meanwhile, for all his newfound celebrity as the impresario of a successful literary magazine, Connolly's personal life was, once again, in tatters. A man newly reconciled with a wife who had spent much of the previous year living apart from him might have thought twice about employing his mistress in the office where both of them worked, but sometime in the spring Diana – now adjudged to have recovered from her injuries – took up residence behind a desk at Lansdowne Terrace. Most of her work involved appraising manuscripts according to the approved Connolly code – 'no good at all', 'doubtful', 'good' and 'outstanding'. Although Jean had disappeared to stay with friends at Malvern Wells – Connolly seems to have left Yeoman's Row to stay at a hotel in Charlotte Street – there were, as yet, no indications that she meant to leave him for good. Judging from the letter in which she proposes a triangular arrangement ('Why don't you and Diana take a cottage in the country and I'll come and stay and we'll all be high-minded and Bloomsbury and the best of friends'), she was still trying to make the best of a bad situation. Not long afterwards she made a new will in which Connolly featured as sole legatee and indicated that she wanted to give him half her annual income for the rest of her days. But the shades were drawing in around Connolly's married life, and in June she left for Dublin ('It is beginning to sink in how very far I am going and for how very long') and then for America. Even here, though, Connolly's powerful magic still worked its effect. 'Darling, darling heart, don't grieve,' runs her valedictory letter. 'I love you and will write you every week and will come back to you.'

Horizon, too, was on the move, a casualty of events taking place across the Channel. Hitler's assault on France began in the second week of May 1940; by 14 June, a fortnight after the British Expeditionary Force's retreat to Dunkirk, there were Nazi troops in Paris. As the fear of invasion grew, Peter Watson decided to lease a house at Thurlestone Sands on the south Devon coast where he, Connolly, Diana and Spender could conduct the magazine's business far away from the threat of war in the comfort of remote, provincial England. Despite the attractions of a hired car and a live-in cook, the relocation was not a success. Connolly spent most of what was intended as a working holiday sulking in his room and complaining about the lack of things to eat and the general inconvenience of being detached from his professional beat. Early in August, Watson informed his friend Cecil Beaton that 'on the 16th the lease is up and HORIZON may move to a famous tropical garden near Dartmouth', but this seems to have been ironic: clearly his editor pined to be back in London, and by the end of that month the editorial team were back in Spender's flat at Lansdowne Terrace.

Connolly, who would otherwise have been homeless, took a furnished apartment high up in Athenaeum Court, Piccadilly, an address so exclusive – Watson lived in the same block – that it was assumed that his patron was paying the rent. It was a time when the realities of war, generally evaded in *Horizon*'s guilt-ridden editorials, became sharply apparent. The London Blitz began on 7 September, watched by Connolly, Orwell and their friend Hugh Slater, from the Piccadilly eyrie. Lansdowne Terrace was hit ('Our office has been bombed and we have been without telephone for three weeks, but we are carrying on', Watson told Beaton.) And then, just as the bombs began to fall, Connolly's emotional life was plunged once more into crisis. Diana, still smarting from the unpleasantness of Thurlestone Sands, resolved to go on holiday on her own. As ever, when threatened by a disturbance in his personal circumstances, Connolly did all he could to forestall it. Threats of suicide; dire warnings of the likely effect of abandonment on his creative powers; interventions from mutual friends: all these were tried and failed. Alone in the furnished room at Athenaeum Court, Connolly was forced to face up to the regrettable fact that both wife and mistress had thrown him over in the space of three months.

It was at this point that the circles in which Connolly and Lys moved began to overlap. The Lubbocks knew Spender. They were also friends with a young student of the Royal College of Music named Natasha Litvin. The Lubbocks' flat in Great Ormond Street boasted a grand piano, to which Natasha was allowed access. One Friday towards the end of August, at almost exactly the same time that Connolly returned from the west country, Tony Hyndman, the bisexual Spender's former boyfriend, dropped by to invite the Lubbocks to lunch on the following day. After some persuasion at the hands of the voluble Hyndman ('Oh come on ducky, you'll love it'), Natasha decided to join the party at Lansdowne Terrace. Here her innocent eye fell 'wonderingly' on the various possessions that Spender had left lying around the office, the small Picasso that hung on the wall, the outsize gramophone, the shiny ebony desk, the records in their sleeves. Ian Lubbock introduced her to Spender, and the evening ended with the pair of them having dinner in a nearby Italian restaurant. Natasha, as she readily conceded, had 'never met people like this before'. The experience was that of being admitted into 'a totally new life'.

Meanwhile, two other people were heading rapidly down the same route. If Connolly and Lys did not meet at Spender's party, then they were introduced to each other shortly afterwards. Certainly, they were on the way to becoming an item by the autumn of 1940, by which time Lys and her husband had moved to a flat in Holland Park. A letter from her around this time brings news of domestic tension ('Ian has been shouting & screaming at me all morning'), canvasses a scheme for Connolly to get her a job on *Horizon*, offers him lodgings while the Lubbocks are away and hatches a plan for a rendezvous: 'I could have lunch with you tomorrow – if you would like that.' 'Everything seems to be so hopeless darling,' Lys lamented, 'but perhaps when I get back we shall have come to some decision.' Clearly husband and wife agreed to separate, for when, in the early part of 1941, Connolly moved into a studio flat at Drayton Gardens, SW10, rented from Celia and Mamaine Paget ('I have the Paget twins' house', he grandly informed Alan Pryce-Jones), Lys came with him.

What was Lys like, and what, aside from her startling good looks, did Connolly find to admire in her? The most obvious answer is that she admired him. ('People say she is dull,' Connolly is once supposed to have remarked about a woman he was pursuing, 'but she is interested in yours truly, and that is what yours truly likes.') At the same time, it takes only a glance at Lys's letters to establish the allure of her personality. Lively, affectionate and dutiful, she was, and continued to remain, a magnet for the opposite sex. Men fell in love with her almost on the spot: years later Connolly can be found complaining about the entourage of male admirers he (wrongly) imagined her to be encouraging. There were complaints about her tendency to prattle and her 'silliness', but her occasional gaucheness seems to have stemmed from an anxiety to please, a deference to the interests of the people around her that, in a world of super-egos and male peacocking, strikes an odd note of humility.

What did the parties to this transaction want from it? Connolly, fresh from his dealings with Jean and Diana, seems to have been fascinated by the regard of an exceedingly pretty woman who not only admired his intellectual brilliance but appeared happy to organise his somewhat chaotic domestic life. Lys, it is fair to say, saw something that her marriage to Ian Lubbock had apparently lacked: a future, a man she respected and for whom she pined to create an environment in which he could feel at home. And so the revolution in Connolly's existence that took place at the end of 1940 was as much administrative as emotional. Lys cooked for him, she arranged luncheons for his friends and relatives, she hired an accountant to explore his complicated finances, did calculations on his behalf and, by submitting details of his entertaining expenses to the Inland Revenue, seems to have ensured that he paid virtually no income tax. The end in view, as she was happy to admit, was a settled relationship, leading to marriage. But this, as she also conceded, was always likely to be complicated by the emotional turmoil that Connolly liked to create around himself.

As soon as Cyril decided he wanted something, he wouldn't rest until he had it. And he was very good at making you feel guilty for not giving him what he wanted. Like a child, he would beg and beg, and then when you gave in, his attention would go to another thing. Sometimes I think he only really loved me when he thought he was losing me. There were endless scenes.

It was inevitable that some of Lys's organisational skills should be brought to bear on the tangled and resolutely ad hoc arrangements of the *Horizon* office. Until now, most of the routine administrative work had been carried out by a floating population of part-time staff. Bill Makins, the original business manager, had disappeared into the army. At various times over the first year-and-a-half of the magazine's existence, secretarial duties had been performed by Diana, a 'Miss Warren', a woman called Liza Mann and a young man barely out of his teens named Michael Nelson. Janetta occasionally helped out and appeared at parties. Far more experienced in the realities of office life than her predecessors, Lys not only brought her managerial skills to the environment in which Connolly conducted his professional life but doubled up as his social secretary. When Spender and Natasha decided to get married in the spring of 1941, the wedding party was held at Drayton Gardens under her supervision.

Tolerant of Connolly's foibles, anxious to make the paths he trod run smooth, ever humble and almost infinitely pliable, Lys was prepared to put up with a great deal, in particular the expansion of the Drayton Gardens *ménage* to include the free-loading Quennell, who had previously been lodging at the flat in Holland Park, and Connolly's protégé Arthur Koestler, a deserter from the French Foreign Legion who had arrived in England after a torturous escape from North Africa and then joined, and been discharged from, the Pioneer Corps. Although there was plenty of space, the premises harboured only a single bathroom. Each morning, with the late-rising Connolly still fast asleep, Lys looked on with amusement as Quennell and Koestler contended for the first bath.

The Drayton Gardens lease expired early in 1942; it was Lys who found a new flat for Connolly at 49 Bedford Square, with a spacious drawing room for entertaining and an attic where the ever adaptable Quennell swiftly established himself. Here and there in the diaries and letters kept by the literary figures of the 1940s come glimpses of their domestic life together. One visitor who warmly approved of Lys was Evelyn Waugh, not least for her ability to overcome the sumptuary privations of the war. 'On Friday I lunched with Christopher and Camilla [Sykes] and dined with Cyril Connolly,' runs a letter to his wife Laura from September 1943. 'His mistress loves me still. Nancy there too. Truffles and lobsters.' Six months later he could be found telling Lady Dorothy Lygon that 'Cyril Connolly and his delightful mistress give dinner parties which I enjoy very much but it always means walking home from Bloomsbury'. The man in the attic was more circumspect, amused by Connolly's airs and finding his companion slightly irritating. A site report from early September 1943 notes that 'at Bedford Square existence is still fairly tranquil: but Cyril is at his most *sensitive* and Lys – in the role of *The Mouse at Bay* or *Battling Minnie* – has been getting slightly on my nerves'. The sharp-eyed Quennell also detected in Connolly a growing sense of his own importance, a determination to live in a way commensurate with his status as an arts-world power-broker: 'Cyril and Lys continue to live a life of conjugal sybaritism, getting up at 12 and entertaining large parties of the intelligentsia, with a slight vanilla flavouring of the nobility and gentry.'

As ever, Connolly's state of mind in the war years oscillated wildly. On the one hand, his star was in the ascendant. The move from Drayton Gardens to the comparative splendour of Bloomsbury seemed to symbolise his newfound status. ('Cyril . . . has taken an enormous flat in Bedford Sq. and is very much on the up-grade', Diana informed her brother.) But however much he enjoyed the benefits of being the editor of a highly regarded literary magazine, he was also restless, dissatisfied with his lot and looking out for fresh opportunities. One promising new sideline came his way early in 1942, when his friend David Astor, proprietor of the *Observer*, appointed him as the paper's literary editor. The salary was £800 a year and the duties minimal, but Connolly's time in Fleet Street was not a success. There were rows with the *Observer*'s editor, Ivor Brown, and an eventual falling out with Astor, who thought the books pages too abstruse and was annoyed by Connolly's habit of criticising him behind his back.

Worse, the end of his *Observer* contract in the summer of 1943 was immediately followed by his fortieth birthday. Connolly took the anniversary hard: a symbol of lost youth; an impenetrable barrier separating him from the consolations of the past. *The Unquiet Grave*, the manuscript on which he was currently at work, a selection of *pensées* infused with the elegiac note of classical myth, is a kind of casebook of accidie, full of inner disquiet and intensely realised longing for days gone by. Years later, Lys would tell him that the only time she had seen him 'completely happy' was when he was working on it. Simultaneously, the days passing by the window at Bedford Square were full of danger. 'This, as you've probably read in the papers, is SECRET WEAPON WEEK,' Quennell told one of his correspondents in June 1944. 'Pilotless planes whizz over the house-tops.' While Quennell affected to be relatively unmoved by the sight of a V1 hurtling over the London rooftops ('It just goes bowling thro' the sky, explodes and there you are'), he reported that Connolly and Lys ('exceedingly buzz-bomb conscious') took refuge in a shelter they had constructed beneath the stairs. The slimline Lys 'fits in as neatly as a maggot into a pea-pod'; her overweight consort, on the other hand, reminded him of a large rabbit trying to squeeze into a rathole.

If Lys was not always on hand in the *Horizon* office – she was called up for war work in 1942 and spent nearly two years working as a secretary in the Political Intelligence Department – then she was a constant presence in Connolly's life, dealing with his affairs, presiding over his entertainments and, it has to be said, running his bathwater and cooking his breakfast. Three years into their relationship, it was still her ambition to marry him, and yet if this feat were to be accomplished, several outsize hurdles had still to be negotiated. One of them was legal, for at this stage in the proceedings both editor and consort were married to somebody else. The other was Connolly's inertia, his deep-seated reluctance to be persuaded into a decisive step, and the obvious satisfaction he got from letting things drift. Some progress was made in 1944 when Lys secured a divorce from Ian Lubbock (Connolly was named as the co-respondent), while Connolly went so far as to inform Jean that unless she returned to England or said that she intended to he would institute proceedings himself, but the turn of the year offered two highly symbolic instances of the way in which Connolly regarded his long-term girlfriend and the role she might play in his complicated existence.

The first was publication of *The Unquiet Grave: A Word Cycle by Palinurus*, brought out in a limited edition of 1000 copies under *Horizon*'s own imprint before being reissued by Hamish Hamilton. 'Palinurus' was the pilot of classical mythology, appointed by Aeneas on his voyage from Troy to Italy, who fell asleep, was swept ashore and murdered by savages. His body was left unburied, and when Aeneas visited the underworld he was petitioned for formal interment by his shade. Lys had helped to type Connolly's manuscript, and yet at least one of his friends interpreted the project as little more than a long-drawn out complaint about the world he now inhabited: 'half commonplace book of French maxims, half a lament for his life,' Evelyn Waugh suggested. 'Poor Lys; he sees her as the embodiment of the blackout and air raids and rationing.'

The second instance was Connolly's trip to post-war Paris, undertaken alone, in which he seems to have been treated as a paladin of English literature hastening back to salute the culture he had been compelled to forsake during the four years of Nazi occupation. ('We've had C. Conelly [*sic*] for three weeks in the house,' Lady Diana Cooper, the wife of the British Ambassador, reported back to Waugh, 'being feted as though he were Voltaire returned.')

It would have been scant consolation for Lys to be asked to reassure Peter Watson that he was missing nothing – 'it is not the Paris we knew but an unreal city' – for most of his friends suspected that he had been vastly enjoying himself: his letter to Lys, as Diana pointed out to Janetta, 'sounded as though he'd had the most wonderful time'. Neither, perhaps, would Lys have been impressed by news of Connolly's recantation of his original view and a wholesale surrender to the delights of French literary life that led to the entire July 1945 number being filled with contributions relating to Sartre, Valéry and other manifestations of French genius. Most ominous of all was an observation that she never got to see – a line in a letter that Quennell, still vigilant in the Bedford Square attic, confided to a friend in November 1944. Connolly, he adjudged, 'is, I fancy pretty bored – but not so bored as to wish to put out onto the wide dark seas of a new adventure'. For Lys, who fussed over his wardrobe, who organised Connolly's parties and haggled for black-market food to delight his friends, the next few years would bring only stasis, frustration and ever diminishing returns.

Interlude: Mapping the Forties Scene

To talk of 'literary life' in the 1940s is faintly misleading. All that remains, three-quarters of a century later, is a number of different literary lives, of which the world inhabited by Connolly and his friends was only one – and that, some neutral observers would argue, not the most important or long-lasting. If the 1940s are the decade of *Horizon*, then they are also, in no particular order, the decade of neo-Romantic poetry, of Eliot's *Four Quartets*, of dozens of crowd-pleasing middlebrow novelists such as Hugh Walpole and J. B. Priestley, whose books outsold anything that Connolly ever put his name to by a factor of fifty to one. Occasionally these categories overlapped – both Walpole and Priestley contributed to *Horizon*'s opening number; Connolly, too, in his *New Statesman* reviewing days, had been an astute critic of such undemanding middle-of-the-road fiction as came his way. At other times, though, the gap between a metropolitan sophisticate and a provincial journeyman, between a bestselling novelist and a recherché little magazine poet, between the prescriptions of highbrow taste and the books with which ordinary readers beguiled themselves on trams and trolley-buses could show every sign of developing into an abyss.

We can see something of the myriad, differing constituencies which forties literature addressed by tracking Orwell's progress through the decade. The *Horizon* regular; the literary editor of the left-wing weekly *Tribune*; the BBC producer; the *Manchester Evening News* and *Observer* reviewer; the pamphleteer; the polemical columnist . . . All these varying ports of call contributed something to the literary persona that he constructed for himself in the ten years before his death, and separating out the 'real Orwell' from this routinely overstuffed workbook is impossible: no such thing exists, and the author of *Animal Farm* and *Nineteen Eighty-Four* was as much at home lunching with a left-wing Labour MP – Michael Foot, say, with whom he enjoyed cordial relations – as chatting to Connolly about their time at prep school. The same point could be made of Evelyn Waugh: happy enough to allow Connolly to shepherd his novella *The Loved One* into print in 1948, but eternally suspicious of the avant-garde artists and the translated foreigners that were a crucial part of the *Horizon* offering, more likely to be seen executing prestige commissions for Sunday newspapers or taking part in religious debates in the Catholic press.

As for what gave Connolly his power, his celebrity, his paralysing influence on upper-brow taste in the 1940s, then the explanation was at least as much social as straightforwardly literary. Critics of the Connolly line – an increasing number as the decade proceeded – usually begin by asserting that in any enterprise to which he put his hand the aesthetic waters have been muddied by affiliations that are, essentially, located in class, that the boundary between the people Connolly printed in his magazine and the people with whom he dined and with whom he had been to school and university was faint to the point of invisibility. Certainly, Connolly's circle at this time can seem horribly homogenous. Scarcely anyone who turned up, manuscript in hand, at the *Horizon* office or made his bow at one of Connolly's parties had failed to attend a public school: Connolly, Watson, Orwell and Brian Howard were Etonians; Spender had been to Westminster; Quennell to Berkhamsted; Waugh to Lancing College. Most of them – Orwell was the exception – were Oxford graduates. None of this made them upper class by the standards of the time – Waugh was a publisher's son from Hampstead, Orwell's father, Richard Blair, had retired from the Indian Civil Service on a pension of £600 p.a. – but it was a key factor in the almost imperceptible closing of ranks that sometimes distinguishes bygone literary life, the suspicion that a poet or a novelist or a short-story writer is being judged not by the quality of his metrics or the suppleness of his prose, but on whether or not he happens to be 'one of us'.

The literary forties are full of symbolic illustrations of this divide, of extraneous talent being welcomed into the exclusive palisades of *Horizon* or John Lehmann's *New Writing* only to quail before some of the social assumptions on display. Shortly before her death in 1941, for example, Lehmann persuaded Virginia Woolf to allow him to print the text of a lecture entitled 'The Leaning Tower', given to the Brighton branch of the Workers' Educational Association. Here the author of *Mrs Dalloway* and *The Waves* spoke loftily of writers occupying 'a raised chair', of benefiting from gold and silver, of relishing their detachment from the workaday world: 'to breed the kind of butterfly a writer is you must let him sun himself for three or four years at Oxbridge or Cambridge'. The former miner B. L. Coombes, who complained of Woolf's snobbery, was himself rebuked by Lehmann. To an Old Etonian, whose first job had been working as the Woolfs' assistant at the Hogarth Press, inclusiveness could only go so far. Or there is the salutary tale of Sid Chaplin, another pitman with literary aspirations, encouraged by Orwell (who printed his stories in *Tribune*) and invited to call should he happen to be in London. Arriving at the very modest maisonette that Orwell shared with his wife Eileen in Kilburn, NW6, Chaplin discovered that a party was in progress on the other side of the front door. Unable to face the metropolitan sophisticates who lurked within, he turned on his heel and fled.

Thirty or even twenty years before, this kind of thing would have passed without comment. But there was a new kind of criticism beginning to establish itself, one less respectful of established reputations, more inclined to interrogate the social underpinning of the work brought before it. Q. D. Leavis – never afraid to name names – had already produced a pioneering essay entitled 'The Background of 20th Century Letters', in which Connolly's *Enemies of Promise* and the memoirs of Logan Pearsall Smith, Edward Marsh and Louis MacNeice were glacially appraised. How to obtain literary preferment in England? According to Mrs Leavis, the 'odious little spoilt boys of Mr Connolly's schooldays move in a body up to the universities to become inane pretentious young men, and from there move into the literary quarters vacated by the last batch. Those who get the jobs are the most fashionable boys in the school, or those with feline charm, or a sensual mouth and long eyelashes.' What gives this assault its kick to anyone in the know is the fact that the final phrases are a direct quotation from Connolly's account of Brian Howard in his Eton pomp. 'The advantages Americans enjoy in having no Public School system, no ancient universities etc., can hardly be exaggerated', she crossly concludes.

Even more than Connolly, Brian Howard (1905–58) would come to be regarded as the villain of the piece, the self-regarding flibbertigibbet whose spectacular lack of success seemed not to have occurred to his well-placed friends, endlessly cosseted and indulged in the hope that he might someday write the masterpiece of which everybody assumed him to be capable. 'Today the gentlemen are on the defensive,' Connolly's old adversary Julian Symons wrote in 1972, 'but there are still reasons for being miffed about (to take a small instance) the seriousness with which a book about the talentless Brian Howard, talentless perhaps but amusing, and one of us, was recently treated.' The book in question was Marie-Jaqueline Lancaster's *Brian Howard: Portrait of a Failure* (1968), a remorseless 600-page compendium of narcissistic play-acting and serial non-achievement, and, as Symons points out, respectfully received by many a newspaper arts critic.

It was Connolly himself who came up with the adjective that still tends to attach itself to the style that he and his friends championed in the era of the Blitz, the Normandy landings and the Attlee government: 'mandarin', which to a Leavisite would have meant detached, ironic and *de haut en bas*. Come the 1950s, the epoch of Angry Young Men, of 'Movements' and grammar-school boys on the make, the mandarins would be in sharp retreat, driven back by the provincial, middle-class tide that produced novels like Kingsley Amis's *Lucky Jim* (1954) or Malcolm Bradbury's *Eating People is Wrong* (1959). A decade later, they were museum pieces. But here in the 1940s, Connolly was a genuine literary power-broker, a grand panjandrum, a maker – and breaker – of reputations. And if one part of his attraction to the Lost Girls – Sonia in search of her great man, Lys in search of security and a settled home life – was his status, then another lay in his familiarity, his ability to shape up to the requirements of their caste. The process worked both ways. Highly individual and distinctive personalities Lys, Sonia, Janetta, Barbara and the others may have been, but like Brian Howard each of them was also 'one of us'.

4.

'Skeltie darling . . .'

Wake up. Foul mood. Detest myself.

Barbara Skelton, diary entry,
12 October 1941

Everything about you interests me and makes me miserable.

Peter Quennell, letter to Barbara Skelton,
1 January 1943

There are several direct routes into the chaotic and impulsive world that Barbara Skelton inhabited in the early 1940s. One is to take a specimen week in her life and examine the extraordinary degree of emotional complexity it seems to have produced. Here she is, for example, drifting through the last few days of 1941. On Christmas Eve her boyfriend Peter Quennell – one of several contending admirers – invites her to dinner with Connolly and Lys. The evening is not a success, largely due to the posturings of the host: 'Cyril always manages to create a strained atmosphere, which is a pity', Barbara records in her diary. For her own part, she feels 'self-conscious and shy'. There is a plan for the party to reconvene the following day for Christmas lunch, but in the morning Lys arrives at the tiny flat in which the pair of them are holed up to rescind the invite. Then, towards the end of the festive period, possibly even on New Year's Eve, there is another supper with Connolly ('Cyril seems more human as he was not being a host at one of his own dinners') and Augustus John. Everything seems to be going well until, back at the flat where she and Quennell are preparing for bed, another boyfriend, the artist Feliks Topolski, turns up unexpectedly. A terrible row ensues, which ends with Quennell smashing a flower vase. 'What a hideous New Year! What exhaustion; what depression!' Barbara laments the next morning. Her low spirits are not improved by Quennell's somewhat arch attempts to cheer her up: 'Oh! Poor thing. Oh! You pretty little thing. You poor dainty pretty', he is recorded as saying. Barbara's diary entry ends with the single word 'Ugh!'

Quite a lot of Barbara, it turns out, is gathered up in this single wartime week: the eternal dissatisfaction; the multiple relationships; the attendance on the great and good; the self-doubt; the sense of existing at the centre of a gigantic emotional mess which it is beyond anybody's ability to disentangle. Another route lies in her highly autobiographical first novel, *A Young Girl's Touch* (1956), which tracks her erratic progress through the Second World War. Barbara, who features as 'Melinda Paleface' and of whom it is said that 'she was far too young and pretty to live in London alone', is first seen working at the offices of a continental government in exile, where she devotes her mornings to 'doing her face or making dates by telephone with all her friends and admirers' and her evenings to being entertained by them at a variety of West End restaurants and backstreet nightclubs.

An unabashed freeloader ('Someone was always there to take Melinda out to dinner'), equally in her element lunching at the Berkeley Hotel or attending blue-movie screenings in Chelsea, her fatal attraction is ascribed to a trick of cupping her chin in her hands and staring abstractedly into the distance to create 'an air of elusiveness that men found irresistible'. At the same time, the deep wells of private unhappiness in which her boyfriends so regularly tumble make her captious and spiteful. Plus, as she frankly concedes, she has a habit of falling for a succession of men every bit as unreliable as herself. Despatched to 'Jubaland' (a thinly disguised Egypt) as a cipherine – a cipher clerk – she is taken up by the local potentate 'King Yoyo' (an even less thinly disguised King Farouk) who delights in thrashing her with a dressing-gown cord. 'Nothing was ever as black as it seems,' Melinda reflects at the close of her tragi-comic picaresque. 'The entire course of our life can change completely at a moment's notice.'

That was certainly true of Barbara, whose abrupt changes of emotional tack became legendary among the people who witnessed her making hay with her countless admirers or were unfortunate enough to be on the receiving end of one of her drop-of-a-hat disappearances. 'Her attachments being multifarious and multiple,' as one despairing suitor put it, ' . . . she could conclude a tiff by walking out of a morning to reappear after some days and re-establish herself, as of right, to be off again at the arising of friction.'

If *A Young Girl's Touch* falls into the category of ingénue confession – one of those engaging books in which a stream of hair-raising events is recounted with a comparatively straight face – then by the time of its appearance Barbara had spent nearly two decades up to her neck in the kind of life it so carelessly describes. Skelton *père* was a regular army officer who had married an Edwardian chorus girl and in doing so alienated himself from grander relations. There was Danish blood – the source of Barbara's ravishing good looks – an ancestral connection to Sheridan, and a germ of temperamental excess that led her aged four to attempt to run her mother through with a carving knife. 'It is doubtful if she had much love for her child', Barbara later reflected. Sent to a convent school from whose disciplinary regime it was thought she might benefit, she was expelled in her early teens for forging a series of love letters to herself signed 'Fred'. All attempts to constrain or otherwise subdue her having failed, she was allowed, aged fifteen, to leave home and live in a London YWCA hostel.

Like her alter-ego Melinda, Barbara was far too young to be left to her own devices. The first of her many admirers had been an Armenian uncle, the husband of her mother's sister Vera, who had arrived in her bedroom one night to plunge a hand down the front of her nightdress and, when out driving, invited her to search for sweets in his trouser-pocket. A guards officer who picked her up in Hyde Park and inveigled her to a louche hotel in Leicester Square was narrowly repulsed. Then, aged seventeen, she was seduced by a millionaire friend of her father's, who took her for a weekend to Brighton and afterwards set her up in a flat in Crawford Street, Marylebone. All the customary trappings of the *poule de luxe* swiftly descended on her teenaged head – an allowance, a Bechstein piano, a fur coat, high-end foreign travel. On her eighteenth birthday, she looked out of the window to see a chauffeur parking a sports car at the kerb. In this equipage she was driven around Europe, taken to stay in Paris ('A suite at the George V. Champagne lunches at Fouquet's. Afternoon drives in the Bois. Shopping in the rue de Rivoli. Josephine Baker at the Folies Bergère') and brought back to London for a discreet nursing home abortion. Most girls in her position would have stuck out for what they could get. Barbara, being Barbara, ended the affair out of sheer lassitude. Bored by the routines expected of the rich man's mistress, she took to modelling for the high-class couturiers Schiaparelli and Hartnell ('Schiap', she always thought, appreciated her 'as my dimensions conformed to the hourglass silhouette'), pining for the bohemian life while acknowledging that whatever society she fell into would always fall short of her expectations of it. Like Melinda, 'for years she had longed to get away into the unreal world of London. Now that she had done so, happiness still seemed far out of reach.'

All this raises the question of milieu, the kind of world Barbara inhabited in her twenty-something heyday and the kind of people she encountered in it. On one level, naturally, it is the sort of existence sketched out in the famous chapter in *Vanity Fair* entitled 'How to Live Well on Nothing a Year', in which a suit of finery or a three-course dinner is all the more enticing for being subsidised by somebody else. It was also a world of stratospherically differentiated removes, in which the Ritz Hotel and the rat-haunted bedsit, the flyblown country cottage and the out-of-season continental resort all play their part, and the next significant other is as likely to be a half-starved painter as a cheque-book wielding millionaire. What stopped her from being a kept woman, pure and simple, was her irritation, her refusal to play any emotional game that failed to suit her highly exacting tastes. Michael Wishart, who knew her in the 1950s, noted that 'she had a tantalising quality of needing a tamer, while something indefinable about her indicated that she was untameable'. Significantly, the most common complaints raised in her boyfriends' letters were not so much of bad behaviour (though there was certainly plenty of that) but sheer unreliability. *Where are you? Why haven't you phoned? Why didn't you meet me when you said you would?* And so, unremittingly and incriminatingly on.

The Skeltons made one final effort to bring Barbara to heel, or at any rate to secure some kind of plausible future for their wayward daughter. Sometime in the mid-1930s, as a cadet member of the tribe of orient-bound inter-war era spinsters known as the 'fishing fleet', she was sent to India to find a husband. The visit took place under the auspices of her Uncle Dudley, who after a distinguished army career had reached the rank of general in the Royal Army Medical Corps. No one suitable could be found, but there was an inevitable besotted young officer named Charles Langford-Hinde who, on her return to England, was discovered to have stowed away in her cabin. Barbara obligingly kept him hidden for the first part of the voyage, smuggling in food and barring the door to strangers, but on the third day out a message came through from army headquarters at Poona and once the ship docked at Aden he was taken off in close arrest. Each of the parties in the romance went home in disgrace: Langford-Hinde to a court martial and banishment to the North-west Frontier, where he died in an ambush by rebel forces led by the Fakir of Ipi; Barbara to a wrathful *j'accuse* from Uncle Dudley, who had written to her father complaining that she was a disgrace to the family and he never wished to see or hear from her again.

The Indian episode seems to have played an important part in Barbara's private mythology, a tantalising lost past she ached to revisit, part of the person she imagined herself to be. Quennell remembered her telling him 'the story of the young man who stowed away on the boat back from India'. There were carefully preserved photographs of Langford-Hinde and of Barbara herself at the time of her Indian adventure, wearing jodhpurs with a half-grown leopard at her feet. Quennell, suspecting embellishment or downright invention, wondered quite how much of the story he ought to believe, but it was a fact that Barbara's voice when she related it and described how, from the rail, she had watched Langford-Hinde being taken off the ship 'was muted, wistful and remotely sad'.

Back in London there was more modelling for Fortnum and Mason, Stiebel and Hartnell, and – courtesy of the art critic Michael Sevier, then married to her friend Louise – an introduction to the bohemian nightlife of the West End. There was also a purchase that came to have a vital bearing on her future life. Sometime in the late 1930s, flush with modelling cash, she laid out £400 on a tiny cottage near Hastingleigh in Kent. Known as the 'Cot', and supervised in her absence by the friendly local policeman, PC Boot, this became important to Barbara in a way that none of her other habitations could ever match. Quennell noticed that while her London addresses were merely 'temporary resting-places', in which she took no interest in decoration or tidiness, in Kent she became an energetic housekeeper, who loved the Cot 'a good deal more than she loved or liked most human beings'. She was twenty-three, and had already got through more experience than half-a-dozen women twice her age.

* * *

The war seemed to make little difference to Barbara's lifestyle. Perhaps in the end it was only that the men with whom she associated became more polyglot – refugees from continental Europe, Free French officers plotting restitution. By late 1939 she was living with her friend Luba Bergery in a tiny top-floor flat in Kinnerton Street. But this bolthole soon gave way to an apartment on Curzon Street whose rent was paid by a French banker named Georges Boris, who was 'desperate for a woman and I seemed to fit the bill'. The Blitz came and the bombs fell but the social round continued: pre-lunch drinks in the Curzon Street Sherry Bar; lunch at the Ritz, the Coquille, the Ecu de France or the Coq d'Or in Mayfair. Then, after the void of the West End afternoon, there might be a trip to the Conga nightclub off Berkeley Square, the Suivi, the Jamboree or to watch the rising young actor Peter Ustinov at the Players' Theatre Club. There were 'scenes' when Georges's wife discovered her husband's infidelity and the idyll – if that was what it was – promptly shattered.

It would take a private detective, here in the war-torn London of early 1941, to trace Barbara's precise movements over the next few months, but they were accompanied by a paralysing lowness of spirits. 'Wept and wept', runs a diary entry from early in January; three weeks later she is 'desperately depressed' and 'so low'. For a time she lived on the top floor of a house in Hertford Street lent her by the dress designer Jo Mattli, escaping its destruction in an air-raid by a providential trip to the country. There were brief periods working at unspecified jobs ('Sacked', the diary reports in mid-February, 'jolly annoying'), stays at Cranmer Court in Chelsea, where the senior Skeltons had now fetched up, with a friend in Ebury Street, and days and nights spent at the artist Feliks Topolski's studio off Warwick Avenue.

Topolski, it has to be said, was fairly typical of the many men whose instinct for beauty, capriciousness and trouble drew them towards Barbara in the early 1940s: at once passionate, sensitive yet not above resorting to physical violence if rivals pressed their suit, and also resourceful, tough and well-connected, quite able to rise to the challenges of living hand-to-mouth in a country that was not his own. Born in Poland in 1907, Topolski had set up home in London in 1935. Here he immediately became a part of the artistic circle of the Café Royal, where such luminaries as Augustus John, Jacob Epstein and Matthew Smith held court. There were valuable connections with D. B. Wyndham Lewis, 'Timothy Shy' of the *News Chronicle*, whose column he illustrated, and George Bernard Shaw, who thought him 'an astonishing draughtsman' and encouraged him to supply drawings for *Geneva* and *In Good King Charles's Golden Days*. By the time he met Barbara he had graduated to the position of war artist, alternating as a war correspondent and a Polish second-lieutenant of infantry. ('Topolski,' General Sikorski, leader of the Free Polish, is once supposed to have twitted him, 'how is it that yesterday you were a middle-aged civilian and today you're a young lieutenant?')

And if the Polish war artist was fairly representative of the kind of man to whom Barbara attached herself in Blitz-era London, then the circumstances of their courtship were more typical still. According to Topolski he first set eyes on her being entertained by a Free French officer in the French Pub in Soho. When, shortly afterwards, they met face to face, she consented to be taken back to the room he was currently renting in Albemarle Street. Here, according to an account written nearly half-a-century later, 'she pressed mutely (her sole/toes signalling through my thigh) for spinning out the deed, to conclude with apologetic whisper "I only need it twice – first thing, and in the morning."' A photograph from around this time shows her lying face down on Topolski's bed, stark naked, eyes raised coyly at the camera. If Topolski assumed that he was to be allowed exclusive access to this new conquest he was badly mistaken. According to Barbara's recollection she was simultaneously involved with a journalist named Anthony Cotterill, an officer called Captain Brien (referred to in her diaries as 'Cold Veal') and a Yugoslav doctor known as 'the Horse Thief'.

Onto this comparatively crowded scene, in the spring of 1941, arrived the figure of Peter Quennell, at this point still married to his third wife Glur, who would bear him a child in the early part of 1942, but to all intents and purposes living the life of a carefree bachelor. Not that any of Quennell's musings on Barbara, who was to alarm, demoralise and obsess him for the best part of two years, could ever be described as carefree. For all his attempts to document their relationship and for all the evidence of his anguished letters, the life they intermittently shared between 1941 and 1943 is almost impossible to reconstitute, largely because of the altogether chaotic conditions in which it was lived: a world of snatched evenings in briefly tenanted bedsitting rooms, missed appointments and long periods of estrangement, where almost everything – from basic chronology to situational detail – is in doubt. According to Barbara they first met at her friend Gerda Treat's house in Culross Street. Quennell, on the other hand, preserved a recollection of being taken by a girl with whom he was having an affair to call on her 'rather dotty little friend', then living with a Free French colonel. Quennell remembered her 'sitting all alone, on the end of the bed but fully dressed, as though she were a good little school-girl waiting to be taken out'. That their relationship proceeded rapidly enough for them to think about living together seems to be confirmed by an undated letter from around this time inviting her to stay with him in Ian Lubbock's old premises ('an otherwise empty rather squalid flat in Holland Park . . . which has few amenities except a constant supply of boiling hot water').

Forty years later, Quennell was still in raptures about Barbara's beauty. He thought she might have had eastern blood. At any rate, 'there was something about her slightly slanted eyes, her prominent cheekbones and smooth olive skin that suggested the youthful concubine of a legendary Mongol chieftain'. For her own part, Barbara reckoned that 'with his Byronic attitudes, wit and blond quiff Peter struck me as being a romantic figure'. On the other hand, this impression 'was soon dispelled when I knew him intimately'. There followed a complex game of hide-and-seek, involving Barbara, Quennell, Topolski and several other men besides, played out among the bedsitting rooms and furnished flats of Mayfair and Chelsea, characterised by suspicion, jealousy and resentment, and rendered yet more complicated by the demands of war work. Quennell at this point had given up his job in advertising for a post at the Ministry of Information. Topolski left the country in August 1941 to accompany the first British convoy to Russia. Barbara, after finally appearing before the call-up board, spent time driving trucks for the Mechanised Transport Corps, was employed as a wages clerk in the factory owned by the millionaire who had first seduced her and then, like Melinda, came to ground as secretary to the Yugoslav government in exile ('a gang of Balkan horse-thieves', Quennell sniffed) at their office in Exhibition Road. Even in ordinary circumstances, pursuing any kind of relationship in the febrile atmosphere of Blitz-era London would have been difficult. But for the men spiralling helplessly in Barbara's orbit, it was practically impossible.

What Barbara felt about it all – a curious mixture of fatalism, self-reproach and a case-hardened determination to enjoy herself while the going was good – may be divined from her fragmentary diary entries: watching Quennell stationed in the telephone booth opposite their flat 'fixing himself up with free meals' before sneaking off to the cinema with Topolski, or candidly acknowledging the extraordinary turmoil of her life: 'What a messy existence! What chaos! What indecision! I feel depressed and unsettled.' Trying to establish what she thought of her two principal suitors, she decided that she liked Quennell for the feeling of 'security' he brought with him and Topolski 'for his company'. Equally, there were occasions when their joint absence alarmed her ('Gloomy gloomy as can be. No Feliks. No Peter') or when both of them managed thoroughly to exasperate her. Thus, buying them presents at Christmas 1941, she exploded: 'Goodness knows why I bother, they will certainly not give me anything. Anyway I am sick to death of both of them.' Quennell and Topolski, meanwhile, were sick to death of each other, conscious that they were being manipulated by a force they could not hope to subdue, both desperate to rise to the top in the struggle for Barbara's favours. Matters came to a head one night at the Gargoyle Club when Quennell, furious at finding 'the ambitious and adventurous young foreign artist' in his girlfriend's company, cornered them by the lifts, swung a punch at his rival and in the ensuing mêlée ended up with two cracked ribs.

An undated letter from Quennell, probably written in the early part of 1942, may be taken as representative:

> Skeltie darling,
> After the ridiculous events of last night, I think I had better leave the initiative to you. Telephone when & if you feel inclined. For some time now you've been becoming more and more difficult & undependable: so perhaps it would be a good thing if you saw less of me or didn't see me at all. You know that I'm just as attracted as I was last autumn indeed much more attracted . . .

Looking at the situation through the prism of Barbara's diaries, one sees immediately just how exasperated she is by her suitors' sulks and insinuations. 'What an insufferably suspicious nature!' she wrote on the occasion when Quennell appeared in her room one morning, shortly after the Horse Thief's departure, and began searching the premises for clues. On the other hand, Quennell clearly had cause for concern: as Barbara acknowledged, 'I must say the bed was in rather a pickle with the bedclothes in disorder and dirty towels strewn about the floor.' But Barbara herself was not above the occasional twinge of jealousy, or rather a faint wistfulness at the thought of a world that she was not yet privileged to enter. A diary entry from around this time notes that Topolski has been seen dining at the Café Royal 'with a very lovely girl'. The suspicion that this was Janetta is reinforced by Barbara's rather rueful gloss: 'It's glamorous to be left-wing these days.' At the heart of the problem, one might suspect, lay a realisation that she could not bear to be with anyone for any length of time. Quennell remembered that, when weekending at the Cot, the atmosphere had usually turned shaky by Monday morning. One early morning start for London with Topolski began with Barbara abusing the taxi-driver, only to apologise with the words, 'I'm sorry, I confused you with my friend.' At the same time, the Kentish weekend offered the chance of many a romantic frisson: four decades later Quennell could still recall a walk in dense August heat when they descended a steep path between fields of barley and wheat that rippled in the breeze. The Greek word for 'Corn-Goddess' is *Chalkokrotos*, Quennell noted: Barbara, stripping off her shirt to wade bare-breasted through the corn, 'made an admirable young Demeter'.

If these mythological visions were always doomed to failure, it was because Barbara could rarely be got to share them, or indeed to tolerate conditions of prolonged intimacy. Not only did close proximity make her anxious and keen to find fault, it also encouraged her talent for homing in on the other half's temperamental weaknesses and frailties. Quennell believed that 'she had acquired a knack, perhaps half-unconscious, of distinguishing her lovers' weakest points, just as certain wasps, accustomed to paralyse their prey, know where to sink their stings'. All this could lead to profoundly embarrassing situations, such as the occasion when the cottage, in which Barbara was staying with yet another boyfriend, 'a gallant young soldier', was visited by the local curate bearing one of Quennell's books for signature.

And so, through the spring and early summer of 1942, the dance went on, an intricate pattern of break-ups and make-ups, spectacular fallings-out and ardent reconciliations in which occasional moments of euphoria ('Barbara darling, thank you so much. I've seldom been so happy – certainly I haven't enjoyed myself so much for a long time') alternated with murmurings of disquiet ('Don't forget me sooner or more thoroughly than you can help') and admissions of the most abject misery.

What did Quennell want, here amid the complications of a life that included the virtual cessation of his literary career, the crack-up of his marriage to Glur and the birth of his daughter Sarah? Despite the serial abandonments and the unignorable evidence of rival suitors, he seems to have believed that, with a fair wind behind them, he and Barbara could plan some kind of future for themselves. The promise of secure accommodation in the rooms above Connolly and Lys's Bedford Square flat in May prompted him to compose a long, reflective letter apologising for yet another recent tiff, revealing, inter alia, why in the midst of his affection for her, he found her so infuriating, and proposing a fresh start:

My darling Skeltie,

I was miserable when I'd rung off in a temper – one always is: but you've worried and disappointed me so much & made me so wretched that a certain degree of acerbity was perhaps not altogether inexcusable. I can't bear all this muddling for muddling's sake – particularly when you're so fond of telling *me* I'm weak-minded & an opportunist. Give me credit for being extremely fond of you: & then decide whether your behaviour later (after the initial shock of the Easter business) hasn't, to say the least of it, been a little inconsiderate. You want people to be fond of you – not to treat you in a casual promiscuous way – but certainly you don't give them a great deal of encouragement. I could be much fonder of you than I am *if* I were given a chance . . .

Let's leave it at this: think things over & if you make up your mind you want to go on seeing me on the same terms and want to make Bedford Square a more or less permanent place of residence, telephone me here on Monday morning. If I don't hear from you I shall assume that the whole thing

is finished: which I may add will make me exceedingly
unhappy but which I shall regard as just another illustration
of the beautiful old couplet:

> La plus belle fille du monde
> Ne peut donner que ce qu'elle a . . .

Darling Skeltie, I hope you ring up but am resigned to the
worst . . .

Goodbye, darling & bless you.

This is a revealing letter, not merely for its exposure of the
paralysing depths of Quennell's unhappiness, but for the light it
sheds on Barbara's temperament: wanting people to like her in a
serious, non-promiscuous way, but simultaneously never giving an
inch in her relations with them; behaving badly and then compounding
her indiscretions by accusing her lovers of shortcomings most of
them believed her to be guilty of herself. The phone call was eventually
made, and Barbara moved into Bedford Square, not wholly to her
landlord's satisfaction. Janetta remembered Connolly complaining
about her using up the supply of hot water – 'That girl he's got up
there's always having a bath.' There were also occasional depredations
on Connolly's quarters. Barbara's diary records 'several grumpy
meetings with Cyril on the stairs . . . I suspect it's due to the pouffe
being removed from his sitting room.'

Meanwhile, as Quennell had reluctantly to acknowledge, her affair
with Topolski was far from over. Most of his letters to her over the
second half of 1942 strike the same anxious, end-of-tether and
frequently paranoiac note, and if at the end of July he was anxious to
tell her that 'I love you very much and look forward to seeing you again',
then by November Barbara found herself stigmatised as 'impossible – at
least as far as I am concerned'. If only, Quennell assured her, she was a
little more normal, 'or understood yourself just a little better'.

Undoubtedly Quennell's agitation was stoked by distance. He was transferred to Belfast at one point, writing nervously home to instruct Barbara – now apparently gone from Bedford Square – to communicate with him 'when you can. I think of you a great deal and wonder – resignedly – what you are up to. How is that Topples?' Back in London, he continued to see her on an almost daily basis, 'though, if a storm blew up – and she was fond of raising storms – she might temporarily disappear'. The wider patterns of Barbara's life, meanwhile, exhibit an almost Thackerayan ability to mingle luxury and squalor from one hour to the next. Coming back one night from dining with Connolly and Lys at a fashionable restaurant to the house in which she was squatting she discovered that the kitchen was infested with vermin: 'Found half a Hovis gnawed away with nothing left but the outside crust.' A storm of particular intensity blew up in December 1942 when she simply disappeared. All Quennell's attempts to contact her over the festive period failed and he was reduced to angry letters. A particularly anguished example survives from three days after Christmas in which Quennell notes sourly that 'Here's another item to add to your file of unanswered correspondence. Will you *please* get in touch with me as soon as possible?'

Another reproachful communication sped forth from the Ministry of Economic Warfare, to which Quennell had recently been relocated, on New Year's Day:

> I suppose you're at cot, dear cot, so frequently profaned, about which I used to feel so romantic!: I imagine you're there with Grub [the military boyfriend] – exploiting the advantage of his interminable farewell. I wish you would telephone me – if only to say that you are now legally Mrs Grub & never wanted to see me again! In 1943 we *must* either separate completely or provide our distracting relationship with some sort of settled basis . . . New Year 1943 was not so bad as New Year 1942, but pretty bad all

the same & I have this morning a dreadful hangover . . . Do appear soon, darling – even for an *Ave atque Vale* . . . I hope you had a nice New Year

A bientot

Why do you spend your whole life cutting off your nose to spite your face? It's far too small a nose to deserve cutting off – & far too pretty a face to be so deliberately & wantonly spoiled . . .

In fact, Barbara had been staying at Topolski's studio, an unhappy interlude which culminated in a decision to separate herself from him permanently. 'Parted from Feliks for good two days ago,' runs a diary entry from early January, 'and am intending to collect my belongings over the weekend.' Quennell's luck turned a day or so later when Barbara telephoned out of the blue and 'unabashed and apparently affectionate', agreed to meet him at the Ritz. Quennell arrived to find a phone message cancelling the date. Twenty-four hours later she finally materialised, 'looking rosy and innocent, with a disarming (if not entirely convincing) story of what she had been up to'. For a week, somewhat to his surprise, Quennell basked in her smiles, though he was careful to remind himself that she '*can* be very difficult'. All this made him reflective, determined once again to work out why he was so smitten with a woman who treated him so capriciously and at times seemed positively to enjoy the experience of making him suffer. Later he would compare himself to Hazlitt in *Liber Amoris*, outlining his humiliations at the hands of Sarah Walker. Both men, he thought, had 'suffered ignominious reverses, and both the young women we loved had an inexplicable attraction.' For the moment, he contented himself with analysing pros and cons, acknowledging that Barbara was extraordinarily quick at detecting her other half's limitations and exposing his pretensions, while admitting that 'There is no one I like sleeping with more – or with whom I find it more agreeable to wake up.'

To balance this was Barbara's fondness for what even the bohemian Quennell reckoned was unsuitable company, her unwavering habit of attracting and sometimes encouraging 'the unlikeliest devotees; and if they were disreputable, eccentric or perhaps a little grotesque, she found them all the more appealing.' Worse still, from the point of view of an enraptured swain, was her duplicity and the delight she took in mocking him behind his back. Coming across one of her diaries, he was forced to acknowledge that he was a 'Chaplinesque figure of fun'. And always, lurking ominously in the margins, was the 'obstinate spectre' of Topolski. Somehow the relationship staggered on into February, when Quennell's diary records 'Telephonings . . . and again more telephonings', in which Barbara 'then proceeded to enlarge on last night's theme and lucidly explained my role as *pis-aller*, with some animadversions on defects in my character . . . She has now concentrated against me in a tight knot of resentment and suspicion.' Once, around this time, they came to blows: 'the bruise on her nose has spread – giving her a darkly spectacled appearance which is not altogether unattractive'. Then on 5 February she disappeared again. Quennell found himself 'oddly calm – almost relieved . . . a load seemed to have dropped off. Independence. Clarity.' Shortly afterwards Barbara rang from Waterloo Station, where she had missed her train, offering 'plausible excuses and a candid friendly voice'. Why carry on? Quennell wondered. The reason, he decided, lay in his isolation and Barbara's charm.

By now, as the spring of 1943 drew nearer, there was a suspicion that none of this – the vagrant lifestyle, the multiple love affairs, the daily attendance at the office in Exhibition Road – could be indefinitely sustained, that too many plates had been sent spinning to avoid the smash of shattered crockery. Meanwhile, the levels of complaint continued to rise. 'Peter irritating beyond belief,' runs a diary entry from this time. 'The cold weather makes him terribly snappy. In fact any time now that his life doesn't run absolutely smoothly he behaves petulantly.' Inevitably, Quennell's petulance was increased by Barbara's frequent disappearances. 'Barbara Darling!' begins a letter from mid-April. 'For the 100th time I feel completely wretched about you . . . *Where* are you anyhow?' It was a good question, that probably occurred to her employers at the Yugoslav government in exile: a ramshackle organisation, according to Barbara's diaries, but one which required basic levels of punctuality from its staff. And so the spring wore on. The letters went back and forth. The meetings were cancelled and rearranged. Finally, there came a day when Barbara arranged to see Quennell at the Ritz. 'Is baby pleased to see Peter?' Quennell hopefully enquired. 'Baby's been sacked for arriving late at the office every morning for the past two months,' Barbara shot back.

What was to be done? Where was Barbara to go, and how was she to earn a living? At this juncture a friend who worked at the Foreign Office suggested that she offer her services as a cipher clerk. The promise of foreign travel and warmer climes worked its effect. Her application for a post in the British Embassy in Cairo was accepted. The cottage at Hastingleigh was shut up and left to the care of PC Boot. In June, after a round of emotional farewells, and with a stream of anguished letters following her north, Barbara caught the train to Liverpool and took ship for the Middle East.

Interlude: Glur

At first glance Glur – Joyce Frances Warwick-Evans, in strict baptismal terms – looks like the Lost Girl to end all Lost Girls, a titan of the species in whose effervescing wake lesser competitors tumbled off into obscurity. There are the coruscating good looks, effortlessly reproduced by the society photographers of the day (Angus McBean's snap from 1938 is so flawless as to make her look almost sinister, with huge and rather startled eyes staring out of a perfectly oval face); there is the chaotic family background (her father jumped ship early on in his marriage, leaving his wife to bring up two small children); there is the string of glamorous marriages (writers, heirs to marquessates, rich young men); the rackety transit through a world where bohemia and the *beau monde* seemed to collide head-on. One by one, year by year, assignation by assignation, each successive scrap of Lost Girl plumage slides neatly into place.

After this, though, the resemblance to Lys, Sonia, Janetta or Barbara runs into trouble. Unlike her contemporaries, Glur had no ambitions to run a magazine office, marry that elusive great man or go to literary parties. In fact, she had no intellectual pretensions whatever. 'I thought it would be fun being married to a writer,' she is supposed to have complained, not long after her first marriage, before adding the fatal caveat, 'but he's always writing.' In some ways Quennell's ever-roving eye was less of a problem than his obsession with Byron. So what did she want? The answer seems to be that, whether living in Chelsea with Quennell or in the stately seclusion of Savernake Forest with the marquess's heir, her principal aim was, as her daughter put it, 'to be the centre of attention'.

As to where the roots of this attention-seeking lie, the strongest candidate is her fractured childhood. Charles Warwick-Evans was a distinguished cellist and leader of the London String Quartet, who absconded while on tour in California, leaving his abandoned wife to marry a Swiss businessman named Werner Glur. There was enough money to send Joyce to St Felix's, a fashionable girls' boarding school at Southwold on the Suffolk coast (where she was marched around the games field by Orwell's girlfriend, Brenda Salkeld), and, aged fifteen, to enrol her at RADA, after which catastrophe struck, her stepfather's business collapsed and she was forced to fend for herself. Her exploits over the next half-decade, here in an England of mass unemployment and deep unease over the coming war, are almost beyond recall. Like Barbara, a year older but indisputably cut from the same cloth, who she came across at this time, she modelled for Norman Hartnell at his premises in Bruton Street. There were very possibly fleeting appearances in a pair of Gainsborough Studios productions under the stage name of 'Camilla Sans', though no film directory of the period has any record of her. And then, aged twenty, there was marriage to Quennell, who according to family legend saw her from the window of the Bruton Street office where he worked and darted out of the building to introduce himself.

There followed a lightning introduction to the upper-bohemian world which was Quennell's professional beat. They spent Christmas 1937 with Connolly and Jean in a rented house whose guests included Spender, the classical scholar and Oxford personality Maurice Bowra, Christopher Isherwood and Brian Howard. What she made of this exotic gathering – Isherwood and Howard are supposed to have amused themselves by dressing up as their mothers – is anyone's guess. Flirtatious, sprightly, the life and soul of any party going, Glur (as Quennell had now christened her) was also a manic depressive – this had been diagnosed in the RADA years – whose flights of over-exuberance alternated with periods of chronic despair. But there was something else gnawing away at her, a second source of unhappiness that made her physiological difficulties that much harder to bear. This was the conviction that her life had taken a wrong turning, that the opportunities she coveted had been denied her, that the pleasures of the world she inhabited were as nothing compared to the path she could have pursued had fate been on her side.

At an early stage this belief seems to have concentrated on Hollywood, on the films she could have made and the starring roles she could have occupied had marriage, children, England, the war – all kinds of obstacles and impediments – not got in the way. But for Quennell, she used to say to friends – and presumably to Quennell himself – she could have taken up that offer from Paramount. There was even talk of her being debarred from an appearance in Carol Reed's wartime biopic *The Young Mr Pitt* (1942), alongside Robert Donat. No hard evidence of either offer exists. 'Tainted by self-pity', a relative once declared, and the self-pitying seems to have begun here, out on the margins of the film world, in London flats waiting for calls that never came, in agents' offices pushing her luck.

Meanwhile, there was Peter, marriage (it was Quennell's third), a rented flat in Flood Street with a maid and an increasing suspicion that none of this was going to last. Not, one should hasten to add, that there was any animosity. Glur liked 'PQ', as she called him, notwithstanding the disbarment from Hollywood and all she could have achieved 'but for you', and Quennell's letters to third parties are full of quasi-affectionate references to 'Glurky' and her latest escapades. What seems to have pulled them apart was the similarity of their temperaments, a refusal to settle down and plan for a future that could only be exacerbated by the privations of warfare, its continual uprootings and situational dilemmas. By the time the bomb fell on Flood Street they had both moved out. Quennell was in Northern Ireland with the Ministry of Information and already involved with Barbara, Glur staying with her mother in north London. Their daughter Sarah, born in 1942, was something of an afterthought, a souvenir from the final day of a long-ago holiday, unexpectedly resurfacing. 'I've just had a sweet letter from Glurky,' Quennell told Barbara, 'in which she assures me that her daughter, besides being ravishingly pretty, looks just like me!' There would be no more Christmases with the Connollys. It was time to be moving on.

But where exactly? If writers spent all their time writing, in addition to being chronically hard up, then what was the alternative? There are some characteristic glimpses of Glur in action in the memoirs of Peregrine Worsthorne, at this point an army subaltern to whom she had been introduced at his Pirbright passing-out parade. Summoned to pick her up at More House, the Chelsea home of the Wilde-era aesthete Felix Hope-Nicholson, Worsthorne arrived to find Brian Howard languidly reclining on a Récamier sofa. When they returned to More House after dinner, Glur, those present observed, was wearing her escort's Sam Browne belt wrapped around her evening frock. Meanwhile, with a divorce in prospect – Barbara was cited as the co-respondent – she had another target in view. 'Glurky has got her Absolute and plans to marry a middle-aged nobleman in March', runs a scrawled PS on one of Quennell's letters to Barbara in early 1944. This was Cedric Cardigan, or, to give him his full name, Chandos Sydney Cedric Brudenell-Bruce, heir to the marquesate of Ailesbury and about as far removed from Quennell in interests, background and demeanour as it was possible to conceive.

Thirteen years older than his prospective bride, a product of Eton and Christ Church Oxford, an enthusiastic flyer and, as such, author of *Amateur Pilot* (1933), the owner of an apparently unique collection of toy soldiers, Cardigan was also a war hero who, captured by the Nazis after the fall of France, had escaped from his POW camp and literally walked home to safety through France and Spain. What he imagined he was getting in Glur, immediately installed in Tottenham House, an outsize mansion hidden in the depths of Savernake Forest where she liked to be known as 'Flavia Cardigan', is anyone's guess. At any rate, no sooner was the marriage solemnised than Quennell was writing to inform Barbara that it 'may spell a good deal of trouble in the not very remote future for the affectionate but uninspiring Earl'. As for what Glur thought she was getting, her obituarist notes only that she 'soon tired of country life'. Worsthorne, misreading his map while out on manoeuvres on Salisbury Plain, turned up one night with his patrol to find the Earl away but his wife and father, the elderly Marquess, in residence and eager for company. Some Italian prisoners of war living on the estate provided musical accompaniment and the evening became a part of regimental folklore. But Glur, too, had misread her map. Her indiscretions with the American soldiers billeted in a wing of the house caught the eye of her husband's servants. When the divorce petition came to court, the Earl's butler was called to give evidence.

Once again, it was time to be moving on. One constant in the Lost Girl's life was her ability to find an escape route: a place to stay; a source of income; an eligible or not so eligible suitor. Sometimes all three came providentially combined. Three years after the war's end, Glur, still barely thirty, was married to a wealthy young man named John Dyson Taylor, living in

Belgravia and expecting a baby. The big house in Savernake Forest was left to the Earl, now hard at work on the bestselling memoir of his great escape, *I Walked Alone*. Three-quarters of a century later, Glur's daughter Sarah could still remember the nursery's red baize door.

5.

Struggling to Go Beyond Herself: Sonia 1918–45

It is as if for Sonia man could do nothing greater than to write books.

David Plante, *Difficult Women* (1983)

Many of the thirty or forty onlookers eating their lunch at the Café Royal on the spring day in 1940 would have known the identities of two of the three people discreetly ensconced at a table in the corner of the room. The stocky figure in the tweed jacket with the coil of proof-sheets protruding from the satchel that lay beneath his chair, fat hand raised to emphasise a conversational point, was the editor of *Horizon*, whose fifth number could be seen outside on the Piccadilly newsstands. The tall, curly-haired man seated next to him was his associate, Stephen Spender. On the other hand, only the restaurant's most seasoned habitués would have recognised the plump, pale-faced girl on the other side of the table. A prodigious new literary talent whose work *Horizon* proposed to launch upon the world? Connolly's mistress? A distant relative up from the country for a London jaunt? In fact, Sonia Brownell was executing what she imagined to be a commission. Although this was not her first encounter with Connolly, Spender was an old acquaintance. It was the second time in a few weeks that she had come here with him, and by his plate lay the letter she had written him a day or so later. 'Last Thursday night at the Café Royal you asked me to edit a number of *Horizon* on Young English Painters. I don't know if you meant this, but I thought about it afterwards and these are my suggestions . . .'

Had Spender meant it? Sonia was barely twenty-one, and although she knew something about art – she had been spending her time with painters since her teens – she had almost no experience of putting pen to paper: in these circumstances, commissioning her to edit an entire number of an upmarket literary magazine in the early stages of its development would have been a gamble, and any failure marked down as a terrific misjudgement on the editors' part. On the other hand, as both Spender and Connolly had acknowledged, the proposals set out in her letter had been assembled with considerable care. The names named – potential contributors included such ornaments of the contemporary art scene as William Coldstream, Victor Pasmore, John Piper and Graham Sutherland – were the right ones. There was a promising scheme to reprint an essay by Winston Churchill to fill in the historical background. An index; a page of small ads offering work for sale . . . Everywhere they looked came evidence of a discriminating intelligence with an eye for some of the practical realities of magazine editing.

Whether or not Spender meant it, Sonia certainly had, and 'Horizon: Young English Painters' might easily have come to fruition had not Peter Watson, an arch-modernist when it came to art, jibbed at devoting a whole number to a style of painting of which he thoroughly disapproved. In the end, and to her considerable annoyance, the proposal was politely declined. But Connolly, with his weather eye for talent, knew that he had chanced on something out of the ordinary. From that moment onward, here in the busy restaurant, with the clamour of Piccadilly resounding in the street outside, Sonia's card was marked.

* * *

What did Sonia want? This was a question that exercised the minds of the people who knew her for upwards of forty years. Spender's diaries are full of disquisitions on what made her tick and the unease and frustration that seemed to lie at her core. On the day of her funeral in 1980 he found himself thinking of the early days of their friendship back in the late 1930s. Then, Spender thought, she had the look of someone 'always struggling to go beyond herself – to escape from her social class, the convent where she was educated, into some pagan aesthete world of artists and literary geniuses who could save her'. Sonia, he decided, had always been on the look out for a great man, a titan of art or literature, to whom she could devote herself and whose interests she could self-denyingly serve. On the other hand, the peculiar, twisted resolve she brought to this determination would always lead her into trouble. 'Undoubtedly she had passionate loyalties – loyalty of some kind was her deepest nature and it transcended her disloyalty, which was the expression of her frustration at none of the people who were the objects of her passionate admiration quite responding'.

There was something misdirected about her efforts, Spender thought, one consequence of which was that the artists and literary geniuses she had in her sights were 'always being faintly embarrassed by an enthusiasm that never quite hit the centre of the target'. What a friend who met her in the early 1940s calls her 'innate rebarbative ways' meant that the connections she wanted to make were rarely established in a manner that made her happy or brought very much satisfaction to the person at whom she had set her cap. And if some of these characteristics were on display at a very early stage in her career, even over lunch with Connolly and Spender at the Café Royal, then, as she grew older, they became more pronounced and made the puzzle yet more insoluble to the people who watched her go about her work.

One of the things Sonia certainly wanted was to escape from the constrictions of her upbringing, a series of advances and retreats in which loss, abandonment, genteel poverty and outright trauma all played their part. She was born in August 1918 in Ranchi, India, a child of the Raj whose early years might have offered promising material for the plot of a novel by Somerset Maugham. Charles Brownell, her father, was a Calcutta freight broker, who died four months after her birth in what looked to be deeply suspicious circumstances: at the early age of thirty-six, apparently of a heart attack while for some reason out at night on a golf course. Beneath the formal record of his death there ran hints of suicide, lost jobs, longstanding business problems suddenly rising to the boil. Within weeks his widow Beatrice had taken her two daughters – there was an elder sister named after her mother but known as Bay – back to England. Within a year she had married a chartered accountant named Geoffrey Dixon, who, coincidentally enough, was a director of Turner, Morrison, her late husband's employers. The family returned to Calcutta, where a son named Michael – always adored by Sonia – was born in 1921.

From an early stage, the surfaces of the outwardly conventional upper-middle-class childhood that followed hid untold fractures and flaws. There was time spent with Vivien Hartley, the daughter of her mother's best friend, who later became known as the actress Vivien Leigh. At six she was sent to board at the Convent of the Sacred Heart, a school in Roehampton made famous, or perhaps only notorious, by *Frost in May* (1933), a novel by its vengeful ex-pupil Antonia White. Meanwhile, things were going wrong in India, where Geoffrey Dixon, a serious drinker prone to erratic behaviour, was about to be sacked by Turner, Morrison.

By 1927 the whole family were in Liverpool, beset by illness – Michael nearly died of emphysema – and lack of money. Although sufficient funds were eventually amassed to send Sonia back to the Sacred Heart, then this, too, was part of the problem, for if the first institution that the teenaged girl burned to detach herself from was bourgeois family life then the second was a Catholic education.

Always contemptuous of her schooling, she later wrote a *Horizon* piece about her 'Jesuitical' training ('perhaps the most perfect weapon devised for trapping the child . . . no area of the human personality is safe from the priests' probing cauterisation'), and is once supposed to have remarked at a hockey match in the hearing of a nun that 'I'm so bored I wish I'd been birth-controlled so as not to exist.' In her mid-twenties she could be found informing Diana Witherby that she still spat in disgust when she saw nuns passing in the street. At the same time, as her biographer Hilary Spurling points out, she was honest enough to realise that the nine years behind the Roehampton privet hedge had made her into the person she was, that as well as a loathing of religion and the people charged with inculcating it, she brought away from the Sacred Heart such virtues as honesty, loyalty and kindness. Work, as Spurling puts it, 'was her substitute for faith'.

But what sort of work? And to what end? Unhappily, her mid-teens coincided with another crisis in the family's affairs when her mother, strongly backed by Bay, walked out of her marriage. With three children to support and no regular income, this was a precarious step, but Mrs Brownell was a resourceful woman. By managing a number of small hotels and boarding houses until her divorce settlement came through, she eventually amassed enough capital to open her own modest establishment at 31 Tregunter Road, South Kensington. There are literary shadings here, for this is essentially the environment of Patrick Hamilton's *Craven House* (1926) and J. B. Priestley's *Angel Pavement* (1930) – a world of travelling salesmen hoisting their suitcases up creaking stairs, muted conversations in the aspidistra's sickly shade and ill-assorted transients eating communally around the long dining table. Perhaps the most ill-assorted of all was Sonia herself. Like many a Lost Girl, her innate intelligence was compromised by the lack of a proper education. On the other hand, if no one at the Convent of the Sacred Heart had ever encouraged her to sit a public examination, then the staff included two zealous young nuns named Mary Allpress and Bertha Meade who gave her books to read and stimulated her interest in the literary world. Under their tutelage she won a leaver's prize in 1935 for an essay entitled 'Man is a Builder', which expressed a belief that 'Poetry . . . is the music and painting of the mind.'

As Sonia's seventeenth birthday loomed, the question of what to do with a girl whose literary and artistic yearnings were balanced by a complete lack of educational qualifications loomed ever larger in Mrs Brownell's imagination. In the end, the money was found to send her to Neuchatel in Switzerland to stay with the sister of a Protestant pastor named du Pasquier, whose daughter Madeleine was her age. Here she could take courses in French literature and language at the local commercial college and, it was assumed, enhance her prospects of employment when she returned to England. Everything went well until the day in May 1936 that changed her life for ever. The drama in which she was caught up was of sufficient magnitude to be reported on the foreign news page of *The Times*:

THREE DROWNED IN SWISS LAKE
ENGLISH GIRL RESCUED
FROM OUR CORRESPONDENT, GENEVA

On the previous afternoon, *The Times* reported, three students of Neuchatel University who had gone sailing on the lake – Madeleine and two boys named Jean-Pierre Roethlisburger and Paul Chappuis – were drowned in a sudden squall. 'The fourth student in the party, a young English girl, Miss Sonia Brownwell [*sic*], of London, swam until rescued by a steamer.' Returning to Neuchatel after a picnic on the far side of the lake, the party had run into trouble when a storm blew up: the boat collided with a beacon and capsized, throwing the occupants into the water. 'They got a footing on the boulder on which the beacon was placed,' the report continued, 'and after 20 minutes righted the boat, but they could not get back into it owing to the violence of the waves. They clung to the boat for some time, the two young men supporting Mlle du Pasquier, who could not swim.'

Sonia, opting to strike out for the shore, was brought back to the upturned boat by the sound of screams. She could only watch as, one by one, the others disappeared into the water. As the second boy began to slip beneath the waves he grasped at her. Without the strength to save him, and knowing instinctively that he would only drag her down, Sonia broke free, and after battling against the waves for over half an hour was herself picked up by a passing steamer and brought back to Neuchatel, together with the body of Mlle du Pasquier, which had been rescued by the steamer's crew. The memory of that afternoon on the Swiss lake, together with its grim aftermath – among other duties she had to tell Madeleine's parents what had happened – stayed with her for the rest of her life.

Back in England, traumatised and disaffected – there were rows with Mrs Brownell and Bay over her reluctance to help out at the boarding house – she enrolled on a secretarial course, moved out of the family home and took a room on the margins of Fitzrovia. Although there was no decisive breach with her mother and sister, Sonia always suspected that they disapproved of her and wanted her to lead a more conventional life. A letter from the mid-1940s describing her presence at a Brownell Christmas notes that she was 'thinking it would be awful but it turned out to be wonderful . . . my family buried all their latent disappointment of me & were very gay + kind'.

Halfway between Bloomsbury and Marylebone, and bisected by the Tottenham Court Road, her new lodgings lay in bohemian territory, the world of faded backstreets and seedy antique shops immortalised by Anthony Powell's *A Buyer's Market* (1952), and the friends she made there – exotic and polyglot – would not have done for Tregunter Road. With two of these attendants – a Russian named Serge Konovalov and the Polish Eugène Vinaver – she set off on a summer tour of the Balkans. Both men were twice her age; each had

115

designs on her. Journeying by car around Yugoslavia, Bulgaria and Romania, their adventures included being chased by a pack of wolves through a pine forest and selling the car's tyres to buy their way out of imprisonment in a Romanian jail.

Then, in the early part of 1938, almost by accident, came a decisive step, when she rented a room in a block behind the Euston Road. By chance it lay immediately behind the disused car showroom and repair shop to whose upper floor the Euston Road Art School had relocated a month or so before. Founded the previous October as a 'School of Drawing and Painting', and bringing together the talents of such young contemporary painters as Claude Rogers, Victor Pasmore and William Coldstream, the 'Euston Road Group', as the Bloomsbury critic Clive Bell would christen them, was known for what its members liked to call 'objective observation'. Keen on such painterly qualities as subtlety and restraint, they aimed at a kind of realism that would be accessible to ordinary gallery-goers. Inevitably, this being the late 1930s, there were political overtones: Coldstream and his friend Graham Bell had recently spent three weeks in Bolton, lodging in a boarding house and painting cityscapes and factory chimneys as part of a Mass Observation art appreciation project intended to establish how local people would respond to paintings of their environment executed in a variety of contending styles. The titles of their best-known works – Coldstream's *St Pancras Station*, say, Pasmore's *The Flower Barrow* or Rogers's *Young Women and Children in the Broadwalk, Regent's Park* – give a good idea of the kind of effects they aimed at: an artistic landscape in which ordinariness, exactitude and formal English exteriors are sedulously combined.

Eighty years after its inception, the Euston Road School's somewhat dutiful style of portraiture has not worn well: 'Euston Road painting had a downbeat, low-key mood,' Martin Gayford has suggested: 'the colours were drab, there was an air of gloom.' But Coldstream, Pasmore, Rogers, Bell and their associate Lawrence

Frances Partridge cuts Janetta's hair, Ham Spray, 1936. *(Estate of Frances Partridge)*

Ralph, Frances and Janetta, late 1930s. *(Estate of Frances Partridge)*

'I envy you the lovely Janetta.'
(Connolly family)

High jinks at Tickerage – Peter Quennell and Glur, late 1930s. (*Sarah Gibb*)

Connolly with (*left to right*) Jean, Angela and Janetta, weekending at Tickerage, late 1930s. (*Connolly family*)

'I will not be faithful, I want love too' – Diana, late 1930s *(Connolly family)*

Connolly and Diana on the rocks, late 1930s. *(Connolly family)*

'[Stephen Spender] was very nice but I can never feel quite at ease or natural with him.'
(Cecil Beaton/Getty Images)

'One of those rich people who without seeming at all dependent on his wealth … manages to get the utmost in the way of pleasure and beauty out of riches' – Lucian Freud's portrait of Peter Watson. *(Victoria & Albert Museum, London, UK/© The Lucian Freud Archive/ Bridgeman Images)*

Lys, 1941. *(Connolly family)*

Joan, early 1940s. *(Connolly family)*

Lys as fashion
model. *(Connolly
family)*

Kenneth Sinclair-Loutit.
(David Sinclair-Loutit)

More high jinks at Tickerage – Quennell and
Barbara. *(Connolly family)*

Charles Langford-Hinde – Barbara's lost love.
(Connolly family)

'Everything about you interests me and makes me miserable' – Barbara sunbathing at the Cot. *(Connolly family)*

Topolski in his studio. *(Powell/Stringer/Getty Images)*

Gowing were Sonia's kind of people. By degrees, here in the months before Munich and the slow, incremental build-up to the Second World War, she became what Anthony Powell, always a shrewd observer of artists and their camp-followers, would have called a 'painter's girl'. The students used to wave at her through the window of her room. Lawrence Gowing never forgot the vision of her combing out her hair as she sat looking up at the painters as they passed above her; Coldstream and Bell once climbed out on the roof to attract her attention.

'With a round Renoir face, limpid eyes, cupid mouth, fair hair', as Spender, who used to paint at the school, remembered her, she was a natural target for painters in search of a model. Sonia can be seen in *Young Women and Children in the Broadwalk, Regent's Park*, although this was not done from the life – she sat for Rogers in his studio and was then painted into the existing canvas. Coldstream produced several 'heads' of her, his concern to reproduce her facial colouring so obsessive, an onlooker remembered, that he asked for samples of her make-up, the better to match the tones with his palette. But for all this resolute immersion in the late 1930s artworld, there are distinctions to be made. She was never a professional model. Neither, despite insinuations to the contrary, did she ever pose nude. As Spurling points out, the nickname she acquired at this time – 'the Euston Road Venus' – had a hint of irony. The artists and apprentices she came across in the Euston Road liked her enthusiasm and her seriousness – her passionate interest in what she regarded as important things – but they also found her overbearing and judgemental, bossy and sometimes presumptuous, with an intellectual reach that often exceeded its grasp.

Meanwhile, there were patterns emerging in her emotional life. Fatherless and erratically brought up, she tended to fall for older men who combined charm, courtesy and expertise, whose talent she esteemed and at whose feet she (sometimes literally) sat. Her first regular boyfriend was Pasmore, who was thirty; there were also relationships with Konovalov and Vinaver. By mid-1939 she had taken up with Coldstream, another man ten years older than herself, recently separated from his wife and their two small children. Much of what we know about her in the period 1939–41 can be divined from the letters they exchanged at this time, an immense thread of correspondence that began when, in advance of call-up, he took a temporary job at a boys' private school while she went to stay at the painter Rodrigo Moynihan's house at Monksbury in Hertfordshire. Coldstream was a punctilious suitor ('You can't think how lovely it was this morning getting a pink parcel of sweets', runs one of her letters from November 1939; 'it was absolutely lovely coming back and finding the roses', begins another), but her replies, though expressing suitable concern for his welfare, are also freighted with hints about the life she was determined to lead. Describing an evening at nearby Sawbridgeworth, she complains that 'There was a perfectly horrible young man called David Green there who was very drunk and gave lurid descriptions of the wonderful time the inhabitants of the offices of *Horizon* were having in London . . .' Already there is combative mention of the special number she later discussed with Spender: 'I hope you are well in on the "Young Painters" issue of *Horizon* because I don't trust either Stephen's or Cyril Connolly's views on Art. Wasn't the advertisement for it depressing in the *Statesman*?'

The courtship continued, with weekends at Monksbury and a secret meeting in London in early December. 'It was lovely at Liverpool Street and I came back safely except that I lost my ticket but they believed me at Stortford when I said I had had one', she reported back on her return. There was a part-time job teaching English to the child of a wealthy foreign family, during which she camped out in a room in Goodge Street, sittings at Vanessa Bell's old studio in Fitzroy Square, and what seems to have been a visit to Dorset, where she remembered a day spent in a countryside deep in winter snow. Back in London, in the wake of her discussions with

Connolly and Spender about 'Young Painters', she was moving ever closer to the *Horizon* world, helping out at Lansdowne Terrace and spending much of her spare time among Connolly's associates.

An undated letter from Goodge Street describing a weekend spent at Lavenham in Suffolk with 'Stephen, Humphrey and Cuthbert' (these can be identified as Spender, Hugh Slater and the writer T. C. Worsley) is full of literary gossip ('Raymond Mortimer is going to the Propaganda Ministry & the lit. editorship of the *Statesman* is free') while giving a first glimpse of the equivocal relationship she would go on to pursue with Connolly's co-editor: 'He [Spender] was very nice but I can never quite feel at ease or natural with him because I feel a most innocuous remark might lead him to condemn one's character entirely. But he is very funny . . .' A later meeting when Spender came to tea produced further gossip about Auden and Isherwood's exploits in America: 'Auden's doing nothing about the War except busying himself with rather inessential and impractical things such as the evacuation of children and so on.'

But the onset of war was rapidly dispersing the artists' colonies of Fitzrovia. Coldstream was despatched to join an artillery unit in Dover, while Sonia acquired a job with a Mobile First Aid Unit attached to University College, London. She was solicitous of his welfare ('Bill, I do hope you are getting all my letters as I do try to write to you quite often but I expect the delivery is very irregular and I wouldn't be surprised if some didn't get there as they seem to be bombing the railways quite a bit') and, as the Blitz reached its height in the autumn of 1940, terrified to discover that Coldstream had been posted to a town immediately beneath the Luftwaffe's flight path: 'I saw a dreadful picture of Dover on the cinema yesterday which made me most alarmed. There didn't seem to be any houses left standing at all. But perhaps as you are on the hill you are a little safer.' As for her own involvement, the Mobile First Aid Unit worked in shifts accompanying rescue crews disinterring bodies from the rubble. Often going without sleep for days on end, frequently forced to confront scenes of utter carnage (Coldstream rated her 'fearless'), Sonia sent regular reports down to Dover. 'Well, we're absolutely in the middle of it now,' runs another undated letter from the early autumn. 'The East End has been on fire for the last two nights . . . One's entire life is quite disorganised . . . The nights here are amazing as everyone is really frightened and we haven't had a proper sleep for three nights.'

And yet, even as the bombs fell on London, Sonia had another end in view. This was the furtherance of her relationship with Connolly and the enticing world of *Horizon*. The catty remarks about Spender go hand in hand with reportage from the Blitz, and in the brief intervals when some kind of social life could be resumed we can see her moving ever closer to the world of Lansdowne Terrace:

31 August 1940

Last night the big raid on London provided great entertainment. It was very exciting watching from the roof of the hospital . . .

17 September 1940

I had rather a gay weekend as I went out to dinner with Stephen on Saturday. We went to the Café Royal and met Cyril Connolly and Erika Mann and Brian Howard. I thought Brian Howard was awfully funny but not very nice, but I was rather disappointed by Erika Mann . . .

The same juxtapositions can be found in a letter sent three days later which notes that on the previous night the firemen feared they would be unable to stop the flames from a clutch of incendiary bombs reaching the hospital, before going on to remark that she hasn't heard from Connolly for a few days and she imagines 'that he + Diana have gone to the country'. The Blitz might be terrifying, or occasionally exhilarating, but the conditions in which she spent her days were also horribly mundane. 'I read detective stories all day long now one after the other + eat sweets', she told Coldstream on the last day of September.

How did she and Coldstream regard each other? The key-note of their correspondence is its dutifulness, Sonia's concern for his wellbeing and safety and her regard for his work. But was he really the great man in whose shadow she yearned to luxuriate? A friend who suggested that she would 'make a good wife for an artist' got short shrift. Coldstream's divorce was coming through, but there were no immediate plans to regularise their union. In the meantime, Sonia was itching to leave the Mobile First Aid Unit. There was a plan to try for a job in the Civil Service, but an undated later from around this time reports that 'I had lunch with Connolly today + there is a chance that I may become secretary of Horizon. I do hope I do.' Another letter notes that 'I saw Cyril Connolly the other day and he suggested that I become part-time secretary to Horizon'. More concrete than these dreams of art and literature were the continuing horrors of the Blitz: 'The All Clear has just gone. It's really rather sinister just waiting for a noise that can go off at any minute without warning! Last night was the first night we haven't had a raid for about a week. They generally last from 9.30 to 5 in the morning + people are getting rather tired and nervy.'

As the Blitz drew to a close, so did her dealings with Coldstream. They spent Christmas 1940 together in London and there was a brief trip to Bristol in the spring, where he was now putting his artistic skills to work on camouflage, but a major fault-line in their relationship loomed into view when his divorce grew nearer. Sonia later said that she had agreed to marry him if her name were kept out of the proceedings, and that when he cited her as a co-respondent she ended the affair. To set against this are the recollections of a friend who first met her early in 1942: even then, he thought, her life was 'still concentrated on Coldstream'.

When the *Horizon* job failed to materialise, she spent a brief period working on its chief rival, John Lehmann's *Penguin New Writing* – Lehmann was pleased to learn that she thought *Horizon*'s organisation 'higgledy-piggledy' – and then accepted a post at the Ministry of War Transport at Berkeley Square: the promise of a regular salary allowed her to move into a tiny flat at 18 Percy Street, halfway between Oxford Street and the Tottenham Court Road. But for all the surface orthodoxy of her Civil Service job, Sonia had proved a point about the kind of person she wanted to be. The next three years might see her occupied with war work, but she remained Connolly's willing accomplice in any schemes he might cook up for the magazine and a highly regarded member of his inner circle. One *Horizon* helper remembered her 'sitting at Cyril's feet'. Janetta and Diana liked her; if Lys suspected her motives (and for that matter Connolly's), then she valued her capacity for hard work, and they later became friends.

There was incontrovertible evidence of Sonia's standing in the *Horizon* world, with the appearance of her essay on the Euston Road School in the May 1941 number. On the other hand, her relationship with both editor and proprietor was far from clear-cut. To Spender her unfeigned devotion to Connolly – Connolly's interests, Connolly's future, Connolly's whims – was a source of mild amusement: 'No one could enter more enthusiastically into the idea that he was the cause of genius personified and frustrated than Cyril . . . Understanding the many ways in which [he] was misunderstood provided Sonia with a tremendous brief, which took up much time and energy.' But was he that great man for whom she pined? Several onlookers – Peter Watson was one – thought that she yearned to be Mrs Connolly, but evidence of any sexual relationship is unclear. Perhaps, when it came down to it, the gap between Connolly's self-propagandising mystique and the reality of Connolly at work at Lansdowne Terrace was too wide for comfort. And then, as several other onlookers were keen to point out, the man whom Sonia most obviously admired on her visits to the *Horizon* office was its proprietor, Peter Watson. On the other hand, delight in any suggestion that Connolly was unhappy with Lys is a feature of her correspondence: 'thoroughly bored with home life, for which I don't blame him!' runs one letter from 1944, while another notes that 'Domestic happiness is more than ever conspicuous by its absence in Bedford Square.'

Years later Connolly would write an unpublished story entitled 'Happy Deathbeds', in which a woman named 'Elsa' becomes infatuated with a rich homosexual called 'Paul' who owns the literary magazine where she works as a secretary. There is a revealing scene in which she telephones him at his flat and afterwards reflects on the life he must live there: 'She thought of Paul's thin sad face, his bath running, the faint backwash from an atonal gramophone record, his money, his distinction . . .' If this, transparently, is Watson then the psychological roots of Elsa's obsession with him are shrewdly drawn out. Subsequently we are told that Paul is someone she can truly love 'because, being homosexual, he inspired no sexual ambivalence, she could not hate him for desiring her or for desiring another woman. In the sex war he was a kind of angel of man's who was on her side.'

If she could never possess Watson then, equally, he could never hurt her: each could bask in the other's regard without the disillusionment of a physical relationship. While Connolly was, in many important respects, the kind of intellectual titan she esteemed and in whose orbit she burned to revolve, then the chaos of his emotional life was something to avoid, if only because close involvement in it was calculated to remove some of his lustre. What lurks at the bottom of these relationships, perhaps, is a faint hint of unreality, a suspicion of Sonia wanting combinations of human behaviour she knew in her heart that she could not have and settling instead for an almost mythological world in which Connolly was a figure of dazzling intellectual eminence rather than a selfish neurotic with a messy private life.

And where did this leave her? Given that Sonia spent the latter part of the war in a government office, there are comparatively few glimpses of her at this time. Such memories as survive recall an underlying hint of purpose: 'a freshness of complexion and a Renoir-ish buxom mien,' a friend remembered, 'she moved with a brisk swirling of her cotton skirts.' But Connolly made sure that he kept in touch, sent holiday postcards ('a lovely torpid time', he reported from Lake Windermere where he and Lys stayed in the summer of 1944), consulted her about *The Unquiet Grave*, which, together with Lys, she typed, and took her advice when he thought it was required: 'I added a paragraph to the book at the spot you suggested,' runs another postcard from the spring of 1944. 'You were quite right.' (Sonia thought 'his Palinurus a very great important book. He is the most wonderful writer. I'm longing for it to come out.')

Quietly and efficiently, though sometimes to the irritation of the people around her, Sonia had succeeded in the task she set herself. Liberated from the Ministry of War Transport in the summer of 1945, she discovered that the post she had wanted four years before was hers for the taking, and she returned to *Horizon* in the role of editorial secretary. Soberly dressed, with her ash-blonde hair dancing off her shoulders, alert to Connolly's instructions but with one ear cocked for the sound of Peter Watson's tread on the stair, she was a formidable proposition. Everyone around her knew that unwanted contributions would be promptly sent back to their authors, and the proofs returned to the printer on time.

Interlude: Angela

Even more than her half-sister Janetta, Angela Culme-Seymour tended to make an instant impression on the people she met. Gerald Brenan, renting a house to her in Málaga in the early 1930s, was so overcome by her beauty that he dropped the price to very nearly nothing. James Lees-Milne credited her with an almost Giaconda-style allure: 'She had camellia-like skin of the softness of satin, large glowing eyes of a dreamy quality, which smiled even when her lips were solemn. Often the only movement of her face came from long bewitching lashes, which, while intoxicating the beholder, gave her an air of complete innocence.' 'A wonderfully beautiful girl', Diana Mosley pronounced. Photographed by Cecil Beaton for the *Tatler* ('Society portraiture at its best', the magazine crowed) in formal dress with a double row of pearls, or, with flower-spray in hand, modelling the 'Tricoleur' outfit for the West End couturier Matita, she looks somehow remote and imperturbable, doing what is expected of her, but in a certain sense going through the motions, impassive, fundamentally disengaged. Significantly, Angela seems to have regarded her stunning good looks with absolute matter-of-factness. 'I have written about my having been pretty and/or beautiful because it would have been false modesty not to do so,' she informed readers of her extensive memoirs. 'I do not feel embarrassed, it was so long ago, as if I were another person. But there it was, beauty that I was lucky enough to be born with and it was part of my life.'

Meanwhile, there lurked the question of what all that beauty portended. Fascinated by a countenance that seemed to give so little away, Lees-Milne noted that 'it was difficult to tell how innocent she was or whether, like a small child, she was amoral'. Most onlookers who came across Angela in her tumultuous prime would have opted for the second diagnosis. In a milieu characterised by its casual love affairs and wrecked marriages, her romantic entanglements quickly became notorious, not merely for the impulsiveness with which they were taken up and cast aside but for the idiosyncrasies that marked their ever-erratic course. 'Commonplace codes of behaviour simply did not apply to her,' Lees-Milne decided. 'Loyalty to one partner even at the start of a love affair appeared not to concern her.' On the other hand, no one could have called Angela scheming, calculating or otherwise out to feather her nest. As was several times pointed out by shocked anatomists, her frequent love affairs rarely brought her any lasting happiness and most of the trappings of mid-century high life – money, luxury, jewellery – left her cold. She was as happy – or unhappy – among the lowlife of a Sussex pub as at the grandest country house weekend. Like 'a ravishing cat', Lees-Milne thought – a description which, coincidentally enough, was several times affixed to Barbara – settling on whichever cushion seemed the softest and then ambling off into the wilderness on a whim, a creature of impulse that, in exceptional circumstances, became a kind of compulsion. 'He dominated me completely and I knew I would do whatever he asked me to,' she remarked of the hugely unreliable charmer for whom she left her first husband. 'Yet I did not really want to go away with him.'

But Angela's early life was a succession of goings-away, of unpremeditated abandonments, of decisions whose authenticating mark is their complete lack of forethought. Contingency meant nothing to her and the oft-voiced determination to 'live for the moment' runs through her recollections like a vein of quartz through rock. If this chronic waywardness had an explanation it seemed to lie in heredity. There was precedent for the deserted first husband, left behind at a bus stop in Málaga, and it came in the shape of her exotic grandmother, Trix Ruthven, a possible model for Nancy Mitford's 'bolter' in *The Pursuit of Love*, who, legendarily, stepped out of a train at Crewe on the way home from Scotland, leaving her children in the carriage with their nurse, and never came back. And always lurking in the background was that question of upbringing, the father dead in France and his earnest young replacement closeted in the drawing room for hours with her mother Jan. Angela's last memories of George Culme-Seymour were of him standing in the doorway of the nursery at Tedworth Square in his Rifle Brigade uniform, and the red and blue plush doll that was his parting gift. Captain Geoffrey Woolley and his stepchildren never got on. Angela remembered her brother Mark leaning over the banisters in an attempt to spit on his head, and of opening the bathroom door and finding Geoffrey trying to manhandle his protesting stepson into six or eight inches of cold water. Did he love their mother, Angela once enquired. 'Oh I love Jan, but I hate father,' Mark shot back.

What Geoffrey thought of Angela is not recorded. As with Janetta, there is only passing mention of her in his memoirs. On the other hand, there were several unmissable signs of his regard: a letter, sent to her at Bedales, confessing that he was in love with her (Angela always remembered the words 'There, now I have told you' staring off the page in his small neat hand); a picnic where he put his hand on her thighs (his stepdaughter 'felt only revulsion, and later pity').

With her schooldays over and the Woolleys about to relocate to Harrow-on-the-Hill, there was a plan to send her to finishing school in Paris, but Angela had other ideas: after three uneventful months of learning to dance and skating at the Palais de Glace she asked if she could live in London and get a job. As with Barbara, she had become part of a demographic sub-group that had hardly existed before the Great War: the well-bred girl who is suddenly superfluous to family requirements, whose presence around the familial hearth means trouble and embarrassment, and whose yearning for freedom is entertained by her parents as the least demanding option available. At seventeen, 'finished' and with a taste for Porto flip – an eye-watering concoction made of brandy, ruby port and a single egg-yolk – which the girls were instructed to drink every day as a tonic, she came back to England and moved into a room at Queen's Gate.

Here in South Kensington, bohemia and the *beau monde* came inextricably mingled. At first she got a job painting boxes, lampshades and wastepaper baskets for a shop called Touch and Go, but a supportive aunt suggested that she should 'come out' and join the debutante charivari of Mayfair dances and presentation at court. Before long there were five evening dresses – white chiffon, scarlet chiffon, green taffeta, shot taffeta and pale gold lamé – to join the clutter of the Queen's Gate bedsit. In this finery, or presumably divested of it, in the course of a clandestine weekend in Brighton, she was seduced by a thirty-two-year-old House of Lords clerk named Henry Burrows. Already, though, discreet murmurings about her character, or lack of it, had begun to surface. Another relative took it upon herself to explain that no decent man would want to marry her 'if you go on the way you have been'. Angela assumed that news of the Brighton escapade had leaked out, but all Aunt Florrie turned out to mean was that her niece should not kiss young men at dances, 'or anyway not different ones each time. Nor at weekend house-parties.' There was an unsuccessful meeting with the two aunts who had brought Henry up, after which they drifted apart, and she fell in with a tall young man, and possible second cousin, named Ralph Jarvis. ('Generally I felt shy when I first met someone, especially if I liked them, but Ralph made it easy to talk, sometimes dangerously so. You told him things you had not meant to,' Angela recalled.)

What did Angela, now in sight of her twentieth birthday, want out of life? Where did her talents lie? And who were the kind of people with whom she enjoyed spending her time? One of her closest relationships was with her brother Mark – a little too close, Gerald Brenan deduced. ('They sleep together, I haven't the slightest doubt incestuously', he told a friend, after meeting them for the first time. Both siblings always denied these rumours.) She liked painting, had been to life classes in Paris, enrolled at the Central School of Art and sold a couple of canvases. There was talk of a novel she might write, and the Spanish trip with Mark was supposedly undertaken with the aim of giving them time for literary work. And always there was her beauty and her highly enigmatic charm, an eternal provocation to the young men she met at debutante balls to propose marriage and the bohemians and chancers she came across beyond them to solicit her phone number and an unchaperoned date. Her mother, now in the throes of detaching herself from her second husband, could offer a spare room in the Battersea flat where she resided when in England ('without the Rev.') but little in the way of useful advice.

One searches for patterns in the file of Angela's admirers and finds only happenstance. Winston Churchill's nephew; a 'golden-haired Russian'; a society gossip columnist; a French count; a downmarket major who offended her relatives by saying 'pardon', 'lounge' and 'dear': it was all the same to Angela, and one of her most attractive characteristics – in a world that, for all its free-and-easy atmosphere was keen on social hierarchies – is her lack of snobbishness. 'Darling it does seem so funny to find you here with all these people,' her brother Mark observed on one of these excursions into debatable lands where other Culme-Seymours would have hesitated to stray. There was an early marriage to the painter Johnny Churchill – a photograph survives of the young artist at work on her portrait – which realised a peripatetic life on the Spanish coast, a baby named Cornelia and a spur-of-the-moment walk-out with a French count, René de Chatellus of the 'enigmatic and uncompromising stare', a departure so unpremeditated and inexplicable that even six-and-a-half decades later Angela had difficulty in rationalising it: 'How could I leave Cornelia? And, in spite of irritations, and even if he was sometimes pompous, and I was not madly in love with him, Johnny and I had not been unhappy together.' Nonetheless, Cornelia was left and Johnny abandoned for a hotel in Málaga, a flat in Alicante and a morning on which Angela awoke to find her paramour gone and only nine pesetas in her purse. Clearly it was time to regroup.

But this was easier said than done. An attempt at reconciliation with Johnny ended with a terse telephone conversation conducted from a call-box at Paddington Station: '"It's too late, Angela," he said, and coldly put down the receiver.' René, temporarily re-admitted to the fold, wanted to introduce her to his parents at their château in Burgundy. Meanwhile, back in England, she had made a conquest of Patrick Balfour, then employed as the *Evening Standard*'s society columnist and an erstwhile homosexual, and accepted an invitation to stay in his house at Warwick Avenue: 'I had nowhere else to go and what could be better . . . than to be with this kind, funny sympathetic person?' A divorce from Johnny having been negotiated, they were married at Chelsea Register Office in February 1938. A somewhat makeshift air hung over the proceedings. 'I suppose it's not very romantic, but I think it's the best thing for you at the moment,' Mark proposed as they stood drinking champagne on the morning of the ceremony. Later that day Angela and her 'safe temporary husband' flew off to Paris to spend the first night of their honeymoon at the Ritz Hotel.

More than one Lost Girl, in the course of her emotional career, experienced what might be called the Balfour Treatment: an attempt, initiated with the most praiseworthy of motives, by a domestically minded man to settle down with a woman of whom, whatever the uncertainties of her previous life, he imagined that something might be made, without realising that her temperamental flaws were liable to doom the scheme to disaster from the start. In Anthony Powell's *What's Become of Waring* (1939), a novel written at almost exactly the same time that Balfour and Angela decided to get married, a character named Captain Hudson jilts the respectable girl to whom he has long been engaged in favour of a fast-living journalist named Roberta Payne. Hudson, another character shrewdly observes, has made a great mistake: 'There he was, engaged to a girl who suited him down to the ground. He meets a bit of hot stuff like Roberta and breaks off his engagement. Then he expects the hot stuff to behave like the girl he was engaged to.' This, leaving aside the fiancée, was essentially what Balfour had done with Angela. What he wanted, according to his old friend Lees-Milne, was 'a permanent Darby-and-Joan marriage around a cosy fireside, with plenty of children to come' and what he got was . . .

Well, what exactly did he get? Within a year of his marriage, the Hon. Patrick's father died and he succeeded to the title of Lord Kinross. As Lady Kinross (in which capacity she was paid £100 to endorse Pond's Cold Cream) and mindful of her husband's job, Angela lived 'a social sort of life, many parties where he might meet people who would be interesting to write about, first nights, newly-opened restaurants'. There were weekends away – to Madresfield Court to stay with the Lygons, to Oxford with Balfour's old *convive* Maurice Bowra, to Tickerage, the Sussex mill house near Uckfield owned by the Wyndhams. A photograph from 1938 shows her in the midst of the Connolly circle: a line of partying figures, drinks and cigarettes to hand, that includes Patrick, the composer Constant Lambert, the journalist Tom Driberg, Cyril Connolly and Stephen Spender. There was also, as Angela cheerfully admitted, a fair amount of adultery: 'I can no longer remember when I first started being unfaithful to Patrick.' This reached a symbolic height on the occasion when she was summoned to Edinburgh to attend her father-in-law's funeral and spent the overnight journey in a sleeper with her 'very good-looking lover, a painter, called David something'.

As with Barbara, the war placed no kind of barrier on her social life. Nursing training at St George's Hospital alternated with nights at the Gargoyle, the Nest and the Café de Paris. But Patrick, his suspicions alerted by gossip overheard at his club and the illusion of a Darby-and-Joan marriage crumbling before his eyes, was already pressing for a divorce. His private life was at an end, he informed Lees-Milne in September 1940. 'I have discovered a whole host of infidelities by Angela over the past year or more and I don't really see it as any good going on with it. It seems that she is incorrigible & perhaps a little mad.' Balfour had assumed that he 'was going to be able to make some sort of job of her, but I see that I have failed, & that perhaps I could never have succeeded'.

Balfour's diagnosis was sheer vacillation. 'I wish that one day you'd grow up and decide what sort of a life you do want,' he told her at their valedictory meeting. But what sort of life did Angela want? The artistic ambitions kept up and she briefly attended an art school in Suffolk, where the youth with curly hair, a pointed nose and darting eyes who sat next to her turned out to be Lucian Freud. WAAF training took her to Kent, where, once again, a chance encounter sent her spinning away on a different course. Walking into a pub in Faversham, she saw an army officer standing in front of the fire whose long polished boots and Great War pilot's wings 'made him look as if he should be different or important in some way'. This was Major Robert Hewer-Hewett, invariably known as 'Brasco' from his military title (Brigade R.A.S.C. Officer), who claimed to have recognised her from the Pond's advertisements, entertained her to dinner at the local pubs and before very long claimed to be 'head over heels' in love with her.

There was a Mrs Major Hewer-Hewett and a couple of children, but such things were no impediment. Neither was a fourteen-year age gap (Angela had just turned twenty-eight, Hewer-Hewett was forty-two). Already pregnant by him, she was photographed by Beaton for his 'Ladies in Wartime' feature for the *Tatler* ('As beautiful as ever,' Beaton remarked, as the session began, 'a little bit heavier, perhaps?') shortly before undergoing an abortion at a Golder's Green nursing home. Brasco, who stumped up the £50 fee, assured her that he would do anything for her and then promptly disappeared on what was represented as a secret mission to France. Angela assumed she would never see him again. Meanwhile, her WAAF training had moved on to radar work. Commended for her interest in her duties, she was transferred to an RAF station at Felixstowe. Unpunctuated letters followed hard on her heels ('Come to me Angela come to me my darling love'). Preparing to take the train to meet him in London for lunch one morning after her night-shift had finished, Angela was struck by a curious feeling of déjà vu ('my thoughts were in a feverish turmoil, just as they had been on that night in a hotel in Malaga five years before, when I had unwillingly left Johnny'). Waking up the next morning, and in her dazed state at first imagining herself to be back in Suffolk, she discovered that she and Brasco had eloped to a Maidstone hotel. Even for Angela, this seems to have been a step too far. 'Oh Christ,' she records herself thinking. 'What have I done?'

What followed has all the makings of a fictional picaresque in which war, bombs, death and relocation crowd in upon each other. It was May 1941 by now, the height of the London Blitz, but Brasco was 'very gay in those days. He used to do imitations of Charlie Chaplin and Buster Keaton and the Marx Brothers, and the people used to hold their sides for laughing'. There was a difficulty with her mother and Janetta, who thought him common and to whom he reacted accordingly ('they never saw this side of him, because with them he was stilted and wary and on the defensive. He said he knew what they were thinking: they were just waiting for the day when I would leave him'). On the other hand, Angela was forced to concede that she had never seen him read a book. Shortly after their elopement he was posted to Yorkshire, declaring that he would send for her when he had found a place for them to live.

And so the cavalcade of Angela's wartime life rolled on, sometimes with Brasco, sometimes without him, occasionally in a state of all-round contentment, frequently in conditions of near penury. Billeted in Dewsbury, and pregnant once more, she went to work in a factory. 'So what was it like being married to a posh Lord?' her landlady's husband wondered, when her divorce case was reported in the *News of the World*. Brasco's military career was coming to an end: after being posted to Scotland, he was invalided out with an injured leg. For a brief period some kind of *ménage* was established in the Surrey countryside near Woking. Jan, after gallantly attempting to get on with Brasco, gave it up as a bad job and left for London: 'Oh darling, I just came to say goodbye. I don't think I can live with Brasco any more. So it's better that I should go.' To Angela, about to give birth to a son named Mark, past and future seemed of no account when set against the chaotic present: 'Already I was learning to live in the moment, to look neither forward nor back.' In her memoirs the tragedies that engulfed the Woolleys in the early part of 1943 are recalled in brief, impressionistic fragments: Angela is clearly moved by the things that are happening to her, but reluctant to confront them head on. Sensation is always there to be grasped at, rarely put under the microscope.

If the tribulations continued to pile up, then an instinct for self-preservation was usually enough to see Angela through. And whatever might happen, whether fetched up with a middle-class major or a French count, in a Spanish fishing village or a London backstreet, there were always friends and family connections on whom she could rely. The capital for Brasco's painting and decorating business, optimistically embarked on early in 1943, came by way of a loan from John Sutro, the film producer, who had been at Oxford with Waugh, Balfour and Howard. But by the end of the year the creditors were massing. 'We have about 40 men now, all doing bomb damage repairs etc! But there still doesn't seem any money over to buy nice things with', laments a letter to Janetta from the summer of 1944. There were frequent visits to the pawnbroker in Kensington Church Street, and once again Angela 'learned to enjoy the happiness of the moment and to put my thoughts in a sort of container, and to look no further than a day, or even an hour'. Members of her family looked interestedly on. 'Thank you so much for your news of Mark + Angela,' the Revd Woolley wrote to Janetta early in 1945. 'I can't help mischievously wondering whether Brasco has paid some of his debts.' On the day the war ended she was giving birth to a second son in Cornwall, where her ever-hopeful boyfriend had invested in a trawler. Shortly afterwards the business collapsed when Brasco was swindled by an associate. With the bailiffs at the door, Angela was forced to sell her Persian lamb coat to buy clothes for the children. 'I've never had any luck with fur coats,' she explained. 'They've all gone, either in wars or revolutions or divorces, or else they've been stolen.'

6.

Blinding Impulsions: Janetta 1940–5

Cyril Connolly has moved into Regent's Park in a decent house of
which he has taken every decent room; the rest go to a Mrs Lootit.
I scared him by saying the crown authorities would expel them all
for living in sin and have made up for it by the gift of a jardinière.

Evelyn Waugh, diary, 1 July 1945,
The Diaries of Evelyn Waugh (1976)

E arly one evening in the spring of 1942, Dr Kenneth Sinclair-
Loutit left the Bloomsbury flat that he shared with his wife and
their young daughter in Great Ormond Street and made his way
down to a Surrey village outside Dorking, where a friend had invited
him to a party. Even at twenty-eight, tall, thin and conspicuous – he
described himself as 'an ordinary but articulate young man' – and
apparently absorbed in the routines of his domestic life, Sinclair-
Loutit had a considerable career behind him. After studying medicine
at Cambridge he had enlisted in the Marxist International Brigades
and served on the Republican side in the Spanish Civil War.
Returning to England, and taking up a position at Bart's Hospital, he
married Thora Silverstone, an operating theatre nurse who had been
his companion since they met in Spain. Here in the third year of the
war, already awarded the MBE for his services during the Blitz, he
was working at the headquarters of the London Civil Defence Region.

Like many another youngish and left-leaning man in the tightly knit world of wartime London, he knew Cyril Connolly: they had come across each other in Spain, and in the early days of the war Sinclair-Loutit had seen him wandering down Great Ormond Street on a visit to their neighbours, the Lubbocks. The events of the next few days were to draw him even closer to Connolly's orbit.

Sinclair-Loutit's host at the party in Surrey was a man named Tom Wintringham, another Spanish Civil War veteran who, after monitoring the conflict as a war correspondent, had ended up commanding the British Battalion at the battle of the Jamara River, where only 225 of the 600 combatants survived the day's fighting. Arriving at Wintringham's house, Sinclair-Loutit discovered that he knew hardly any of the guests. On the other hand, one of the women made an instant impression. Over sixty years later, he could still remember their first encounter in almost photographic detail. 'She was wearing white wool knitted knee-high stockings and she had straight hair, little make-up as well as an economic, accurate vocabulary. She was beautiful, and in her quiet manner she had immense presence.' The girl – barely out of her teens, he divined – was called Janetta. Though not long married to a man named Hugh Slater, she was apparently 'alone'. In the moment they met, Sinclair-Loutit experienced what he described as a '*coup de foudre*, a blinding impulsion' altogether impossible to resist. As he later put it, 'what passed between us at that party had presaged, in its total ease and in the idiom and intimacy of our contact, something that I was unable to deny'.

Janetta was staying at an address in Dorset Street, Marylebone. Sinclair-Loutit acquired her phone number. Ten days later, in an agony of indecision ('I had been sure of myself but I knew and feared the consequences of taking a road on which there could be no turning back'), he made the call. The telephone was answered on the instant – Janetta confessed that she had barely left the house in the week and a half since they had met – and Sinclair-Loutit's fate was sealed.

Faced with what he called the 'all or nothing' option, he went unrepentantly for the all, with the personal and social consequences that the throwing over of one's wife and child in mid-twentieth-century England entailed. Old friends registered their disquiet. Janetta was widely regarded as a husband-snatching scarlet woman, unfit for polite company. 'You came to London, you lived with Sinclair-Loutit, you were *asked* to give him up but you refused', Diana remembered two years later when divorce proceedings were in train. Even worse, Sinclair-Loutit recalled, his betrayal of Thora and their child was also seen as a betrayal of political principle, the embarrassing spectacle of a tribune of the left abandoning his duty at the siren's call of an upper-middle-class seducer. Happily, the object of these aspersions knew his Freud. 'Many of those making this diagnosis were at least bourgeois stock and I realized that their reactions were best explained in terms of their own personal psycho-analytical state.' In any case, such was the state of Sinclair-Loutit's romantic excitement that he was prepared to put up with almost any insult flung his way. Janetta, he recalled, 'made me feel a new and different person'.

Janetta, at this point, had just celebrated her twentieth birthday. The social circles she and Slater frequented in the early 1940s, symbolised by her attendance at Tom Wintringham's party, were impeccably left-wing, with a tendency towards Spanish Civil War veterans. Much of their joint contribution to the war effort in the first year of hostilities had been governed by lack of money. The stay in Devon came to an end when war regulations prohibited the transfer of the £10 a month that Jan allowed her daughter through a French bank; Slater's income, too, was in jeopardy after his once-indulgent former lover, Elizabeth, decided to stop subsidising him. At first the couple decamped to Bristol to work in an armaments factory, but their prospects improved with the receipt of an invitation from Wintringham asking Slater to join him in setting up the Osterley Park training centre for the Home Guard. A blatantly political undertaking founded

on the belief that the hundreds of thousands of local defence volunteers should constitute a 'people's army', and strongly deprecated by
military traditionalists, the scheme was warmly approved by a third
Spanish veteran whom Janetta met at this time. George Orwell's
New Statesman review of Slater's *Home Guard for Victory!* (1941) is
not only highly enthusiastic ('The best of the Home Guard manuals
issued hitherto') but notes that the book touches on political problems
that are inseparable from the details of military organisation. 'The
reforms it suggests all have the implied aim of making the Home
Guard more definitely into a People's Army and breaking the grip of
the retired colonel with his pre-machine-gun mentality.'

A second review, filed for *Horizon*, claims that if the Home Guard
achieves anything at all, it will be down to the efforts of 'Mr Slater . . .
and Tom Wintringham and his other associates at the various Home
Guard training schools'. Orwell's enthusiasm for Slater's training
routines is also a feature of some Home Guard lecture notes, compiled
in the period 1940–1 and intended for his own comrades in the
organisation's Regent's Park unit, where he officiated as sergeant
('Describe method given by Slater . . . Pass on Slater's hints . . .
Emphasize agreement with Slater here', runs the section on 'Street
Fighting'). The cumulative effect is enough to suggest that the
Osterley Park set-up had a considerable influence on Orwell's long
essay *The Lion and the Unicorn: Socialism and the English Genius*
(1941), with its insistence that 'only a socialist nation can fight
effectively' and its implication that only a revolution in social and
political life could bring the defeat of Nazi Germany.

The success of the Osterley Park experiment had important
consequences for Janetta's private life. Anxious to regularise an
institution that looked dangerously unofficial, the War Office drafted
the highly experienced Slater into the army with the rank of private.
When the absurdity of this was pointed out in the House of Commons
by a Labour MP, he was promoted to captain. At the same time he
was also encouraged to formalise his relationship with his teenaged

girlfriend. The ceremony took place at Reigate Register Office on 6 December 1940. The Revd Woolley, whose permission Janetta had to obtain, sent a wedding gift of £50. Most of the evidence suggests that Janetta saw the marriage to Slater as a temporary arrangement. A diary dating from the early weeks of 1941, when they were living outside Dorking, combines remorseless domestic detail and the to-ings and fro-ings of guests ('Papa brought apples and a mauve flower in a pot for Humphrey') with accounts of trips to London, lunches at the Café Royal ('Lucian Freud standing glumly waiting in hall for someone who never came') and references to Connolly and his friends ('C coming here Saturday . . . met Cyril in Lyons. Went to see Peter Wattie . . . Met Cyril in Majorca Restaurant but Orwell didn't turn up. Peter Q did'). To the teenaged girl Orwell and Connolly seemed ominously alike ('not an easy man to talk to,' Janetta later recalled, 'being, for me in the category of people who silently inhibit one with a strong message that every word you say is unbelievably dull and stupid. Cyril, with his silences, was very good at this'). Early in February she spent the day reading *Enemies of Promise*, '& thought a lot of it very good'. None of this interest in the intellectual life of the metropolis boded well for a relationship with Hugh, lived out in a Surrey community whose relaxations seem to have consisted of political debates with Wintringham and his wife Kitty ('I won victory in supporting Orwell whom Tom is inclined to attack'). As early as April 1941 she was talking about the likelihood of its ending in divorce.

The same thought had occurred to Frances Partridge who, whenever Hugh was brought down to Wiltshire, welcomed him, as she candidly acknowledged, for Janetta's sake 'while thinking him hardly good enough for her'. There is a glimpse of the couple in late September 1940, when they arrive at Ham Spray for the weekend 'to have a rest from the bombing'. Frances noted that Janetta 'with the most remarkable candour and realism said that she felt far more terrified than she would have believed possible, and flung herself on the floor trembling all over'. Six months later Janetta rang to announce her arrival at Hungerford Station and the news that Hugh was in camp ('and it is horrible trying to live alone'). She also filed a report of a recent dinner party in Fitzroy Square where, with an air-raid in full spate, Cecil Beaton stood at the window marvelling at the spectacle: 'It's *too* fascinating, *too* extraordinary.'

The Partridges were also keeping up with other members of the Woolley family. Jan was trapped in German-occupied France, having failed to make her escape in the summer of 1940, but there was an ominous visit from Janetta's brother Rollo, then training to be an RAF pilot. Frances recorded that her Great War veteran husband wondered whether the young man 'fully realizes the suicidal nature of his career. I don't know.' Rollo came a second time, shortly after he had passed his pilot's exams: 'He touched both R. and me very much by his friendliness and charming manners and I suppose by the pathos of his position.' But their principal concern, as ever, was Janetta. In the summer of 1940, Frances had noted that she was 'someone of whom I am fonder and more closely linked to than anyone except R. and Burgo'. Slater, clearly, was a short-term expedient, an also-ran in the high-class emotional steeplechase on which Janetta now seemed launched. But who was to succeed him? For the next twenty years, Frances's diaries come crammed with analyses (and, for the most part, pained dismissals) of likely candidates for her young friend's hand, hugely exacting yardsticks that the vast majority of aspirants had little chance of satisfying.

Most of the Slaters' married life seems to have been lived out in hotels, which Janetta disliked. With Hugh, increasingly immersed in his military career ('restless & impatient'), detached, critical and also, his wife suspected, drinking too much, Janetta found herself drawn to the smart London world to which she had been introduced by Connolly and his friends. The maisonette at Drayton Gardens was a perpetual lure, as was her new friend Diana Witherby, now more or less detached from Connolly, whom Janetta admired for her 'wonderfully clear & perceptive mind' and her 'great sensitivity'. By the summer of 1941 the two women were sharing a flat in Dorset Street, NW1. Slater arrived there one evening to have the situation explained to him – a sad and rather touching figure, Janetta recalled, 'without the superiority and arrogance which had begun to exasperate me'. By early 1942 – about the time of the Dorking party – Frances was able to congratulate herself that Slater had finally been dispensed with: 'The slight veil that swathed her during her subjection to Humphrey has floated away, and I am confirmed in my view that she is one of the most intelligent, beautiful and sensitive young creatures I know.' Come mid-May, she notes that Janetta has written asking 'if she could bring her new friend Kenneth for the weekend'. Nothing was said; the young lovers were welcomed into the Ham Spray fold; but Kenneth Sinclair-Loutit, alas, was not what the Partridges had in mind. Thereafter, though treated with every politeness, his candidature was suspect. Were the relationship to go wrong, it was abundantly clear whose side Frances and Ralph would take.

Here in the summer of 1942, these intimations of disquiet ran far below the surface of what appeared to be an idyllic relationship. Janetta admired her new partner's war work among the bombed-out houses, and found him 'enormously practical & organised & brave'. She found a flat near Regent's Park, filled it with some Woolley family furniture from the store where it had lain since Jan departed for the south of France, and subsidised the rent by persuading Diana to occupy the spare room. Some of her time seems to have been spent at Osterley Park, rather less of it helping out at Lansdowne Terrace. Janetta would always maintain that her practical involvement with *Horizon* was negligible, but she remembered sifting through the piles of unsolicited manuscripts and she was certainly present at one famous episode in the magazine's history when the December 1942 number was found to contain Julian Maclaren-Ross's short story 'This Mortal Coil', from which Connolly had forgotten to remove several appearances of the word 'bugger'.

The Curwen Press, fearful that any scandal arising from this lapse might compromise their government contracts, were aghast and a censoring party, consisting of Connolly, Watson and Janetta, set off by tube to the printing office at Plaistow to erase the words by hand. As they reached the East End an air-raid began and the train came to a halt, leaving them 'horribly vulnerable in that sea of railway lines'. (Orwell refers to the 'bugger' incident in an 'As I Please' column for *Tribune*, 6 December 1946: 'Recently it has become possible in England to print the word in full in a book, but in periodicals it still has to be B dash. Only five or six years ago it was printed in a well-known monthly magazine, but the last-minute panic was so great that a weary staff had to black the word out by hand.')

None of this was enough to stop Janetta being gathered up by the war effort. Sometime in 1942 she was conscripted into the ARP, and set to work at the Rising Hill First Aid post, on the boundary between Islington and Finsbury: 'I went to Islington and sat in the basement of a school and was supposed to bandage people when they got hurt but nobody got hurt at all; I never bandaged anyone.' If this employment was short-lived, it was probably because, within a few months of setting up home with Sinclair-Loutit, she discovered she was pregnant. As with Slater, there was talk of an abortion, but Janetta decided she wanted the baby ('This time something inside me had physically taken over'). Frances's diary from early November records a 'lovely visit' from her, in which she talked about 'dreading' not doing her best for the child and wanting to have it without anaesthetic. Meeting her again in London a few months later, Frances – more protective than ever – was in ecstasies over her attitude to impending motherhood. Old-style Bloomsbury had never been very keen on the idea of what Lytton Strachey had called *le petit peuple* gate-crashing the seemly pursuits of their elders and Janetta's determination not to become a tiresomely adoring mother secured her warm approval. 'One finds very few people these days to hold out against children and say they aren't suitable company for adults', Frances enthused.

Simultaneously, there came warning signs from a personal life that would be increasingly subject to trauma. One of them was the return of Jan, whose slow journey from German-occupied France via neutral Lisbon was advertised in a letter to the Partridges. The effect of this ordeal on Jan's habitually frail constitution was catastrophic: 'I'm so thin that I rattle in the bath, and my bones have actually come through my skin in some places', she told Frances. Janetta left a heartfelt account of meeting her on the platform at Paddington: 'Tall & very thin & very brown, with her characteristic slightly bent & awkward stance. Oh, how I hugged that thin body.' She arrived at Ham Spray in May 1942, reporting that conditions in France were bad, with little to eat and the street cafés devoid of anything to drink or smoke but still crammed with people desperate for company ('I used to take a fan and fan myself, so as to have something to do'). Watching her depart after a second visit in August, Frances thought her appearance, hair belling out under a little blue cap 'like a young man in an Italian fresco', strangely poignant. 'As she turned to wave one saw her fine eyes set in a deeply-wrinkled face; they have lost none of their beauty with age and even gain by the contrast.'

The tragedies that struck in the early part of 1943 can be followed in Frances's diaries. Janetta was anxious about Rollo, now serving with the RAF in North Africa. In the second week of January came a postcard from Janetta and a letter from Jan conveying the same news: that Rollo was missing and that the Revd Woolley, who also happened to be in North Africa, believed him dead. 'Rollo always seemed to have a doomed air, as if he knew himself not to be long for this earth', Frances grimly reflected.

Hastening to London, the Partridges found Jan with her husband's letters on the table before her. As passionately convinced of the non-existence of God as they were about the futility of war, Frances and Ralph were unimpressed: 'Geoff's letters were maddening: instead of definite details about the exact wording of the report, he wrote crazily about feeling Rollo near him, and the stars, and God, and how kind everyone was being to him. So much for his Christianity.' On the following day, they had lunch with Janetta at the Ivy – 'her courage was as remarkable as Jan's, but different'.

Worse was to come. A month later a telegram arrived at Ham Spray announcing that Jan was dead. Telephoning Janetta, a shocked Frances learned that her mother had been recovering from influenza, suffered a relapse and died shortly afterwards in hospital to the bewilderment of her carers. Janetta reported that 'when I took her there I suddenly saw that she was dying. The hospital couldn't understand why she had died and said she should have had every chance, but seemed to have no resistance at all.' The suspicion was that Jan, already enfeebled by her journey back to England, traumatised by Rollo's disappearance and convinced that he would never return, no longer had the will to live. Janetta had lost both mother and, potentially, brother in the space of five weeks.

Friends tried to raise her from the pit of depression into which she quickly subsided and remained for many months afterwards. 'It was appalling how much I cried,' she remembered. 'Everything, everywhere brought on uncontrollable floods of tears.' There was more trouble before the funeral, when Jan's brother, the Conservative MP Ian Orr-Ewing, shouted abuse at her over the telephone. He had probably heard something 'about all his sister's family being thoroughly disreputable', Janetta deduced. Those who offered consolation were grimly aware of how little comfort it would bring. 'Rollo you will get over,' Connolly later assured her, 'for it is not so much what he was as what he might have become . . . you will get over that. Jan is a different matter . . . Try writing down your worst moments of regret & nostalgia – it makes them seem worse at the time but it helps to get them out of the system.'

Absolute proof that Rollo was dead – a letter from the Revd Woolley revealing that his papers had been found on the body of a dead soldier – arrived in early May (the ever-observant Frances noted that Sinclair-Loutit handed it over in 'rather an off-hand way').

A month later, in June 1943, Janetta went into labour and produced a girl named Nicolette, having shortly beforehand changed her name to Sinclair-Loutit to produce what her partner termed 'a nice elegant birth certificate'.

By this time the couple had moved from their original lodgings to a much bigger flat above a shop named 'Claire's', selling handmade chocolates, opposite the gates of Regent's Park. The atmosphere, as Sinclair-Loutit remembered it, was determinedly Gallic, with French earthenware bowls and *café au lait* much in evidence. There were dinners with Elizabeth Bowen, who lived nearby at Clarence Terrace, a trip to the Wigmore Hall to hear Natasha Spender give her first recital, and a social life in which Connolly and his *Horizon* cronies played a significant part. Sinclair-Loutit would recall the memory of Orwell, eating alone at the Majorca in Soho, seeing them pass by on the pavement and calling them inside, 'though it would not be me he wanted to talk to'. (Orwell, who had fought with the Trotskyist POUM militia in Spain, was eternally suspicious of Sinclair-Loutit's International Brigades Marxism.) And there was a curious encounter with Lucian Freud, then in the Merchant Navy, whom Janetta invited to dinner to discuss his worries over the receipt of a summons to an army medical: he and Sinclair-Loutit devised a strategy in which Freud painted his black shoes white, and by dint of constantly drawing attention to them, was diagnosed psychiatrically unfit for military service.

In Sinclair-Loutit's recollection, he and Janetta were blissfully happy, living as they chose, untroubled by social convention: 'It was our affair and ours alone.' Nineteen forty-three, he later decided, 'was the happiest year of my life'. Janetta, he recalled, 'had an admirable mastery of the small things of life, so our days were comfortable and trouble free. With her, problems vanished as soon as they emerged'. Janetta herself was less sure. Childcare was hard work, she decided, made worse by Connolly's 'jeering "pram in the hall" attitude'. But Sinclair-Loutit was convinced that he dwelt in a domestic nirvana.

Even the Partridges, he thought, had come to accept him, 'treating my emergence into their world with tolerant kindness'. If there were any seeds of doubt they lay in the fact that, as Sinclair-Loutit acknowledged, all this domestic harmony made him 'absurdly self-confident and far too pleased with myself'.

Meanwhile, the tocsin of family history clanged in his ears. There had, after all, been 'two generations of bolters'. Would Janetta make a third? But the catalyst for the unexpected downturn in their relationship turned out to be poor, dead Rollo. Sinclair-Loutit had liked the younger man, and considered him an ally. The arrival of his personal effects in the mail had a sobering effect, making him feel 'how undeserved was my relative security'. This realisation coincided with a summons, sometime late in 1943, to an interview with Air Vice-Marshal Sir Victor Richardson and the news that he was being considered as a candidate for a staff officer's job in the Balkans.

Whoever obtained the post would proceed to it by a rather circuitous route. The immediate need, Sinclair-Loutit discovered, was for an Allied Military Liaison Officer based in Cairo. But this would be an interim step, leading – it was assumed – to United Nations agency work in Yugoslavia or Romania as the Allies set about the task of cleaning up parts of Eastern Europe previously occupied by the Nazis. Still haunted by the memory of Rollo, dead in the skies above Tunisia, Sinclair-Loutit expressed an enthusiastic interest. Janetta, on the other hand, was furious, detecting in his behaviour only 'a perverse reversal of all our priorities, a silly incomprehensible seeking for adventure on my part for which our little family would have to pay the price'. It was an interesting and exciting job, she later reflected, 'and there was every reason to say yes, except for me'. None of this boded well, but after looming alarmingly above the horizon for a week or two the spectre of separation then dwindled away to nothing. There were no further instructions from the authorities and life in the Regent's Park flat and at Ham Spray went on more or less as before. Frances's diary for late 1943 notes that 'Janetta and family are here', while mother and daughter enjoyed a three-week holiday in the spring of 1944 in which 'Nicolette slept in the garden, crawled all over the lawn and grew fatter, browner and more energetic before our eyes'.

Then, without warning, in the third week of July, Sinclair-Loutit's embarkation orders came through. There was one last weekend at Ham Spray, but the newly appointed Lieutenant-Colonel, Military Liaison Office attached Minister Resident Cairo, was given to understand that his departure was regarded as 'a desertion'. The Partridges, too, were appalled, and Sinclair-Loutit was glumly aware that in their eyes he qualified for the 'pacifist anathema'. The embarkation order directed him to Newquay, where a plane would take him to the Middle East. Arriving at the Cornish town he spent three days wandering the streets and awaiting instructions, telephoning Janetta several times but never being able to have a proper talk, owing to the blanket of security that hung over his impending journey. On one of these excursions he found a glazed earthenware figure from 1820, a 'sweetheart's token', that he thought might appeal to his lost love, and commissioned the shop to post it to her. Then on 24 July, dimly aware that he had created a problem that it might be beyond his ability to solve, he left England for the Middle East. A letter sent just before he embarked assured Janetta 'how much I think + think about you + how I long to hear from you + how I remember that last warm ½ hour with Nicky roaring with laughter at the edge of the bed'.

Like many another military man posted to North Africa in the 1940s, Sinclair-Loutit enjoyed his time in Cairo. He stayed at Patrick Balfour's flat with its view over the Ibn Tulun mosque and, in the intervals of assembling what was to become the first units of the United Nations Relief and Rehabilitation Administration (UNRRA) Yugoslavia, relished the 'extraordinary liveliness' of a city that made London seem dowdy by comparison. These diversions included the presence of Topolski, a notorious gossip, whom Sinclair-Loutit blamed for 'spreading piquant stories about myself when he returned to London'. A stream of letters sped back to Janetta at the Regent's Park flat, but he was conscious that the issues that really mattered to them were unlikely to get an airing, given that she 'could never get over her disapproval of my being so willing to depart overseas'. 'I can feel your warmth + kindness so well,' he wrote in mid-August, 'please don't get unhappy – please don't hate me for not being there.'

Anxious to conciliate her, he bought an expensive wristwatch and commissioned Topolski to bear it home, but this, too, was a source of disquiet as the messenger seems to have imagined that the errand would be a good way to insinuate his way into Janetta's affections. There was confusion over the identity of the donor and in the end Janetta had to be reassured that it was Kenneth rather than her Polish admirer who had sent the gift.

Meanwhile, in the diary entries being sedulously filed at Ham Spray, Janetta remained a constant source of anxiety. During a visit in early September Frances saw her face become 'grey and set' as she read a letter from her father announcing that Rollo's body had been found in Tunisia, buried beside his aeroplane, and re-interred in a military ceremony. 'Thought a good deal about the passing of youth,' Frances recorded later in the autumn. 'Here is Janetta in the full bloom of youth and beauty, able to make anyone's heart beat faster, yet does she seem to realise the advantages of her lot? Or its impermanence? Not a bit.'

Already there was a suspicion that in departing for the East, Sinclair-Loutit had fallen into a pit from which he would never be able to extricate himself. Janetta's friends wrote to commiserate and fish for information. 'I am afraid that by now Kenneth will have gone + do hope you are not feeling too low', Diana wrote consolingly. A second letter, sent from the nursing home in which she was about to give birth to her first child, asks 'if he has said anything yet about what he wants to do'. But whatever Janetta may have said in her letters to Cairo – none of which survives – was making Sinclair-Loutit steadily more uneasy. 'Oh darling wolfers don't get the idea I'm no longer a factor in your life or you in mine,' he consoled her at the end of September. 'I do see a very good chance of your coming out as a private person soon after we get in, say in the New Year.' They must 'try not to fret' he counselled a month later.

Sinclair-Loutit continued to balance the responsibilities of his new position with a lurking realisation that his emotional life required him to return to England. Late in November 1944 he left for Bari, by way of Athens, as UNRRA made contact with the Yugoslav partisans. In the early part of the New Year he was confirmed as director of Yugoslav health and relief services. By this stage the majority of Janetta's friends were still supportive. Sonia reported that she had recently been talking to the writer Arthur Calder-Marshall who had 'seen Kenneth both in Cairo + at Bari, + he said . . . he thought there was every chance of K. resigning + coming back'. Diana professed herself 'convinced that the old boy will find a way of getting you out or coming back himself, so I do hope you are not feeling too despairing about this'.

Meanwhile mother and daughter had been spending Christmas at Ham Spray amid a select Bloomsbury gathering that included the critic Raymond Mortimer. Snow fell and Frances recorded Janetta 'stalking about on Burgo's stilts with her long hair swinging; Nicky trotting purposefully about, a tiny Father Christmas, in her red siren suit frosted with snow'. On New Year's Eve the company celebrated Janetta's twenty-third birthday. Writing to a friend she noted that 'we all sat down to write forecasts for the year to come. Somehow when it came to the point I couldn't think of anything likely . . .' If Ralph Partridge and Mortimer were 'insanely optimistic' about the prospects for an end to war and prophesying an armistice within 3–6 months, then Janetta was, understandably, weighed down by her private troubles. The situation was 'hopelessly unsatisfactory', she declared, but she had resolved to 'slog on'.

By this stage Sinclair-Loutit had a plan. 'Things have looked up quite a bit here + next time I write I expect to have something pretty definite to say', he wrote early in the New Year. His idea was that Janetta, possibly accompanied by their daughter, should join him in Yugoslavia. To this end he applied for compassionate leave ('Dear Wolfers . . . I am determined that you shall never feel unsupported, forgotten, neglected, side tracked, secondary or anything else'). But the ground was slipping away from beneath his feet. Arriving at Ham Spray early in spring 1945 he found that whatever credit he might have amassed with the Partridges had altogether disappeared. Frances was 'utterly opposed to any thought of Janetta and Nicolette moving out of England into a newly liberated Belgrade'. The returning lieutenant-colonel reckoned his leave 'paradisiacal', even if Janetta was largely silent ('I no longer loved him, no longer wanted him, no longer even liked him'), but he realised that in underestimating Frances and Ralph's influence on her view of the world he had made a fatal mistake.

When VE Day came on 8 May, the couple were once again half a continent apart, Sinclair-Loutit carousing at the French Embassy at Belgrade and arranging the Free French air-flight that he was still convinced would bring his family out to join him, Janetta sending accounts of the London celebrations back to Frances and Ralph. Ever a Bloomsbury girl, for whom the sight of massed humanity would always be faintly suspect, she reported that she found the crowds 'very depressing indeed, and the flags and decorations pathetic although often very pretty'. If the bonfires were 'wonderful, bringing back the old ecstasies of staring into a fire', then they also stirred terrible memories of the Blitz. As for the war-weary Londoners, 'I so loathe the masses of boiling people with scarlet dripping faces, wearing tiny paper hats with "Ike's Babe" or "Victory" written all over them.'

The early summer of 1945 also heralded a change in Janetta's domestic arrangements. Significantly, and emphasising the hold he continued to exert over her, they involved Connolly. The lease of 49

Bedford Square was about to expire; Cyril and Lys needed somewhere else to live. It may well have been Elizabeth Bowen who told them that 25 Sussex Place, an elegant Nash house near Regent's Park, was available for lease from the Crown Commissioners. To acquire the property, the underfunded Connolly realised that he needed an additional lessee. He found her in Janetta. The obvious assumption is that Janetta took this step to escape from a relationship that had begun to turn sour. In fact, Sinclair-Loutit recalled being involved in the negotiations and signing some of the papers. Having looked over the premises – so spacious and well-appointed that Frances, visiting them for the first time, was stunned by their 'grandeur and beauty' – the new leaseholders divided up the accommodation, with Connolly and Lys allotted the master bedroom, study, dining room, drawing room and kitchen, and Janetta and Nicky occupying the top floor and basement. The division struck at least one onlooker as unfair. Evelyn Waugh, supplying a conspectus of Connolly's activities to Patrick Balfour, reported that 'He and Mrs Lubbock have imposed on a dead-end kid called, I think, Jacqueline [*sic*], a former connection of yours, half-sister of Angela; she has bare feet like a camel . . . and a baby by a communist doctor.' Waugh, attending one of Connolly's lunch parties at Sussex Place, where Janetta had been pressed into service in the kitchen, had been fascinated to discover that she went about her work without shoes. Thereafter she appears in his diaries and the letters exchanged with Nancy Mitford as 'Mrs Bluefeet'.

Connolly's father, too, objected to the shared lease: 'I am sure that divided ownership *cannot* possibly be a success or work smoothly,' he told his son, 'you will grow to hate each other every time you meet on the stairs or the other gives a noisy party'. There were to be plenty of noisy parties, but Sinclair-Loutit's immediate difficulty with regard to Sussex Place was the question of whether he would ever get to occupy it. Frances's diary for the summer of 1945 is full of warning signs. In mid-June, she noted that Janetta 'still sees no solution of her relation with Kenneth – he never refers to returning from Belgrade and she feels the position is hopeless'.

Five days later came a yet more ominous entry, recording the visit to Ham Spray, under the auspices of their mutual friend Nicko Henderson, of Robert Kee, 'a delightful young man, just back from three years in a German prison camp'. A former bomber pilot whose plane had been shot down on the Dutch coast in 1942, tall, saturnine and melancholically intent, Kee made an instant impression on the Partridges. Almost from the point of meeting him, they began to wonder whether he might do for Janetta. ('That's the man for her', Ralph is supposed to have exclaimed.) That a subsequent introduction swiftly bore fruit is confirmed by an entry from mid-July 1945 in which Frances notes that 'Kenneth is suggesting that they go out to Belgrade, but she doesn't want to, resists thinking about it', and adds, in the very next sentence, the information that 'She has been seeing Nicko's friend Robert Kee, but I don't know how much.'

By mid-September, Frances was reporting that while Kenneth has arranged a permit for Belgrade, he has begun to realise that 'something is the matter'. Janetta and Robert's relationship had by this stage advanced sufficiently far for them to be able to go on holiday together in the Welsh mountains. Shortly afterwards Frances was taken to inspect the newly refurbished house at Sussex Place. The contrast between Janetta and Nicky's rooms, with their well-chosen colours and freshly painted fixtures, and the apartments grandly colonised by Connolly and Lys was a source of bewilderment: 'he has stuffed them with symbols of success and good living'. Neither the heavy furniture nor the sideboards groaning with decanters, silver coffee pots and antique porcelain had any attraction for the high-minded Frances: 'I think the worse of him after seeing it.' The visit coincided with another 'pathetically anxious' letter from Sinclair-Loutit, who had clearly got wind of the Welsh interlude, and whose representations caused Janetta to sink into a chair with 'a lost tragic expression', remarking that 'I feel I shall really have to go on with him. I can't face it all.'

As very often happened when Janetta's complicated *amours* reached boiling point, another interested party was manoeuvring into position. A fortnight later, Frances noted that Janetta had sent a 'useless, awful letter' to Belgrade 'saying she wouldn't go . . . and he must come back to London'. Connolly, on the other hand, urged her to depart, on the plausible grounds that this would be more likely to sabotage the relationship than renew it: 'As Janetta has the sense to see, [Connolly] would like her to be always unattached.'

There was also a suspicion, gradually amounting to certainty – a subject on which Sinclair-Loutit's memoirs are unforthcoming – that he was involved with another woman in Belgrade. The heap of photos brought back in the summer had contained several incriminating shots of a pretty girl in a driver's uniform.

By the final week of October, a crisis loomed. As a torrent of letters and telegrams continued to arrive from Yugoslavia, Frances professed herself bewildered by Janetta's unwillingness to give up the relationship, 'for it is plain that all trace of love for Kenneth has gone, and that what is left is liking, pity, some respect and a sense of responsibility'. With Sinclair-Loutit on the point of returning home, Robert Kee seems to have decided that he would be better off monitoring the proceedings from afar. Then, while staying at Ham Spray, Janetta was called to speak to him on the phone. She returned, according to Frances, with her face beaming to report that 'Everything seems to have changed.'

Whatever Janetta's precise situation with regard to Sinclair-Loutit and Kee, Frances was still able to report the receipt of a letter written 'in a frame of mind as near as lunacy' as she had ever been in. Sinclair-Loutit, returning to England in the last week of October and joining the household at Sussex Place, noted that 'there certainly was a welcome, but something lacked'. There was also a ghastly moment when he picked up the telephone extension and heard the male voice at the other end ask the silent Janetta if she was still there. At this point Sinclair-Loutit seems to have believed that Janetta would accompany him back to Belgrade, leaving Nicky behind. Matters came to a head on 2 November, when Janetta announced that she would be taking Nicky to Ham Spray and expected Kee to join them there. Clutching at straws, Sinclair-Loutit asked if he could escort them to Paddington.

At Ham Spray, a domicile which had seen its fair share of trauma – Lytton Strachey had died there in 1932 and Ralph's first wife Dora Carrington had killed herself as a result – the day seemed to be filled with 'a feverish disquiet'. It began with Janetta telephoning to report that everything was 'too awful', that she had decided against Belgrade and thought she ought to leave Sinclair-Loutit on the spot. An hour or two later the cortège reached Paddington, to find Kee lurking on the platform: 'I could not have been confronted with a clearer demonstration of my loss', Sinclair-Loutit admitted. Long before the party could have reached Newbury, he rang Ham Spray to ask the Partridges to take care of Janetta and Nicky, to remark that he thought Kee a weak, immature character and not fit to be trusted with their happiness, and, it appears, to be told a few home truths about how Ralph and Frances truly regarded him.

Ralph answered the phone: 'his cold unhelpfulness and sudden brutality was cruel. He made it aggressively clear that my call was unhelpful.' Frances, a shade more sympathetic, assured him that it would all work out for the best, 'as the two of you are so very different'. Sinclair-Loutit decided that he had been deceived by the Partridges' good manners. Ham Spray *politesse* 'had concealed from me the shallowness of their acceptance of me as the right partner for their truly beloved Janetta'. Not long after this, Ralph and Frances drove to fetch their three guests from Newbury ('a pathetic group on the dark station platform'), Sinclair-Loutit made two more heart-broken phone calls ('the old house is bursting with all this drama and tension', Frances noted) and went off to drown his sorrows in Connolly's eagerly proffered claret ('a great help but it is not a cure').

Though buffeted by the emotional typhoon that had blown through their house, the Partridges could not help exulting in its aftermath: 'When Ralph and I are alone together we chorus Robert's praises . . . I don't remember Ralph ever before taking such a liking to a younger man.' Convinced that Janetta had made the right decision, they did their utmost to dissuade her from briefly returning to Sussex Place a day or so later, and were highly relieved when she came back to report that 'Kenneth had been quiet and matter-of-fact and accepted everything'.

The usual recriminations flew back and forth, and the customary positions were taken up: Frances's diary gives short shrift to the mutual friend who had suggested that the couple ought to stay together for the sake of their child ('is there not great cruelty in condemning a girl of twenty-three to spend the rest of her life with a man she doesn't love and who has for some time been living with someone else?'). The child, now two years old, was, as Frances puts it, 'reacting to the situation in her own way', entering the dining room at Ham Spray at breakfast time 'at a red-faced tearful gallop, one arm outstretched towards Janetta, her hair flying, a tiny Tintoretto bacchante'.

From the sidelines, gossips fastened eagerly on whatever tantalising scraps Connolly chose to let fall. Nancy Mitford wasted no time in conveying details of a visit from 'Smarting Smarty' to Evelyn Waugh: 'His description of the final Bluefeet parting beats everything . . . He says in the end it was so mixed up with who should have the electric boiler that sentiment & feeling seemed no longer to exist.' And Connolly, she reported, had another source of anxiety: 'He is very cross because now Mrs Hugefeet will be very poor & Smarty foresees lodgers, & worse.'

How had Sinclair-Loutit failed? Where, apart from the obvious mistake of leaving for Belgrade and taking up with another woman, had he gone wrong? Like many another incomer who had presumed to infiltrate the world of the Lost Girl here in the early 1940s, he had assumed that he could do so on his own terms. Three years down the line, it was not that he had been betrayed, or that any one – with the exception of the Partridges – thought his credentials inadequate: after all, his friendship with Connolly pre-dated his relationship with Janetta and Connolly had even printed his essay 'The Prospect for Medicine' in the June 1942 number of *Horizon*. Rather, it was that he had failed to understand how efficiently the denizens of the milieu he had wandered into could close ranks if they imagined that the principles on which it was founded were somehow being imperilled. However much Connolly might have liked the younger man, he preferred the women in his circle to revolve, in a greater or lesser degree, around himself. However much the Partridges might be prepared to tolerate Janetta's emotional attachments to men of whom they disapproved, the fact remained that what they thought was good for her and what she thought was good for her did not always coincide. The Lost Girl might at various times in her career be vagrant, impulsive, detached and indecisive, but the people who organised her professional and social lives – Connolly in particular – were generally anything but.

By now it was Christmas 1945. Having divided up the contents of his former home, Sinclair-Loutit retired to Yugoslavia. Janetta and Nicky spent the festive season at Ham Spray, where Nicky was fascinated by the elderly Bloomsbury veteran Saxon Sydney-Turner. The post-war world loomed, and with it a new kind of Lost Girl life.

Interlude: Anna

Not all the Lost Girls precariously at large in wartime London were in their early twenties. If the *Horizon* secretaries tended to be young, stylish and good-looking, then the outer margin of Connolly's circle also extended to older women, middle-aged veterans of the Jazz Age and the thirties reckoning up the cost of many years' bitter personal experience. None of them, it might be said, was as odd, as demon-haunted or ultimately as talented as the slight, silent and deeply traumatised figure of Anna Kavan.

Nearly forty when the Second World War broke out, the battered survivor of many an agonising breakdown and painful rehabilitation, Anna – Helen Emily Woods, as she was baptised – exhibits all the classic features of Lost Girl ancestry. Her father was a Tyneside landowner; her physician grandfather had attended Queen Victoria; but to cancel out the domestic grandeur – the family lived at Holeyn Hall near Newcastle – came bumper helpings of neglect and unhappiness. Starved of parental affection and left to the care of nurses and relatives, she was despatched to an American boarding school at the tender age of six. In her early teens her father, for whom she had warm feelings, committed suicide by plunging from the steps of a ship bound for South

159

America. 'By dying he seemed deliberately to have destroyed this hope and condemned me to lifelong loneliness', runs a line in one of her unpublished short stories.

Having apparently ignored her in infancy, her overbearing mother now began to interfere in her daughter's life. Among other interventions, shortly after the end of the Great War she persuaded Helen/Anna to turn down the offer of a place at Oxford and – she was now eighteen – marry a man who may very well have been one of her own former lovers. Shortly afterwards the teenage Mrs Donald Ferguson was shanghaied out east to Burma to a married existence whose only memorial is a scene in her third novel, the ominously titled *Let Me Alone* (1930), in which the heroine resists her husband's advances on their honeymoon out of sheer physical loathing. There was a son named Bryan, a return to England and marital estrangement.

Already the patterns of Anna's life seem set in stone: a fear of oppression and constraint; a hankering after bohemia; an urge for independence and space to write and paint – her pictures were proficient enough to be exhibited at the Wertheim Gallery in London in the 1930s; and a deep-rooted inner disquiet. In her mid-twenties, in the paralysing depths of a love affair with an artist named Stuart Edmonds, she tried to kill herself. A second attempt saw her packed off to a private clinic in Zurich. Meanwhile, there were books – half-a-dozen novels, published in an eight-year stretch under the name of 'Helen Ferguson' – several of them containing barbed little hints of the mirror through which she saw herself and the things she needed from life. Beryl in her first novel, *A Charmed Circle* (1929), runs away from her father's vicarage to live in a room in Knightsbridge and work for an upmarket female milliner. Is this what Anna wanted? Who can tell.

Plenty of novelists from the inter-war era wrote about vicars' daughters pining to escape the thraldom of country rectories:

one thinks of F. M. Mayor's *The Rector's Daughter* (1924) and Orwell's *A Clergyman's Daughter* (1935). On the other hand, not many of them were full-blown heroin addicts, as Anna had become by the mid-1930s. If her literary career can ever be said to have taken off, then it did so in 1940 with the publication of *Asylum Piece* – her first book as 'Anna Kavan' (the name of the disgusted newlywed in *Let Me Alone*), frankly autobiographical, Kafka-esque and, in its designating of the characters by their initials, thoroughly avant-garde. As ever, the course of her life seemed entirely detached from whatever else might be going on around her. While the world slid into war she went off travelling – to Norway, America, the Antipodes. At one point, staying at a hotel in San Francisco with a man who announced his intention of returning to New Zealand, she found herself on the fourteenth floor 'trying to decide whether to walk out of the window or swallow a large number of sleeping pills which I kept by me for this sort of emergency'. The sleeping pills won out, and she travelled home via Singapore and Fiji. But worse was to come. Back in England she discovered that Bryan was missing in action: there was another suicide attempt, after which she was installed at St Stephen's Hospital under the care of the psychiatrist Dr Karl Bluth, who became her mentor and also, as her biographers dutifully point out, her supplier.

The introduction to Connolly seems to have come on the back of *Asylum Piece*'s success. In early 1943 the magazine accepted her short story 'I Am Lazarus' and shortly afterwards she was installed as a secretary-cum-editorial assistant in place of Lys, then temporarily absent at her government ministry. Like most of the *Horizon* girls, she took a shine to Watson, who enjoyed her company, sympathised with her afflictions, introduced her to his gay friends and was sufficiently impressed by Dr Bluth to join the patient roll himself. It was Watson who, one day in the spring of 1943, arrived at Lansdowne Terrace to find her seated at her desk with one arm dangling limply at her side after overdoing her daily fix and sent her home so that Dr Bluth could be summoned to effect one of his 'cures'. Not to be outdone, Connolly encouraged her to join his team of reviewers, and got her to write on Virginia Woolf, Denton Welch, Henry Green and Aldous Huxley.

The job lasted until Lys's return to full-time duties; the reviewing continued until the relocation to Bedford Square. And then, for some reason – in fact, a very obvious reason – Anna's *Horizon* days came to an end. By the summer of 1944 her ill health had reached the point where Watson felt compelled to contact her mother – Mrs Tevis, as she had since become, was then in South Africa – to warn her that there was a strong chance her daughter might die. A letter despatched to Connolly from Torquay, where she had been sent to convalesce, maintains that its author is 'much better physically and have decided to come back to town tomorrow', complains about the boarding house in which she has been quartered ('It's filled with old ladies of 95 who relate details of their illnesses all the time') and asks Connolly not to suspect her 'of coming back to buy coke. I just feel a craving for a short spell of comfort.'

The letter ends on an optimistic note: 'I ought to be well enough to come back to work in about a week: if you want me anymore.' But shortly after this the review-page assignments dwindle away and the trail goes cold, or rather swings off into the bleak institutional hinterland that invariably lay beyond the edge of her engagements with literature and art. There were still books to delight the critics – her short-story collection *I Am Lazarus* (1945) was judged a success – but a year after the war's end she was undergoing another detox at Sanitorium Bellevue in Kreuzlingen: the appearances on a masthead otherwise occupied by Waugh, Orwell and Huxley ground inexorably to a halt.

7.

Cairo Nights: Barbara 1943–4

It is worth remembering that most English-speaking people in
Cairo at this time were under thirty, and involved in the immensely
significant task of winning the war. It gave their world a glamorous,
magazine feature quality; and within it, women were a privileged
minority.

Artemis Cooper, *Cairo in the War 1939–1945* (1989)

Here in the summer of 1943, the Mediterranean was still closed
to most non-military shipping. The preferred route to Egypt
took in a voyage to the west coast of Africa, followed by a trans-
continental aeroplane flight. As the ship headed north to its rendezvous
with the rest of the convoy, Barbara's sense of geography began to
desert her. 'We are now passing a long stretch of land rumoured to be
either Scotland or the Isle of Man', she informed her diary. All the
evidence suggests that she was in low spirits. When Melinda, her
alter-ego of *A Young Girl's Touch*, takes ship at Liverpool she is
immediately 'afflicted with a deep sense of melancholy, and so intense
was her feeling of isolation and loneliness that she could have cried
out with despair'. Visiting the dining room she notes 'with misgiving
the oblong table set for six or eight', reflects that 'this would be her life
now on for several weeks' and slinks miserably off to bed in her cabin
without bothering to eat. Then, on the third day, when the ship

reached the north of Scotland, the Hebridean scenery began to have a soothing effect. Diary and novel contain a near-identical account of the curious feeling of exhilaration Barbara/Melinda experiences as the convoy assembles in the grey North Sea.

> It was a bright, palpitating morning with a clear, blue sky and hot, caressing sun; going through the minefields each ship followed close behind the other, the last making a great spurt forward before the file broke up and fell into formation. After facing north the convoy glided into position and with perfect timing veered due west. There was a short gun practice from each one in turn and the passengers were ordered to take cover. Trace flashes gleamed in the sunlight as the machine-guns fired and curling puffs of smoke dissolved into the cloudless sky.

When the firing stops and calm is restored, Melinda discovers that she 'could not have felt more content and rested. She had not a single care or unpleasant association to mar her state of mind'.

Meanwhile, there were letters following Barbara south. Anguished importuning letters that urged her to remember the lovers she had left behind and hasten to reassure them of her regard. To judge from the evidence of surviving correspondence, Topolski seems to have been allowed to see her off from London but, not to be outdone, Quennell wrote from Tickerage assuring 'My darling Skeltie' of the enormity of the gap she had left behind. Three more letters followed in quick succession, the second offering a gloomy conspectus of bachelor life in a deserted Bedford Square ('Mrs Pope [the charwoman] is taking a week's holiday & Mrs Lubbock has gone off to stay with her aunt; & Cyril and I are alone & helpless . . . No one to make the beds or remove tea-cups or cigarette ash or old copies of the *Daily Mirror* . . .') but claiming to be in 'fairly good spirits', and the third issuing an ultimatum: 'No more letters will you get from me – till I get at least a post card.'

By this point Barbara was somewhere off the west coast of Africa. Here she endured 'several days of gloom and persecution, imagining the dried-up officials consider me stuck up'. At Freetown, where the ship remained in harbour for some time and the passengers were forbidden to disembark, she commissioned an obliging purser to replenish her stock of hair-grips, cold cream and perfume: 'He returned frightfully pleased with himself, laden with vanishing instead of cold cream and bottles of Soir de Paris.' But already a trail of emotional havoc had begun to wind itself around the ship, extending from captain's table to armaments store, as male members of the crew competed for Barbara's favours. The 'inevitable amorous complications' culminated in a fist-fight between the purser and a French sailor named François who was sometimes put on duty in the gun turret. In its aftermath, both suitors ordered her to choose between them. For such an experienced man-handler as Barbara, this should have been an easy call. She offered to toss a coin, which François called correctly. Then, seeing the purser skulking grimly about the ship, she decided she felt sorry for him and told him to forget about his abandonment. But this act of charity had unfortunate consequences.

> Later I found François sitting in a deckchair in the sun, reading, and confessed what I had done. He immediately rose in a fury, dragged me off to a remote corner of the ship, banged my head very hard against a spare engine that is being exported to the Congo, threw two of my combs in the sea and then ran as fast as he could in the direction of the kitchen.

This confrontation with François raises a question about Barbara that hangs over nearly all her dealings with men. Was she a victim or an aggressor? An agent or a patient? The answer seems to be that she was a mixture of both, sometimes desperate for male company and resigned to the power that the male sex wielded over her, at other times anxious to devote her energies to demonstrating just how shaky were the foundations on which that power rested, but at all times capable of giving quite as much as she got. There is a suspicion – confirmed by other episodes later on in her career – that she was attracted to violence and violent men and stimulated by physical conflict, that she enjoyed seeing just how far she could provoke her other halves and was prepared to put up with some of the likely consequences. Significantly, within the week she was slipping out to meet François on deck at midnight: 'He interpreted my amiability as encouragement and tried to hurl me against the rails.' On the other hand, her account of being beaten up by the French sailor has a comic side, what with its ingenuous supporting detail about the engine that is being exported to the Congo and the combs tossed into the sea. To this can be added the scent of fatalism – men are awful, but what can you expect once you become involved with them? – and also, it has to be said, an overwhelming sense of boredom.

Freetown to Takoradi. Takoradi to Lagos. Picturesque lagoons and mangrove swamps. Bright mornings and overheated nights. The doubtful reputation that Barbara had by now acquired was enhanced by the behaviour of the travelling companions with whom she shared a cabin. Joan, a married woman off to join her husband, and Sheila had standing dates with two of the ship's officers. Even Audrey, the fourth member of the *ménage*, a prim girl who wore large sunhats and spent most of her time disinfecting the premises with insect repellent, was somehow suspect. 'On entering the dining room, we arouse immense interest, particularly at breakfast, when each of us troops in looking increasingly dishevelled.' Having exhausted the possibilities of the purser and François, Barbara now 'made friends' with a young Russian engineer called Vladimir, who was twice caught by Audrey trying to climb through the porthole.

Finally at Lagos, they disembarked and were put on the two-day flight to Cairo. All signs of human habitation vanished from the 'flat red country' and the view from the plane's windows became 'rocky, sandy and desolate'. Conditions were cramped, and Barbara found herself sharing a mattress with a rabbi on his way to Israel ('You go Cairo? Me go Televiv') who spent much of the journey sedulously combing out his beard. Like the ships manoeuvring in the North Sea, the sight of Cairo stirred something in her and produced an intensely felt descriptive passage in her diary.

> Cairo was oppressive, dusty and colourless. Trams ran in all directions hooting, limp little donkeys loaded with fruit trailed along the gutters surrounded by horseflies. The pavements were crowded, women with frizzy black hair hurried along on taloned cork sandals, and tarbooshed men shuffled with limp arms or stood picking their noses and spitting into the dust. Gary carts drawn along by bony, glistening horses clopped by full of American soldiers on leave.

She took a taxi to the British Embassy, where an elderly lady showed her the deserted cipher room: 'Lipsticky cups of half-drunk tea were scattered about amongst used carbons, despatch books, partly chewed slabs of chocolate and countless cigarette ends.' Later, a second taxi ferried her to the Continental Hotel and a fellow-cipherine showed her to her room. After examining the view from her window onto the square nearby, where Gary cart and taxi drivers congregated in a 'spitting huddle' and moustachioed men in uniforms sat in basket chairs drinking lemonade, she pulled down the blinds, climbed onto the bed and lay staring at the ceiling.

Cairo in the early autumn of 1943 was an odd mixture of movement and inertia, grandeur and subterfuge, shameless opulence and stark privation. The war in Egypt had officially ended with the surrender of the Axis forces in Africa four months before: Allied military interest was now concentrated on the Italian campaign, which had moved into gear on 10 July with the landings in Sicily. Politically

Egypt – a British protectorate since 1914 – was administered by the government of Mostafa El Nahas: corrupt, ineffective and, it was thought, ripe to be overthrown by an opposition that had tolerated British occupation during the battle against the Afrika Korps but were now turning against the ambassador, the recently ennobled Lord Killearn. Little of this intrigue would have registered with the great mass of English men and women – military personnel, civil servants, intelligence experts – currently on the Cairo staff, who regarded the city as they would any other outpost of empire. The British garrison was housed in the Citadel of Muhammed Ali, a vast administrative centre that included married quarters, tennis courts, stables and training grounds. Officers spent their leisure time at the highly exclusive Gezira Sporting Club or such expatriate watering holes as Shepheard's Hotel, founded as long ago as 1841, with its Moorish hall and pillared ballroom.

Violet Powell's grandmother once observed that if you sat in the lobby at Shepheard's for long enough, almost everyone you had ever met in your life would eventually walk by. Certainly, most of the memoirs written about wartime Cairo emphasise its curious intimacy: delighted cries of recognition sounding across hotel foyers; friendships begun in childhood on the Wiltshire Downs eagerly renewed in the shadow of the pyramids. Off-duty officers and their dates enjoyed a vigorous social life – dinner at Fleurent's, the St James's or Le P'tit Coin de France, say, followed by dancing at the Scarabee, the Deck Club or the Kit Kat. The Continental, at which Barbara was now installed, had a celebrated rooftop restaurant complete with dance-floor, cabaret, belly-dancers, acrobats and a 'Mr Cardyman', who did card tricks. It was open season for husband-hunting – there were stories of girls who kept wedding dresses in their kit-bags on the off-chance of striking lucky.

At the same time, none of this gracious living could altogether subdue the background of dust, noise and squalor that Barbara had noted on her arrival. Artemis Cooper has observed of Olivia

Manning's *The Levant Trilogy* (1975–80), which draws on memories of the time that she and her husband Reggie Smith spent in Egypt between 1940 and 1942, that 'the feeling of what it was like to be in wartime Cairo is not, for her, the pleasant recollection of glamorous parties where all the men were in uniform: it is the physical sensation of enervated liverishness, brought on by the heat, which makes everything seem tawdry and insubstantial.' Lawrence Durrell and his wife Nancy were similarly unimpressed: 'Such a country,' Durrell complained, 'cripples, deformities, ophthalmia, goitre, amputations, lice, flies.'

Astride the summit of this mountain of dirt, clamour, antiquity and imperial prestige sat the larger than life figure of Egypt's titular ruler, King Farouk. A mere seven years into his tenure – he had succeeded his father, King Faud, at the age of sixteen – Farouk was already a legendary presence in his country's life, and gossip, rumour and scandal attached themselves to him like iron filings obeying the magnet's call. Many of the stories told about him had to do with his incorrigible appetite: put on a diet by his father in his early teens he was supposed to have eaten food put out for the palace cats. Others took in his enthusiasm for collecting: hunting trophies, cars, pornography, jewels, weaponry, coins and matchboxes all attracted his magpie's eye at one time or another, and his private rooms were full of negligently accumulated junk. Still more revolved around his enthusiastic womanising: though married a month before his eighteenth birthday to the sixteen-year-old Safinaz Zulficar and the father of two small children, he liked showing off the row of latchkeys which admitted him to his girlfriends' apartments. Overshadowing them all came a weird streak of eccentricity, symbolised by the occasion on which he announced that he intended to present a gift to the royal princesses, George VI's daughters Elizabeth and Margaret, which could be distributed to children in British hospitals. When embassy representatives arrived to inspect the benefaction, they discovered that Farouk had ordered 230 lb of chocolates from Groppi's, Cairo's most famous café, had them piled up on a large table and now stood waiting to sample them, flavour by flavour.

As for the daily round of Cairo life, newcomers from London were always amazed by the availability of fresh food. 'The war is non-existent in Egypt,' the actress Vivien Leigh wrote home to her mother in early September, 'and to see huge tables spread with every sort of deliciousness, and bowls of ice-cream was extraordinary.' With military operations transferred to the farther side of the Mediterranean, Barbara's arrival coincided with an upping of the social tempo. *Spring Party*, a revue produced by John Gielgud and starring such imported talent as Leigh, Beatrice Lillie and Dorothy Dickson had been playing at the Opera House during the summer. Noël Coward was much in evidence. A luxury nightclub, the Auberge des Pyramides, newly opened on the Mena Road, featuring an open-air courtyard with a dancefloor in the centre, had soon acquired the reputation of the city's best nightspot, and the patronage of the King.

Barbara seems to have taken up all these opportunities with gusto. At any rate there is scarcely any mention, either in memoir or novel, of time spent at work on her official duties decoding telegrams about incoming ships and their cargo. Escorted to lunch at the Gezira Sporting Club on her very first day, she began a whirlwind romance with a 'bumptious major' that came to an abrupt end in the back of a taxi several weeks later. Meanwhile the diplomatic bag had begun to disgorge letters from home. PC Boot wrote with news of the Cot ('I despatched two old razors to Mr Quennell but have not heard if he received them. Is Mr Topolski still in London? Give him my respects when you write . . . I was pleased to see Mr Topolski in this week's *Picture Post* with our prominent friend Mr Bernard Shaw.') For his part, Mr Topolski sent reams of gossip, while Mr Quennell, though delighted by a letter Barbara had sent him en route, was alarmed by the thought that she might have been misbehaving in his absence:

Your letter – posted at Sierra Leone – has arrived – almost exactly
a month after your departure. So all is forgotten and forgiven . . .
A nice letter it was too, tho' I couldn't help wondering just what
had happened on that boat and being a little disturbed – quite
unreasonably – by the background you rather vaguely filled in of
sultry nights, and scandal, and fisticuffs etc etc.

Quennell had also been pondering the question of Barbara's
launch into local society, for a second letter, written a fortnight later,
contains an introduction to Patrick Balfour, who had arrived in
Cairo late in 1942 as press attaché to the RAF. 'Use it or not as you're
inclined,' he instructed. 'At the worst you could meet him for a drink
& give him some gossip about Cyril'. Remembering that Balfour was
in the throes of his divorce, he advised that 'whether Angela is still a
tender object I'm not quite sure: it would probably be wise to allow
him to take the initiative.' There remained the question of how
Barbara, several thousand miles away and prey to all kinds of male
temptation, might feel about him and vice versa. 'Tomorrow I hope
to be at Tick & will moon around looking at old photographs &
examining your signature in the visitors' book.' There had clearly
been a second letter, sent from Nigeria, offering details of her romantic
exploits, as Quennell goes on to add, somewhat ruefully, that 'I've
accepted the black lamb at Lagos with resignation: tho' your gun-
turret activities stick in my gullet a little even now.'

Not that Barbara, now transferred from the Continental to new
quarters at the Villa Moskatelli at Zamalek, seems to have needed
very much help in insinuating herself into the Cairo *beau monde*.
Fresh admirers gathered on all sides: Oxford-educated 'Freddie', a
Bentley-owning Copt who introduced her to the local nightlife;
'Victor', an international polo player who claimed that his idea of bliss
was to make love to a woman on a bed of tuber roses. In the midst of
these diversions, the letters home dried to a trickle and then stopped
altogether, so that Quennell could complain, early in December, that

it was 'a very long time since I heard from you – & I fear a very long time since you heard from me'. Topolski, meanwhile, was fretting at the news that Quennell was still in the game, sending his very best love and, in his capacity as a war artist, planning a descent on the Middle East. That Topolski now had a confederate seems clear from an enclosure from PC Boot. ('Just a line from Mr Topolski's studio. I am on my way home from Blackpool & have just looked him up. Wish you were here too. I do hope you are enjoying the life in Cairo.') To add to the confusion, 'Grub', the military boyfriend, was also thought to be on his way to Egypt. Either Freddie or Victor is presumably the subject of a letter from Quennell written at the end of January 1944:

> My darling Skeltie,
>
> I was much struck by your news, & gather that you are perhaps a little more flustered by the whole affair than you're prepared to let on. Don't go marrying him for God's sake! Grub arriving too! He met little Lys in a pub & told her that he expected to see you soon; & little Lys had, of course, great pleasure in telling me – adding 'Poor Topples, I'm afraid he may find Skeltie rather *surrounded*, mayn't he?' She seems to have been righter than she knew. But seriously . . . I hope you are not too unhappy & bothered – or too much enamoured. What is he like? Spherical – solid – black – or slow & moon faced? Thank you for saying that, were we to meet tomorrow, the situation, so far as you are concerned, would not have changed greatly. Who can tell . . . I had a *twinge* – yes, a distinct twinge – when I read of your latest adventure . . .

Quennell's letter is revealing in several ways. On the one hand, Barbara's account of her latest *passade* had clearly gone into considerable detail ('Your last letter was both the nicest & most informative you have yet sent me'). On the other, it seems to have betrayed a certain amount of disquiet at the prospect before her. There were good reasons for this, the most obvious being that Barbara was an employee of the British government and that the men she was now associating with operated at the upper level of what, if not a fully fledged imperial possession, was a British Protectorate whose internal power-brokers were jockeying for position in what they knew would very shortly be a post-war world. At the very least, Barbara's association with Freddie and Victor was woefully indiscreet. At worst, it was a security risk. All the evidence suggests that Barbara, for all her customary self-possession, was slightly out of her depth.

As to what actually happened when, where and with whom, all this is more or less impossible to reconstitute. Topolski headed east early in 1944 – there was a minor confrontation with Quennell in London when news of the trip went public – and a single room was eventually procured at Shepheard's Hotel for their reunion. Here, too, there was trouble. The fact that the pair were unmarried outraged public morality: coming back to the hotel one night, Barbara used the back stairs in an attempt to evade the hotel authorities, only to find that they had got wind of her presence. Their efforts to evict her turned into what Topolski remembered as a 'slapstick chase – the horde of long-gallabiahed and tarbooshed *safragis* and Nubian porters racing up after her, and, finally, gathering outside the room with bangs and shouts'. Professional duties then took Topolski to China and India, and his second visit to Cairo was less successful. Although he took care to book a double room, by this time it was too late: Barbara's affections were engaged elsewhere.

At some point in the summer of 1944, somebody – presumably the faithful Freddie or the tuber-rose loving Victor – took Barbara to dine at the Auberge des Pyramides. The royal party sat at an adjoining table, where the King, in one of his playful moods, was amusing himself by scattering coloured pom-poms. (In *A Young Girl's Touch*, Melinda dines at the fictitious 'Hotel Flamboyant' and watches King

Yoyo decant a cauldron of roast peanuts onto his plate, which he then begins to flick at the guests.) An introduction was effected, with Barbara professing to find 'his infantile side rather endearing, even this kind of thing'. A few days later an equerry arrived at the embassy bearing an invitation to join a royal house party in the desert. Picked up at the Villa Moskatelli by a royal aide, she was taken to a private train that 'ran like a centipede through the desert' to a station where a convoy of cars waited to transport the twenty or so guests to Farouk's summer palace. Of the night that followed, Barbara remembered that:

> We were told we all had to sleep on the Palace rooftop where mattresses had been laid. Farouk never stopped chatting in Arabic and laughing with his underlings at his guests' discomfort, as we all trooped onto the roof in our respective nightwear. When I appeared in a green dressing gown he said I reminded him of a cabbage. At sunrise, we were awoken by the inevitable bugle call. I had a pair of earrings in the shape of curly fish that I had bought in Moosky. Farouk took them, saying he was going to give me a surprise. One night I was getting into bed when I found a jewel box tucked under the pillow: the curly fish had been copied in gold with emerald eyes, and a clip to go with them . . .

A Young Girl's Touch adds a few corroborating details, in which the King gives Melinda a tour of the palace, shows her his stamp collection, his apostle spoons and the contents of the royal armoury ('We're nearly out of Brasso') and beats her with a rolled-up newspaper ('Tensely she awaited each thud with a forlorn feeling that was not unpleasant'). There is also a rather wistful exchange in which he invites her to take up residence.

> 'You could live here if you wished.'
> 'Wouldn't I get lonely?'

'You'd soon get used to it . . . I should very much appreciate finding you here whenever I came with some guests.'

'A permanent member of the harem?'

Over the next few weeks, Barbara was constantly, if covertly, in the King's company – dining and watching films at the Abdin Palace in Cairo, being driven back to the Villa Moskatelli by him in the small hours and ducking out of view as the car passed the night-watchmen at the palace gates. Set against popular caricatures of Farouk as a sybaritic debauchee, her memories of him are unusually downbeat. She thought he had simple tastes in food, while 'in spite of the rather dull sycophantic people surrounding the King, I must confess I was never bored'. Quennell, previously reduced to fragments of Bedford Square gossip ('Did I tell you that little Lys now has a pink & grey Australian parrot, which makes the hours of daylight hideous . . . loves only Cyril (of course) but as soon as it is out of its cage, descends like a dive-bomber yelling with fury on the heads of those (including myself) who it does not care for'), had been told about the jaunt to the summer palace.

I was delighted to get your very funny letter about King F's week-end party. It is just how Eastern Monarchs are supposed to behave & I thought your description particularly – tho' not unexpectedly – brilliant. Whether King F. eventually got his beady (?) way you leave a little doubtful. Perhaps he did – or has done – since you wrote. However, it is a little late in the day to appear possessive: & I suppose that to have been a royal mistress at least once in her life is an attractive woman's privilege.

This, too, is a revealing letter, for it hints at a change in the way that Quennell regarded Barbara. His letters from the early stages of their relationship are ardent, but also faintly superior, full of rather sickly pet-names ('Baby', 'Skeltie', 'Wombat') and prone to patronage.

Three years later there is a sense that Barbara has gained an extra dimension, turned into a royal mistress with a literary style to match. You suspect that Quennell, though clearly admiring of the new Barbara, is nonplussed by her, not quite sure how the transformation has been effected, and at the same time anxious about its implications for the small matter of himself, wondering if his own recent successes – the reviewing job for the *Daily Mail*, the editorship of the *Cornhill Magazine* – might not be considered inferior to the accomplishments of a woman who was being wined and dined by the King of Egypt.

But the wining and dining, the swimming sessions in the palace pool and the late-night lifts to the Villa Moskatelli were about to come to an end. Before very long she found a polite note on her desk at the embassy suggesting that, in view of her professional duties, she might be associating too much with non-Britishers. ('Did it mean Farouk, myself or others unknown to me?' Topolski wondered.) In much the same way, Melinda in *A Young Girl's Touch* is

> aware of a hostile atmosphere; everyone made a note of the time she came and went; how often she left the room and the amount of tea she consumed and, whenever the telephone pealed, the girls would exchange grave looks. They reserved the longest telegrams for her, with lists of ships and cargo to be unloaded at some port, or the dreariest, that were unravelled with the aid of an enormous tome, which could be found in the post office of any provincial town. She was considered a security risk.

One of the last passage migrants to set eyes on Barbara in Cairo was Sinclair-Loutit. Meeting her for a drink in mid-August 1944, he found her 'either thro' dumbness or niceness . . . unaffected by the intolerable Cairo female vanity'. That Barbara had by this point become a focus of expatriate gossip is confirmed by Sinclair-Loutit's account of a conversation with an old Cambridge friend, who 'thinks the amount of attention she gets is a tribute to her real qualities rather than to her biological scarcity. When treated without avid supplication at her real value she exhibits a petulant boredom.' Coming across her again a week or so later, Sinclair-Loutit was less impressed. 'Skelton is unbelievably dumb + I think knows it', he informed Janetta, 'is, I think, genuinely gone on Topolski . . . + they say she is being sent home for having an affair with Farouk . . .'

In this regard, the gossips were right. Shortly afterwards she was summoned by the first secretary at the embassy, Bernard Burrows, and informed that if she went on seeing Farouk she would have to leave Egypt. Burrows was by no means a martinet. And, as one of Farouk's own British friends, he would probably have appreciated the irony of having to forbid another British subject his company. To Barbara this reaction was understandable, if misguided. After all, as she later put it, 'I was in a sensitive position, and they were convinced Farouk was setting me up just to get information from me.' Her own view was that, on the contrary, the King had no interest in politics. 'What they never could understand was that Farouk couldn't have cared less. The only communications to England that mattered to him were his telexes ordering silk neckties from Hawes and Curtis.' In the end, Burrows decided to give his wayward cipherine a fortnight's leave. Nothing loath, Barbara opted to spend her two weeks hitch-hiking round the Middle East. A day later she could be found eating her supper at a cheap hotel in Ismailia ('A strange contrast to my dinner of last night with the Monarch!'), sousing her food with ketchup to disguise its nastiness. It was amusing being alone, she reflected, as people were encouraged to come up and talk 'as though I were an old friend'. Later she would retire to a room that overlooked the railway terminus, where trains rumbled past the window, children's voices screeched and there was a clatter of plates from the hotel kitchen.

If anything irked her, it was the physical consequences of her last meeting with Farouk. She was deadly tired, she wrote in her diary, and ached all over 'from a flogging last night on the steps of the Royal Palace'. Barbara would have preferred a splayed cane, 'but instead had to suffer a dressing-gown cord which created a gentle thudding sound over an interminable period'. A day or two later she was in Jerusalem, drinking with a 'small lecherous Frenchman' who had picked her up in a taxi outside Gaza. There was a tussle in the cab on the way home after dinner, but Barbara, fresh from her experiences with a royal flagellant, could handle a lecherous Frenchman. After hitting him twice on the head with a volume of Virginia Woolf she happened to be carrying with her, she made her escape.

Interlude: Joan

O n first inspection, no one could look less like a Lost Girl than Joan Eyres-Monsell. Lys was an orphaned teenager forced to carve out a career by way of the typing school and the mannequin parade. Sonia's mother kept a South Kensington boarding house. Joan's father, on the other hand, was a one-time Conservative Party Chief Whip who by the early 1930s had risen to the dizzying political heights of First Lord of the Admiralty. The *Honourable* Miss Eyres-Monsell – after papa was raised to the peerage in 1935 – was brought up on the family's estate at Dumbleton, Gloucestershire, where hunting, shooting and other rural pursuits were enthusiastically pursued. Joan enjoyed a thoroughly conventional upbringing, in which genteel poverty and bohemian shadings were conspicuous by their absence. From an early stage, though, there were hints of a personality that pined to escape from the world of debutante dances and enforced leisure and set up camp in less orthodox climes. When she married in the summer of 1939, it was not to a landowner or a Tory MP of the kind of whom her parents might have approved but to a recently divorced journalist named John Rayner, one of Lord Beaverbrook's bright young men, who had just become day assistant editor of the *Daily Express*.

And even before her trip to the altar came evidence of a different kind of person, more at home on the margins of inter-war era literary life than letting rip among the Gloucestershire fauna. Spring 1937, for example, found her on a trip to New York in the decidedly mixed company of Peter Quennell – already married to Glur but keenly interested in his fellow traveller – and Tom Driberg, the *Express*'s gossip columnist. Driberg's 'William Hickey' column commended her fashion sense, for coming down to dinner wearing a purple dress, a scarlet and gold Eton jacket and 'a single extraordinary earring. It consisted of a bunch of 42 small gilt safety pins.' One by one, the marks of Lost Girl affiliation stack up. By the late 1930s, she and Rayner were weekending at Tickerage Mill. As an accomplished semi-professional photographer, proficient enough to have her work featured in the *Architectural Review*, she took the celebrated group portrait of Dick Wyndham, Angela Culme-Seymour, Connolly, Spender and their friends. Above all, she was a chum of Connolly's, and as such a fixture of the King's Road dinner parties he gave with Jean. 'The Connollys are marvellous people to know,' James Lees-Milne wrote of one of these gatherings:

> They are quite rich, about £1,200 p.a. I should think, and they like to spend it all on their friends. They are both extremely intelligent; he is brilliant, untidy, dirty and ugly. They give lots of dinners at which 8 or 10 people sit down to the most gorgeous meals . . . They never go to cinemas or plays after, instead one sits round the fire and drinks . . . Above all they know and invite all the people one likes best in England.

On this particular evening, the favoured few included Nancy Mitford and her husband Peter Rodd, Quennell and Glur, John Sutro, Lady Dorothy Lygon, the writer Christopher Sykes and his sister Angela, the Countess of Antrim, the publisher Kenneth

Rae . . . and Joan. If Connolly admired her photographs – he was to print her picture of the bomb-wrecked Chelsea Old Church in *Horizon* – then he relished her stupendous good looks. As the 1930s went on she joined Diana and Janetta at the hub of his personal myth, a constant stimulus to his romantic day-dreaming and the alternative worlds where he wandered endlessly with the women of his choice; when she married Rayner he remarked that it was the unhappiest day of his existence.

The Rayners began their married life in a flat in Blue Ball Yard, off St James's Street, Piccadilly, but from an early stage they were an integral part of the Connolly circus. They stayed with him at Driberg's house at Bradwell in Essex. When the Blitz came and their new home near the Gray's Inn Road was bombed out, they relocated to a flat in Palace Gate next door to Peter Watson. For Joan it was the wartime Lost Girl life *in excelsis*, in which days spent working for the Holborn Division of the Red Cross alternated with evenings in bohemia and a fair amount of extra-marital dalliance. Connolly, naturally, was included. With her marriage in ruins, abroad looked a better bet than war-torn Bloomsbury, and, after training as a cipher clerk, she followed Barbara's route to Cairo and became yet another of the lodgers in the house shared by Patrick Balfour and Eddie Gathorne-Hardy. Come September 1945 she was working in the Athens Embassy as secretary to the press attaché, Osbert Lancaster, making the best use of her opportunities and reflecting on the considerable distance she had managed to travel from her early life. 'I can't complain,' she wrote brightly to Balfour, 'as I am having a gay time here and I do think Greece comes up to my expectations. There is also a delicious pagan atmosphere of NO GUILT, which I appreciate very much having suffered too much of it on account of my upbringing.'

Part Two

8.

Ways and Means: Lost Girl Style

On New Year's Eve she was meeting Darcy at the Ritz. Arriving at seven o'clock she seated herself in a corner of the bar and ordered a crème de menthe. This evening she had taken trouble with her appearance, mascaraed her eyes and combed her hair so that it overlapped the high cheek collar of the pleated dress that she wore. She felt self-conscious waiting alone.

Barbara Skelton, *A Young Girl's Touch* (1956)

Not many photographs survive of day-to-day life in the *Horizon* offices. Judging by the uniformity of the dress styles on display, most of them date from a single shoot, in all probability from the autumn of 1949 shortly before the magazine's closure. In one a bow-tied and besuited Connolly stares rather absently out of the high windows onto Bedford Square. You get the feeling that it is all the same to him. Governments will rise and fall, literary magazines will come and go, but still middle-aged *litterateurs* will be able to smoke their cigars and exult over their collections of Sèvres china. In another, some kind of editorial conference is in progress. Connolly looms over a table. Lys sits to his right in modish, tweed-jacketed profile. Sonia, at the opposite end, throws out an elegant hand that almost obscures the fourth participant in the tableau – a balding bespectacled man stationed alongside Connolly who looks as if he may be the writer T. R. 'Tosco' Fyvel. In a third, Sonia and Lys are sitting side by side in cane-backed chairs, Sonia in close-up, Lys placidly regarding her from the further end of their shared workspace. Each is sporting an elaborate Veronica Lake-style hairdo of ridges and swept-back scallops.

As for their clothes, Lys's costume looks like a home-grown approximation of Dior's celebrated 'New Look', variations on which had begun to flood the London rag trade a couple of years before. Sonia, in jersey and sensible skirt – there is a suspicion that the photo was taken on her last day at work – looks pensive, clearly exercised by the thought of one kind of life coming to a close as another kind grinds inexorably into gear. Behind them, somebody unidentifiable with a great deal of fuzzy hair is labouring away at a desk. Each element of this portrait – from the sitters' get-up, to the attitudes they strike and the way they address the camera – raises the question of what might be called Lost Girl style. What did they look like? How did they talk, and what did they talk about? How did they spend their leisure time, and who with? What were the dimensions of the world they inhabited, and how did they attempt to make sense of it?

As ever with the Lost Girls, nearly every generalisation that can be made about them as a collective unit needs some kind of qualification. Seated in the office at Bedford Square, telephone to hand, and Connolly (presumably) lurking in the editorial sanctum, Lys looks, as she always does, like a fashion-plate; Sonia seems a touch less modish, more like a girl on a country weekend who fears that the central heating may not live up to expectations. Most contemporary or near-contemporary observers who reported back on Lost Girl style were concerned to emphasise their bohemianism: a make-do-and-mend approach to dress that in most cases was the result of sheer poverty. Quennell, puzzling over the question of Barbara's elusive charm, noted her habit of bundling her graceful body into a 'blue horse-blanket coat' and piling up her brown hair into 'an untidy poodle coiffure' secured by half-a-dozen badly placed clips. Here in the early 1940s, when a substantial percentage of women sported perms or three-day sets, unruly hair was a signature mark of the bohemian's disdain for propriety. Feliks Topolski remembered Janetta's hair 'overhanging her face and shoulders'; he deduced that she was 'one of the progenitors of this bohemian, later universal style'. In the same way, Evelyn Waugh's fictional account of the *Horizon* staff notes that they 'wore their hair long and enveloping in a style which fifteen years later was to be associated with the King's Road'.

Physically, the Lost Girl tended to be tallish, slim to the point of skimpiness, her good looks accentuated by habitual pallor. Spender's description of her in her early twenties – the Renoir face, the cupid's mouth – is trailed by 'a bit pale perhaps'. There were occasional complaints (exclusively from men) about Sonia's plumpness and the size of her legs: 'They were enormous, quite inappropriate for what was on top', Woodrow Wyatt cruelly alleged. When the going was good, or in Barbara's case when the significant other possessed the necessary resources, an innate sophistication immediately declared itself that found expression in the usual appurtenances of upper-class female style. In a world of rationing and clothing coupons, Peter Watson, for example, kept Sonia supplied with French perfume and silk stockings from America. In these circumstances, only the best would do: Barbara, when she was presented with 'Soir de Paris' en route to Egypt, was quick to sneer at what she regarded as 'French tart scent'. In general, bohemian tendencies in dress were usually extinguished by the onset of prosperity. In the mid-1940s, Janetta had once arrived at Topolski's studio on a bicycle with a rucksack strapped to her shoulders, but by 1947 Evelyn Waugh could report to Nancy Mitford that she 'has a new look: silk stockings, high heeled shoes, diamond clips everywhere'. Frances Partridge's diaries monitor this upward path. Spotted at a party in 1949 she is 'looking lovely in a dress of grey watered silk'. A year later she is 'looking so trim' in a camel coat with 'new shoes, skirt and pullover'. By 1951, with a new and well-heeled husband in tow, she is reported as wearing 'nothing but a little short green corduroy jacket over camel's hair trousers', the acme of Attlee-era *ton*.

As to how a Lost Girl might communicate, the words she might employ and the emphasis she might choose to put on them, these were products of the mid-twentieth-century middle to upper-middle class, the daughters of public school masters, army officers and old India hands, with a vocabulary and a vocal style to match: not quite the world of Nancy Mitford perhaps, in its caste-sanctioned prohibitions, but running it close in its emphasis on laconicism, understatement and irony, a clipped precision that could occasionally shade into outright disdain. One of Barbara's boyfriends remembered her habit of dropping shrewdly perceptive comments into the conversation in 'the flat, monotonous drawl of a ventriloquist's dummy'. Disparagement was conveyed in Edwardian nursery-talk: 'beastly', 'awful', 'ghastly', 'maddening', 'madly' (to Janetta, the sight of people falling over in the winter slush was 'madly dangerous'), 'desperately' (Barbara's 'desperately depressed' or 'desperately dejected'); a pressing personal dilemma – the arrival of one boyfriend, say, while another was still on the premises – might be described as a 'pickle'; the death of a close friend or major trauma might be greeted with the comment that 'I minded most frightfully.'

If this suggests a damming up of sentiment, a determination to batten down the emotional hatches and repress any feelings that might be stirring within, then most Lost Girls were happy enough to call a spade a spade when the circumstances demanded it. Sex was 'fucking'; a homosexual 'a bugger'; menstruation 'the curse'. 'A touch of commonness is absolutely indispensable, don't you think?' Barbara once pronounced. Janetta, too, had her no-nonsense, abrasive side. Angela remembered an evening in 1942 when she and her half-sister, together with Jan, Brasco and Sinclair-Loutit, went out to dinner. 'Did you see me, darling, driving along in my fast open sports car?'

Sinclair-Loutit wondered. 'Yes we did.' 'What did I look like – rather dashing?' 'You looked an absolute shit,' Janetta told him.

Naturally, there were widespread individual variations, some of them nearer to traditional upper-class flamboyance (Glur's cry of 'Darling!' as she greeted a friend was thought to echo through the average drawing room like a klaxon), others closer to middle-class neurosis. Sonia, in particular, could sometimes come across as a rather earnest schoolgirl. There is a (possibly apocryphal) story of her being chased round the garden by a lustful fellow guest at a country weekend and finally taking refuge in the pond. 'It isn't his trying to rape me that I mind,' she is supposed to have told Quennell, as he helped her from the water, 'but that he doesn't seem to realize what Cyril stands for.' A not terribly well-informed schoolgirl, either: certainly a tactlessly worded rejection letter that winged out from the *Horizon* office to the distinguished American poet Theodore Roethke ('It seemed to us that your poetry was in a way very American in that it just lacked that inspiration, inevitability or quintessence of writing or feeling that distinguishes good poetry from verse') caused lasting offence. In contrast, Barbara's epistolary style is blunt, rueful and matter-of-fact. 'Thank you very much for having us to stay,' runs a thank-you letter to a hostess from the early 1950s. 'I am sorry you had to do so much work and never a complaint. So unlike me.'

There would always be plenty of thank-you letters. Apart from Lys, who spent nearly a decade in Connolly's company, the Lost Girl was essentially peripatetic, moving from place to place and billet to billet as the demands of work, romance and inclination took her. If Barbara's trail is so difficult to follow in the 1940s, it is because she lived at so many addresses, an eternal passage migrant continually flying from nest to nest. In the nightmare world of the Blitz, with its bombed-out flats and constantly shifting personnel, the practical difficulties of working out where one might be staying on a particular night, or how to make contact with the person you were supposed to be spending it with, could be all but insuperable. Quennell's letters to Barbara are full of these impediments: rooms that may or may not be available; beds that may or may not be free. For all that, the Lost Girl's professional beat still had its boundaries, its oases and its favoured ports of call, its routines and its attendants. She tended to live in places where rents were cheap and accommodation easier to procure: Bloomsbury, or its margins; Chelsea; South Kensington, with occasional forays beyond. Rising early, or in Barbara's case, sometimes not, she would proceed to her place of work – between 1939 and 1945 this would often be a government office – to answer telephones, take dictation or attend meetings. Lunch would be eaten at her desk, in a staff canteen or, if there were a male escort available, anywhere from a Lyons restaurant to the Ritz Hotel. Then came a long, fatiguing afternoon in a badly ventilated office dense with cigarette smoke, whose tedium was relieved only by the promise of the evening's entertainment.

As for how the Lost Girl occupied her leisure hours, this, too, depended on her current level of prosperity. One of the distinguishing marks of most Lost Girl existence is its lack of funds. Barbara's lifestyle would not have been sustainable without men to subsidise her meals and offer her presents. Diana's letters from the early 1940s are a litany of sorely needed £2s, of 30 shillings that are owing, meetings with unfriendly bank managers and County Court judgements on unpaid debts. Angela was an habitué of the pawn-broker's shop, while even Sonia and Lys – employed by government ministries during the war and less reliant on handouts – were used to living on a shoestring. Yet, once a sponsor declared himself, their surface life could seem relatively upmarket. Janetta recalled how much she liked dining at the White Tower in Percy Street, provided that there was someone to pick up the tab. With a rich boyfriend on hand to settle the bills, Barbara seems to have spent much of the early part of the war in ceaseless transit from one upmarket Mayfair watering hole to another: the Ecu de France, the Coq d'Or, the Curzon Street Sherry Bar. Lunches might be taken at the Berkeley

Hotel or the Café Royal, evenings spent at private establishments such as the Theatre Club or the French Club.

Two or three years later, on the other hand, in the company of the famously improvident Quennell, her haunts became more bohemian: nightclubs such as the 400, the Jamboree or the Nut-house. Quennell's diary records a grim-sounding evening spent at the Jamboree in January 1943, 'the whole room wrapped in a hot clammy grey fog that seemed to be rising from the floor: in all directions prostrate drinkers; a woman with cascading blonde hair . . . being carried from a table'. Desperate for entertainment, most of those present scarcely noticed what onlookers diagnosed as the 'tenseness' of a social world made up of smoking, drinking and sleep deprivation. Slightly more congenial, perhaps, was the Gargoyle Club at 69 Dean Street, founded by David Tennant in the 1920s and intended both as a chic nightspot for dancing and a daytime refuge for the avant-garde, where, as the original press release put it, 'still struggling writers, painters, poets and musicians will be offered the best food and wine at prices they can afford'.

Thus conceived, the club managed to combine an authentic smartness with a sentimental attachment to bohemia. Honorary membership was available for the 'deserving artistic poor'. No less an authority than Matisse, asked to advise on décor, had suggested that the walls of the main room on the first floor should be covered with a mosaic of mirrored tiles assembled out of the fragments of antique French looking-glasses. All this had a magnetising effect, and most Lost Girls and their consorts can be found at one time or another at the Gargoyle, drinking at the bar with elderly Soho celebrities such as Nina Hamnett or Augustus John or taking to its teeming Saturday night dancefloor. Barbara, Sonia and Janetta were all seen there at one time or another. As 'Mrs Peter Quennell', Glur was photographed there by a society magazine at one of Tennant's parties in 1939 talking to Lady Julia Mount. It was by its lift shaft, sometime in 1941 or 1942, with Barbara looking on, that Quennell and Topolski came to blows.

If the focus of Lost Girl life was essentially metropolitan, then there were several rural retreats where weekends and holidays could be spent. Barbara had her cottage in Kent; Janetta her bolthole at Ham Spray. Tickerage, the Sussex mill house near Uckfield owned by Dick Wyndham, was another favoured locale: Peter Watson rented it for a year in 1944; Connolly and Lys spent Christmas there in 1947. Weekends there offered a tantalising alternate world where the privations of wartime London instantly disappeared. 'Had a heavenly 2 days in the country with my bosses Connolly and Peter Watson,' Anna Kavan reported early in 1944. 'It snowed the whole time so that one could hardly go out at all, but I can't say how marvellously peaceful and relaxed one felt with no alerts, no bombs, no queues, no crowds.' And beyond clubland and the country weekend lay an alluring landscape of taxi rides to parties in far-off suburbs, vagrant journeys through the outer London dawn and a series of entertainments that ranged from the questionable to the downright illegal. *A Young Girl's Touch*, for example, has Melinda being taken by a man named Darcy to an address in Chelsea to watch a pornographic film. On arrival she is shown into a room where several people are gathered around the projector, 'two well-known actors, a famous cartoonist, a popular second-rate portrait painter and a black-marketeering restaurateur on intimate terms with the host'. Also present are some 'sexually avid young women stimulated by social success, grateful if in return they were occasionally taken to an expensive West End restaurant'.

Gradually the evening unfolds. The host introduces his wife ('a big, smiling blonde with wide apart front teeth') with the assurance that 'She has a first rate pussy and if she likes you I'm sure we could arrange something good.' Having sat through the first two films, one of which involves a flagellation scene at a girls' school, Melinda finds herself alone with an over-excited Darcy in a blacked-out room. Desperate to escape she sprints back along the main hall ('deserted except for a naked man asleep on the floor') to the front door but finds it locked shut, mounts a chair and tries to get out through the skylight and is eventually thrown out into the street by the host. Glancing back at the house as she turns the corner, Melinda sees 'a row of angry men silhouetted in the doorway; each one in a threatening attitude; some were waving clenched fists while others just stood naked and grim and shivering'. Given that much of *A Young Girl's Touch* is barely ornamented autobiography, there is every reason to suppose that this happened exactly as described.

If the Lost Girl's daily round can seem uncomfortably frenetic, a matter of snatched assignations, exhausted late-night carousing and the relentless grind of unappetising day jobs, then this was a consequence of the wider atmosphere in which it was conducted. These, after all, were lives lived during wartime, the world of the London Blitz (September 1940–May 1941) and, as hostilities drew to a close, the V-1 and V-2 flying bombs which could fall almost without warning, reducing a row of terraced houses to rubble; a world from which no one who moved in the *Horizon* circle emerged without some degree of psychological damage. In the aftermath of a bomb blast in which they had seen a woman killed in front of them, Connolly and Lys came across a severed hand lying in the street. 'I'm sorry I haven't written for a few days,' Sonia explained to Coldstream from her ambulance station at University College Hospital in September 1940, 'but life here is so odd at the moment that it's difficult to concentrate on anything.' The peculiar atmosphere of London in the early 1940s – its sinister individuality, its lurking sense of existential dread – is a constant of almost every diary written at the time, whether by a young woman or anyone else. 'I am melancholy and terrified of the celebrated Blitzkrieg,' the twenty-two-year-old Penelope Fitzgerald wrote in mid-October 1939. 'I start at noises in the street, sleep with my head under the bedclothes and listen to the owls hooting.' Twelve days later she noted her feeling of inertia in a world of panic-stricken movement: 'Everybody seems to be so mobile nowadays, and to flash to and fro past or through the metropolis leaving me glued to my desk.'

Fitzgerald, who was working at the BBC, recreated her time there in the novel *Human Voices* (1980). Here the barrage balloons tethered above Green Park ascend like a flock of sheep in the evening light, 'fixed and grazing in the upper air'. The breeze is full of 'fine, whitish dust'. At night people in transit through the murky London streets count their steps in the darkness, passing 'doors with tiny slits of light, just enough to catch the eye'. In an atmosphere of constant uncertainty, civilians survive by focusing on their everyday routines, deliberately excluding from their minds the thought of 'helpless waves of flesh against metal and salt . . . the soundless fall of a telegram through a letter box'. If you can't face living your life day by day, Fitzgerald observes at one point, 'you must live it minute by minute'. This compulsion to 'live for the moment' is a feature of Lost Girl reminiscence. 'People don't realise how strange it was to live in London in the war, with so many things happening and such uncertainty and desperation', Janetta recalled. At bedrock level, life during the Blitz was simply a question of facing up to a series of unrelenting logistical demands: getting from place to place in the blackout; securing transport to take you through the bomb-cratered streets. As for the psychological consequences, Janetta thought 'people behaved very differently and recklessly and with a sort of abandon . . . because there was always a possibility that every single thing was going to go wrong'.

Inevitably, much of this abandon had a sexual side. The novelist Mary Wesley, at this point in her late twenties and employed in tracking Soviet and German call signs from an MI5 office near St James's Park, later remarked that however much she might have been ashamed of the fact, the war offered young women from her upper-middle-class background the prospect of an intensely exciting time: danger, exhilaration and a degree of sexual freedom that would have been unthinkable in the days before 1939. By 1941, the mother of a child who was not her husband's, Mary was living in an ancient manor house near Land's End and making hay with the personnel of the nearby RAF base. 'War is very erotic . . .' she remembered. 'We thought why the hell shouldn't we do what we want . . .? They were all going to get killed . . . It got to the state where one reached across the pillow in the morning and thought, "Let's see. Who is it this time?"'

If none of the Lost Girls ever quite reached these heights of promiscuity, then some of them came fairly close: Angela, after all, had two illegitimate children while still married to Balfour, and the roster of Barbara's boyfriends in the early part of the war – even the ones whose trails endure – runs comfortably into double figures. Questioned about contemporary morals by Frances Partridge, Janetta called up 'a (to me) dreary vision – of hopping into bed at the smallest provocation, no gradual approach or Stendhalian crystallization, much unkindness, that utterly useless emotion jealousy, of course, and desperate attempts to preserve a cynical outlook'.

On the other hand, there is a suspicion that at least some of this behaviour is exaggerated. 'Whenever things were hard, they simply sent Sonia out to sleep with a few advertisers or possible backers', Stephen Spender is supposed to have told the publisher John Calder of *Horizon*'s financial arrangements, but Spender always denied it and lodged a note to this effect in the Orwell Archive after Sonia's death. Equally, you have a feeling that an environment of blackout curtains and falling bombs was only an incidental stimulus to such free and independent spirits as Angela and Barbara, and that they would have behaved in exactly the same way whatever might be going on in the world beyond. Certainly, the Barbara of the 1950s does not seem so very different from the Barbara of 1941. All the same, the romantic pass-the-parcelling of the 1940s left ineradicable scars. The interior damage wrought by Barbara's several abortions meant that she was never able to have children. And hanging over the question of Lost Girl sexual behaviour is the unignorable fact that most of the judgements passed on it were made by men, for the most part men with axes to grind. The myth of Sonia's lesbianism, for example, was apparently put about by Connolly in retaliation for her refusal to sleep with him: the only Lost Girl with authentic lesbian tendencies was Barbara, who remarked of one of her experiences in this line that 'I just saw her as a man with breasts.'

There is a wider question here, which lies at the heart of young women's emotional lives in the 1940s. However liberated and self-determined, what was the degree of freedom that they actually managed to achieve? On the one hand they were independent spirits suborned by no one ('their lives went as they wanted them to', Janetta remarked of Barbara and Sonia), who believed that they were making their own choices. On the other, it is difficult to proceed very far through the tangle of their romantic careers without divining just how little they liked being on their own and how few inner resources they harboured when it came to coping with isolation and abandonment. 'They felt you had to have a man in your life otherwise you had no justification', Glur's daughter remembered of her mother's circle. 'Without one, you were somehow a second-class citizen.' Men could be taken or left, picked up or walked away from on a whim, and yet it was men who authenticated you, supposedly made your lustre shine brighter, could confirm or deny the sparkle of the personality you brought to the society in which you operated. All this offered a dilemma that some Lost Girls took decades to solve. There is a suspicion that Barbara never solved it at all.

Meanwhile, there was the practical question of how that independent, free-spirited life might be lived in a wider world where, for the most part, traditional moral standards still applied and hotel receptionists shook their heads over unmarried couples who applied for a night's lodging. Years after her affair with Connolly, married now and with a small baby, Diana wrote a rather revealing letter to Janetta canvassing the advantages of taking the name of the man you were living with rather than marrying him. 'I absolutely agree with what you say about name & marriage,' Diana assured her friend. 'For so long now ever since I was 18 I have been false-naming & though I haven't minded all that, it is a relief from strain now to have to wonder whether it might be bloody; as I've had scenes in hotels etc.' The interest of Diana's letter lies in its disavowal of anything that might be construed as a mercenary motive. 'I suppose if one was nasty & wanted money one would get more from a husband but life is not worth living if one has to get married for that! How dreadful it would have been to have had to divorce Cyril instead of just going – it was bad enough as it was.' In the vast majority of cases, what seems to have mattered most to the Lost Girl was not material comfort but her own autonomy.

If the world through which the Lost Girls wandered was one of living for the moment, of sexual recklessness and social opportunism, then there were other ways in which it differed from the arrangements of 1918–39. One of them was the high degree of intermingling encouraged by an environment in which the barriers of social class suddenly seemed a great deal less impregnable. The war novels of Anthony Powell and Evelyn Waugh, for example, are full of what, in an earlier age, would have been regarded as societal meltdown: middle-class subalterns polluting regimental messes with their 'common' accents; temporary gentlemen sweet-talking, and sometimes disappearing with, upper-class girls whom chance had sent their way. Whether in government offices or in the course of after-hours socialising, all kinds of unlikely people were brought together in circumstances which could throw their original affiliations sharply out of kilter. The eighteen-year-old Jaqueline Hope-Nicholson, who had acquired a secretarial job at War Office Intelligence, was startled to find Brian Howard cruising its chilly corridors and to embark on a friendship that at one point encouraged this life-long homosexual to hazard, 'You know, sweety, you and I could get married.' Nothing came of the proposal, if proposal it was, but such declarations were almost routine in a series of environments full of anxious and dislocated people taking solace wherever they could find it.

The social heterodoxy of the war took several forms. Most obviously, it allowed the men and women at large in Blitz-era London to expand their range, to contract alliances with people that they would be unlikely to have met in peacetime. Inspecting Sonia's acquaintances in the later 1940s, for example, one finds everyone from novelists and painters to young Labour MPs and arts-world patrons. Even Barbara seems to have emerged from the war with a raft of attachments that would be useful to her in later life. To examine the Lost Girls' social landscape as a whole is to marvel at the number of different levels it incorporated. There were Bloomsbury connections, mostly through Frances and Ralph Partridge, literary links to *Horizon* regulars such as Orwell and Waugh, oblique – sometimes less than oblique – hints of aristocratic drawing rooms, the donnish salons of Oxford and Cambridge, and City lucre. The standard description of this kind of world, the world in which, albeit in somewhat artificial circumstances and for a brief period of time, a duchess can exchange small-talk with a homosexual painter or a man-of-letters carouse with an up-and-coming tycoon in conditions that are agreeable to them both, is 'High Bohemia' (significantly, this was Waugh's label for the world of the Bright Young People in which he was intimately involved in the late 1920s). Each of the Lost Girls, in their individual ways, washed up on the shores of High Bohemia in the 1940s, and the friendships they forged there would be invaluable to them once the decade was over.

Once again, there are substantial qualifications to be made. However tightly drawn together by occupation or social life, the Lost Girls were, at heart, very different women, whose idiosyncrasies seemed abundantly clear to people who knew them at the time. Waugh, for example, revered Lys both for her cooking and her appearance ('beautifully neat'), treated Sonia with grudging respect ('quite presentable') but regarded Janetta as a dangerous left-wing nuisance and Barbara as not much more than a prostitute. Among these four, Sonia was probably the toughest-minded and the cleverest, while remaining a target for criticism from men who found her bossy, interfering or, having had their advances rebuffed, declared that she was frigid. There were also complaints about a relish of life beyond the English Channel that led her to pepper her conversation with Gallic phrases and encouraged a small child, meeting her for the first time in the late 1940s, to deduce that she was a native Frenchwoman: 'given to using French instead of English whenever she thought she could make a literary effect, or to impress Cyril', Woodrow Wyatt remembered. Janetta, meanwhile, was the most artistically minded – she went so far as to illustrate a book on child-rearing in 1946 – and also the most instinctively radical. 'My mother's circle was left-wing, arty, intellectual', one of her daughters remembered. When Waugh remarked to Nancy Mitford a few months before the war's end that he feared Connolly had 'lived too much with Communist young ladies', Janetta would have been one of the prime suspects. But in a political world keen on orthodoxy and resolute toeing of the party line, close friends tended to stress her reluctance to be told what to think or do. Frances Partridge believed that 'though surrounded by communist-minded young, she still is . . . an individualist'.

Matched against the intellectual playmate of the great and the left-inclined bohemian, Lys seems much more conventional, much more consciously ladylike (Janetta's daughter Nicky remembered writing an essay for her school magazine 'about playing at posh ladies' inspired by the thrill of watching Lys in action), keener on creating the kind of domestic environment in which Connolly would feel comfortable rather than jousting with his highbrow friends. Friends recalled her practical skills, her resourcefulness, her practised attention to detail. It was Lys who, wherever she happened to be established with Connolly, saw to such mundane necessities as paying the tradesmen and seeing that the milk was delivered. But if, like Sonia, she was a regular victim of male condescension (Quennell's letters to the Egypt-bound Barbara carry slighting references to 'little Lys', who 'continues to twitter dutifully in the background'), then some of her sharpest critics were other women, who found her horizons too limited and her conversational style too tame. Janetta complained that her role in Connolly's life was simply to take the lead from him and echo what he said. Lys's somewhat high-pitched voice led Diana to nickname her 'Squeaks'. Barbara, too, was bored by her company. 'He [Connolly] was very sweet with Lys,' runs a diary entry from late in 1941, 'who was as tiresome as ever, trying to make the apt reply to everything.' 'Lys is very pretty,' sniffed the Bloomsbury bluestocking Frances Partridge, on meeting her in 1946, 'and she prattled of housewifely things, like linoleum and dry rot.'

Barbara, the most wayward and the least sortable of the group, attracted even less in the way of sisterly solidarity. As Connolly's biographer Jeremy Lewis has noted, for all her devotion to him there was a way in which she never really belonged to his world. 'She was a good deal cleverer than most of the upper-class groupies who hung on his every word, and unlike them she could put pen to paper to lethal effect; but she was, in the last resort, considered to be both common and tarty, and as such she remained an outsider.'

Something of the deep suspicion, sometimes amounting to outright disdain, with which many of Barbara's contemporaries regarded her may be divined from Frances Partridge's admittedly second-hand account of a winter weekend she spent with some friends named Robin and Mary Campbell at their house in Stokke, Wiltshire in the early 1950s. After sulking in her room and refusing to come down to meals, Barbara asked to be taken to the station first thing on Monday morning to catch an early train to London. The Partridges, who happened to be delivering their own house-guest Janetta to the same station later in the day, were surprised to find the Campbells on the platform, their faces lavender with cold. Robin told me in tones of stifled horror that they had got up at seven and called Barbara, only to be told . . . that she was sleepy and had decided to take the next train. So there they were, but Barbara refused to get into it, saying that she had left some kind of basket behind at Stokke. 'She's going on the 1.17 though,' Robin said between clenched teeth.

Writing up the visit in her diary, Barbara was unrepentant: 'a horrid four days at the Campbells. I never wanted to go but was tricked into it.' Indifferent to the company – her fellow guests included the philosopher A. J. Ayer – unimpressed by the cuisine ('A succession of meaty-coursed meals into which we all troop like penancing monks') and resenting the arctic atmosphere of the unheated house, she decided to invent a Monday morning dentist's appointment. Then, in a moment of classic Skelton negligence, she took two strong sleeping pills and fell into a stupor, further antagonising her hostess by leaving the fire on all night. 'Come again when you're not so cross,' Mary Campbell instructed as she waved her off. According to Barbara's account, she 'spent the rest of the day crying from one train to another'.

Interlude: On Not Being Boring

The externals of Lost Girl life are relatively easy to decipher. In so far as these things can ever be truly reconstituted, we have a fair idea of how Barbara, Lys, Janetta, Sonia and the others spoke, what they wore, how they went about their daily round and the kind of social promontories from which they regarded the world. Much less easy to determine is what went on inside their heads. What were the value systems they espoused? What, when it came down to it, were the qualities they esteemed? What sort of behaviour had them signifying their approval or registering their disgust?

Loyalty, naturally, stood at the head of the queue. If a single factor united the various women who worked on *Horizon*, or were gathered up in its slipstream, it was their regard – at once emphatic, paralysing and unconditional – for Connolly. It was not so much that they loved him, which at least half-a-dozen of them at one time or another professed to do, rather that his interests, endlessly interrogated and analysed, were so transparently their own. The reportage of the period is full of Lost Girls springing to Cyril's defence, taking his opinions on trust, turning on anyone beyond the circle who has dared to call them into question. If bad behaviour could be detected, then it was theirs to rebuke: outsiders could keep their distance.

Almost as highly rated was intellectual ability, although – as with loyalty – there were substantial distinctions to be made. Just as the latter did not necessarily extend to sexual fidelity, so the former had to be cautious in its exercise. While 'cleverness' was an advantage, any descent into 'showing off' was likely to be roundly deplored. In *Horizon* terms, the ideal intellect – the ideal *male* intellect, it has to be said – was one that made a virtue of self-deprecation, hinted at profound depths of expertise and creativity while keeping its powder dry. The glancing remark was nearly always preferable to a gush of learned expostulation, and 'wit' could be guaranteed to trump rational sobriety.

All this leads us to one of the wartime literary world's most salient characteristics: its faint air of amateurishness. Orwell, with his three articles a week and his day-job in the BBC's Eastern Service, seems the doughtiest of professionals when set against a band of fellow-practitioners who sometimes seem to have made a positive virtue out of their non-achievement. Brian Howard's shortcomings in this line are practically legendary, but Connolly, too, can sometimes look like a talented dilettante, a writer of almost limitless capacities who for some reason prefers never fully to extend himself and whose potential is never properly realised. This, after all, was a man whose attainments at the age of forty consisted of a slim novel, a critic's autobiography, an even slimmer book of *pensées* and a file of book reviews.

Not that Connolly ever saw himself in this light. He belonged, as did Howard and many another literary gentleman of the time, to a tradition that prided itself on bringing off the well-nigh impossible trick of trying hard without being seen to do so, or in some cases deriving superiority from not trying at all. The Oxford philosopher Richard Pares once wrote a revealing letter to A. L. Rowse along these lines in which he complained about the success of such contemporaries as Quennell and Waugh, on the grounds that 'I know I could do much better than they and I don't want the trouble of doing so.' This is the authentic note of the gentleman-amateur, who awards top marks for effortlessness and obliquity, wit and conversational pizzazz and would be appalled by anyone who commits the unpardonable sin of making a special effort to draw attention to themselves.

And what about the substantial percentage of the population for whom conversational pizzazz and personal resonance – the knack of irradiating a drawing room or an editorial sanctum merely by walking into it – are just a distant dream? They, alas, will always be found wanting, judged for their ability to keep the ball rolling and summarily dismissed.

If the Lost Girl and her admirers believed in loyalty, intellect and modesty, then their greatest enthusiasm seems to have been directed at those who could keep boredom at bay. Sincerity, perseverance and kind good humour were all very well, but of all the compliments directed at friends and lovers the warmest was the somewhat negative quality of not being a bore. 'The only thing that concerned him,' a relative once recalled of Eddie Gathorne-Hardy – born into an earlier generation, but the friend of several Lost Girls – 'was whether people bored him or not.' The women of Connolly's circle could put up with a great deal: in the end, ill treatment, desertion, indifference, spite and jealousy could nearly always be tolerated. What they could not abide was tedium. 'You see that dreadful old bore,' Laura Waugh once remarked to her son Auberon about his father, a decade after the *Horizon* era had come to an end. 'He used to be so witty and gay.'

9.

Sussex Place: Connolly, Lys, Janetta and Others 1945–9

I see signs of mounting hubris, I am afraid.

Peter Watson, letter to Cecil Beaton,
7 April 1946

If one key Lost Girl meeting point was the *Horizon* office at Lansdowne Terrace, then another – at any rate in the second half of the 1940s – was the big, multi-tenanted house at 25 Sussex Place. Connolly, Lys and Janetta all lived there for several years; Sonia was a regular visitor; guests came and went; and it was an ideal location for parties, whether of the informal kind, conjured out of half-a-dozen bottles of red wine and a telephone directory, or the more lavish, meticulously planned affairs in which Connolly delighted, such as the reception given to mark T. S. Eliot's award of the Nobel Prize for Literature late in 1948. Elegantly furbished, home to Connolly's collection of rare first editions, Connolly's fine china and his elegant furniture – all the symbols of gentlemanly detachment by which their owner set such store – Sussex Place had the reputation of a high-class bohemian hotel, and yet the day-to-day life that went on behind its doors was far from idyllic.

As ever, it was Lys who did most of the work, telephoned the gasman, argued with Janetta over whether to sack the charwoman, Mrs Gough, organised the entertainments and tried to ensure that *Horizon*'s editor got to the office on time the following morning. Connolly was often late in settling the rent: Janetta, his co-tenant, was frequently reduced to leaving embarrassed notes on the stairs. Meanwhile, Major Connolly's warning about the dangers of house-sharing had proved to be uncomfortably prescient. Connolly and Janetta were old *copains*, always able to subdue the momentary irritation that each occasionally felt for the other when living at close quarters, but her friends – younger and sometimes less respectful – were not always Connolly's idea of agreeable company. It was Evelyn Waugh who noted, in the aftermath of one of Connolly's visits, that 'his joint tenure of the house in Regent's Park is proving irksome. He maintains his habitual bewildered resentment when bohemians behave like bohemians.'

Other aspects of Connolly's life seemed equally problematic. For all his delight in the newly expanded landscapes of the post-war world, the chance to travel and make plans, these were difficult times for the sage of Bedford Square. However much he had hated the war, with its dietary privations, the gloom of the blackout and the buzz-bombs falling on the Bloomsbury pavements, it had at least given his life a structure: *Horizon*, after all, had been intended to represent the values that Nazism imperilled. In Nazism's absence, he seemed faintly directionless, unsure of his destiny, fearful that he might not be making the best use of his talents. To add to this disquiet was his relationship with *Horizon*'s readers, whom he sometimes suspected of resenting the high-class pleasure garden which they believed Connolly and his circle to inhabit. A piece about Osbert Sitwell that Alan Pryce-Jones intended to cast in the form of a letter stoked some characteristic fears about the gap between Lansdowne Terrace and the world beyond it.

I don't think we can possibly publish it as it stands, you have no idea of how irritable and envious our public is. They can't stand being left out of anything. You leave them out both of your pleasant holiday in Vichy and your cosy upper-class coterie life with 'Osbert', 'Willie Maugham' etc. This in 1946 is unforgiveable . . . You probably think I have gone off my nut, but the more I am attacked the more I study the psychology of these little folk whose whole life is spent in tying up us Gullivers.

All this begged the question of what might be happening to his own inner voice. One key aspect of Connolly's progress through the 1940s was the gap between what the world thought of him and what he occasionally thought of himself. Coming across him sitting in panelled drawing rooms pronouncing on the literature of the day, most contemporaries saw a man who hobnobbed with the great writers of the era and was regarded by them with an esteem that sometimes bordered on adulation. Connolly, on the other hand, was increasingly conscious of his idleness, lack of commitment, inability to get things done. One aspect of this profound unease was the deterioration of his relationship with Peter Watson. The trip they took to Paris in July 1945 was intended as a triumphal return to the city that both men had loved, but a shock awaited them at Watson's flat in the rue du Bac, now filthy and neglected, with most of its valuable collection of artworks gone missing and a pile of pawn tickets casting into doubt the Romanian caretaker's claim that they had been stolen. All this was 'terribly depressing', Connolly complained, not least for its effect on Watson, whose commitment to style and sophistication seemed to have been replaced by a 'morbid discomfort'.

But worse was to come. In Switzerland, on the next leg of their continental tour, Watson went down with jaundice. It was a debilitating attack – so serious that he was confined to bed for six months and at one point restricted to a diet of spaghetti and rice with mashed turnips and carrots. In this enervated state, from a clinic in Lugano, and with his travelling companion returned to London, he wrote several letters to his old friend Cecil Beaton, the principal topic of which is Connolly: Connolly's sulks, Connolly's character defects and, if only by implication, Connolly's lack of interest in the work that Watson was paying him to undertake. 'Cyril writes very gloomily of London, of being tied down to Lys, Horizon and his new house and complains of the cold dirt and dullness,' runs a note from October 1945. 'However he complains so much that one doesn't understand much.' A second letter, responding to something Beaton had written, is sharply critical. 'I found his greed and his snobbery got terribly on my nerves in Switzerland,' Watson began.

> He is so vain, so touchy, so anxious all at the same time. I am quite the wrong person to deal with such a mixture over a busy period. He used to lose his temper with me in front of other people which I find quite inexcusable. Of course I know he is everything I am not, impulsive, enthusiastic, quickly deceived & satiated, easily distracted from one thing to another. He can never get over the fact that I *won't* behave like a conventional rich man, always go to the best restaurant hotel, travel first class etc. I suppose the rich reassure him but it is horrifying to watch him making up to them & his contempt for people with different standards.

A third letter, undated but apparently written shortly afterwards, offers corroborative evidence: 'I must just mention that Douglas Cooper who was here for the night yesterday & who knows a lot of Swiss people told me that everywhere he goes people ask him if Mr Connolly is only interested in food & they found they couldn't raise a spark of enthusiasm when they mentioned literature or anything else, so my impression cannot only be due to bias.' Much of this, naturally, was simply Connolly being Connolly, taking a positive relish in biting the hand that so generously fed him, celebrating the security of his position (beautiful girlfriend, elegant house, much-coveted job) one moment only to disparage it the next. The people who dealt with Connolly knew what he was like, and in the great majority of cases were prepared to put up with his temperamental shortcomings in return for the chance to luxuriate in the dazzle of his personality. All the same, Watson's letters from Lugano strike a new note, in which a rueful acceptance of Connolly's contradictions is replaced by something very close to exasperation.

The same ambiguity hung over Connolly's relationship with Lys, now deep into its fifth year. The Paris trip with Watson was the longest stretch of time he had ever spent apart from her, and a letter sent back towards its end is practically lachrymose in its fervour: 'I really can't bear being away from you for so long, and I hope it will never happen again – a fortnight is the limit, after that one finds out the loneliness of everything in life except being with the loved one.' It was not that Connolly was being insincere when he wrote this; he was merely playing his habitual trick of failing to see his life in context, so devitalised by his separation from Lys that he could not bring himself to consider what he really thought about the existence he had left behind him in London. But if Connolly was a creature of impulse, a short-term profligate bent on satisfying any emotional whim the moment it presented itself, then Lys had more definite objectives in view. At this point, after several years of stasis, her plan to persuade Connolly to marry seemed to be drawing closer to fruition. Her divorce from Ian Lubbock had come through. Simultaneously, a packet of legal papers sent from Reno, Nevada, the divorce capital of the United States, demonstrated that Jean was taking steps to separate herself from Connolly.

The only legal requirement that now remained, here at the end of 1945, was for Connolly to pilot the divorce through an English court. But this presupposed a fixity of purpose that Connolly had never possessed. Offered clarity and commitment instead of haziness and drift, he naturally back-tracked. 'Did not ask you to divorce me but to come back,' he cabled plaintively to America. Unable to chart a course to the altar, Lys did the next best thing, which was to change

211

her name by deed poll. This transformation was effected on 10 January 1946, and come the spring the happy couple set off for Europe on a mock-wedding tour. ('Lys has become Mrs Connolly (deed poll not the church!) and they have gone off to Zurich for their honeymoon! Can you beat it?' Watson informed Beaton early in April.) After calling at Paris and Corsica, the Connollys ended up in Switzerland in the company of the artist John Craxton.

Meanwhile, back in England grand literary eminences continued to amuse themselves with such scraps of Connolly gossip as came their way, much of it cruelly attuned to what was assumed to be Lys's subordinate role in their relationship. Nancy Mitford's new nickname for Lys, borrowed from Quennell, was 'the Mouse at Bay', as in a letter to Evelyn Waugh from late February: 'Have you heard about the Mouse@Bay? Some other women were saying how the virility of men is in relation to the size of their noses & the M@B jumped out of her chair & said "It is quite untrue. Cyril has a *very* small nose."'

In the Connollys' absence, the big house was left to Janetta and Robert Kee. Once again, the principal adult witness to the progress of their emotional life was Frances Partridge. Everything had been going 'wonderfully lovely well', one of Janetta's regular letters to Ham Spray reported late in January, until Robert was threatened with a court martial for writing newspaper articles about his time in the POW camp, which he had forgotten to submit to the RAF censors. And Janetta had her own professional project in view to provide the illustrations to a childcare primer by her friend Dorry Metcalf. Issued in 1946 by the Pilot Press, *Bringing Up Children* was a particularly ironic commission when set against the accounts of life at Sussex Place later filed by its youngest inhabitant, Nicky Loutit. Intrigued by Connolly ('Cyril was the king, even I knew that, and if he bothered he was nice to me'), fascinated by Lys and the perfume bottles that could be found in her bedroom, Nicky discovered that the main impediment to a settled existence in Sussex Place was Robert Kee, or rather Janetta's infatuation with him. 'He was

Landscape with Figures – Osbert Lancaster's drawing of the Café Royal, 1942. Barbara, Quennell, Connolly and Lys are clearly identifiable in the bottom left-hand corner. Brian Howard is top left on the balcony. Lancaster himself is to the left of the central potted plant. *(Clare Hastings)*

'My dear, I have done the most incomparably foolish thing' – Brian Howard, early 1940s.

'She's a real minx, this one' – King Farouk, 1940s. *(© Illustrated London News Ltd/Mary Evans)*

Nicky Loutit, mid-1940s.
(Nicky Loutit)

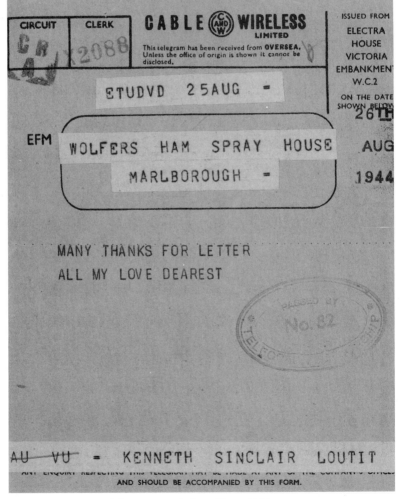

ETUDVD   25AUG   =

EFM   WOLFERS HAM SPRAY HOUSE

MARLBOROUGH   =

MANY THANKS FOR LETTER
ALL MY LOVE DEAREST

AU VU = KENNETH SINCLAIR LOUTIT

Kenneth keeps in touch from Cairo, 1944. *(Nicky Loutit)*

Horizon's new editorial secretary, Sonia, 1945.
(Orwell Archive)

Julian Maclaren-Ross.
(Nick Jaeger)

Evelyn Waugh, 1940s.
(Bettmann/Getty Images)

Lucian Freud, 1945.
(© *National Portrait Gallery, London)*

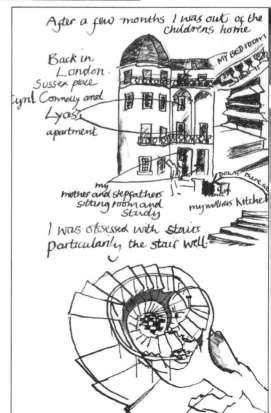

After a few months I was out of the childrens home

Back in London. Sussex place Cyril Connolly and Lyas apartment

MY BED room

my mother and stepfathers sitting room and study

Down there

my mothers Kitchen

I was obsessed with stairs particularly the stair well

'Cyril Connolly has moved into Regent's Park in a decent house of which he has taken every decent room: the rest go to a Mrs Lootit.' – Nicky's drawing of Sussex Place.

Lys, Connolly and
Sonia, mid-1940s.
(Connolly family)

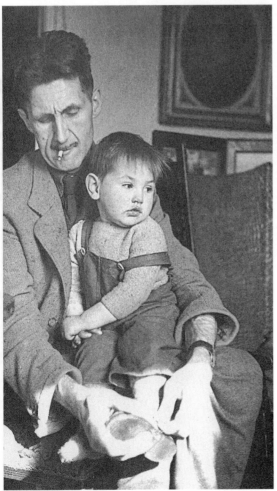

Barbara with John Sutro, 1947.
(Connolly family)

'You see, I've always been good with
animals' – Orwell and his adopted son
Richard, 1946. *(Vernon Richards)*

Post-war literary society. Lys in chair, flanked by Sacheverell Sitwell, Quennell and Connolly. *(Connolly family)*

'My stepfather wanted to kill me' – Robert Kee, late 1940s. *(Estate of Frances Partridge)*

(above) 'As for the secretaries, Lys was beautifully neat and, as I remember her, Miss Brownell was quite presentable' – *Horizon* office, late 1949. *(Orwell Archive)*

(right) Evidence of Connolly's regard. *(Orwell Archive)*

Osbert Lancaster's view of the trip to France, 1950. *(left to right)* Barbara, Farouk, Connolly as pasha.
(Clare Hastings)

Dear Tony,
Just to remind you to keep Nov 14.
[Flowerdew Lawson's benefit] firmly fixed
in your diary. White tie, 6.30 for 7,
I will call for you at 6.25. Love to
Violet . Yrs. Osbert.

Lys on the beach,
America, late 1950s.
(Michael Shelden)

handsome and charming and angry,' Nicky remembered. 'My mother loved him, though he wanted to kill me.'

Halfway through her third year Nicky was despatched to a children's home 'for my own protection'. She returned to a domestic life in which, as she put it, 'Robert and my mother continued wanting to be rid of me.' According to Janetta, the move was allowable 'because Robert no longer seemed so resentful of her existence'. Solace lay at Ham Spray, a permanent refuge and place of safety always remembered for its flower-filled gardens and its communal meals, being read to by Frances or collected at the station by Ralph in his car. If the house was haunted by the ghosts of old Bloomsbury – from an early stage Nicky knew that there had been a violent death on the premises, though she did not yet associate it with Carrington – then the Bloomsbury artefacts that lay around the place could be oddly consoling: 'At Ham Spray at breakfast time – quiet and a little tense – usually just me, Ralph with his pink *Financial Times* and Frances with her letters – I'd look at Carrington's painting of the mill at Tidemarsh – green water reflecting the sky. I'd hold that image in my head and body. If things were hard I'd remember a print of a waterfall in the passage upstairs.'

Undeniably, things were hard for a small child whose mother found it difficult to show affection and whose prospective stepfather seems barely to have tolerated her presence in the house. Seventy years later, Nicky could still remember the terror of being shaken by Kee when he was in one of his fits of temper. *Bringing Up Children* contains a photograph of an infant being suckled at the breast. 'The love and affection a baby enjoys from being held in our arms is as important as the food he takes,' runs the caption. In the memoir she wrote of her early life, Nicky recalled her mother remarking of her father, 'in a hopeless tone of voice', 'I simply couldn't bear to touch him – too awful', adding the gloss 'And I don't remember my mother touching me.' Plenty of evidence exists of Janetta's deep-rooted affection for her children, but the fact remains that her absorption with the men in her life was such that domestic responsibility invariably came off worse. Nicky remembered, as a small child, being left alone at Sussex Place and other locations while her mother disappeared to assignations and parties. Several years later, when Nicky's situation was repeated with a second child and another man, even so loyal a supporter of Janetta's interests as Frances Partridge could be found noting that 'It is clear from her letters that Janetta is missing her children badly, but she has made no mention of their missing her.'

That Robert Kee, with his volcanic temperament and his four years in a German POW camp, was as psychologically damaged as Janetta, with her fractured childhood and the bereavements of her early twenties, was no help to their dependants. As for their own prospects, a romantic idyll soon gave way to furious rows. In July 1946, for example, Frances recorded the 'beautiful and charming' couple bringing Nicky to stay at Ham Spray for the weekend. Deciding to walk to the top of the downs, Janetta and Robert came to a halt in a nearby field where they stood talking for an hour, and 'something in the attitude of their drooping heads struck a chill into my heart'. Nicky, too, remembered endless disputatious circuits of the Partridges' garden. 'We should have been very happy', Janetta wistfully recalled. Unfortunately, the 'emotional rage' that was tearing Kee to pieces had a similar effect on his other half. Self-contained, impulsive and at all times trailed by a stream of other admirers anxious to fill a vacated place, neither of them was the least put out by the temporary separations of which their life together consisted. Feliks Topolski, always susceptible to Janetta's allure, remembered ringing her up on the spur of the moment at around this time. She arrived at his studio in Maida Vale shortly afterwards on a bicycle with a bulging rucksack, 'having meant anyway to leave her man on that day'. There followed what Topolski called 'a charming and calm seven days of courteous bed-sharing'. Forty years later he could still recall seeing her from a bus walking back to the studio 'through the mean Edgware Road crowding, uniquely unaffected, blonde, undeniably my mate, very beautiful, very desirable'.

There were other extra-curricular relationships of this kind. On a 'paid holiday' picking apples in the country, Janetta attached herself to a vacationing sailor, 'more to prove to myself that somebody could still want to be with me than because I was in any way attracted to the young man'. If some of Janetta's friends suspected that Nicky might be getting a raw deal out of her new domestic arrangements, then they were united in their admiration for Kee. Ralph was unstinting in his praise. Coming across him for the first time, the old Bloomsbury hand Clive Bell enthused that 'It's a long time since I met any male creature to whom I took a more immediate fancy.' Finally, and to general satisfaction, their differences were patched up and a Register Office wedding arranged in London for 20 January 1948. Afterwards, the guests – Connolly, Angela Culme-Seymour and Diana Witherby among them – assembled to consume oysters, smoked salmon, chicken mayonnaise and champagne. Exalted by the varieties of food and drink on offer, the heat of the fire and the scent of mimosa, an uncharacteristically mellow Frances recorded that 'the whole experience merged into one, and I was borne on the wings of semi-intoxication, combined with the sympathetic feelings I had been simmering in all day'.

The newly married Kees were not the only couple on whom Frances Partridge's shrewdly observant eye fell in 1948. A diary entry from the spring offers a neat little cameo of a visit to their neighbours Robin and Mary Campbell, where the Connollys were staying. Lys was 'untiring in her wifely deference', Frances noted, constantly flattering her other half with admiring references to 'Clever people like Cyril' or 'Good talkers like Cyril'. But clever, talkative Cyril paid her little attention. The same characteristics were on display later in the year when the Campbells brought the Connollys over to Ham Spray. 'Oh, that must have been wonderful Cyril,' Lys would chirp, as Connolly gamely reminisced, or would proudly inform the assembled company, 'Oh, do you know Cyril was remembered by the waiter at the *Chapon Fin* who hadn't seen him for twenty years?' Frances noted that Connolly 'doesn't snub' Lys even when she tried to 'produce' him. On the other hand, none of this seemed to augur well for their life together.

With and sometimes without Lys, Connolly had continued to avail himself of the new freedoms available to the post-war traveller. The long mock-honeymoon of 1946 was followed by an end-of-year trip to New York with Watson, ostensibly to gather material for an *American Horizon* special number booked for the autumn of 1947. ('I am told he is now at work in America telling the Yanks of his sufferings', Evelyn Waugh reported to Diana Cooper early in January, having previously assured Nancy Mitford that 'S Boots Connolly has fled the country. Some say from his debts.') When he travelled alone, or with his proprietor, letters from Lys followed him around the globe like homing pigeons, to tell him that he is much missed, that renewals circulars are about to go out to *Horizon*'s subscribers or that the dinner parties convened in his absence have been a great success ('Orwell was quite gay!'). Predictably, a joint spring visit to Paris – where Nancy Mitford had taken up residence – produced a torrent of gossip and insinuation about 'S Boots whom I met accompanied by Mrs Boots when walking through the Louvre on my way home'. Staying in England later in May, she reported that Connolly was 'very touchy' about Janetta ('Love I expect'), before alleging that Lys had been sent home early 'so that Connolly could entertain intellectuals on her £75'.

'I see Cyril's boom fading,' her fellow-conspirator pronounced at Christmas 1947, '*Horizon* losing subscribers, income-tax officials pressing him, inertia, luxury and an insane longing to collect rare things.' By this stage in *Horizon*'s seven-year history, the question of its probable future was being discussed well beyond Connolly's immediate circle. It was not only Waugh and Mitford who wondered whether Connolly had shot his bolt. What was his attitude to the creation that had sustained him since the early days of the war? *American Horizon*, which appeared towards the end of September 1947, with contributions from Marianne Moore, Wallace Stevens and John Berryman, had been well received in a post-war England untouched by any new-found luxuriance in the arts, but more than one critic alleged that none of its contents was in the same class as Connolly's introduction. Certainly, Connolly was still prepared to fight his corner, to publish new writers who caught his talent-hungry eye and champion work that might not have been to every reader's taste – the decision to devote an entire special number to Waugh's *The Loved One* early in 1948 was brought off in the face of stiff opposition by an unimpressed Peter Watson. The arrival of the hundreth issue in April produced the usual volley of complimentary remarks and testimonies to his status as one of the great cultural paladins of the age, but Connolly was restless, ripe for diversion. The American publisher Cass Canfield, meeting him in New York the year before, reported back to Hamish Hamilton that their distinguished English visitor had said that he thought the job of editing a monthly magazine took up too much of his time.

Clearly, the restlessness was as much domestic as professional. But the early part of 1948 brought several indications of quite how much Connolly relied on Lys and quite how indefatigably she managed his affairs. In January, alarmed by his listlessness and chronic exhaustion – a whole vista of vague but disturbing symptoms that at one point included blurred vision – she installed him in a health farm at Tring. Solicitous letters quickly followed. 'I miss you so much and am wretched to think of what you are going through. The first week is probably the worst. After that you will probably slide into a dull routine and time will go more quickly,' Lys reassured him. Alert to the comic potential of Connolly's infirmity ('Cyril has had an apoplectic seizure & gone to take the waters. The bare footed partisans have got his dining room') and keen to profit from its possible aftermath ('If he had another seizure it is really all up with him.

I wish I could get Lys as a cook'), Waugh and Mitford were also seriously alarmed about his health. 'Awful about Smarty's stroke', Nancy wrote from Paris early in February, adding that 'at luncheon Lysey disclosed that Cyril had one in a train . . . But as a lover of Smarty I feel sad about him, I thought he seemed wretched the night I dined alone with him.' Whether or not he had had either a stroke or, as Waugh suspected, a heart attack, the Connolly who lay sequestered at Tring, slowly recovering his strength and steadily losing weight – he shed 25 lbs in the course of his stay – knew who to thank for his redemption. 'But for you I would have no eyes and no teeth', he fervently, if melodramatically, assured Lys.

Another mark of her practical, problem-solving side emerged in the spring when London County Council decided that it wanted the flat at Lansdowne Terrace for new housing, effectively leaving *Horizon* homeless. It was Lys who secured the two elegant rooms at 53 Bedford Square, which became the magazine's final resting place. However genuine Connolly's gratitude for this piece of resourcefulness, there were signs that the relationship was coming to an end. Twice Watson found her in tears at the *Horizon* office. Sonia, always matter-of-fact about her friends' emotional setbacks, reported that she was 'more like a sad and bedraggled sparrow than ever, keeping up an unceasing chirping about "true love" while contemplating the ringless finger – and there's NOTHING one can do about it'. There was an intensely sad and symbolic episode in which Lys bought herself a small ring, showed it to Janetta and then betrayed the depths of her emotional hurt by exclaiming, 'This is all I've got and I've had to buy it myself.'

The catalyst for the events of the next six months was Dick Wyndham, for so long Connolly's host at Tickerage, killed in May 1948 while exercising his talent as a professional photographer by covering the fighting in the newly created Jewish state for the *Sunday Times*. At his funeral Connolly was introduced to yet another of the very young women who continued to wreak such havoc on his emotional life. Eighteen years old, immensely pretty and at this point being courted by Lucian Freud, Anne Dunn had approximately the same effect on the middle-aged editor as Janetta had produced almost a decade before. The first seeds of his infatuation were sown as Connolly set about planning a new and unrepentantly extramural project – a travel book, to be published in England by Hamish Hamilton and in America by Canfield, which would take him to the area around Bordeaux that, even in the pre-Jean days, he had always regarded as his spiritual home. In June he undertook a reconnaissance trip, returned to Paris to collect Lys and then headed south to the Villa Mauresque to stay with Somerset Maugham. Luxuriously entertained and gratifyingly deferred to, Connolly, as his letters home to Sonia make clear, was in his element. Maugham was a considerate and reassuring host ('Willie is in excellent form & makes one feel that at seventy five one enjoys, if one is careful, *rather more* everything one likes at thirty five'), not averse to flattering his younger acolyte ('I know what you are, Cyril, a BRIGAND') and delighting him with the grandeur of his other guests ('Great efforts to-day to get Lys to go to the hairdresser as the Windsors are dining here tomorrow').

With the Duke and Duchess disposed of, the Connollys moved on to stay with Lady Kenmare at Cap Ferrat. Subsequently Lys returned to London and the office, while Connolly repaired to Bordeaux and, it was anticipated, some serious work on his book. The original idea had been for Wyndham to supply the illustrations that Canfield and Hamilton required. In his absence, Connolly engaged Joan Rayner, who combined the advantage of being a talented photographer with the drawback of being one of Connolly's old loves, after whom he continued intermittently to pine. Lys, assured that the new relationship was strictly professional, would not have been reassured by some of the letters Joan sent back to her current boyfriend, Patrick Leigh Fermor. 'Cyril is being very sweet & easy & is heavenly to travel with', ran an early note. Afterwards the atmosphere declined. 'The only blot on this (& this, my darling, is for your ears alone) is that things are getting a bit tense', Joan complained some weeks later. Why did these complications have to spoil things so often? she wondered. 'I feel like a boringly monogamous bitch but I can't do anything about it.' As very often happened with Connolly's amours, high emotion and low farce uneasily contended. At one point she agreed to take part in a mock-wedding in a cave, only for the proceedings to be interrupted by the arrival of a party of boy scouts and the rumble of falling rocks. By early autumn, bored with having to sustain the all-too demanding role of Connolly's 'lovely boy-girl . . . like a casual, loving, decadent Eton athlete', she returned to Leigh Fermor.

The Bordeaux trip offered a pattern demonstration of Connolly's capacity for vacillation, his inability to accomplish a task or conduct his emotional life without wounding the people who were closest to him. There was no prospect of his French holiday leading to anything, but Joan's presence encouraged him to embark on one of his regular exercises in compare and contrast, in which the tantalising ghosts of the past sprang up to contend with current obligations. As he explained to his mother, the trip with Joan 'made me realise that I could not marry Lys at present because I should only be unkind to her – she is so devoted to me and belongs to all the every-day part of my life – but Joan is like Jean, a very intelligent and remarkable person in her own right . . . and the one person who could have got me over the Jean years earlier if we had had better luck'. Many of Joan's letters to Leigh Fermor over the autumn refer to 'the Humanist', as they christened him, and his rekindled interest in her. There was a scheme for her to return to Bordeaux, but divining the real purpose of the offer she cried off. In these circumstances, even a trip to London was fraught with embarrassment. 'I may stay at Sussex Place', she told Leigh Fermor in October, adding that 'it's safer than anywhere since Lys is always there – but I don't really want to if I can get anywhere else nice'.

The travel book was quietly abandoned, leaving Canfield and Hamilton with an exorbitant expenses claim but nothing they could satisfactorily publish. Meanwhile, back at Sussex Place Lys's already frail emotional state was further undermined by a visit from Brian Howard. It was by now the end of October 1948. Connolly was in Paris, irritating her with letters describing how much he was enjoying himself. What happened was set out in considerable detail in a letter to Sonia, framed in Howard's inimitable high-camp style.

'My dear, I have done the most incomparably foolish thing. And although it was not a deliberate piece of naughtiness on my part it must seem exactly as if it was.' According to Howard, he happened to find himself in the vicinity of Sussex Place, 'and as I really do like Lys, very much, I rang up, and asked if I could come round and see her'. Here, by his own admission, he made 'a complete ass of myself. I said I couldn't believe she really loved Cyril (such a silly, vulgar thing to say – and she does) and then I gaily said "And what's all this I hear about Cyril and Joan?"' It was meant to be a 'jolly remark', but Lys was devastated. Howard, swiftly enlightened by Peter Watson as to the true facts of the case ('He tells me that Lys had no idea that Cyril and Joan were having a flirtation even. As a matter of fact I don't even know whether they really *are*'), added a handwritten PS in his letter to Sonia with the information that a friend had just arrived to tell him that 'Peter said you were furious + would never speak to me again . . . God knows I did NOT intend to hurt Lys. It was just my bloody tongue running away with me . . . Try not to think too badly of me. B.'

Although Connolly and Lys would continue to live together for more than another year, this was effectively the end of their relationship. While Connolly went on throwing parties in the big house at Sussex Place, what he and his co-host said to each other once the guests had gone home can only be guessed at. Professionally and personally, nearly a decade's worth of relative stability was drawing to a close. In January 1949 Watson went to New York for four months, but there was no suggestion that Connolly was holding the fort in his absence.

He went less and less to Bedford Square, left most of the work to Lys and Sonia, and continued to haunt West End nightclubs in pursuit of Anne Dunn. At the same time, the long diminuendo of his relationship with Lys was accompanied by prodigious bouts of soul-searching, psychological back-tracking and peevish complaints. When Lys, deciding that she could stand the situation no more, disappeared to Florence he bombarded her with anguished letters, accused her of 'playing about' with his desertion complex and claimed that he could imagine her 'casting me off like an old shoe and marrying a rich American or an Italian count'. To friends he continued to maintain a party line of unshakeable fealty. Shortly after a solitary Whitsuntide stay at Piers Court, Evelyn Waugh reported to Nancy that 'Smarty Boots has just left, having spent the weekend in torpor . . . Whenever Cyril woke up it was to tell me of his undying loyalty to, and devotion to, Lys.'

There were others close to Connolly who were reaching the end of their tether. On the far side of the Atlantic, Watson was beginning to lose interest, not so much in *Horizon* but in the man who was supposed to be conducting it. 'A rather terrible showdown with Cyril is about to happen,' he told his lover, Waldemar Hansen. 'Either the magazine will end in November or continue under very different auspices. He has behaved with shocking cynicism and it has upset me very much.' Although there were one or two half-hearted negotiations with potential successors – Spender, John Lehmann and Alan Ross were all sounded out at one time or another – it was eventually decided that the magazine would close at the end of the year. Watson, reading the penultimate editorial, accused Connolly of compiling 'the most dishonest series of reasons for stopping'. In this context there is something horribly disingenuous about Connolly's famous and much-quoted foreword to the final number with its intimations of cultural drift, autumnal shadows falling over a once sunlit lawn: 'it is closing time in the gardens of the West and from now on an artist will be judged only by the

222

resonance of his solitude and the quality of his despair'. If Connolly had been able to stir himself into action, then *Horizon* would have gone on.

Lys hung on until the end, overseeing arrangements for the final, double number of December 1949–January 1950 and assisting with the last rites of closure when, as Connolly theatrically described it, 'We closed the long windows over Bedford Square, the telephone was taken, the furniture stored, the back numbers went to their cellar, the files rotted in the dust. Only contributions continued inexorably to be delivered, like a suicide's milk.' Elsewhere there were other long windows closing, and other furniture going into storage. Lys's letters from the early part of 1950 are full of intimations of the damage done to her in the eight years she and Connolly had been together. 'Please forgive me for going away', begins a note from early spring, 'but I feel if I stay I shall have some kind of a breakdown, which would only make you feel guilty, and therefore hate me . . . My feelings have been played around with so much that nothing remains except a desire to escape.' 'P.S.,' runs a codicil, 'Please ask Mrs Shaw to do laundry . . . I've put everything in the box. Her wages will be £2. I'll leave some money for you on Sunday.' Even in the depths of her despair, Lys was determined to keep an eye on Connolly's domestic wellbeing.

Friends of the couple who had been disposed to poke fun at the relationship knew where their loyalties lay. Nancy Mitford, to take the most obvious example, might have been endlessly amused by Lys's strivings on Connolly's behalf, but she liked her, sympathised with her and, somewhat perversely, wanted her to obtain a prize that she suspected to be scarcely worth the having. 'I love Lys . . . ,' she told Waugh in reply to his letter about Connolly's Whitsun stay, 'it would be a horrid shame if he turned her off now.'

No doubt the small girl who lived at Sussex Place thought so too. During Lys's absence in Italy, Nicky had taken to visiting the Connollys' rooms after breakfast. Now past her sixth birthday, she had developed a talent for mimicry. One morning she fixed her eye on Connolly and informed him, 'Now I'm going to be Lys.' The middle-aged man in the dressing gown looked fascinatedly on. 'Get up Cyril and go to your office,' Nicky shrilled at him. 'You're lazy. Now come along to the office with me.'

Interlude: Office Life

Goodness the things sent in were dull.

Janetta, remembering her time at *Horizon*

If a certain amount of the Lost Girl's time was spent in West
End watering holes or in the bedsitters and furnished flats of
Chelsea and South Kensington, then far more of it was eaten up
by daily attendance at her place of work: at institutional tower
blocks allied to the war effort; at requisitioned hotels occupied by
Balkan governments in exile; above all at the *Horizon* office. Lys
laboured there, on and off, for nearly seven years, Sonia for almost
five, Anna for two. Diana and Janetta helped out when required.
Cumulatively, the whole enterprise can sound horribly depressing:
unending, infinite: thousand upon thousand of hours employed
in the not terribly exciting job of answering telephone calls, typing
letters, administering Cyril's hectic social life, fraternising with
the other employees – these included an editorial assistant named
Benedicta and the business manager, Mr Harris – eyeing up the
bundles of manuscripts that arrived each day in the morning's
post, dealing with callers, and . . . doing what exactly?

That so little survives of *Horizon*'s daily routines is, from one
angle, a consequence of their utter mundanity. However dazzling

the lustre that shines off a literary magazine, what goes on in its editorial sanctums is tedious in the extreme, and for every contribution that might just find a place in the next issue but four there are generally two or three dozen that are sent back by return of post. The glamour is all abstract, and the reality a mixture of half-drunk cups of coffee, intermittent raids on the petty-cash tin and the reek of cigarette smoke. Janetta recalled trackless hours 'putting rejection slips into stamped envelopes & slightly less abrupt ones into any more promising mss'. And so the countless letters that Lys and Sonia despatched to Connolly when he was away from the office are horribly matter-of-fact: word counts; advertising slots; subscriber offers; whether or not to accept Antonia White's new story lest she take it elsewhere. Reconstituting the interiors of Connolly's two command centres at Lansdowne Terrace and Bedford Square is more or less impossible. Maclaren-Ross's famous sketch is more interested in the editor, 'the folder with my stories which lay upon his desk' and the prospect of lunch at the Café Royal, than the rooms in which he sat. Natasha Litvin, equally understandably, is beguiled by high-end paraphernalia – Spender's Picasso, his gramophone, his boxes of records – not the piles of page proofs and the rectangular brown envelopes. The late-period photographs of Sonia and Lys at work show, well, what you would expect – desks, cane chairs, telephones and efficient young women waiting for the next call, the next importunate young writer bursting through the door with a parcel in his hand.

So, what went on at Lansdowne Terrace and Bedford Square? What did Lys, Sonia and the others actually do? Anna Kavan once mentioned trying to get hold of 'cake', forties-era slang for cocaine, for her colleagues but there is no other evidence that drug-taking was a part of *Horizon*'s daily round. On the other hand, there is general agreement that the atmosphere of the office was irradiated by the presence of its proprietor. Spender would recall Connolly's complaint that Sonia loved no one but Peter Watson, that he, Connolly, would always know if Peter were there as Sonia reserved 70 per cent of her smile for him. Not that the editor himself was a permanent fixture. Connolly usually arrived after lunch, by which time his handmaidens would have spent a good five hours dealing with whatever the morning had thrown up. This was Lys's favourite time: 'People were always coming by to talk. London seemed a lot smaller then, especially in the early part of the war when so many people left to avoid the bombing. But life went on, and you could never tell who would turn up.'

And who were these visitants, *Horizon*'s passing trade, Connolly's friends and protégés come to file copy or simply exchange small-talk? Lys remembered a violently hungover Evelyn Waugh, regular appearances from Dylan Thomas, who came to borrow money from Watson, and occasional visits from Orwell, whose habit it was to argue with her about Connolly: 'He thought that Cyril shouldn't go to fancy dinner parties at the Dorchester when there was a war on.' Years later Lys decided that Orwell's disapproval of his editor's vigorous social life was merely a way of flirting with her, that the glint in his eye denoted faint romantic interest rather than the twinge of conscience. 'He was more handsome than his photographs make him appear,' she thought. As for the visitors, no aspiring literary man or woman received *Horizon*'s call with anything less than profound satisfaction. But for his encouragement, Angus Wilson informed Connolly a quarter of a century after the acceptance of his first short story, his writing might have petered out 'as the unfertilised hobby of a man who was looking for some means of self expression but never found it . . . I know that my life would have been emptier and more futile if I had never written . . . *None* of it could I have done without your encouragement and I must be only one of many'.

Experienced Connolly-watchers often noted an element of performance. The editor, it was said, knew the effect that his personality produced on people and played up to it. Together he and Watson were a formidable team. 'They are the best people one could possibly work with,' Anna Kavan decided, 'intelligent, sensitive, tolerant, even a little gay occasionally, wh. is quite something right now.' Undoubtedly, the faint air of being part of a public spectacle rubbed off on his assistants. What began as routine could transform itself, almost without warning, into a highly self-conscious ritual, in which supporting roles were expected to be gamely filled, and cues instantly supplied. The suspicion that one was acting in a play under Connolly's direction could occasionally be a bit too strong for comfort. Older visitors were sometimes less than impressed. It was Evelyn Waugh, on a visit to London in October 1949, who telegraphically remarked to Nancy Mitford that he had seen 'the inside of *Horizon* office'. What enticements were on offer? Waugh noted only 'horrible pictures collected by Watson & Lys & Miss Brownell working away with a dictionary translating some rot from the French'.

10.

The Man in the Hospital Bed: Sonia 1945–50

Boots's boule de suif what was her name? Sonia something is engaged to marry the dying Orwell and is leaving *Horizon* so there will not be many more numbers to puzzle us.

Evelyn Waugh, letter to Nancy Mitford, September 1949, in
The Letters of Nancy Mitford and Evelyn Waugh (1996)

One evening early in the autumn of 1949, on his way through the West End, Kenneth Sinclair-Loutit stopped for a drink in a Charlotte Street pub. It was four years since his relationship with Janetta had stumbled to a halt, but the London world he inhabited was still full of the friends they had made together in the early 1940s. Here among the Charlotte Street bohemians, the advertising copy-writers and the used car salesmen – Warren Street, home of the second-hand motor trade, was a stone's throw away to the north – another of these old connections loomed into view, when a pale, buxom girl at the bar revealed herself as Sonia Brownell. There was something odd about her, Sinclair-Loutit thought, a hint of nervousness and suppressed agitation. She was getting married, she explained. Then, out of the blue, she asked him: could he lend her £5? This, too, was odd, Sinclair-Loutit deduced, for the way in which she made the request seemed

229

somehow loaded, 'her manner indicating that she had no intention of paying it back'. As a medical man with an interest in psychology, he decided that borrowing the money had something to do with stress, that here in the weeks before her wedding this was her way of dealing with the state of chronic emotional upset in which she found herself. He never saw her again, and the loan remained unpaid.

One of Connolly's first tasks as *Horizon* prepared to greet the post-war world in the autumn of 1945 was to introduce his new editorial secretary to the magazine's contributors. In the case of George Orwell, this was technically a re-introduction: Orwell was a *Horizon* mainstay, a fixture of its columns since the appearance of 'Boys' Weeklies' in 1940, and Sonia had almost certainly become acquainted with him three or four years before. As their mutual friend Celia Paget put it, she 'couldn't not have come across him' in the early days at Lansdowne Terrace. As Sonia remembered it, their first meeting had taken place at one of Connolly's dinner parties in 1941, shortly after she had read a library copy of his first novel *Burmese Days* (1934), lent to her by Diana Witherby. Orwell's memory of their conversation is not recorded, but Sonia had been far from impressed, recalling that when dinner was served, 'he was very quiet and said something about you've put foreign stuff in the food but sat down and enjoyed it'. The accepted version is that their re-encounter took place shortly before Christmas at Orwell's bolthole in Canonbury Square, a cold and comfortless flat that was also home to his adopted son Richard, then eighteen months old, and the boy's nanny Susan Watson. The plan was for Connolly and Sonia to be entertained to drinks, but they arrived to discover that the sherry had run out: Susan had to be despatched for a fresh bottle. Alternatively, they may have met earlier in the autumn, as Michael Sayers, who had shared a flat with Orwell in Kentish Town in the 1930s, remembered intro-ducing them at a *Horizon* dinner on the grounds that his old friend 'needed looking after'.

Whatever the precise circumstances of the reunion, Sayers was right. Orwell badly needed looking after. Here in the latter part of 1945, his career had reached a watershed. *Animal Farm*, published in the summer, had been a considerable success – the first book he had ever written to have sold more than a few thousand copies – but even before it had appeared in the bookshops his personal life had been thrown into turmoil, when his wife Eileen, undergoing what was alleged to have been a routine operation, died on the operating table, leaving him with the care of a baby in sight of his first birthday. However traumatised by his wife's death, Orwell was determined to do his best by Richard, although visitors to Canonbury Square noted that the domestic arrangements sometimes had a rather cack-handed air, and that paternal enthusiasm for the job in hand was frequently undercut by lack of attention to detail. Would it not be a good idea to close the bathroom window, the wife of a friend invited to watch Richard having his bath diffidently suggested, as freezing January air blew in to mingle with the clouds of steam? And why not dry the child beforehand rather than simply scooping him up in a bath towel and carrying him off along an unheated passage to the sitting room?

Orwell accepted these suggestions with the same matter-of-factness that he greeted compliments about his manifest absorption in the business of child-rearing: he had always been good with animals, he explained, without irony, to a sympathetic friend. None of this, though, could compensate for the emotional desert in which he found himself, or subdue his curious psychological response to Eileen's death. This was to propose marriage, more or less on the spot, to any remotely suitable young woman who came his way in the course of his daily life. The first of these candidates was Arthur Koestler's sister-in-law Celia Paget, who admired his work but wanted nothing to do with him romantically. Another was a girl named Anne Popham, who inhabited another flat in the Canonbury Square block. Given the slightness of their acquaintanceship – they had done no more than exchange the occasional word on the staircase

– Miss Popham was startled to receive an invitation to tea, and even more surprised when her host sidled meaningfully up to her to enquire: 'Do you think you could take care of me?' It was in this fraught and emotionally charged atmosphere that Sonia came properly into Orwell's life.

What did she make of it? As anyone who knew Sonia well might have predicted, all her fundamental instincts of duty and fellow feeling were aroused by the sight of the lonely widower and his adopted son in the freezing flat. She took to calling round on Susan Watson's day off to babysit and cook in rooms that, as she later recalled, stank of 'cabbage and unwashed nappies': Anne Popham discovered her there one day, very much at home and talking to her host about Stéphane Mallarmé. On the other hand, the respect in which, taking her cue from Connolly, she held Orwell as a writer – a prodigious talent who showed every sign of becoming more successful still – was seriously undermined by his physical shortcomings. She later confessed to being 'appalled' by his advances, and although there was probably a brief affair in the early part of 1946, like Celia and Anne she turned down the inevitable proposal of marriage with barely a second thought.

But there was something else about Orwell that Sonia, bustling around the Canonbury Square flat as the short winter afternoons faded into twilight, may not have grasped. Once the psychological effect of his wife's death had been discounted, his life seemed full of purpose. As well as being absorbed by the responsibilities of looking after his infant son, he was also brooding about a new novel and planning to relocate to the Scottish island of Jura where, he fondly imagined, the book could be written and Richard brought up in a world of unspoilt landscapes and clean air. On the other hand, the man busy planning a future as a part-time Hebridean smallholder was also seriously ill. In February 1946, shortly after *l'affaire* Popham, Susan Watson, hard at work in the kitchen and disturbed by noises elsewhere in the flat, found him walking down the passage with blood pouring from his mouth. Following her employer's instructions, she fetched a jug of chilled water and a block of ice from the Frigidaire, wrapped the ice in a piece of cloth and placed it on his forehead, and sat holding his hand until the bleeding stopped.

Clearly, Orwell had suffered a tubercular haemorrhage. Equally clearly, medical help had to be summoned. But here Susan ran into a problem that many of Orwell's friends had been forced to contend with over the years, especially when his health was in doubt: his resolute inflexibility of will. Admitting to TB would have meant immediate hospitalisation; the priority, he reasoned, was to start work on what would become *Nineteen Eighty-Four*. By the time the doctor arrived, Orwell, well wrapped up beneath the bedcovers, and deflecting awkward questions, was able to pass off his illness as a bad attack of gastritis. Amazingly, the imposture worked, and he spent the next two weeks in bed, maintaining the pretence, to Koestler and other friends, that he was suffering from a severe stomach complaint – 'quite an unpleasant thing to have, but I am somewhat better and got up for the first time today', he informed Anne Popham, now in Germany working for the Control Commission.

The letter to Anne, addressed to 'Dear Andie' ('I call you that because it is what I have heard other people call you'), is an immensely gloomy performance, apologising for the embarrassment he had caused ('I thought you looked lonely and unhappy, and I thought it just conceivable that you might come to take an interest in me . . .') and claiming that 'There isn't really anything left in my life except my work and seeing that Richard gets a good start.' At the same time, as he readily conceded, neither of these interests made his loneliness tolerable. 'I have hundreds of friends, but no woman who takes an interest in me and can encourage me.' As it turned out, the woman who would eventually take an interest was nearer at hand than he thought.

From its earliest days, and for all its editor's monomania, *Horizon* had always been a geometry of people. Connolly; Watson; Spender;

Bill Makins, the first business manager; assorted helpers and sponsors: all these had played some part in shaping the face that the magazine presented to the world and the kind of cultural currency in which it dealt. Here in the post-1945 era, even more so as the decade wore on, some of the angles began to shift. It was not so much that Connolly had lost interest in his creation – he enjoyed being the editor of a highbrow monthly, and relished the prestige that came with it – more that the circumstances of the post-war world conspired to divert his attention from what most observers would have regarded as the one true business of his life. Despite, or perhaps because of, his non-combatant status, Connolly had taken the six years of hostilities hard. 'FUCK THE WAR', runs one of his letters to Janetta. In their aftermath, pleasurable diversions loomed on all sides. There was a newly liberated Europe to re-explore. America beckoned. There were books to write, or rather – as Connolly was no less a procrastinator than he had always been – to think about writing, and women to cultivate. All this made him much less interested in *Horizon*'s day-to-day management, its finances and even the writers and artists who appeared in its pages. When travelling abroad, he became an increasingly erratic correspondent, all too ready to assume that those left behind him had the situation in hand. It was in this atmosphere of drift, laxity and the want of a controlling purpose that Sonia came into her own.

From one angle the three-way correspondence between Connolly, Watson and Sonia from which *Horizon*'s post-war history can be pieced together has a single theme: the devolution of responsibility. A responsibility, more to the point, that the editorial secretary in her Bloomsbury eyrie was very anxious to see devolved. As she puts it in a letter she wrote to Connolly and Lys in the summer of 1946 when they were away on their self-styled honeymoon: 'I was rather sad to hear that you're coming back so soon – not because I'm not longing to see you both – I am, but because I hope it doesn't mean that everything isn't delicious or that you've run out of money or something horrid. Please don't worry about Horizon because everything is magnificent.' There were occasionally complaints of high-handedness – Francis Wyndham remembered how 'established poets would send in stuff . . . and get sent a rather patronising letter from this blonde girl they'd never heard of' – but the notes and postcards that Connolly sent home from his travels are abundant evidence of just how much he was beginning to rely on her judgement: 'I sent comment to Curzon [*Horizon*'s printers],' runs a letter from 1946, 'please correct it against manuscript in case they misread it, please also alter the tone if it seems to you too flippant OR too serious anywhere.' By 1948, reliance was turning into outright delegation. 'How is the September number?' Connolly enquired from the Villa Mauresque, where he and Lys were staying with Somerset Maugham. 'Do accept anything you think good . . . Will you write and ask Mary MacCarthy to review the Kinsey Report for us?' The same letter notes, a shade wistfully, that 'It seems a long time since I had some Horizon news – do write to me & send any interesting letters that don't need an answer. I liked the last number very much.'

And if *Horizon*'s editor was increasingly detached from the publication on whose masthead his name appeared, then so, to a certain extent, was its proprietor. Peter Watson, too, was not the man he had been two or three years before. Part of this was due to the long and debilitating illness that had kept him abroad in the early part of 1946. A little more could be ascribed to an increasingly complex love-life. But like Connolly, Watson's professional eye had begun to turn elsewhere. Suspicious of his editor's long-term intentions, conscious that his love of the arts might benefit from a wider focus than a monthly magazine with a limited circulation, he seems increasingly to have regarded Connolly as someone to be put up with and reminded of his duties rather than a bright star permanently agleam in literary London's firmament. Still, he was *Horizon*'s guarantor, it was his money that subsidised its weekly appearance on the newsstands and paid for Connolly's foreign jaunts, and he liked and warmly approved of Sonia. If the relationship between proprietor and editor was showing its age, then the bond between proprietor and editorial secretary grew ever closer.

Much of this involved engaging Sonia for surveillance duties, monitoring Connolly's comings and goings, using her to keep him up to the mark, chide him for bad time-keeping or question such hints of the editorial forward planning as had come Watson's way. 'No news from Cyril,' complains a letter sent from New York early in 1947. 'Is he turning up every morning at 9.30? (nothing left in the In Tray at 5.30.) I wonder.' From Jamaica, two years later, he expresses a hope that 'the Auden stuff by Spender isn't included in the next. Auden told me in N.Y. that it was simply factually untrue & would be most upset if Cyril published it too.' For most of the time, en route from one continental resort to another, Watson is simply in pursuit of information of a kind that only Sonia could supply. 'Please send me the latest HORIZON to Hotel Inghilterra Rome' instructs a letter sent from Sicily in the summer of 1947, 'also proofs of Malta photos & anything else you may have to direct me – and I hope a newsy letter.'

At the same time there was more to their relationship than a shared fixation on Connolly, Connolly's whereabouts and Connolly's (presumed) lack of commitment. In Peter Watson, Sonia had found a man who, though romantically unavailable, was genuinely solicitous of her interests, worried about her wellbeing and her finances, anxious that she should be rescued from the lure of overwork, take proper holidays and enjoy herself. Three letters sent back from Europe in the summer of 1947 are full of offers of extra money and time off, and concern for her health.

This little cheque is for you and I hope will have its uses. I don't think you get enough of what you deserve and it is a constant source of regret to me your holiday was so short and so unlike a holiday & I didn't think you looked at all well just before I left

London. Where is this happiness you should certainly have and do not seem to get – I mean the real kind and not that pasha's idea of it?

I have written a letter to Cyril which I fear will make him cross with me. I didn't mention anything about you except to suggest that you had his £5 a week expense nonsense added to your screw while he is permanently absent as you do *all* the work.

I really think you should just disappear to where you want for 3 or 4 weeks. *Please* do. It can make no difference when a number has just gone to press.

Quite as blatant as Watson's concern for Sonia is his subtext. Connolly, clearly, is the 'pasha' whose idea of happiness is bogus, and helps himself to expenses payments to which he is not entitled while harassed assistants drudge on in his absence. Sonia, we infer, deserved something better and, throughout the later 1940s, Watson was constantly at work to provide it. He arranged cinema visits and evenings out. To an England mired in the depths of austerity, he returned with silk stockings from America. ('Is your stocking size 9½? I forget. Let me know & I'll get some more.') Above all, he introduced her to the members of his social circle, predominantly, though not exclusively, homosexuals whose company Sonia very much enjoyed. She made a particular friend of Watson's American boyfriend Waldemar Hansen, one of whose poems she took for *Horizon* and whose letters are full of approving references to her charm. After Hansen's return to America, and a year after a Halloween party he had hosted, she sent a postcard sorrowing over their lost friendship: 'Peter and Lys and I are sitting here in tears in the gloaming . . . We miss you and wish we could have another party.'

Several of Sonia's shrewdest observers from this period are from Watson's entourage, and their appraisals of her have a delicacy that heterosexual friends occasionally struggle to achieve. Above all, they were sympathetic to the emotional predicaments of a forthright and outwardly self-confident woman who struggled to achieve satisfactory relationships and whose assertive manner could sometimes set prospective boyfriends back on their heels. 'So sweet,' Hansen wrote at about this time to his friend John Myers, 'and I wish we could find a lovely man for her.'

But where was this paragon to be sought? Sonia's romantic life in the mid-1940s is more or less beyond recovery. She is known to have had brief affairs with Koestler and Lucian Freud, both of whom have been plausibly canvassed as the father of the unborn child that took her to an abortion clinic sometime in 1947, and she was fruitlessly pursued by suitors as various as Maclaren-Ross and G. W. Stonier, the books editor of the *New Statesman*. Naturally, these rejections did nothing for her popularity. As Hilary Spurling notes, much of the disparagement that followed her around literary London – the complaints about her bossiness, her overbearing manner, her perceived sexual coldness – was down to outraged *amour propre* and wounded male vanity. But in the summer of 1946 came the first glimmerings of what began as a friendly attachment but was to turn into one of the most important relationships of her life. The catalyst, appropriately enough, was Peter Watson, the setting was Paris, where Watson had taken her on holiday, and the context could be found in the admiring looks directed by *Horizon* at the literary culture of post-liberation France.

To the Francophile Connolly, French literary life had everything that its post-war English equivalent lacked: confidence; passion; style and swagger; the whole effortlessly overseen by a succession of titanic reputation-brokers such as Jean-Paul Sartre and Raymond Queneau. *Horizon*'s May 1945 number had featured part of Sartre's manifesto for his new literary magazine, *Les Temps modernes*. Here on the Left Bank, a year later, Sonia found herself being introduced to a member of the magazine's staff, the philosopher Maurice Merleau-Ponty. In his late thirties, and shortly to take up a professorial appointment at the École normale supérieure, the author of *La phénoménologie de la perception* (1945) was instantly smitten by his English counterpart, claiming to have detected in her 'a mixture of gaiety and sorrow which is something unusual and, as I think, fine'. By his account they discussed Orwell, Koestler and the young philosopher A. J. Ayer with an eye to a *Horizon* essay. A few days later, even before Sonia had returned home, came a letter, addressed to 'Dear Sonia Brownell', complimenting her command of the French language ('I wish I would be able to write this letter in English from the beginning to the end, – as a proof of my gratitude for your perfect French'), recalling 'talks with you about Orwell, Ayer etc' and proposing 'a paper about their so-called humanism'. Merleau-Ponty signed off with an elegant personal flourish. He would be delighted to meet her again, he declared, 'at the beginning of the week and afterwards in your own country, with your own friends and performing your own behaviour'.

There would always be difficulties about Merleau-Ponty, who in addition to living on the further side of the English Channel had a wife and a child and little interest in giving either of them up. To Sonia, more accustomed to the clumsy importunings of the *Horizon* contributors or being stalked around the streets of Bloomsbury by Maclaren-Ross, he was a *beau idéal*. 'I never longed for anything in my life so much as M.', she once wrote on the blank page of a notebook. The proposal for a paper on Orwell's so-called humanism was turned down, but by the summer of 1947 she was back in Paris, delighting Maurice with her English irony and the gimlet eye she trained on the antics of his more politically minded friends. A letter headed 'Sunday' and typed on *Horizon* paper conveys both the depth of her infatuation and her lack of sympathy with her boyfriend's colleagues on the French Left. 'I terribly want to write to you this evening, although I wish you were here so that I could talk to you instead', she begins, before going on to register her anxiety over the political situation and describe a lunch with two French socialists, Roland Barthes and Dionys Mascolo: 'they talked about the civil war as one talks about a visit to the dentist. When they came to discussing how to make efficient bombs out of bottles with petrol I could have knocked their heads together with impotent rage, and I only refrained from screaming when they said that any form of personal pleasure was a waste of time because they were so busy getting tight and so pleased with the clothes they had bought on the black market that it became rather touching.'

Sympathetic friends signalled their approval. 'If you're madly in love & don't want to come back, say so', Connolly advised. As for the prospects of some kind of shared existence, with or without the impediment of Madame Merleau-Ponty, there was talk of Sonia acquiring a job in Paris, or of Maurice getting Ayer to fix him up with an academic post in London. When neither of these schemes came to fruition, Merleau-Ponty decided to spend the last few days of 1947 in England ('Arriverai Victoria Vendredi 18 heures 30 Yours Maurice,' runs a telegram dated 23 December). They saw in the New Year at the flat in Percy Street, where Sonia – always keen on presenting her young men with items of clothing – gave him a waistcoat for Christmas.

Meanwhile, another of Sonia's admirers was continuing to press his suit. After establishing himself on his Hebridean island, together with son, housekeeper and sister Avril, Orwell had spent the winter of 1946/7 in London. Returning to Jura in the spring, he waited only a day to inform 'Dearest Sonia' of his arrival, offer details of his house and its surroundings ('There are daffodils all over the place, the only flower out. I'm still wrestling with more or less virgin meadow, but I think by next year I'll have quite a nice garden here'), and suggest that Sonia, perhaps accompanied by Janetta and Nicolette – a possible playmate for Richard – should come and stay with him. 'I wrote to Genetta [sic] asking her to come whenever she liked & giving instructions about the journey. So long as she's bringing the child, not just sending it, it should be simple enough.' His aim, he assured her, was to impart 'the complete details about the journey, which isn't so formidable as it looks on paper'. But Jura, whatever Orwell might think about its comparative ease of access, was a remote spot. There followed seventeen lines of meticulous instruction, including a paragraph on the necessity of writing well in advance and problems that might arise along the way: 'If you come by boat, you could probably get a car all right by asking at the quay, but if you come by air there wouldn't be a car at the ferry (which is several miles from Craighouse) unless ordered beforehand.' A further paragraph advertised the need for a raincoat, stout shoes or boots, and how it would help if she brought that week's rations. 'I am afraid I am making all this sound very intimidating,' Orwell gamely concluded, 'but really it's easy enough & the house is quite comfortable. The room you would have is rather small, but it looks out onto the sea. I do so want to have you here.'

Sonia's reply to this forensic account of the Road to Jura has not survived, but she did not take up the offer. The next eighteen months, in any case, were to be devoted to what she frankly acknowledged was the love of her life. All this begs the question of what Merleau-Ponty, plainly bedazzled by the bright English girl he had met among the Existentialists of the Left Bank, made of her when they were reunited on her own territory. Sonia was 'an uneasy partner' where men were concerned, a friend once pronounced. If Merleau-Ponty was captivated by the force of her personality, then he was less keen on her wary, obstructive side: their last night together at Percy Street in the January of 1948 ended in a raging quarrel. And hanging over this cross-Channel affair was the spectre of Madame Merleau-Ponty. At an early stage in the proceedings, Maurice seems to have made it clear to Sonia that he was not prepared to divorce his wife. Neither was Madame prepared to turn a blind eye to his infidelity. No doubt she had got wind of the nights her husband had spent in Sonia's hotel in the rue Jacob when she stayed in Paris in the spring of 1948, for when Sonia came back there later in the year it was to find a note from Madame Merleau-Ponty returning a letter to Maurice and explaining that he had left town.

If there was no decisive break between Sonia and Maurice – they continued to meet, correspond and scheme in the hope of reconciliation – then it was also clear that the relationship had no long-term future: geography, temperament and Madame Merleau-Ponty had seen to that. It was in this febrile atmosphere, returned to England and plunged into her *Horizon* work – Peter Watson was away for the first four months of 1949, which increased her responsibilities – that her life took a wholly unexpected turn, and Orwell, peripheral to her existence for the past three years, gradually became central to it. In the year-and-a-half since he had attempted to inveigle her to Jura, Orwell's professional star had waxed as his health had waned. *Nineteen Eighty-Four*, completed shortly before Christmas 1948, was with his publishers, acclaimed as a masterpiece and awaiting publication in the summer. But the effort of finishing the book – typed sitting up in bed while chain-smoking in a room warmed by a noxious-smelling paraffin heater – had been too much for Orwell's damaged lungs. By the spring of 1949 he was installed in a sanatorium in Cranham, Gloucestershire, his mind bent upon his physical condition, his book but also, as a letter to his publisher Fred Warburg makes clear, the faint stirrings of romance.

'As she may have told you, I had to put Sonia Brownell off,' he told Warburg. 'I am in the most ghastly health & have been for some weeks.' He had been so feverish for the last few days, he explained, that he had been unable to walk to the X-ray and stand against the screen. But this was merely to postpone the inevitable. 'When the picture is taken, I am afraid there is not much doubt it will show that both lungs have deteriorated.' This prognosis was correct: when he asked one of the doctors if she thought he would survive, she would say only that she didn't know. Yet in the midst of this uncertainty, Orwell remained curiously optimistic. 'The one chance of surviving,

I imagine, is to keep quiet. Don't think I am making up my mind to peg out,' he assured Warburg. 'On the contrary, I have the strongest reasons for wanting to stay alive.' One of them, clearly enough, was Sonia. She was at Cranham to celebrate his forty-sixth birthday on 25 June. Another letter to his friend David Astor from mid-July reports that he is in better health and that 'when I am well & about again, sometime next year perhaps, I intend getting married again. I suppose everyone will be horrified, but it seems to me a good idea. Apart from other considerations, I think I should stay alive longer if I were married & had someone to look after me.' As for the name of his intended, 'It is to Sonia Brownell, the sub-editor of "Horizon," I can't remember if you know her but you probably do.'

What had happened to bring this match about? One crucial preliminary was a visit that Sonia had made to Paris earlier in the month with Peter Watson: it was here that she seems to have decided that all was over between her and Merleau-Ponty. Orwell probably asked her to marry him in mid-July 1949: his first words after registering her acceptance were apparently, 'You must learn to make dumplings.' Thereafter, the progress of their relationship can be tracked through Orwell's letters. Early in August, he asked for copies of *Burmese Days* and *Coming Up for Air* to be sent to Sonia at *Horizon*. In the first week of September, by now transferred from Cranham to University College Hospital in Bloomsbury, he wrote a long letter to Astor expressing a hope that he would soon be able to meet his bride-to-be. 'Sonia lives only a few minutes away from here. She thinks we might as well get married while I am still an invalid, because it would give her a better status to look after me, especially if, eg., I went somewhere abroad after leaving here.' As to the general reaction, Orwell declared himself 'much encouraged by none of my friends and relatives seeming to disapprove of my remarrying, in spite of this disease. I had an uneasy feeling that "they" would converge from all directions & stop me, but it hasn't happened. Moreland, the doctor, is very much in favour of it.'

Naturally, such an engagement was highly newsworthy. *Nineteen Eighty-Four*, now three months on the bookshelves and avidly reviewed, had been an enormous success both in Britain and the United States. Several newspapers interested themselves in the romance between the bestselling author, now confined to a hospital bed, and the blonde young woman who ministered to him. 'A specialist's verdict will decide whether fair-haired Miss Sonia Brownell, engaged to novelist George Orwell, will have a bedside wedding in hospital', the *Star* informed its readers on 17 September 1949. A reporter had called at the *Horizon* office in Bedford Square, where 'Miss Brownell, in a white lace-work blouse and grey flannel skirt, was wearing her Italian engagement ring of ornamental design with rubies, diamonds and an emerald. She chose it herself because she thought it pretty.' On the same day Orwell wrote to tell his friend Richard Rees that he had felt 'distinctly better' since coming to UCH. 'Sonia comes & sees me for an hour every day & otherwise I am allowed one visitor for 20 minutes.'

The question of why Sonia – aged thirty-one and in the pink of health – consented to marry Orwell – forty-six and, it was generally agreed, on his deathbed – has been chewed over by biographers for seventy years. Something of the consternation it produced may be seen in the reaction of his friends, who if they did not actively disapprove, as Orwell had feared, were, almost to a man, nonplussed. Inevitably, the root of this mystification lay in the fact that many of them barely knew who she was. Malcolm Muggeridge's diary for 5 September records that Anthony Powell is intrigued by 'the curious information I had received that George Orwell is going to marry a girl called Sonia Brownell who is connected with bringing out the magazine *Horizon*'. That very few people were, at this stage, prepared to take Sonia at all seriously is confirmed by Muggeridge's gloss: 'she is what Tony calls an "Art Tart" . . . it will probably be a rather macabre wedding, I should suppose'. To the majority of Orwell's male acquaintance, Sonia was merely a face at a *Horizon* desk, a girl glimpsed momentarily at a party, ripe for patronage and belittlement. Powell, who went on to become one of Sonia's greatest friends, later recalled that he had 'only met her once before she got engaged to George, an occasion when, owing to the bad light, I thought she was about 18 and gave her a terrific lecture on Classicism and Romanticism. She was a bit taken aback, having no mean opinion of her own qualifications in such spheres. My host, white and shaking, followed me out into the street and explained what I had done.'

Other observers were prepared to go further even than this. Woodrow Wyatt, who liked Sonia while ridiculing what he imagined to be her pretentious, highbrow side, was frankly incredulous: 'Somehow she snuggled up to George Orwell . . . before he died and got him to marry her. Why he did so is a mystery . . . I hope the poor man did not die to a barrage of French phrases.' In Wyatt's defence, Sonia's own friends were equally bewildered. 'And Sonia's engagement?' Peter Watson ruminated in a letter to Waldemar Hansen. 'It is all rather a shock to me. This week's Time reports it in the People section under the heading "That old Feeling." Mmm – I'm not so sure.' Hansen's own view was expressed in a letter to John Myers: 'Nobody seems to approve, since they all feel she is doing it as a Florence Nightingale gesture. There is some truth in that, but the real truth is that she doesn't love M.P. any more, and since any choice she makes would not really matter . . . her marrying Orwell is okay. I, at least, approve.'

Female friends professed themselves startled by news of the engagement. There had been no hint of impending marriage. Neither was there any sign of sexual attraction. According to Janetta, Sonia confided to her they had slept together only once, at the Cranham sanatorium, and that the experience had been 'disastrous'. There was a cultural drawback, too, in that Sonia preferred French writers. Although she admired Orwell's work it was a pity, as Janetta put it, 'that he was so English'. Looking back at the affair from the vantage point of old age, Janetta diagnosed a coming together of several quite different emotions: affection, interest, concern for his wellbeing and 'guilt that she hadn't deeper feelings of love'.

Establishing Sonia's precise state of mind in the summer of 1949 is far from straightforward. Of the various motives that biographers have ascribed to her decision to marry Orwell, who can tell which carried the most weight? Certainly, she was on the rebound from Merleau-Ponty, anxious to exorcise the demons of the last two years and start afresh. On the other hand, part of her reasoning may have been narrowly expedient. With Connolly and Watson now increasingly detached from each other, it was clear by this time that her job at Bedford Square was unlikely to last into the New Year. Friends remembered her saying that, when *Horizon* folded, she would marry George. Connolly himself, who regarded the marriage as a 'grotesque farce', told Evelyn Waugh that he thought it 'a panicky acceptance of a new job because she is losing the old one'. As for the skeletal figure whom she visited each day at UCH, there have been several attempts to characterise her as a gold-digger with one eye on her husband's posthumous royalties. But the Orwell who asked her to marry him in the summer of 1949 was, at this stage, merely a moderately successful writer whose latest work had clearly scored a hit: no one could have envisaged *Nineteen Eighty-Four*'s continuing success throughout the decades that followed or the income it was likely to generate. Much more plausible is that incorrigible sense of duty and responsibility – 'I felt sorry for him', she once remarked in later life – coupled with the instinctive desire that her friends had noted as long ago as the 1930s to sit at a great man's feet and organise his life to their mutual satisfaction. More than one onlooker noticed how at home she seemed at UCH, vigilant at her post by Orwell's bedside, alert to his needs, dealing with his post and hobnobbing with his visitors. 'She loved it,' Janetta remembered, 'and it was all to do with being in control.'

A shrewd investment or an act of self-sacrifice? Most onlookers were divided. Sinclair-Loutit, for example, thought it a 'gross mismatch' but also 'the kindest and most generous act of Sonia's life'.

Only Koestler, whom Sonia disliked, was unequivocally in favour. 'I have been saying for years that she is the nicest, most intelligent and decent girl that I met during my whole stay in England', he declared. The significance of Koestler's vote of confidence lay in its barbed assessment of the milieu she inhabited. She was 'very lonely in that crowd in which she moves,' he suggested to Orwell, 'and she will become a changed person when you take her out of it. I think I had a closer view of the Connolly set-up than you did; it had a fairly stultifying effect which left its mark even on a tough guy like me.' To Koestler, it was not that Sonia might be rescuing Orwell from a lonely widowerhood and giving him a reason to go on living, but that he was salvaging her from a life spent as Connolly's handmaiden, permanently in thrall to his whims, forever dealing with the consequences of the administrative, and sometimes the emotional, problems he could not be bothered to solve himself.

It was all very well for friends to speculate. How did Sonia envisage her future? The optimistic view of Orwell's condition, sometimes canvassed by sympathetic doctors on the UCH medical staff, was that he might improve sufficiently to be considered a 'good chronic'. In this semi-convalescent state he could be allowed to retire to a cottage in the country where Sonia could nurse him, keep unwelcome visitors at bay and type his manuscripts. The less optimistic view, presumably unvoiced in Sonia's presence, held that he was unlikely to survive. As the autumn wore on the friends who visited him grew increasingly pessimistic about his chances. Malcolm Muggeridge, who arrived at Room 65 in the last week of September, thought him 'inconceivably wasted, and has, I should say, the appearance of someone who hasn't long to live'. It was Muggeridge's first encounter with Sonia – 'a large, bouncy girl, quite pleasant', he decided, who, if dressed in a tweed suit, would be the epitome of a philanthropic village lady, had she not chosen to 'mess about' with *Horizon* and 'intellectual circles'. Shortly afterwards, he received a letter from her informing him that the wedding would take place on 13 October.

There could be no question of Orwell leaving his bed. A clergy-man – the UCH chaplain, the Revd W. H. Braine – was summoned to preside; David Astor procured a special licence from the Archbishop of Canterbury. Muggeridge and Powell, commissioned to buy something suitable for the groom to wear, came up with a crimson corduroy jacket. Orwell approved of this dandy-ish gesture. Propped up against the pillows, he had, Powell thought, 'an unaccustomed epicurean air'. And so, with half-a-dozen guests crammed into the tiny hospital room, the ceremony took place. Astor officiated as best man; Robert Kee gave away the bride; Janetta acted as witness. The night nurses had signed a congratulatory card. There was something unbearably poignant about the scene, those present recalled. Half a century later, Robert Kee retained a memory of Orwell 'in bed but wholly participating and showing real attachment to Sonia'. Janetta lingered just inside the door, desperately upset, she remembered, and aghast at the austerity of the setting, yet for all her long-held suspicion of marriage and religious observance, deeply moved. The atmosphere was one of 'bleakness and touching sadness', she recalled, the bottle of champagne Sonia had brought with her sitting awkwardly amid the medical paraphernalia: 'I think I had tears in my eyes watching that ill smiling face.' Leaving the groom to reflect on his newly married state, the party then decamped to the Ritz for lunch.

The peculiar circumstances of Sonia's marriage occurred to more than one literary diarist. Frances Partridge, who met the Kees later in the day, noted that they were 'just back from a strange wedding party: Sonia Brownell had that afternoon married George Orwell in hospital where he lies seriously ill with T.B. He is said to have a fifty-fifty chance of recovery, and as he is much in love with her everyone hopes the marriage will give him a new interest.' The Kees, Frances observed, 'had obviously been much moved by the event.' A few days later, armed with the comments of interested friends, she returned to her theme: 'Many people regard the Orwell marriage cynically and remind one that Sonia always declared her intention of marrying a Great Man. I see it principally as a neurotic one, for a marriage to a bed-ridden and perhaps dying man is as near no marriage as it's possible to get.'

This may have been true. Equally, there was no doubt that the marriage had improved Orwell's spirits. Powell reckoned that for all his bed-bound and emaciated state in some respects 'he was in better form than I had ever seen him show'. Muggeridge, who visited him in late October, found him 'remarkably cheerful'. But he was growing steadily weaker – so thin now, he told a friend, 'that it's beyond the level at which you can go on living'. That Sonia seems to have grasped that the situation was beyond saving seems clear from a note sent by Lys to Connolly in the second week of November: 'Poor George has had a relapse and Sonia now thinks the only thing is to send him to Switzerland.' Meanwhile, sharp-eyed visitors noted the symptoms of nervous strain. Muggeridge, for example, was present one evening when Orwell's supper was brought in on a tray. He had had a wonderful life, Sonia briskly informed him as the orderly set down the plates, waited on hand and foot, compared to her struggles with the temperamental Connolly.

Meanwhile, a stream of visitors continued to beat a path across the Bloomsbury squares: old comrades from the Spanish Civil War; *Tribune* colleagues; platoon-mates from the St John's Wood Home Guard. Janetta brought Nicky to sit at his bedside: when her mother demurred at the noise the six year old made with her toy car, the gaunt figure in the bed solicitously intervened: 'No, no, it's all right. It's all right. Let her be, let her do that,' Nicky remembered him saying. But time was running short. On Christmas afternoon 1949 Powell and Muggeridge came to see him. He looked like a picture he had once seen of Nietzsche, Muggeridge thought, raging and furious at his deteriorating health, his mind roaming unappeasably back in time and forwards to the unknowable future. 'Poor George. He went on about the Home Guard, and the Spanish Civil War, and how he would go to Switzerland soon, and all the while the stench of death was in the air, like autumn in a garden.'

The Swiss excursion – transfer by plane to a sanatorium in the Swiss Alps – was little more than a palliative. No amount of alpine air could save him now. But still, preparations for his departure went on. Lucian Freud, mildly fixated on hospitals and medical procedures, was invited to join the party as a surrogate male nurse. A bundle of fishing rods lay in the corner of the room. Sonia's friends continued to worry about her. 'I hope you are NOT having a nervous breakdown and that you do get away for a change very soon,' Peter Watson wrote early in January. 'Also that George is better & able to leave by now for a better climate.' And still the visitors came – five-year-old Richard, who had been brought down to London by Avril and taken to the zoo by the Powells; Orwell's anarchist friend Vernon Richards, who recalled how his 'thin, drawn face lighted up and his eyes shone' as he described Richard's account of the trip; Muggeridge, who, calling on Thursday 19 January 1950, thought him 'at his last gasp'. The Swiss trip was now scheduled for 25 January. All that week, the visitors remembered, Sonia had been suffering from a cold and not always present at the bedside, but on 20 January, feeling better, she spent most of the day in Room 65. Then, early in the evening, she decided to go home. Sometime in the small hours an artery burst in Orwell's lungs; he died within minutes.

Sonia seems to have kept very few of the letters she received in the following weeks, but she preserved Peter Watson's note from Jamaica. 'I have read the sad news in Time when I arrived here from Haiti. In these circumstances it is impossible to offer condolences & so extremely difficult to convey sympathy I know but I do want you to know how much I have been thinking about you the last days and how shocked I am.' Watson would have been still more shocked to discover that something else had died in the room at University College Hospital. This, it is fair to say, was the old Sonia: the teenage girl that Coldstream and Pasmore had wanted to paint; the aspiring art critic proudly unveiling her plans to Connolly and Spender at the Café Royal; the keen-eyed custodian of the *Horizon* office. Her place would shortly be filled by a very different proposition: the Widow Orwell.

Interlude: Sonia's Things

Like the man she married in the hospital bedroom in October 1949, Sonia left little behind her. Or rather, little in the way of physical artefacts. Not counting the books and the pamphlet collection, Orwell's leavings could be fitted into a couple of cardboard boxes: the fishing rods the dying man had planned to take to Switzerland with him; a fragment or two of the Blair family silver; the tie Sonia had given him for Christmas four weeks before he died; assorted odds and ends from his bedbound, post-Hebridean life. Seventy years after his death, this notional pile has dwindled almost to nothing. Even the handful of artefacts featured in the last photographs of him ever taken seem to have vanished from the earth. I once asked Richard Blair what had happened to the antique Burmese sword his father can be seen unsheathing from its scabbard in Vernon Richards's photograph taken at the Islington flat in 1946, and received the answer that it had been used for bringing in the Jura harvest in the 1950s and then disappeared, been left to rust at the field's edge or thrown out with the rest of the superannuated ironmongery.

With Sonia, the trail seems even sparser. Her correspondence is mostly restricted to the letters she sent to William Coldstream in the early years of the war, her petition to Spender about the number on Young English Painters, and a fragment to Merleau-Ponty, written on *Horizon* paper, that may not even have been sent. Here and there, though, in the box files devoted to her in the Orwell Archive, something stirs. There is, for example, the celebratory card, signed 'The Night Nurses', offering 'Congratulations on Your Wedding Day', and a National Provincial Bank cheque, signed by Connolly jokily dated 22 January 1999, and promising to 'Pay Sonia Brownell one million pounds & no more.' Even better, perhaps, are the occasional hints of the role she played in managing Orwell's affairs in the last six months of his life. Working in the Archive one day, I turned up a small padded box that looked as if jewellery might once have been kept in it. From beneath its gingerly prised-up rim came fluttering two or three scraps of paper, each of them bearing Orwell's signature.

What were they doing there? Why had Sonia hoarded them? To what use had she wanted them put? Most of the other items in the file dated from 1949, the year in which Orwell lay flat on his back at the Gloucestershire sanatorium or at University College Hospital supervising the publication of his last novel and then monitoring its reception. Unsurprisingly, given the state its author was in, very few signed copies of *Nineteen Eighty-Four* survive. It seems reasonable to suppose that the signatures were for volumes that Orwell aimed to present to his friends, that this was the residue left over when the ever-efficient Sonia had finished the job of sticking them in.

11.

The Destructive Element:
Barbara, Connolly and Others 1944–51

Thirty today. Christ!

Barbara Skelton, diary, 26 June 1946

G. Orwell is dead and Mrs Orwell presumably a rich widow. Will Cyril marry her? He is said to be consorting with a dingy demi-mondaine called Miss Skelton.

Evelyn Waugh, diary, January 1950,
The Diaries of Evelyn Waugh (1976)

Most Lost Girl lives in the 1940s are to a greater or lesser degree trackable. Lys, after all, was by Connolly's side, or at any rate a pace or two behind it, for the best part of a decade. If not reconstitutable on a day-to-day basis, the outlines of Sonia's career are a matter of record, and should Janetta ever threaten to slip beneath the surface of Blitz-era London for a month or two there are always Frances Partridge's diaries to drag her unresistingly back.

The exception to this rule is Barbara. There are whole stretches of the late 1940s where she simply vanishes, disappears from the face of the earth, tugs free of the diary entries and letter exchanges that kept other Lost Girls at the forefront of her friends' imaginations and slips off into a kind of sub-world of out-of-the-way vacations and lying low, an obscurity so unmonitored that at times even her closest friends scarcely seem to know where she is. As to how this had come about, and why the one-time ornament of the Ritz Bar and the Ivy should be spending her time on furlough in the Alpes-Maritimes or roosting in some anonymous London hotel, the most obvious explanation lies in the changing shape of the post-war world. People were growing older, staider and more respectable. The patterns and the congeries of the early 1940s were breaking up. Not long before he died, Feliks Topolski reflected on the landscape through which he, Quennell and Barbara had wandered nearly half-a-century before:

> She was this beauty, an odd beauty, because it was not real beauty, but tremendously desired by all men all round. And being utterly silent and not offering really anything and not going along with any situation but at the same time, in consequence, being the most desirable object in existence. In the early days she was mysterious with this lovely cat-like attitude of not settling anywhere but just carrying the basket of essentials and moving from one person to another. At that time she was mostly using as bases, Peter Quennell and me. And so, if she stayed with me and after a few days became unbearable – because she was unbearable, basically – she would simply without much explanation take her basket, slink off along the wall and go to Peter; and then reappear in a week or two to stay in my bed with no things said. And that's how it went on for a while, for quite a while – for years, actually.

There was a suspicion that this kind of life was no longer sustainable in the age of Mr Attlee, Ernest Bevin and the National Health Service. Quennell had settled down into the routines of (reasonably) upmarket journalism, editing the *Cornhill Magazine* and reviewing books for the *Daily Mail*. Topolski, though still hungry for whatever crumbs Barbara let fall from her plate, had a career to pursue. The Free French officers had gone back to a newly freed France; and where did that leave Barbara? Her first task, naturally, was to see out the war. A letter survives from November 1944 in which Topolski, writing from London, imagines the two them together on an Egyptian beach some years hence, comparing notes on their past marriages. That old rivalries endured is confirmed by the information that he saw Quennell at the Dorchester cloakroom, and the theatrical manner in which he turned towards the lavatories annoyed Topolski so much that he abandoned his own visit and sat out the dinner he was attending with a full bladder.

By this time Barbara was long gone from Cairo. Coming back to base after her two-week tour of the Middle East, she discovered that the European situation was in flux. The German army was in retreat across the Greek border; the British Embassy in Athens was expected to reopen and, as the war moved on, there was a demand for cipherines. The route led north via Italy and the next four months offer tantalising glimpses of Barbara in action: the meet-ups with old friends (one of them was Janetta's half-brother Mark, whom she visited in hospital in Salerno where he was recovering from TB); the legion of male admirers (these included an obliging USAF colonel who provided access to PX stores and spent Christmas with her in Naples); and the customary difficulties involved in calibrating the demands of her personal life to the call of duty. Brought back to England by the Foreign Office early in January 1945, she was booked for redeployment to Lisbon in the summer, but 'for some inexplicable reason' missed her flight and was promptly suspended from the service.

In the meantime there was the question of finding somewhere to live. It is a mark of her elusiveness that virtually the only clue to her whereabouts in the immediate post-war period comes in the letters sent to her by friends. In February 1945, newly returned from Athens, she was staying at the Eccleston Hotel in Eccleston Square, a stone's throw from Victoria Station. There was a brief stint at the Park Village

East house, which Quennell was sharing with the publisher George Weidenfeld. ('Turned out. Move to Peter.') One of the notes to Topolski from January 1946 is sent c/o the literary critic John Davenport at Rossetti House, Flood Street, Chelsea, but by the following month she seems to have moved on again, as a letter sent in late February by her friend Gerda Treat suggests that 'Your Sydney St abode sounds like something in a play. Screamingly funny, but I suppose not so funny to live in.'

As for the existence being lived out in Pimlico, Chelsea or elsewhere, the early part of 1945 saw an instant resumption of her pre-Cairo routines. She lunched with Quennell on each of her first three days back in England, and Topolski's name turns up in her diary in the first week of February. If there was any satisfaction to be gained from once again playing off Quennell against Topolski and vice versa, it seldom surfaces in her diaries. ('Went to the cottage alone and desperately dejected . . . Saw Feliks. Very upsetting. Think of nothing else all day.') What did Barbara make of the news from Europe, where the war was now reaching its endgame? The diaries are merely a succession of one-line entries: 'Mussolini dead . . . Hitler dead . . . Germany surrenders'. Clearly, she had her own problems, in which the necessity to earn a living – she started work at the BBC in November 1945, capacity unspecified – contended with growing unhappiness: 'Gloom gloom. Polished off the gin . . . Depths of despair . . . Loneliness and awfulness.'

The answer, if there was one, lay abroad. As early as September 1945, Topolski could be found writing to her at an address in Cagnes-sur-Mer in the Alpes-Maritimes, a picturesque Riviera town where she spent three winters in the immediate post-war period with her friend Poppet John; there was at least one summer holiday in a villa co-owned by François Villiers, whom she had met in Lagos. One obvious question that hangs over this peripatetic lifestyle with its intermittent and at times non-existent employment is: who was paying for it? The prime candidate would seem to be John Sutro, who certainly funded the top-floor flat in Queen Street, SW1, where she established herself towards the end of 1947 and whose correspondence hints at a fairly close relationship. A letter from Poppet John from this time sent to Cagnes records that she 'has seen John S. twice, he never stops talking about "our little friend" – this is you – and seems to want to find some kind of a flat or room for the winter . . . He can't wait to see you again.' The Queen Street landlord's own letters are full of polite expressions of sympathy ('I am sorry that your sojourn at the Rock Pool [Cagnes-sur-Mer] is proving unsatisfactory; the milieu (or that horrid word "*ambience*") sounds most disagreeable'), with little flashes of emotion breaking out from under the surface ('I confess I miss you very much . . . I simply *must* see you for a few hours').

Sutro was an odd character, an Oxford friend of Evelyn Waugh known for his elaborate impersonations who went on to make a career as a film producer: one of his letters to Barbara is addressed from the Venice Film Festival. If his activities on Barbara's behalf seem to cast him in the old-fashioned role of gentlemanly 'protector', offering subsidy and accommodation in return for sexual favours, then he was understandably sensitive to another aspect of her life in the later 1940s: regular bouts of ill-health. 'I am very sorry to hear you have been ill,' runs a letter from the summer of 1949; 'it's the second time you have been ill on your arrival at Cagnes.' A letter from the previous September strikes a similar note – 'I hope you are well and not having any relapses' – and presumably refers to the illness mentioned by Gerda a few weeks before. 'You poor kid. A couple of incoherent letters from you. You never told me what's wrong, just about operation. Where? + how did it all come about?' There are no references to health problems in Barbara's memoirs, but the trouble may well have been gynaecological: a brief diary entry from May 1945 notes that 'the doctor professes sterility'.

Ill-health notwithstanding, Barbara's emotional life was every inch as complicated as it had been in the days when Quennell and Topolski fought for her favours at the Gargoyle Club; Topolski, at least, was still on the scene, for the letter in which Gerda enquires about the operation notes, 'So that Felix [sic] is still around. Is he divorced yet?' Whatever her relationship with Sutro, she spent much of her time at Cagnes-sur-Mer in the company of an ex-Resistance leader named Pierre Savaigo, another one of those enticing hooligans in whose company she always delighted. Possessive and prone to violence, Savaigo once beat her up after seeing her in the company of a cheque-forger and afterwards took a knuckleduster to her bedroom walls. After he lost his temper at the sight of her engagement-strewn diary during a visit to Queen Street and produced a gun from his suitcase, Barbara decided that the relationship had probably run its course and notified the police. The following morning two plain-clothes men rang the doorbell 'and how sad I felt when Pierre was politely extradited'.

And so the 1940s ran on. A little modelling for her old sponsor Mattli at his salon in Carlton Place. Late evenings at the Gargoyle in the shadow of David Tennant's Matisse. Bohemian parties at Queen Street. Weekends at the Cot, where the ever-faithful PC Boot still acted as unpaid security guard when its owner was away. Riviera vacations, with the wind blowing through the pines and the blue of the Mediterranean stretching out into the distance . . . And a curious episode remembered by an Australian girl called Robin Dalton at large in post-war London, and dated to 1947, in which Miss Dalton, out on the town with the society photographer Baron Nahum, whose name recurs in Barbara's engagement diaries, found herself in Feliks Topolski's studio together with Barbara ('very drunk') and another girl of the same name: 'The two Barbaras were enjoying themselves in what appeared to me a most curious fashion, indulgently watched over by Felix [sic] and Baron, before Barbara Skelton turned her attention to me. Baron took pity on my prim lips, murmured protestations and firmly crossed legs and took me home.'

A suspicion that some of the company Barbara kept here in the half-decade after the war was not of the choicest is confirmed by her diary account of a trip to North Africa in May 1949, undertaken with a pair of unidentifiable male friends called Vasco and Graham, jointly referred to as 'the boys'. The excursion began on a whim: 'Vasco turns up at luncheon & suggests going to Tangier. Pack bags and depart.' After a night in Paris ('Woke up in bed with both the boys'), the party left for Barcelona and then flew south across Spain to the Mediterranean. The next few days were devoted to sex, drugs and quarrelling: 'I bicker with the boys. Vasco & I end up in the hole in the wall smoking hashish . . . Swim in the morning. 3 fucks from V.' There were visits to Casablanca and Algiers; the final entry reads, 'Graham & I pass out on the bed clutching a bottle of wine.' Pierre and his knuckledusters. Waking up with the boys. Bickering in the Tangier cafés. Clearly, it was time to be moving on.

If the two centres of Lost Girl life in the later 1940s were the *Horizon* offices in Bedford Square and the house in Sussex Place, then Barbara at this point in her life was detached from both of them. What brought her back, shortly before the magazine published its final number, was a meeting with an old friend named Natalie Newhouse. Natalie, then living with her future husband, the actor Robert Newton, at Tickerage farm, confided to her that, as Barbara guilelessly put it, 'Cyril was bored with Lys and was seeking someone new.' That this someone might be Barbara was made abundantly clear when Connolly invited the pair of them to lunch at L'Etoile. The ex-editor was in low-ish water. Despite having pocketed substantial advances from publishers on both sides of the Atlantic, he had failed to write the masterpieces expected of him. The invitation to review books for the *Sunday Times*, which would set his post-*Horizon* life back on course, would not arrive for nearly another year. At the same time, he was darkly conscious that the world he had moved through so effortlessly for the past decade – a landscape of high-end entertaining in comfortable surroundings, with Lys always present to deal with his moods and raise his spirits – was coming to a close. Funds were low, his association with Peter Watson was coming to an end, and Lys – faithful, attentive and put-upon Lys – was searching for an escape route.

If Connolly was looking for a change of partner, as opposed to someone to trifle with whenever he grew weary of Lys, then why did he turn to Barbara? And why, if it comes to that, should she turn to him? They had known each other intermittently for eight or nine years, and neither had particularly enjoyed the other's company; Connolly irritated by the thought of his lodger's sullen girlfriend in the upstairs flat using up the hot water and stealing his furniture; Barbara unimpressed by Connolly's stage management of the social occasions at which he appeared and amused by the details of his domestic routine sent out by Quennell to the Middle East. All of this, though, is to ignore both the highly individual way in which Connolly conducted his emotional life and Barbara's positive relish of domestic unease. From Connolly's point of view, Barbara was a superlatively good-looking woman who, while alluring in herself, might also serve as useful ammunition in his dealings with Lys or, for that matter, with anyone else who might stray into his orbit. From Barbara's equally idiosyncratic viewpoint, here was a man who, while lacking in physical attraction – no great hardship to a woman who once confessed that 'I never really appreciated conventional good looks' – had wit, flair and a wide range of amusing friends: just the thing to ginger up her social life and keep boredom at bay.

At the end of February 1950 Topolski, then on a tour of the Far East, wrote to inform her that he would be back in the beginning of May and asking whether she would spend time with him. But by this stage Barbara was already pursuing a clandestine affair with Connolly. According to her diary he telephoned on 9 March 'in a terrible self-pitying state' to report that Lys had gone out to dinner leaving him on his own, that there was no money and that it was all her – that is, Lys's – fault. Fearing the worst, Barbara packed a basket and hastened round to Sussex Place, only to find him 'prancing about the bedroom barefoot . . . said he was pleased to see me, whipped off his dressing-gown, sprang into bed and was asleep in no time'.

Discovering that Barbara's plans for the spring included a continental trip, Connolly decided to gate-crash the party. Their relationship, consequently, began as it would continue: in an atmosphere of subterfuge, sarcasm and divided loyalties. Accompanied by Quennell, Barbara set off for France in a red convertible Sunbeam-Talbot, possibly supplied by Sutro, and was met by Connolly in Paris. When she moved on to Geneva to stay with Sutro, Connolly booked himself into a hotel on the far side of the lake and amused himself by signalling to her from his room. If this hot pursuit was a sign of Connolly's genuine interest in her, then their covert meetings also brought out a less attractive side. Barbara noted the first of his 'deflating quips' when, as she lit up in a restaurant as the cheese course came into view, he remarked: 'I suppose you think the hollows in the gruyere are there for you to stub out your cigarette.' Shortly after this he began to pine for Lys and went off to meet her in Marseilles.

Although there was a subsequent reunion at Sussex Place in the early summer of 1950, none of this boded well. Neither did the phone call in which Connolly revealed that he had spent the greater part of the previous night allotting marks to all the women he knew according to their suitability as wives. Barbara got fewer than anybody for 'spirituality' but achieved top score for sex appeal, followed by Sonia. Lys and Joan Rayner were awarded top marks for loyalty and giving a sense of security. And yet, amid the point-scoring and the mutual antagonism, it seems clear that Connolly and Barbara had more to bring them together than to drive them apart and that from an early stage in their relationship they seem to have understood each other pretty well. Each, for example, was a natural melancholic. Both seemed to have pined for some ideal mode of existence without really knowing of what it might consist. And in the end, the net result of their inbred sulkiness and dissatisfaction was a curious affinity. It was as if each was drawn to the turbulence that the other created, basked in the winds that blew over their wounded dignity, disliked and resented the face on the other side of the breakfast table but would have lost an essential element of their life if it had been suddenly removed. To put it in a way that Barbara would instantly have comprehended, Connolly liked things to be difficult too.

He was also – a crucial factor in his relationship with anybody, whether male or female – at his most vulnerable. In July 1950 came the news that Jean had died, a few months short of her fortieth birthday. Lys, steadily detaching herself from his orbit, had taken a job in the London office of the *New Yorker*, found a new boyfriend and moved out of Sussex Place – a furious Connolly was at one stage discovered watching from the street as the couple talked in Lys's office. Janetta was on the point of leaving Robert Kee for Derek Jackson. Joan was with Patrick Leigh Fermor. Everywhere around him, friends were moving on and old alliances splitting apart. There was a depressing trip to the Cot during the course of which Barbara told him that she was sick of life. They couldn't possibly marry, Connolly told her, 'as we don't get on at all well when things go wrong and you couldn't bear being poor. After all, it's not as if anyone is likely to leave you any money we can count on.' Back at Queen Street, Barbara's low spirits continued, made yet more irksome by Connolly's idleness. ('Wake up with terrible gloom . . . Spend all morning cleaning while Cyril soaks in the bath.') A second weekend in Kent was enlivened by Connolly's unselfconscious memorialising of his romantic past: 'He is always telling me of the number of women he nearly went to bed with and when I say "Why didn't you?", he says their scent put him off.'

Another question worth asking about these transactions is: what did each of the parties to them want? Connolly, by this time, was clearly contemplating marriage, although – Connolly being Connolly – his steps towards it were tentative in the extreme. 'Talk of our living together, preparatory to marriage,' Barbara noted in mid-August.

'He said that if two people who live together don't marry within the first year, they never will.' Half an hour after this exchange, he returned to say that 'he thinks he has been in a married state too much in his life'. If this sounds as if all the decisions were being made – or rather not being made – by Connolly, then Barbara, too, was capable of giving as good as she got. 'B. is certainly unhappy, but she is tough and she is so horrible to me that I don't feel guilt about her,' he wrote at about this time. But what did Barbara want? Establishing what she felt about Connolly is made more difficult by the fact that her diaries and memoirs are clearly written for effect, intended to memorialise the dumpy figure found marinating in the bath or sprawled over the bed as a great comic character. Beyond this a yearning for security, that eternal wish to stave off boredom and the sense of some elemental coming together uneasily contended, together with a suspicion that both would happily have walked away from the relationship had a better offer presented itself.

The stage was set for the first great drama of their life together. It began one summer day in Queen Street when, with both Connolly and Quennell conveniently on the premises, the telephone rang. The call was from Paris. The caller was Farouk, not seen for six years, who, according to Barbara's account of their conversation, remarked: 'It would be nice to see you again. Why don't you come out and join us?' A less sophisticated man might have baulked at the idea of a woman he wanted to marry disappearing to France to reacquaint herself with a former lover who happened to be the King of Egypt, but Connolly urged her to go: 'After all, a king's a king.' Barbara left London more or less on the spot, was met at La Baule in Brittany, to which Farouk had moved on, by Freddie of ancient memory and taken to join the royal entourage, at this point quartered on two floors of the Hermitage Hotel. Her host, fatter and seedier than when they had last met and resembling 'a huge sawdust teddy bear badly sewn at the joints', tweaked her ear affectionately and told the assembled company 'She's a real minx, this one.' With her customary sangfroid, Barbara settled down into a routine that involved accompanying her host each evening to the casino (she was given a thousand francs but expected to stay seated beside him as a kind of mascot once this was lost) and being summoned each morning by a member of the royal bodyguard to join him for breakfast.

Connolly, meanwhile, was working hard to monetise the trip. The *Daily Mail*, possibly instigated by Quennell, was prepared to commission a piece about the royal visit to Brittany, although any face-to-face interview would, as Connolly knew, be problematic: Farouk detested journalists. When he arrived in La Baule, the King refused to see him, although he and Barbara were allowed to meet for drinks. Shortly afterwards, Farouk announced that he and his entourage were leaving for Biarritz. Desperate for something that would give his copy bite, Connolly cooked up a plan, told Barbara that he would be sitting drinking coffee outside the last café out of town as the cortège passed by and she should try to persuade her escort to stop. Sure enough, as the fleet of cars sailed into view, a fat, chair-bound figure with a suitcase could be seen on the pavement, but no amount of pleading on Barbara's part could induce Farouk to halt. The royal party proceeded to Biarritz, where she was pursued by reporters 'wanting to interview the English mystery woman'. Barbara, too, was determined to make a profit out of her holiday. Although large sums continued to be lost at the roulette table, she managed 'to put enough aside to give Cyril some cufflinks and provide for our eventual trip back'.

As for her dealings with Farouk, one notes once again her complete inability to be anyone other than herself: sardonic, unimpressed, never likely to wilt in royalty's shadow. Farouk, praised for his driving skills, declared that 'a compliment from you is a rarity, I'll take it'. As well as the thousand francs a night gambling stake, the royal bounty included a ring with emerald chips and a gold cigarette holder, but Barbara was unmoved by 'a large vulgar clip inlaid with multi-coloured stones that was pinned onto my evening dress like some badge of merit'.

Subsequently the party moved on to Cannes and Barbara, her unlooked-for holiday at an end, returned to England by way of the Dordogne. Visiting the Egyptian Embassy to collect her suitcase, which had been despatched in the diplomatic bag, she discovered a crate of mangoes which Farouk had sent as a present for Connolly.

By now marriage was definitely in view, even if friends and former lovers counselled caution ('Don't do anything in a hurry,' Lys advised. 'If you and Barbara are really suited . . . then marry her in six months' time) and Barbara's behaviour sometimes seemed calculated to forestall it. On a September trip to Paris, where Connolly arrived with a ring, they attended a nightclub where Barbara, conspicuous on the dancefloor, went out of her way to be agreeable to all the men present except her future husband. Still the ever-indecisive Connolly hesitated to commit himself, fearful of what marriage to Barbara might entail, still more fearful of what he might be missing if he let the opportunity go by. 'After a year's talk of marriage, we have decided that that is to be the day', runs an entry in Barbara's diary from 5 October 1950.

They were formally united at Elham Register Office, with PC Boot as the main witness. When at one point Connolly was found to have disappeared from the room, the clerk took Boot for the husband to be. 'If I weren't a married man, I'd take his place readily,' the policeman declared. The wedding breakfast – in fact a lunch – took place 'in sullen silence in Maidstone'. A gigantic basket of exotic plants later arrived from Farouk. Friends of the couple looked on with a mixture of mock and genuine horror. 'There is I believe no doubt that Boots has married the Sultan's Circassian slave', Evelyn Waugh informed Nancy Mitford later in the year.

The evidence is conclusive tho it is not known whether he gave her a ring. A Mrs Hulton gave him a wedding breakfast. After the fifth course, Boots had a seizure, fell off his chair frothing & gasping, was carried straight to a waiting van & whisked off to Tring where he spent the first fortnight of married life in a padded cell being hosed and starved and worse . . . Their total capital is £5 . . . two sacks of sugar and a cottage in Kent which belongs to the sultana . . . He writes daily to Lys begging to see her & saying how wretched he is, but she is adamant.

As with nearly all the elaborate fantasias with which Waugh entertained Nancy Mitford, there is more than a grain of truth in this conspectus. The Connollys' income as they embarked on their married life would be severely reduced. Sussex Place, now in need of substantial repairs, was becoming too expensive to maintain. Sutro had presumably intended the flat at Queen Street for Barbara, rather than Barbara and a husband. Even more ominous, perhaps, was the fact that almost from the moment that he emerged from the Register Office Connolly began to feel that he had made a mistake. The post-nuptial atmosphere can be gauged from an entry in Barbara's diary three days after the wedding when they were staying at Queen Street. Still worrying that there might be headlines of the WRITER WEDS FRIEND OF FAROUK kind, Connolly began the morning by going downstairs to fetch the newspapers. Finding none, his anxiety switched immediately to faint disappointment. Barbara suggested that he make some toast. 'Don't know how to make toast.' After drinking half a cup of tea he sank back into bed 'like a dying goose, still in his dressing gown'. Two days later, she found him standing stark naked in the bedroom and staring into space 'in an attitude of despair'. What was the matter? Barbara wondered. 'It's marriage. I feel trapped.'

Barbara's suspicion that her newly married husband was pining after Lys was confirmed by Quennell, and also by an argument about Sussex Place, where Barbara declined to live on account of its rundown state: 'What you don't realise is that it's like that because its chief ornament has gone', Connolly told her. 'I feel very badly about Lys and therefore very badly about marrying Barbara,' Connolly guiltily informed Hamish Hamilton a few weeks later, 'though I think it will turn out all right hence my general furtiveness and persecution mania.' Barbara declared herself restive and dissatisfied, saddled with a man who spent his time either soaking for hours in the bath or plodding off to his club to study the racing form. Only a month after the wedding ceremony another argument about whether they should live on the top floor of Sussex Place and let the rooms beneath turned into 'a heated discussion until we are screaming at each other'.

Christmas was spent among relays of Connolly's grand friends – a stay at the Faringdon estate in Oxfordshire which Lord Berners had bequeathed to his companion Robert Heber-Percy, dinner with the Mosleys, another supper with John and Penelope Betjeman. It was all too much for Barbara, who recorded herself suddenly turning on him with a shout of 'My God, you are a bore'. On New Year's Day she woke at noon with 'screams for food from Hubby who has put on an inch of jowl since Christmas'. On what she called 'bad guilt days' he took to lying in the bath groaning, 'dense steam seeps from under the door and spreads round the flat, and I hear an ecto-plasmic voice crying "A million miles from here," pause. "A million miles from here," or "I wish I was dead."' Two days later he went off to have a drink with Janetta. Shortly afterwards, Barbara noted another 'pining-after-Lys phase. They have had secret meetings every afternoon this week.'

But Lys's door was now firmly shut. At about this time she announced that she had been offered an assistant editor's job at the US firm of Doubleday and would shortly be leaving for America. Here, she thought, she might be able to clamber out of the emotional sink to which eight years of living with Connolly had condemned her: 'I cheer myself up by thinking of the excitement of going to America. I have several admirers, but am not in the mood for love or sex – nor do I want to entangle myself with anybody. If I can remain free for a while I have a chance of growing up and stopping the arrested development.' Connolly responded with a desperate letter declaring how much he wanted her back, but it was too late. The fog of mutual antagonism that hung over the Connollys' relationship can be gauged from Joan Rayner's account of a dinner party to which she had invited the newly married couple early in the New Year:

> Skelton left before C, the only one not to enjoy it in a furious temper of course, although C could not have been kinder to her, and when he got home about 4 she had locked him out of the flat. It took him about an hour to get in after nearly being arrested, and then apparently he socked her good and proper and slept on the sofa in the sitting room. Robin [Campbell] and I were going to lunch there but C met us at an exhibition in a frightful state, asking us what he was to do, longed to leave but nowhere to go, couldn't be alone etc, Barbara was still in bed crying so C went home to lunch alone to make up his mind . . .

There is a suspicion that at least some of the reports of Barbara's bad behaviour in early 1951 are slightly exaggerated, if only because the people who filed them tended to be Connolly's friends rather than hers. Neither Joan nor the Campbells, with whom she and Connolly spent an uncomfortable weekend in mid-January ('Had a sleepless night in a too-narrow bed with Hubby heaving about like a giant seal'), regarded her as anything more than a dangerous nuisance, a poor substitute for Lys when it came to the vital task of providing Connolly with the kind of settled domestic existence that would enable him to make best use of his talents. By the spring Connolly and Barbara were back at Sussex Place, part of a curious household that included the journalist Philip Toynbee, Toynbee's young American wife and the abandoned Robert Kee. 'He is in great trouble,' Waugh gleefully reported to Nancy Mitford:

Absolutely hates his wife whom he has taken to live in Sussex Place (telephone cut off for non payment & water too by the look of him) with Toynbee, whom he absolutely hates because he has a steady job, and Toynbee's new wife – a juvenile American typist – and Mr Somebody who is the broken hearted last husband of Blue Feet . . .

It was the beginning of April 1951, and they had been married for a little over six months.

Interlude: Parents and Daughters

Most groups of youngish people end up defining themselves by way of opposition to their parents, or at least to the generation that their parents may be thought to represent. The history of the Bright Young People is a succession of anguished stand-offs, occasionally conducted in print, more often at house parties across a no-man's-land of smashed glass, purloined brandy bottles and badly behaving guests.

With the Lost Girls this generational divide is at once more ambiguous and more intense. Nearly all of them, by their late teens, had either purposely removed themselves from family homes, been encouraged to depart, got on badly with relatives with whom circumstance forced them to live (Diana) or, in the case of the orphaned Lys, found themselves driven out into the world by sheer force of circumstance. Their relationships with the people they left behind them were correspondingly flawed. Barbara always assumed that her mother had no love for her. Janetta claimed to dislike her father, the 'bogus' Revd Woolley, adored her mother Jan but remained a victim (or so we infer) of the benign irresponsibility of a woman who allowed her teenage daughter to travel halfway across France with a man twice her age. Sonia, having flounced out of the Kensington boarding house to begin a new life among the artists' garrets of Fitzrovia, seems to have been closest to her half-brother.

Undoubtedly, amid the tart remarks and self-conscious throwings-over, a fair amount of cake was being had and eaten too. Whatever individual Lost Girls might have said, or thought, about their fathers and mothers, the family home nearly always served as a refuge when funds were low or emotional crises loomed. Barbara's progress around war-torn London was punctuated by visits to her parents' home. For all her complaints – see the letter to Janetta from January 1945 which talks about her family 'burying their disappointment' – Sonia seems to have enjoyed her Christmases *chez* Brownell. The idea that Janetta was estranged, or at any rate kept at arm's length, from her clerical father is disproved by her habit of keeping his letters and the number of appearances he makes in her wartime diaries. 'Geoff' addresses his 'darling Janetta' from camp in Pirbright in the early part of the war; he visits the house near Dorking and discusses military strategy with his son-in-law; he enquires humorously about Angela and her prospects; he sends gifts to his grandchildren (Nicky remembered an inscribed copy of *Winnie the Pooh* lying on the nursery shelf at Sussex Place: 'I think he had more to do with us than Janetta makes out.') It doesn't *sound* like a generational impasse although, naturally, such things are in the eye of the beholder.

On the other hand, the contrast between a Lost Girl and a representative of the world she had left behind was instantly apparent to disinterested observers. The biographer Jeremy Lewis, driving Barbara through Kent towards the end of her life, was suddenly made aware that he would 'shortly experience something not vouchsafed to any of her husbands, lovers or friends'. This was Barbara's sister Brenda, then resident in Hythe. Barbara's aim was to abstract a painting which she had presented to Brenda but now wished to reunite with a similar artwork owned by her god-daughter. Arriving at the house, where they lunched frugally on supermarket ham and salad, Lewis inventoried their respective dress styles. Barbara, then in her late seventies, was wearing a cowboy shirt with the top three buttons undone, skin-tight jeans and a pair of cowboy boots. Brenda ('homely, familiar and very easy to talk to') sported a maroon twin-set, a plum-coloured tweed skirt and fur-lined suede boots. The two sisters talked desultorily for a while, after which Barbara, unable to nerve herself to execute the theft, told Lewis that he was eating too slowly, got up from her chair and stalked out of the house.

12.

The Invisible Worm:
Cyril and the Women

I am very frightened and only if you made me feel you really loved me & needed me could I have the courage to marry you. For the eight years I have known you, you have been the only person in my life.

Lys, letter to Connolly,
early 1950

If anything brought the Lost Girls together, it was their relationship with Connolly and, by extension, the world through which he strode. Whether they were living with him, employed by him, pursued by him or merely wistfully regarded by him from afar, he was the fulcrum on which their existence turned. To read their correspondence – the hundreds of letters that Lys addressed to him during the eight years they were together, the dozens of earnest notes from Sonia that followed him around continental Europe in the later 1940s, the countless intimations of reproachful regret filed by Diana after the end of their love affair – is instantly to become aware of something that can only be described as a collective obsession, a grand, communal passion sweeping up half-a-dozen individual consciousnesses in its net.

To begin with, there is the fervour of their salutations – 'Dearest Cyril' (Sonia), 'Darling Love' (Lys), 'Darling Strident Squeaking Mouse' (Diana), 'Darling Squiggie' (Lys), 'Darling Moobly' (Diana), so many pet-names and terms of endearment that it would take a wall-chart to track their progress. Then there is the terrible self-abnegation of their gratitude. It is not simply that all those present are fixated on the man at the desk in Lansdowne Terrace or Bedford Square, but that they seem to be in a state of permanent thankfulness. They are grateful for the gifts sent to gloomy sickbeds, the 'delicious limes and grapes which have just arrived' (Diana). They are grateful for his morale-boosting regard. ('Thank you again, dearest Cyril, for being so wonderful to me', as Sonia once guilelessly put it.) They are grateful that he acknowledges their existence, still more that he recognises their abilities. ('I am very glad you liked the review,' Diana once assured him. 'It has given me a feeling that perhaps I am not so half-witted as you have sometimes thought.') Even when relationships are going badly or trouble is in the air they are missing him profoundly, longing to see him, pining for his shadow in the doorway, sending 'love, love Sonia', 'love from Lysie' or 'love and kisses from Diana.'

What did Darling Strident Squeaking Mouse make of this ceaseless gush of admiration and flattery? Did he calmly accept it as his due? Or did he sometimes pause to marvel at the extraordinary regard in which he was held by a group of beautiful young women who were prepared to go to almost any length to conciliate him and keep him by their side? Certainly, the Lost Girls' devotion to Cyril's health, wellbeing and mental equilibrium is practically fathomless in its intensity. Should he be engaged on cultural pursuits abroad they are there to encourage and console. ('Have a lovely wonderful time and eat a whole grapefruit for breakfast and do write and say which of all the writers you like and everything.') Should he desire some entertainment to be arranged on his behalf, a postcard will wing in to offer help. ('I suggest we have a kind of upstairs sit-down buffet supper at 9 p.m. I will bring the food.') Requests for information are instantly attended to. ('Harris has just had your message . . . So I am writing at once to tell you all the news.') Sonia's letters sent to him from the *Horizon* office are extraordinary documents, straining for approval in every sentence, in which no detail of pagination or print order is too trivial to be omitted. The slightest hint of illness – a cough, the onset of a cold – has them clamouring to hear of his symptoms, counsel rest, relaxation or recommend expert help primed to effect a cure. ('Why don't you try Mr Neal for fibrositis?') On one level, Lys, Diana, Sonia and the others are lovers, editorial assistants and concerned friends, but there is sometimes an irresistible temptation to see them as nursery maids with a vigilant eye trained on the pudgy figure hanging over the playpen rail.

One mark of the esteem in which Connolly was held is his infallibility. Even in extremis, he can do no wrong, and excuses will nearly always be found for bad behaviour or the paralysing attacks of wistfulness and self-absorbed forward planning to which he was perennially subject. The remarkable thing about the letters Lys wrote to him when their relationship was breaking down is how often she apologises for something – for leaving him ('Please forgive me for going away'), for disturbing his domestic arrangements, for having the temerity to be seen with someone else when Connolly is stalking her ('It must have been painful when you were watching from the street to see Andrew with me in the office, but you did say you were not jealous about him'). Whatever he says goes, and the most fanciful exercises in selfishness and destiny-broking are meekly encouraged: 'You are quite right to live intensely for the next ten years, welcoming every pleasure and new experience that comes your way. That will leave you the best years of your life for creative work.' The Lost Girl may have been traduced, insulted, deserted or abandoned for somebody else, but Cyril's point of view is invariably the one that counts: 'I am not blaming you,' Diana reassured him, after he had gone back to his wife, 'It is quite understandable that you should prefer Jean's assets and drawbacks to my assets and drawbacks.'

Such are the depths of the emotional investment that the Lost Girls have made in Connolly that nearly all his ill-treatment has to be underplayed. 'It is unreasonable to want back a person "who has bored you for eight years." Why not find someone who doesn't bore you?' Lys tentatively suggested sometime in 1950. It was worse than unreasonable, but Connolly's callousness was something Lys could rarely bring herself to admit. And yet as the instances of deceit and the high-handedness pile up, there is a sense that Connolly is being found out, that his girlfriends and his helpmeets are beginning to take the measure of some of the emotional patterns on which his life is based and not liking what they reveal. A particular annoyance was the sight of Connolly established in one relationship but unable to stop himself from making injurious comparisons with the relationships that had preceded it, often to the point of making lists which exposed his current love's inadequacies when set against the glory of a rapidly receding past. Diana wrote him a furious letter in response to some remarks comparing her with Jean and Lys:

> You have the tact of an elephant a rhinoceros a mole. You write a long description of all the things Lys does to make you happy . . . You talk as though I did not cook a meal for you at Thatched C[ottage] – instead of breakfast lunch tea dinner for 2 months. You say she 'enjoys it' – Well I did NOT enjoy doing it for you after a time but I DID enjoy doing it for Peter W. Why? Because he helped & was considerate of backache. I broke my pelvis – remember?

There follows a highly sarcastic summary of all the ways in which Diana imagines herself to have fallen short of Connolly's ideal, tailed by a bitter acknowledgement of the reasons that will always stop her from returning to him:

> You can't have everything so don't harp on other people's good qualities, harp on mine if you want me which I really & truly

doubt. I cannot face it – if I lived with you I should be told how Lys cooked you breakfast how Jean was a wonderful tart in bed ALL OVER AGAIN. You are doing it all over again, making me feel unwanted. If you had really been clever & wanted me to live with you, you would have written me love letters, you would not set up another menage & then expect me to be faithful.

To tactlessness could be added the charge of self-destructiveness, an assumption that no relationship was really worthwhile unless it hung teetering on the edge of a precipice, an unconquerable urge to subject any liaison of which he was a part to more emotional pressure than it could stand, whatever the consequences for the people caught up in it. 'I now see that I set myself an impossible task,' Lys once informed him. 'You seem to have an "invisible worm" inside you which compels you not only to destroy your own happiness but also the happiness of anyone who loves you.'

No less irksome, perhaps, were Connolly's double standards and his hypocrisy, failings to which Lys and Diana's letters return with a kind of homing instinct. Why, they wondered, were they expected to be faithful to him when he never reciprocated the compliment? And why did he expect this faithfulness to be maintained even when he had moved on to someone else? Lys offered a particularly anguished account of Connolly's inadequacies in this department: 'It is wrong of you to try & make me equally responsible for the failure of our "marriage." I only left you after the most blatant infidelity on your part, whereas I was faithful to you for a whole 8 years with only one exception . . . & that occurred when you had thrown me into despair by your behaviour towards me'.

Diana, too, files some withering remarks about Cyril's keenness on having his cake and eating it. All very well, she informs him, to complain about her brief liaison with Lucian Freud, 'BUT please remember that you have never been faithful to me & it is too absurd that you should tick me off for Lucian when at that very moment you were having Jean!' Cyril, she tells him, can count her out. 'I will not be faithful, I want love too.'

And so, over the years, it goes on: a groaning catalogue of reproach, recrimination and regret in which fury at the way Cyril has behaved is nearly always tempered by an awareness of the dreadful conse-quences of letting him go and then recharged by a consciousness of moral rectitude. The girls know that they are 'better' than Cyril, more trustworthy, more reliable, more selfless, more kind and yet, even when the door of the flat closes behind them and the cab lies waiting in the street, they are still anxious to give him the benefit of the doubt, to find explanations for his behaviour, to acknowledge, even amid their own misery, that his interests – and his success – are what mat-ters. Part of this stems from their belief in his genius, the thought that romantic disappointment is as nothing compared to the prospect of Cyril writing a masterpiece. 'I do think it's very important whom you marry,' Lys instructed him, not long after he had left her for Barbara, 'if only from the point of view of your writing.' And why so? 'If you marry someone who keeps you in a state of ferment and anxiety, you will not have the necessary calm when it comes to the time that you want to write. Your work is really more important than any woman'.

Ultimately, Lost Girl anger at Cyril will always be replaced by a kind of self-abasing resignation, an acceptance that this is how the world works, that however hard they laboured the effort will have been insufficient. 'I will always fall short in some ways,' Diana told him, 'even if I tried like I tried. When we first went to Paris, you were dissatisfied then . . . But I behaved badly I know because instead of going on trying I gave up.' Lys's letters strike exactly the same note ('You must not forget that I tried really hard and that I weathered your pining for the ghosts'), constantly dwell on her 'struggles', her unavailing attempts to calibrate her responses to whatever happened to be going on in Connolly's head, a battle that could never be won if only because of the constant realignments of the army drawn up on the other side.

But there was another imbalance that separated Connolly from most of the women to whom he paid court in the 1940s. This might be defined as the contrast between their expectations. The girls want comparatively little – a home, security, a man to love and be loved by in return, with the proviso, as Diana once put it, that the man should love them 'more than they love anyone else'. Connolly, on the other hand, wants everything: autonomy, the freedom to come and go, to vacillate between one love and another, to keep his options open whatever the nature of the ties that supposedly bind him, to procrastinate endlessly about where his true loyalties lie, to compile another of the incriminating lists in which girl a is informed quite how prodigiously she falls short when compared to girl b or even girl c who preceded them both. One sometimes feels that Connolly could only have been happy if he had managed to create a kind of composite being made up of all the women he had known in the previous ten years, all of whose disagreeable qualities had mysteriously disappeared to leave an exceptionally beautiful playmate with the wit of Madame de Staël and the culinary skills of Elizabeth David.

If no such paragon ever declared herself, then the women who made do as substitutes would nearly always compound the bad hand that circumstance had played them by dint of their humility. Deep down they suspect that resistance is futile, that Cyril knows best, that even in the depths of their despair his are the sensibilities that matter most, that in the last resort they are not worthy of his regard. Lys's letters are full of this terrible, self-lacerating doubt.

I know I shall never find anybody else like you again. It is unlikely that I shall ever love anybody as much – but I am no good to you, conscious of my inadequacy, and this makes me nervous and gauche. You should have a self-confident companion.

I have no wish for revenge, darling, nor do I put the blame for the failure of our relationship on you.

It is because I am convinced that you will be better off without me that I am making this great effort to detach myself.

As for that process of detachment, no one took longer to conclude a relationship than Cyril. Rather than coming to an abrupt halt, his love affairs stutter on, waver and stop only to be diffidently renewed and then, in their death throes, agonised over for months on end. You suspect that, as well as being cast down by this constant re-evaluation of motive and desire, Cyril also took pleasure in it, that his reluctance to let go of a significant other was a species of game-playing, full of anxiety and disquiet but also capable of affording him an odd kind of emotional satisfaction. His separation from Lys, for example, went through at least half-a-dozen individual phases, and even in the months before his marriage to Barbara he seems convinced that he can have her back if only he truly wants it. But Lys, by this time, was beyond persuading. Or rather, not *quite*. Of the countless letters she addressed to Connolly through the latter part of 1949 and the early part of 1950, perhaps the saddest was written from Orthez sometime in the spring: 'You are the only person I love – I cannot "beg you to take me back" because I only left you when my spirit was completely broken by your passionate affairs with "destroyers."' Lys goes on to assure him that 'If you will only stop blaming me and see things as they are we can make a fresh start.' But the effort will have to come from Connolly: 'As my feelings for you have never wavered – and yours for me have – then surely we can only come together again if you are able to convince me that, after all, I mean more to you than Barbara etc. If I don't then it would be much better for us to live as if the other were dead.' He will not find it easy to replace her, she warns. 'But I would rather live alone than relive the last two years.' There follows the usual note of self-deprecation: 'I know this kind of letter is a bore, but I feel I must explain all this – and now I need never refer to it again.'

Ironically, at the time this was written Connolly was reconnoitring his way around the one woman who at this stage in his career seems to have been able to deal with him. Holed up in the Kentish countryside with a companion who remained resolutely unimpressed by his posturings and his wistful romantic dreams, the plump, middle-aged despoiler of so many female hearts had finally met his match.

13.

Projections: The Lost Girls in Fiction

'How are you enjoying political life?'
'Like any other form of life – sheer hell.'

> Conversation between Nick Jenkins and
> Pamela Widmerpool in Anthony Powell,
> *Books Do Furnish a Room* (1971)

The twelve volumes of Anthony Powell's novel sequence, *A Dance to the Music of Time*, a vast conspectus of English life between the end of the Great War and the late 1960s, appeared between 1951 and 1975. Barbara seems to have come late to the books: at any rate there are no references to them in her letters to Powell until the early 1980s. On the other hand, when she did begin to read them she was in no doubt as to where Powell might have got his inspiration for the sullen, man-eating and terminally disaffected Pamela Widmerpool (née Flitton). 'I shall follow Pamela's fate. Does she come to a sticky end?' enquires one letter. 'I have just read *The Military Philosophers*,' runs another. 'I thought you were very subtly funny with Pamela, she gets worse, I'm told, but I do not have the sequel here. Naturally, I shall sue.'

Powell's response to this challenge was characteristically oblique. Reading the first volume of Barbara's memoirs, on their appearance in 1987, he noted that she 'makes no bones about causing trouble for its own sake, indeed resemblance to Pamela Flitton could hardly be more emphasized'. Rung up by an inquisitive journalist and asked to confirm or deny the identification he 'replied with guarded affirmative'. Years later, learning there were plans for a TV programme on the subject of 'real people' in fiction in which Barbara might appear, he conceded that it 'certainly might be funny'.

Many of the people attached to Connolly's circle in the 1940s were writers. It was inevitable that as they moved into middle age and sought to re-cast some of their experiences in fiction that the world of *Horizon*, its contending personalities and its emotional intrigue, should play a part in half-a-dozen novels that touch on the subject of literary life in wartime London and that, individually and collectively, the Lost Girls should take on a variety of incidental roles.

If Waugh, Powell and Nancy Mitford were all sharp-eyed observers of Connolly's foibles, then by far the cruellest portrait of him in action was written by a *Horizon* insider. Michael Nelson (1921–90) had worked on the magazine in the early days: *A Room in Chelsea Square*, first published anonymously in 1958, is a curious example of a novel that shoulders its way out of one cultural background into another while leaving many a trace of its original framing for the reader to puzzle over. Originally written in the late 1940s, at which point its gay themes were carefully concealed beneath a top-coat of heterosexuality, and then called *A Room in Russell Square*, *A Room in Chelsea Square* was culturally updated for the late 1950s to include faintly incongruous references to such Eden-era fads as Existentialism and Teddy boys. At the same time, no one with a working knowledge of conditions at Lansdowne Terrace could fail to spot that 'Ronnie Gras', its magazine editor, is Connolly, that 'Patrick', his rich, homosexual backer, is a bitchy caricature of Peter Watson and that several other *Horizon* mainstays are cruelly reimagined in some of the supporting parts.

Nelson himself appears as 'Nicholas', an ambitious youngster working for a provincial newspaper but anxious to make a career for himself on the London arts scene. Ronnie, alternatively, is represented as a former painter whom Patrick thinks of setting up as editor of a fashion magazine in the style of *Harper's* or *Vogue*. One of the attractions of the project to beady-eyed Patrick is that Nicholas can be employed on it. ('He would bring him to London and launch him on a career.') As a preliminary move in what is clearly intended as a campaign of seduction he gets a friend who edits a popular newspaper called the *Gladiator* to offer him a job. If any doubt remained as to Ronnie's original, it is immediately dispelled by mention of his fat and protruding stomach, his (highly successful) womanising, his status as a gourmand and wine buff, his Connolly-esque habit of spending long, meditative hours in the bath and his tendency to say things such as 'My *Angst* has been absolutely dreadful this last week.' Among many injurious comparisons, it is said of him that 'he can sniff out a bottle of champagne like one of those clever animals that can smell water hundreds of miles away'. Seeing him at dinner, Patrick is pleased to notice 'that the extraordinary creature at the head of the table with the physiognomy of an ape and a mind of the most intricate and delicate pattern, was in a large measure one of his own creations'.

While most of *A Room in Chelsea Square*'s carefully contrived plotlines come to nothing – the magazine never takes shape, Ronnie ends up supervising the *Gladiator's* women's page, Nicholas is thrown over by Patrick in favour of a good-looking shop assistant – then there is a dreadful fascination about the relationship between Ronnie and his highly attractive girlfriend, 'Lily'. Patronised and dominated by him ('Ronnie's slave girl', according to Patrick), lined up to act as his secretary when the magazine launches, Lily is thought to be 'much too beautiful for that slug Gras'. Nicholas's friend Michael wonders, 'How has someone as hideous as Ronnie managed to get hold of someone so beautiful?' There is a ghastly evening *chez* Gras which begins with Lily bounding out of the drawing room at Ronnie's call and executing drinks orders at his direction. Michael, offering to lend a hand in the kitchen, is told that Ronnie wouldn't approve. As well as officiating as secretary, Lily has also been recommended for the magazine's business side, as Ronnie imagines that her salary can be put towards his household expenses. According to Patrick, an amused spectator, 'I'm sure Michael's just the boy to lick the stamps which Lily is going to put on all those letters you're going to write.' Ronnie's final words after dinner are a condescending: 'You can lock up now, Lily. I shall go and work in the study. You needn't wait up for me. Breakfast about eleven, I think.'

The suspicion that on his journeys around Lansdowne Terrace, Nelson saw scenes like this being enacted is enhanced by an exquisitely awful moment in which Ronnie wakes up to find that Lily has placed a bunch of grapes by his bedside. Asked if she would hold them for him ('I find it so tiring to the arm'), Lily dangles them before his open mouth and then wipes his face with a napkin. At bath-time Lily wonders: would he like to play with his boats today? 'Of course. But you're not to refer to my tummy as a sandbank.' Underlying this badinage lurks the thought that Lily's personality has been squashed flat by Ronnie's treatment. When Michael contrives to sleep with her, in Patrick's flat, the experience is a sad disappointment. 'It had been like going to bed with a corpse. Every ounce of vitality must have been squeezed out of her long ago by Ronnie.' Lily's confession of her infidelity produces an even ghastlier exchange:

'You don't want to leave me?'
'Oh, no, Ronnie.'
'Then you'd better go and see about lunch. I don't know whether I shall be able to eat much. You've probably ruined my digestion. You'd better concoct some particularly light and appetizing dishes.'

By the time that *Horizon* limped to a close at the end of 1949, Evelyn Waugh and Nancy Mitford had been swapping jokes about Connolly and his entourage for nearly half a decade. 'Smarty-Smarty'; 'Smarty's Own Mag'; 'Mrs Bluefeet'; 'Mrs Barefoot': no letter exchanged between Nancy's Parisian eyrie and Waugh's Gloucestershire fastness seems to have been complete without its teasing reference to the cultural panjandrum of Bedford Square. It was not that the teasing came to a halt in the post-war era, rather that it had a different focus and was recalibrated to include fictional re-castings of Connolly as well as straightforward mockery. The most obvious aspect of the novels that Waugh and Mitford published in the decades after the war which relate in some way to *Horizon* is their sense of complicity, the thought that both writers are working from a store of allusions and jokes laid down years before, picking up batons that will be handed on again further along the track.

And so Nancy's *The Blessing* (1951) – dedicated to Waugh – seems to carry on where her letters left off. Grace, its heroine, has two suitors, one of them an Old Etonian theatrical impresario named 'Ed Spain'. Known to his friends as 'the Captain' or 'the Old Salt', Spain is described as a 'charming, lazy character', keen on his food and French wines, whose ambition is to make enough money to lead 'the life for which nature had suited him, that of a rich dilettante'. There is also a punning joke about his keen blue eyes, which 'looked as if they had been concentrated for many years on a vanishing horizon'. As a taste-maker and highly rated intellectual presence, he has accumulated a band of acolytes, 'clever young women all more or less connected and more or less in love with the Captain'. Spain calls them 'My Crew' and leaves the management of his theatre increasingly in their hands, 'a perfect arrangement for such a lazy man'. The Crew have such hifalutin names as 'Oenone', 'Ulra', 'Fiona' and 'Phaedra' and inhabit the Captain's rambling house on the river, where they do the housework, living in the attics and the cellar, 'which no servant would have tolerated for a moment, but which the clever Captain had invested with romance'. The girls themselves are punctiliously described:

They looked very much alike, and might have been a large family of sisters; their faces were partially hidden behind curtains of dusty, blonde hair, features more or less obscured from view, and they were all dressed alike in duffle coats and short trousers, with bare feet, blue and rather large, connected to unnaturally thin ankles. Their demeanour was that of an extreme sulkiness, and indeed they looked as if they might be on the verge of mutiny. But this appearance was quite misleading, the Captain had them well in hand; they hopped to it at the merest glance from him, emptying ash-trays and bringing more bottles off the ice.

As for their political views, following Waugh's earlier remarks about Connolly's 'Communist young ladies', Mitford notes that they 'could not be the clever girls they were without seeing life a little bit through Marxist spectacles'. Put to work on a communist play translated from 'some Bratislavan dialect', they sit about 'in high-necked sweaters, shorts, and bare, blue feet, their heads bowed and their faces entirely obscured by the curtain of hair'.

In *The Blessing*, Connolly masquerades as a theatre manager. In Waugh's *Unconditional Surrender* (1961), the final volume of his *Sword of Honour* trilogy, he reappears as 'Everard Spruce', who conducts a magazine named *Survival*, funded by the Ministry of Information, and lives 'in a fine house in Cheyne Walk, cared for by secretaries to the number of four'. Spruce, who wears Charvet shirts and a bow tie, is said to display 'the negligent elegance of a fashionable don'. The significance of Waugh's portrait of Spruce and his entourage lies in its deliberate echoes of Mitford's sketch. A visitor to his house remarks on the bohemian get-up of the girls.

The secretaries were dressed rather like him though in commoner materials; they wore their hair long and enveloping in a style which fifteen years later was to be associated with the King's Road. One went bare-footed as though to emphasize her servile condition.

They were sometimes spoken of as 'Spruce's veiled ladies.' They gave him their full devotion; also their rations of butter, meat and sugar.

The secretaries have names such as 'Frankie' and 'Coney'. Frankie, the bare-footed one, offers a cocktail made of South African sherry and 'Olde Falstaffe Gin' and tells one of the guests that it is a relief to meet 'a real writer instead of all these smarties Everard wastes his time on'. The *Survival* office ('a smaller room austerely, even meanly furnished') adjoins Spruce's drawing room. Here, when not engaged on domestic tasks, 'the four secretaries stoked the cultural beacon which blazed from Iceland to Adelaide; here the girl who could type answered Spruce's numerous "fan letters" and the girl who could spell corrected proofs'.

Naturally, some of the situational details are exaggerated – at no time were Lys, Sonia and Janetta all working and living together under the same roof – but there seems little doubt that Waugh and Mitford were using them as models. That Waugh, who owed Connolly many a professional debt, felt guilty about this cannibalising process is clear from a letter he wrote him shortly after *Unconditional Surrender* was published. Here Waugh professes himself 'greatly annoyed' to see that reviewers have attempted to identify *Horizon* with *Survival*.

That magazine was the creation of the Ministry of Information. *Horizon*, of course, was Watson's benefaction. It is true that you had a semi-literate socialist colleague, but he was not 'Spruce'; still less you. As for the secretaries, Lys was beautifully neat and, as I remember her, Miss Brownell was quite presentable. Some time later you had a bare footed landlady but (surely?) she had no part in *Horizon* and very little part in the delightful parties you gave. The whole identification is a fantasy.

Waugh's defence would have seemed much less disingenuous had he and Mitford not spent long years exchanging injurious gossip about Connolly framed in exactly the same language as their novels. Meanwhile, *Sword of Honour* harbours another Lost Girl, whose career Waugh follows in some detail. This is Guy Crouchback's first wife Virginia Troy, a once stylish ornament of the *beau monde*, who, by the time the insinuating Lieutenant Trimmer comes across her in a Glasgow hotel in the early part of the war, is badly on her uppers. Trimmer is aware of a woman in her early thirties, dressed in clothes that two years ago had come from a *grand couturier*, 'with all the requisites for attention, who was not trying to attract'. Virginia's latest man, she explains, has just disappeared: 'He's a sailor. I haven't known him long but I liked him. He went off quite suddenly. People are always going off suddenly nowadays, not saying where.'

How has Virginia come to be the person she is? Like Barbara, she turns out to have been seduced by a friend of her father's, 'who had looked her up, looked her over, taken her out, taken her in, from her finishing school in Paris'. There follows marriage to Guy, a second marriage to his replacement, Tommy Blackhouse, and then a succession of sugar daddies: 'London hotels, fast cars, regimental point-to-points, the looming horror of an Indian cantonment; fat Augustus with his cheque-book always handy; Mr Troy and his taste for "significant people . . ."' Only the here and now has meaning: 'It was the present moment and the next five minutes which counted with Virginia.' Later passages dwell on her feeling of isolation, the younger brother with whom she 'never got on', now dead in the war, a stepmother ('She never approved of me and I can't get at her now') living in Switzerland. It is said of her that 'Whatever the disturbances she had caused to others, her own place in her small but richly diverse world had been one of coolness, light and peace.' From the day of her marriage to Guy and desertion of Mr Troy until her meeting with Trimmer, 'she had achieved a *douceur de vivre* that was alien to her epoch; seeking nothing, accepting what came and enjoying it without compunction'. Significantly, when she dies in a doodlebug blast, it is left to Spruce to pay tribute to a life in which half-a-dozen real Lost Girl lives seem to have been gathered up: Virginia, he tells Frankie and Coney, 'was the last of twenty years' succession of heroines. The ghosts of romance who walked between the two wars.'

Waugh, Mitford and Nelson were using the Lost Girls as ammunition in their satirical war against Connolly, useful evidence in a campaign to expose what they regarded as his bogus side, his vanity, self-absorption and ability to surround himself with impressionable acolytes who lacked sufficient cultural knowledge to stop themselves from a wholesale swallowing of the Connolly myth. But there were other novels of the period in which the Lost Girl takes centre stage, ceases to be a satirical instrument and becomes something more enduring – a behavioural enigma, a psychological puzzle for the author to fret over, particularly if, as occasionally happened, the author had his own emotional scars to display.

Getting wind of Patrick Balfour's plan to write about his failed marriage, Waugh was unimpressed. 'He is trying to write a novel about Angela,' he informed Nancy early in 1948. 'It won't be any good.' Reporting back on the finished product early in 1950, he was slightly, but only slightly, more emollient. 'Poor Patrick has written a novel in praise of Angela. Quite good about her but the rest *Forsyte Saga*.' The real significance of *The Ruthless Innocent* (1949), it might be argued, lies in its back-dating. Rather than giving it a contemporary setting, Balfour emphasises his heroine's spiritual attachment to the pleasure-seeking world of the Bright Young People by placing most of the action in the period 1928–31. Like the Balfours, the Heriots are aristocratic Lowland Scots, their family prestige assured by a tyrannical grandfather. Martin, his grandson, a painter-aesthete in line to inherit the barony after his older brother's death in the Great War, has an entrée into smart bohemia by way of his interior-decorating chum 'Ozzie'. It is in Ozzie's Bruton Street shop that he first sets eyes on Angela's alter-ego, 'Sally'.

Several passages dwell on Sally's guilelessness, her apparent naivety, her stunning good looks ('Her eyes glowed with pleasure. They were large and deep and blue'), her love of such sensual diversions as lying in the sun, and her complete inability to resist an emotional impulse. Her childlike qualities are repeatedly emphasised: she is said to have a child's head on a woman's body, to talk without expression – 'it was a child's voice which has not yet developed its tone'. This air of sexy infantilism is enhanced by her ingenuous vocal style. 'It's nice and cuddly,' she observes of her white fleece coat. 'I call it my little lambkin.' Sally's early life is as rootless as her current existence and includes an unknown father, an actress mother who abandons her in childhood and a fleeting career on the stage. After coming across her at a country weekend, where, in the approved Bright Young Person manner, she has stationed herself 'under an apple-tree on the brink of the lawn, dressed as an Austrian peasant girl', Martin has no trouble in pressing his suit. 'What lovely things do happen!' Sally remarks before consenting to come and live with him in Cheyne Walk.

Simultaneously, there are family pressures at work, in the shape of Martin's parliamentary father and his stockbroking Uncle Kenneth. Sally, we swiftly infer, is not just a glamorous halfwit but a symbol of inter-generational tension. Like many a mid-century novel by an erstwhile Bright Young Man, *The Ruthless Innocent* soon declares itself as a battle between the old world and the new, between duty, heritage and the family fortune, and love, living for the moment and pleasing yourself. But Martin, however besotted by his girlfriend, drawing and painting her endlessly in the studio at Cheyne Walk ('The child's head on the woman's body, the cloudless face with its intent, still eyes, continued to fascinate him'), is ever more conscious of Sally's lack of emotional ballast. The story of their romance, consequently, is largely the story of his efforts to work out what is going on in her head. After carefully logging her relish for film magazines, her fixation on a succession of actresses whose looks she aims to replicate, her susceptibility to passing whims – learning the guitar, getting a dog – he concludes that she is a 'nomad' for whom none of the conventional rules in life apply, for whom stray impulses and fleeting attractions will always mean more than long-term plans.

One senses that Martin, like his long-suffering creator, is deeply bewildered by Sally/Angela, cannot understand why she behaves as she does or clings so desperately to a life without strings at a time when, with family money lost in the 1929 crash and Uncle Kenneth's firm enmired in scandal, his own existence is increasingly subject to upset. There is a rather ominous moment when, after their marriage and the birth of a son, Sally laments the number of relations the child will acquire: 'I'm beginning to think that relations are rather nice to have, if they're dead or you don't have to see them.' Martin demurs. For a short time the idyll continues in a Cap Ferrat villa owned by Ozzie's rich American friend Mrs Sprint. But once again the tocsin of familial obligation is clanging in the shape of Martin's Aunt Susan, who lives in the hills nearby, and a discussion as to whether the newly married couple should join her. Vagrant spirit Sally fears being tied down ('It's nice to be able to go away and know you'll never come back') and, when told that you can't always be on the move, counters with the claim that 'It's exciting not to know at all where I'll be or what I'll be doing this time next year.' Then, when Susan falls ill and Martin is summoned to her bedside, Sally allows herself to be squired off to Venice by his Uncle Geoffrey. 'Darling, darling M,' runs the letter conveying this unexpected news, 'I have *had* to go with Geoffrey. I tried very hard but simply couldn't help it . . . when something like this happens to one there's nothing else to be done, I couldn't not go with him.'

Martin's sense of bafflement is brought to boiling point by a final meeting in Paris, where – Uncle Geoffrey having been quickly thrown over – Sally arrives in the company of an Italian admirer named Giovanni. Her explanation – if explanation it is – echoes the relevant passages in Angela's memoirs, a hankering for excitement coexisting with a wish to carry on with existing arrangements: 'I feel as if I don't want a safe sort of life all the time, like before. But I feel just the same about you as I always did.' When Martin, not unreasonably, objects that 'Sally, you must know. Being unfaithful's not just something that happens to you, like having measles. It's something you decide to do or decide not to do.' Like Angela, Sally instantly returns to her default position: the ungovernable impulse, impossible to resist, in whose grip she is simply swept up and borne unhesitatingly away: 'With Geoffrey, it just seemed to happen.'

If Sally/Angela is simply unfathomable, a kind of elfin sprite wandering a lost pre-war world and mostly unaware of the havoc she causes, then the Lost Girl psychology on display in Powell's *A Dance to the Music of Time* has an altogether different focus. For Pamela Flitton, first glimpsed in *The Military Philosophers* (1968), then found contemptuously making hay of the Labour MP Kenneth Widmerpool in *Books Do Furnish a Room* (1971), and finally coming to the immensely sticky end that Barbara had predicted for her in *Temporary Kings* (1973), is not a romantic figure but a modern version of one of the Furies – brusque, vengeful and utterly uncompromising, keen on male company but determined to cause as much pain as possible. 'Giving men hell is what Miss Flitton likes,' someone shrewdly diagnoses early on in her career. A wartime boyfriend maintains that 'She's cross all the time. Bloody cross. Thrives on it. Her chief charm. Makes her wonderful in bed. That is, if you like tension.' The air of icy deliberation that she carries around with her, together with her casual attitude to sex, is confirmed by a character named Bob Duport: 'I only stuffed her once. Against a shed in the back parts of Cairo airport, but even then I could see she might drive you round the bend, if she really decided to.'

Given that *Books Do Furnish a Room* contains at least two men who are driven to distraction by Pamela's goings-on, this strikes a prophetic note. In one of the journals written in his old age, Powell notes Barbara's conviction that she 'is' Pamela, but the life into art projections of his novels are rarely straightforward. It is not that Pamela is an unvarnished portrait of Barbara; rather, that Powell mingles some of Barbara's characteristics and incidents from her life with a fair amount of invented material to produce something which, though hugely exotic, contains enough traces of the original to alert the reader to its grounding in some kind of lived existence. There is, for example, no physical resemblance. (Pamela is described as 'one of those girls with a dead white complexion and black hair'.) Neither does Pamela pursue any of Barbara's employments. When first glimpsed by *Dance*'s narrator Nick Jenkins in *The Military Philosophers*, she is an ATS driver. Although, like Barbara, she is transferred to Cairo, she ends up working for 'a secret service outfit'. Simultaneously come hints that Pamela's capacity for causing trouble is of far higher order than the dawdling siren turning up late every day at the offices of the Yugoslav government in exile. After being mixed up in 'a rather delicate situation' with some Free Poles, then withdrawn from driving duties after her car goes missing, her conquests include 'two RAF officers . . . court-martialled as a consequence of a fight about which was to drive her home after a party', a Lieutenant Commander given 'a severe reprimand' and a Treasury official who gives her a lift in his car at Richmond Station, thereby 'starting a trail of indiscretions that led to his transference to a less distinguished ministry'.

There is even a hint that her powers may be practically diabolic. When the clairvoyant Mrs Erdleigh tells her fortune one night, as the displaced residents of a block of flats gather in a basement while bombs fall overhead, even this practised overseer of female destiny is shocked: 'You must be careful, my dear . . . There are things here that surprise even me.' On the other hand, another of Pamela's distinctive features – her complete indifference to the age and status of the men she decides to fascinate – brings her closer to the early 1940s version of a Barbara who once declared that her male ideal was the thickset actor Erich von Stroheim. She is, Nick tells us, 'just as happy deranging the modest home life of a middle-aged air-raid warden, as compromising the commission of a rich and handsome guards ensign recently left school'. Then there is the matter of her procedural attack, 'the unvarying technique of silence, followed by violence, with which she persecuted her lovers'. Like Barbara, she has an infallible trick of sniffing out male weakness, picking a significant other's vulnerable spot and twisting the knife. 'You don't think I'm going to take orders from a heel like you?' she tells Odo Stevens, her escort on the night when Mrs Erdleigh examines her palm. 'You're pathetic as a lover. No good at all. You ought to see a doctor.'

What does Pamela want? An obvious answer would be power: the power to ensnare and humiliate, revenge herself on men who have failed to match her exacting standards, a category in which all members of the male sex can be thought to repose. Even if what Jenkins calls her 'iciness of manner' is a constant, then, as he acknowledges, 'there was no denying she was a striking girl to look at. Many men would find this cosmic rage with life, as it seemed to be, an added attraction.' Even the normally prudent Widmerpool, when despatched to Cairo on War Office business, is no match for her wiles: 'He managed to make a fool of himself about some girl . . . She was absolutely notorious.' Transferred – as Widmerpool's wife – to the snowbound English winter of 1946–7, the setting for *Books Do Furnish a Room*, Pamela shows an unexpected side. Her first appearance, escorted by her hapless husband, is at Thrubworth, where members of the family of Nick's wife Isobel have gathered for the funeral of her brother Erridge. But the obsequies are only a secondary consideration to the much more pressing problem of what makes Pamela tick.

Observing her at close quarters for the first time, and struck as ever by the 'pent-up sullen beauty', Nick tries to establish what marks Pamela out as more than just a beautiful girl. Perhaps, he muses, it lies in 'her absolute self-confidence, her manner of expressing without words that to be present at all was a condescension'. There is a revealing scene in which, feeling ill during the service and retiring to the house, she chatters tersely to Nick: 'Are Kenneth and those other sods on their way here? The Kraut got me some tea.' Nick looks on as Siegfried, the German prisoner of war employed at Thrubworth, and the deceased's Uncle Alfred stand staring at her, 'expressing in their individual and contrasted ways boundless silent admiration. Her contempt for both of them was absolute. It seemed only to stimulate more fervent worship.'

There is a final *pièce de résistance* when, taking ill again on her way out of the house, Pamela is violently sick into an antique Chinese vase. Is she pregnant, somebody wonders. Nick decides not: 'I think it was just rage.' Much of the novel, established in the literary London of the immediate post-war era, takes in the founding of a literary magazine called *Fission* – much more left-wing and 'committed' than *Horizon* – and it is here that Pamela comes into her own, extending her reputation for extreme bad behaviour yet revealing some hitherto unsuspected artistic interests. Again, Powell can be found elaborating the scope of a landscape he had observed at close hand in the late 1940s for the purposes of fiction. One of *Fission*'s contributors is the writer 'X. Trapnel', transparently a version of the dandy-novelist Julian Maclaren-Ross, who was one of Connolly's early discoveries. The particular object of Maclaren-Ross's desire among the *Horizon* staff was Sonia, so much so that Maclaren-Ross was eventually banned from the office. Here, Trapnel confesses to Nick that he is in love with Pamela: 'I'm mad about her. I'd do anything to see her again.' Arriving at the Widmerpools' flat one night, Nick discovers that Trapnel and Pamela have eloped together.

Again, Nick struggles to understand Pamela's motivation. Why has she gone off with the deeply unreliable and narcissistic Trapnel? Why, if it comes to that, did she marry the vainglorious and self-obsessed Widmerpool? The only explanation he can find – practically cosmic in its implications – is that 'She had done it, so to speak, in order to run away with Trapnel'. These 'two unique specimens' – husband and lover – 'as it were brought into collision, promised anarchic extremities of feeling of the kind at which she aimed, in which she was principally at home.' All this, naturally, returns us to Barbara and her dealings with Quennell: 'I *like* things to be difficult.' But Pamela, we soon discover, regards her relationship with Trapnel as far more than a means of taunting her husband. Holed up with her paramour in a dingy flat in Maida Vale, she takes a keen but critical interest in his work-in-progress, a novel entitled *Profiles in String*, informing Nick, who chances upon them there, that she is 'not satisfied' with its merits. Neither, it turns out, is she satisfied with Trapnel. Coming back along the towpath of the Regent's Park Canal from the pub in which Trapnel reveals that she has abandoned him, Nick and his friend Bagshaw stumble upon the evidence of her parting shot: the pages of *Profiles in String* floating in the water.

Powell is not quite done with Pamela. In *Temporary Kings*, still married to Widmerpool and still giving off that 'instant warning of general hostility to all comers that her personality automatically projected', she turns up at a cultural conference in Venice in the company of an American publisher named Louis Glober. By now the aura of notoriety that envelops her has darkened to include necrophile involvement in the death of a French intellectual named Ferrand-Seneschal ('the implication is that she was in bed with this Frenchman after he was dead'); her own death, in equally doubtful circumstances, is not far off. By this stage Pamela has lost her grounding in Barbara's comparatively modest exploits of the 1940s and become something not far short of a figure in classical mythology, a kind of elemental force, malign and unappeasable, beholden to no one but herself.

If Barbara's appearance in *A Dance to the Music of Time* involves the application of almost infinite layers of malevolence, not to mention some coruscating special effects, then Sonia's part seems much closer to her real life function at *Horizon*. In *Books Do Furnish a Room*, she can be identified as 'Ada Leintwardine', a doctor's daughter said to be 'keen on making a career in . . . the world of letters', and employed as secretary to Sillery, the elderly and intrigue-ridden Oxford don. Ada, as Nick describes her, is 'in her twenties, fair, with a high colour, a shade on the plump side, though only enough to suggest changes in the female figure then pending'. Capable, industrious, with a faintly bossy side, Ada moves on to work at Quiggin & Craggs, the publishers of *Fission*, where she rapidly wins golden opinions. As Bagshaw remarks, echoing what was said about Sonia in *Horizon*'s last years, 'Ada's the king-pin of the whole organisation. Maybe I should say queen bee. She provides an oasis of good looks in the office, and a few contacts with writers not sunk in middle age.' But while Ada is only a minor attendant on *Dance*'s thronged and constantly evolving cast, there is another novel – possibly the most famous work ever produced by one of Connolly's satellites – in which Sonia is always supposed to play a starring role. This is Orwell's *Nineteen Eighty-Four*, published a bare four months before she became the second Mrs Orwell in October 1949.

To Hilary Spurling, her biographer, Sonia is transparently 'Julia', the 'girl from the fiction department', who spends her working hours in a government office helping to produce pornography for impressionable proles and her leisure hours conducting a doomed affair with Winston Smith. Anxious to begin on the novel's second draft after a hard winter's journalism, Orwell, according to Spurling, returned to Jura in the spring of 1947 with the aim of 'recreating' Sonia as Julia and a determination to 'take her as his model'. Certainly, Sonia would have been in Orwell's mind at the time he resumed work on *Nineteen Eighty-Four*: why else would he have invited her to visit him? Watching her enter the room in which the two-minute hate is being staged, Winston sees

> a bold-looking girl of about twenty-seven, with thick dark hair, a freckled face and swift, athletic movements. A narrow scarlet sash, emblem of the Junior Anti-Sex League, was wound several times round the waist of her overalls, just tightly enough to bring out the shapeliness of her hips.

In fact, Julia's age is later given as twenty-six (Sonia, by the time that Orwell invited her to Jura, was twenty-eight). Much is made of the contrast between her youthful zest and Winston's advancing decrepitude: 'I'm thirty-nine years old. I've got a wife that I can't get rid of. I've got varicose veins. I've got five false teeth.' Orwell, at the time he first asked Sonia to marry him, would have been forty-three. Later on, Winston notes that 'Except for her mouth, you could not have called her beautiful.' Like Sonia, she has a forceful demeanour, is said to 'burst' into rooms, and has a briskly assertive vocal style that stops only just short of bossiness: 'I do voluntary work three days a week for the Junior Anti-Sex League. Hours and hours I've spent pasting their bloody rot all over London. I always carry one end of the banner in the processions. I always look cheerful and I never shirk anything.' Unlike Sonia, she is resolutely unintellectual, 'didn't care much for reading' and falls asleep while being entertained with selections from Emmanuel Goldstein's critique of the Oceanian regime, *The Theory and Practice of Oligarchical Collectivism*.

There are circumstantial factors, too, which might call this identification into question. One is that Orwell had started thinking about *Nineteen Eighty-Four* well before his re-encounter with Sonia in 1946. Another is that he had asked several other women to marry him at this time: it might equally be the memory of Anne Popham or Celia Paget that he carried back with him to Jura. A third is that, with the exception of Winston's opening remarks and one or two speculations about Julia's interior life ('She was very young, he thought, she still expected something from life . . . She would not accept it as a law of nature that the individual is always defeated . . . She did not understand that there was no such thing as happiness, that the only victory lay in the far future, long after you were dead'), we learn very little about her, how she operates as a human being and what goes on in her mind. However attractive to ageing, moth-eaten Winston, there is a way in which she is more important for what she symbolises – youth, rebellion, free-spiritedness – than for what she actually is.

To Spurling, Sonia is not merely a physical presence in *Nineteen Eighty-Four*; she is also a decisive influence on its intellectual framework. In July 1946, for example, she wrote a long *Horizon* review of *Les amitiés particulières*, a novel by the French writer Roger Peyrefitte which turns on the friendship between two boys at a Catholic boarding school. The book reawakened all Sonia's hostile memories of her own upbringing, and the strategies of treachery, betrayal and what Orwell would have called 'doublethink' that she imagined to lie at Catholicism's heart:

> When you have seen through [this] world you can never become its victim, but can fight it with the only unanswerable weapon – cynical despair; when you have learned the lesson of the double vision, action and emotion are equally meaningless. This is the heritage of Catholic education . . . one which those who went to Catholic schools always recognize in each other, members of a secret society who, when they meet, huddle together, temporarily at truce with the rest of the world, while they cautiously, untrustingly, lick each other's wound.

While there is no proof that Orwell ever read the issue of *Horizon* in which this appeared, Spurling thinks it 'hard to write off as coincidence the fact that, at the very moment when he started work on *Nineteen Eighty-Four*, his ex-mistress outlined in print precisely the scenario that would become the central section of his plot'.

Certainly, *Nineteen Eighty-Four* was properly begun no more than a month after these lines were written (Orwell told his friend George Woodcock in August 1946 that he had 'just started' another novel). And certainly, whether Orwell read it or not, there is a clear connection between the 'double vision' and 'doublethink'. On the other hand, a trawl through the journalism Orwell was writing in the period 1944–6 suggests that the possibility of a link between the Christian Church and secular dictatorships had been exercising his imagination for at least two years. One might note his unpublished review of Harold Laski's *Faith, Reason and Civilisation*, written for the *Manchester Evening News* in March 1944 but rejected, or so Orwell assumed, for its 'anti-Stalin implications'. Laski's book is an attempt to square his belief in democracy and freedom of thought with his conviction that the highly authoritarian Soviet Union is 'the real dynamo of the Socialist movement in this country and everywhere else'. According to Orwell, Laski does this by drawing an analogy between the USSR and Christianity in the period of the break-up of the Roman Empire; Soviet socialism 'aims at the establishment of human brotherhood and equality just as single-mindedly as the early church aimed at the establishment of the Kingdom of God'.

In the end, Orwell rejects Laski's analogy as false, but there are several other meditations of this kind in the journalism he produced towards the end of the Second World War, and his attempts to equate religious faith with left- and right-wing forms of autocracy go at least as far back as 1938. Meanwhile, there is another reason for wondering if, in the end, the girl in the fiction department is the girl in the *Horizon* office. O'Brien, the member of the Inner Party whom Winston believes to be his saviour, is ultimately revealed as an *agent provocateur*; Winston's rebellion against Big Brother is a put-up job; there is at least a suspicion that Julia is O'Brien's willing accomplice, primed to entice Winston into a net of subterfuge whose eventual consequence will be his re-education at the hands of the Thought Police. If *Nineteen Eighty-Four* is a love letter from Jura to a girl left behind in London, then one of its overriding messages is that in the end the people we love will betray us.

Interlude: Barbara's Style

Dear Tony,

Thank you very much for taking the trouble to write and say you enjoyed the book. I read your letter just after running into Peter Quennell on the train, who was so depressingly evasive and po-faced that I anticipated nothing but further scathing and shocked reactions, and was very consoled and pleased indeed by your enthusiasm.

> Barbara to Anthony Powell, shortly after publication of
> *A Young Girl's Touch*

Barbara published five books in her lifetime: *A Young Girl's Touch* (1956); a volume of short stories primed by her experiences in America entitled *Born Losers* (1965); and two volumes of memoirs, *Tears Before Bedtime* (1987) and *Weep No More* (1989). A second novel, *A Love Match* (1969) perished at the hands of the libel lawyers – the litigants were her old supporter John Sutro and his wife Gillian – and was eventually withdrawn from sale. Literary friends occasionally complained that her efforts were marked by laziness, that age-old amateur reluctance to do justice to promising material. 'As with so many female writers with a touch of talent, she will not take sufficient

307

pains', Anthony Powell rather testily pronounced. On the other hand, it could be argued that this tendency to throw the words down any old how is what gives her writing its kick, the breezy impressionism of the style made all the more compelling by the hint of darker things beneath. In *A Young Girl's Touch*, Melinda takes a train to Teddington, where she eavesdrops on a pair of fellow travellers loudly conversing across the carriage:

'My husband's lost all his money in this war,' said one of the women. 'Nearly all,' she added, flashing a square-cut diamond. 'He's really very hit. What with no supplies . . .'
    'My husband lost all his money in Austria before de war.'
    'This war . . . ?'
    'You know what it means, Gestapo? De English people have no idea what they're like. If a Gestapo man he sees your coat and he likes . . . well.'

Comically pointed – note the contrast between the feigned deprivation of the woman with the square-cut diamond and the genuine predicament of the Austrian émigré stripped back to its bones – the dialogue also strikes an oddly sinister note: two middle-aged housewives chatting on a train, maybe, but with all the horrors of pre-war *mitteleuropa* welling up beneath the tracks. When the Austrian woman, staring from the window, declares that 'I like life . . . In the morning there come de birds to pick up der crumbs. And the baker he comes with de bread. And look at de river. Lovely, isn't so?' the reader is likely to be pulled up short by the realisation that wartime London, with its ration cards and piled rubble, is a kind of Elysian field compared to Anschluss-era Vienna. Or there is her description of 'Roger' (possibly based on Quennell), one of Melinda's countless boyfriends, reduced to silent anguish by her bad behaviour and refusal to turn up on time:

Roger had spent over an hour pacing the station. At first he had been very worried, but, after experiencing similar treatment on a previous occasion, he realized that she had wished to ditch him. He had been through a severe crisis and was beginning to feel the better for it. Convinced that he was thoroughly hardened and that nothing she did now could affect him, he soon repented of his decision. Pacing his father's study Roger suffered conflicting emotions. In the course of the last ten years he had fallen for a number of girls but always at some point they were the infatuated ones and he it was who backed out.

Clearly Barbara had been reading Powell's early novels, not to mention Nancy Mitford, whose deadpan tone she faithfully reproduces. The Mitford connection, in particular, is worth pursuing. Evelyn Waugh once wrote of Nancy that she belonged to the category of the mid-twentieth-century English writer 'who can write but cannot think'. By this Waugh meant that his friend's considerable intelligence was largely home-grown, denied the benefit of a proper education and to a certain degree instinctive. 'She is purely idiosyncratic,' he pronounced, 'a survival of the time when it was thought feminine to be capricious.' Growing up in the years before girls of upper-class families went to university, 'her syntax is shaky. But her essential quality is that she can write.' Much the same can be said of Barbara, whose astringent, high-visibility prose has exactly the same inconsistency that Waugh detected in the author of *The Pursuit of Love* but tends to redeem itself in sheer high spirits.

But there is something else boiling away in *A Young Girl's Touch*, a stealthy undercurrent of irony, which simultaneously mocks the exasperated Roger with his 'severe crisis' and his conviction that he is 'thoroughly hardened' to Melinda's wiles, while quietly sympathising with his inability to commit himself. 'Squinting and puzzled, staring into the Empire mirror, heedless of his sticking out ears and dimples, he wondered why it was that he should be so obsessed by Melinda.' The answer, it turns out, is threefold. Not only is Melinda 'remarkably pretty', but to add to the fact that 'one never quite knew what went on in her head' is the question of her indifference to him. Roger's real problem, alas, is that he is not up to his inamorata's fighting weight, that her attentions to him will always verge on the perfunctory, that she can take him or leave him, whatever his own feelings about being left.

What inspired Barbara to pick up a pen in the first place? To a genuine desire to explore some of the emotional complications of the world she was a part of can be added a straightforward wish to settle scores. If Quennell got off comparatively lightly, then other old friends were not so fortunate. 'In this book two of the characters are portrayed in such a way as to have led a number of readers to identify them with the Sutros', the plaintiffs' QC insisted when *A Love Match* came to court. 'Shameful behaviour on the part of the two characters is described, which as far as Mr and Mrs Sutro are concerned is completely without justification.' Mr Justice Thesiger agreed: damages were paid and surviving copies disposed of. But for sustained, score-settling bitchiness, the memoirs are in a class of their own, not least for their portrait of vainglorious, layabout, sheet-chewing Cyril. At one point Connolly is pictured lying in recumbent misery with the bedclothes seeming to spew out of his mouth 'like ectoplasm'. At another, a domestic crisis threatens to derail his social plans.

Still delicious blazing hot weather. Cyril has a lunch in London, so I take him into Ashford to catch the train. As usual, the stove is blocked and not drawing sufficiently to make hot water. Have to boil kettles to add to bath. A few drops of boiling water fell onto scowl-jowl-face's Chinese coolie legs which he had dangling over the side of the bath; fearful abuse. Both part at the station delighted to see the last of each other.

Or there is Barbara's account of the grand party, attended by Princess Margaret, to which husband and wife were invited in December 1951, an extraordinary comic set piece in which amusement and straightforward contempt both play their part. Grimly aware that more fuss is being made about Cyril than herself, she rushes up to him at the moment when he is being 'hustled away to the Royal Dwarf's table' and screams, 'It's no good turning your back on me.' She tries to talk to an unresponsive Lucian Freud, who is swiftly dragged off to safer havens by Lady Rothermere. Excluded and distressed, Barbara finds a chair and, sitting down with a glass in her hand, announces to the room at large that 'There's only one thing to do. Get drunk.' Later Cyril and his friends return from supper: 'They all emerge with a healthy tan, the acclaimed heroes of a Shackleton expedition, and mingle with the throwouts. I turn on Cyril, but we are interrupted by Orson Welles, so I try to be offensive to him but he doesn't notice.' The evening ends with a glimpse of Quennell making eyes at Lady Elizabeth von Hofmannsthal. His 'puce-tinted face was trying to express ardency,' Barbara savagely concluded, 'but he seemed to me to be just a dreary old zombie putting on airs.'

What did Barbara hope to achieve by these high-octane displays of temperament? Nothing, probably, rather than the adrenalin rush of a slight avenged. But if there is something rather impressive about her complete disregard for what people might think of her – one of her most mystifying tricks as a memoirist is to spin out stories that present her in a bad light – then there is no getting away from the deep-rooted vulnerability, the sense common to nearly every account of her in no-holds-barred, man-quelling action that here is someone who not only makes life harder for herself with each self-protecting twist of her personality but who knows it as well. And while the merits of her books can be overstated, she remains a classic example of the woman writer inhibited by the company she keeps – a genuine stylist who deserves to be taken out of the context of the world in which she was compelled to operate and given something rarely allowed her by her teeming horde of male associates: a life of her own.

14.

Afterwards

I thought the demise of Horizon would make some changes for all concerned. It is not a bad thing, I think. It must be a relief for Cyril who can now become more himself which in a sense Horizon (more especially you and myself) was preventing.

Peter Watson, letter to Sonia, 4 January 1950

The first Lost Girl to detach herself from the life of literary London, and indeed from Connolly's orbit, was Lys. By the spring of 1950 she had moved out of Sussex Place to temporary lodgings at Sonia's flat in Percy Street and accepted a job as editorial assistant in the London office of the *New Yorker*. Already there were more ambitious plans afoot, in particular a move across the Atlantic. Peter Watson, writing to her late in April, noted that he is 'worried in case I was wrong to advise you not to go to the States. At certain moments any change can be a good thing in one's life but in one way the struggle for life is far worse out there than it is in Europe.' But the strain of presiding over *Horizon*'s last rites and the emotional struggles with Connolly had seriously affected her health. Early in April, underweight and exhausted, she left London for a recuperative holiday with her friend Lauretta Hugo at the Château Bellevue in Orthez. Here in the warmth of Gascony she spent most of her time gardening, pausing, she informed Sonia, only to 'read, eat, drink and sleep – I think I am getting a little fatter and certainly look better'. If Lys had thought that by leaving both his house and his place of work she could separate herself from Connolly, she was sadly mistaken. Though by now deeply embroiled with Barbara, the ex-editor was still busy constructing castles in the air. According to Watson, shortly before he left for a stay in Paris, 'Cyril asked me . . . should he marry Lys?'

But Lys, by this time, was beyond marrying. Watson had tried to dissuade her from relocating to America on the grounds, he told Sonia, that 'she will spend so much money getting there and on a New York hotel and she doesn't have a definite job or even many friends there. It would surely be a mistake?' Such reports that reached Connolly of the new life she was establishing for herself among the local society hostesses while working as an editor at Doubleday were calculated to make him seethe with envy: 'Lys has been adopted by Alice Obolensky and given a suite at the Regis (2nd best hotel in New York),' Evelyn Waugh informed Nancy Mitford in April 1951. 'That makes it much worse for him.' For several years afterwards, Connolly continued to bombard his lost love with letters of fervent devotion and elegiac reproach. 'The other night I had a sudden vision of you walking towards me along the edge of the pavement in the brown coat I bought you with the velvet collar and a yellow scarf round your head,' he told her in 1953, 'it was not a dream but like a shot in a film sequence. Ever since I have tried to start this film going again but with no success.'

Tokens of esteem, as well as letters, sped westward across the Atlantic. Waugh, sending news to Nancy in the spring of 1954 of a 'very happy day in London with Cyril Boots', reported that he 'bought a silver knife, fork and spoon in a leather case to send to Lys. Poignant.' Whatever Lys may have thought of these gifts, she was determined not to repeat the mistakes of the previous decade, and in 1956 married a Duke University psychologist named Dr Sigmund Koch. Stephen Spender, who met the couple at a party in London six years later, was unimpressed. 'Dr Koch is bearded, has a carved-wooden semitic profile, a smirking expression and a very loud voice. He called everybody "old boy" which he seems to think the right therapeutic approach to the English.' Subsequently, he got drunk and embarked on a series of imitations of English speech in which he delivered attacks on English food. Lys, Spender thought, was 'just as silly as 25 years ago' and 'told interminable stories at dinner about uncles and aunts all of which were to illustrate her new attitude to England derived from Sigmund K.'

Subsequently Lys vanished from the literary world, ceased to write to old English companions and devoted herself entirely to domestic life. Beginning work on *Friends of Promise*, his study of Connolly and the *Horizon* circle in the early 1980s, the academic Michael Shelden was told by one source that she had died years ago, and by another that she had disappeared into the rural wilderness of North Carolina, unreachable by post or telephone. Eventually, and with the help of Spender, Shelden tracked her down to the University of Boston, where her husband now held a professorial post. Visiting her home in the Boston suburbs in the autumn of 1984 and remembering the celebrated portrait by Lee Miller, Shelden was shocked to find 'all that beauty had gone. Her complexion was pasty, her eyes dull. She was wearing a shapeless pants suit made of dark green fabric, and she spent a lot of time pushing back the sleeves, which were too long.' The contrast between her present existence and the life she had led in Bedford Square were further emphasised by a trip to the local grocery store where, as Shelden watched the cashier ring up the items Lys had purchased for their dinner, he thought 'how commonplace she looked in these surroundings'.

After the evening meal had been eaten, and encouraged by her guest, Lys descended to the basement and returned at intervals with handfuls of Connolly's letters. 'She did this several times, and each time I could see that she had been crying . . .' Shelden recalled. 'There was no mistaking the pain it caused her to read those letters again.'

Lys died in 1989, three months after the publication of *Friends of Promise*. 'Well, I've had my seventieth birthday,' she told Shelden in their final telephone conversation, 'which is something, don't you think, in this polluted world of ours? I mean, just to live that long.'

The patterns of Janetta's post-war career may be followed in Frances Partridge's diaries. A daughter, named Georgiana, was born in 1949, but by the early summer of the following year Frances had begun to suspect that the marriage was in trouble. When the Kees paid a weekend visit in May 1950, Frances noted 'certain symptoms . . . that have revived a buried disquiet. Why aren't they happier, I wonder?' To the chatelaine of Ham Spray the problem seemed to lie in Robert Kee's constant criticism of his wife and her reluctance to defend herself. 'This ghost train running along old railway lines is very disturbing,' Frances concluded. 'If Robert goes on writing down her character she will go off with someone who thinks her wonderful, and there are plenty who will.'

This was a prophetic remark. In London in the summer of 1949, Janetta had been introduced to the mercurial figure of Derek Jackson. A brilliant physicist, who combined a private fortune with an overbearing personal manner, Jackson held political views so extreme that during the Second World War, in which he served with distinction in the RAF, he was very nearly lynched by the members of a bomber crew to whom he had suggested that they were fighting 'against the wrong enemy'. At this point Jackson, married to his second wife, Pamela Mitford, was living the somewhat peripatetic life of a tax exile. By September 1950 Frances reported that the Kees' marriage had broken down and that Janetta had left for France. From here arrived a letter announcing that 'she hoped never to return to married life'. Then, in December, came the news that Janetta had been seen in London, and that 'Derek Jackson was pressing her to marry him'.

Early in January 1951, Frances contrived to meet Janetta in London. She appeared at the Great Western Hotel 'looking very charming, and more like the Bohemian of past days than I had expected'. Jackson seemed to be the main figure in her life, Frances noted during a subsequent visit to Ham Spray, 'but I would guess that "love" is not what she feels for him'. Whatever Janetta may have felt, both parties took immediate steps to divorce their other halves; she and Jackson married in 1952. The marriage, however, was short-lived. Shortly after Janetta had given birth to their daughter Rose at a nursing home in Welbeck Street in August 1954, Derek announced that he was leaving her for her half-sister Angela. Janetta's explanation of the timing of this bombshell was that it stemmed from the perverse reasoning that 'if you're going to be beastly to someone you might as well be really beastly'. The half-sisters did not speak to each other for the next twenty-seven years.

Nevertheless, her separation from Jackson produced considerable material benefits. On the proceeds of the divorce settlement, of which the *Evening Standard* reported that she 'cites a relative but is allowed to keep the name secret', she was able to install herself and her three children at a house in Montpelier Square, Knightsbridge. It was here that she embarked on a brief but intense relationship with Arthur Koestler. The affair, described by Koestler as 'a month of hell and heaven', included a ten-day trip to Cornwall, visits to Paris, Salzburg and Vienna, a proposal of marriage (this was declined), outright physical violence, and Koestler's eventual decision to leave London on the grounds that if he had not done so 'I would at least have had a nervous breakdown, if not a car accident or a similar self-destructive manifestation. For the first time in [my] life I felt it would be worthwhile to hang or do 20 years in jail for killing a woman.'

Janetta's later attachments included Ralph Jervis, Patrick Leigh Fermor, Lucian Freud, the Duke of Devonshire and a much younger man who subsequently became her son-in-law. Her daughters regarded the succession of stepfathers – real and protemporaneous – with misgiving. Nicky, re-encountering Derek Jackson later in the 1950s and being asked if she remembered all the wonderful times they had had together, volunteered the single word 'No.' Yet the prospect of emotional stability lay at hand. Staying in Málaga with the Partridges in the winter of 1957, she was introduced to a Spanish nobleman named Jaime Parladé. Frances was impressed: 'a young, slender Spaniard, with an oval face and long-lashed twinkling eyes'. A month later, Frances noted that she and Ralph had been 'charmed . . . by his intelligence and gaiety'. By the mid-1960s Janetta was spending most of her time in Spain with Parladé, the latter using his professional expertise as a decorator to create a house at Torre de Tramores around the ruins of a Moorish castle. In 1971, Frances received a phone call announcing that 'Jaime and I are going to do that marrying thing tomorrow.'

In later years, the Parladés constructed a second house at Alcuzcuz near San Pedro de Alcántara. James Lees-Milne, visiting in 1990, left an admiring account of 'a grand Spanish villa belonging to the (today) absent husband Jaime, said to be Spain's leading decorator of international repute', the décor so artfully contrived that even such a practised connoisseur as Lees-Milne could not decide whether the house had been recently decorated in the Edwardian style or was a 'genuine' house of 1910. As for his hostess, Janetta, he decided she was

a once-beautiful, sophisticated, intellectual moll . . . She frightened me to death on the two or three times I met her at Ham Spray in the early 1950s, is now a bad seventy, straight hair pulled back like a skull-cap, one drooping eye, raddled skin, hollow chest and bulging stomach. But nice and welcoming and undoubtedly clever. Very anti-Christian, which upsets me rather. She destroyed the chapel in the house – 'I can't abide such things . . . had to take away cartloads of saints.' Fanny Partridge staying and the only other guest present. She has long been a sort of mother to J.

The party lunched off foie gras with truffles, fish in *brochette* and chocolate cake. Afterwards a fascinated Lees-Milne looked around the house and its contents – the easy chairs covered with pieces of Turkey carpet, the leather-seated fenders and the Edwardian lamps and shades – examined the pictures, watched a grey parrot in the courtyard imitating the ninety-year-old Frances as she capered before it, and wandered through a garden crammed with exotic plants brought back from abroad. Jaime died in January 2015, after which his widow returned to London and a final resting place in a ground-floor flat in Cadogan Square. She died in June 2018.

Orwell's funeral took place on 26 January 1950 at Christ Church, Albany Street, London NW1. The body was subsequently interred at a plot in the village graveyard at Sutton Courtenay, Oxfordshire, secured by David Astor. Sonia's distress was palpable: 'dazed', thought Malcolm Muggeridge, who decided that he would always love her for her 'true tears'. Afterwards, in the company of Janetta, she departed on a restorative holiday in the south of France. There was a brief re-encounter with Merleau-Ponty and a trip to Saint-Tropez, after which they quarrelled again and parted for good.

Far from lessening Sonia's sense of responsibility, the vast posthumous sales of *Animal Farm* and *Nineteen Eighty-Four* may be said to have increased it. 'Of course, the money's not really mine', she reputedly told a friend who had congratulated her on some charitable act. Certainly, her work-rate during the 1950s and 1960s was prodigious. Among other activities, she held down an editorial job at the firm of Weidenfeld & Nicolson, co-edited the Paris-based journal *Art and Literature* and organised a highly successful international writers' conference at the 1962 Edinburgh Festival attended by such luminaries as Norman Mailer, Rebecca West and Mary McCarthy. Ever anxious to preserve her late husband's memory, she established an Orwell Archive at University College London and, together with her collaborator Ian Angus, began work on the four-volume edition of his *Collected Journalism, Letters and Essays*. Appearing in 1968, this won high praise for the scrupulousness of its editing and the compilers' determination to bring out little-known items from the Orwell canon into the public gaze.

Sonia's personal life was much less successful. A second marriage in 1958 to Michael Pitt-Rivers, who had spent eighteen months in prison on a homosexuality charge, ended within two years. 'The young man won't like all this booky talk', the novelist Ivy Compton-Burnett cautioned when Sonia brought her husband to lunch. Thereafter, opinions of her were sharply divided. To her admirers she was a loyal, devoted and generous friend, always happy to encourage a fledgling talent or support a writer who had fallen on evil days. To her detractors she was a bossy, 'difficult', self-pitying drunk, ready to fly off the handle at a moment's notice. Frances Partridge's diary records an evening in December 1965 at which Janetta described the critic Raymond Mortimer leaving a party of Sonia's and innocently remarking, 'Aren't you a lucky girl to have this lovely house?' According to Frances 'she was drunk as usual and blazed out with: "*Lucky* – a house! You don't think *that* makes any difference when all the time . . . etc." I don't know exactly what the words were but they were delivered with a shriek and she banged the door angrily on him.' Sonia's only comment was 'After all, I've never really liked Raymond.'

Sonia's last years, mostly spent in Paris, were a decline. Her unhappiness had two principal causes. The first was regret at her decision to allow Professor Bernard Crick to write a biography of her first husband. The second was her growing suspicion that she had been swindled by the firm of accountants, Harrison, Son, Hill & Co., who administered the affairs of George Orwell Productions, the company formed immediately before his death. A long letter sent to Janetta in November 1979 sets both these anxieties in sharp relief. 'It all started in December 1977,' she explained. 'It's all so amazing and literally terrifying and even after all this time I can hardly believe it. But the fact is that I'm now involved in a huge, lengthy law-suit with them and I'm living in a very distressing world . . .' As for Crick, she claimed to have been 'bullied into commissioning a biography of George because people were writing such bad and stupid ones all round the place and the person I picked, much abetted by the publisher, has turned out to be quite ghastly, incapable of writing properly, bent on somehow needling George and making him out an unpleasant person'.

At the heart of her troubles lay an overpowering sense of guilt. 'I really do wish I was dead,' she told Janetta, 'but I feel I must fight this law-suit and do my best to get the biography as accurate as possible in a desperate effort to right some of the wrongs I seem to have committed.' This was highly unfair to Crick, whose *George Orwell: A Life* was praised for its even-handedness and the punctiliousness of its research.

Sonia died late in 1980, a few weeks after the book appeared. The court case was settled a few weeks later. Most of the money had been lost by the accountants in foolish investments. So little remained that there was barely enough to defray the expenses of the funeral. Reflecting on a friendship that had endured for nearly forty years, Janetta noted that she was 'very sad and touched by it all . . . It's very much a part of me that's died with her.'

Sequestered in their Kentish cottage, together with several guinea fowl, some geese and a South American coatimundi named Kupy of uncertain temperament, Cyril and Barbara Connolly continued to fight, as Cyril once put it, 'like kangaroos'. Punctuated by outsize doses of husbandly melancholia and periodic crises in the pet department ('His Animal has been sacked from the zoo and sent home to Oak Cottage in disgrace', Waugh reported to Nancy Mitford late in 1954), the marriage limped on until early 1955. It was at this point that Connolly became aware of his wife's infidelity with the publisher George Weidenfeld, apparently by walking on a whim through the front door of the latter's house in Chester Square and finding them *in flagrante*. The situation was complicated by the fact that Weidenfeld, already installed as Connolly's publisher, was about to issue Barbara's first novel, *A Young Girl's Touch*.

Though represented as something very near to farce – Janetta remembered the affair as a case of 'people literally hiding in cupboards in hotels' – the swerve to Weidenfeld is a classic instance of Barbara's fatalism, her tendency to take the worst possible option when experience counselled caution. 'The situation is getting more insoluble and distressing,' she wrote in her diary at around this time. 'I find it increasingly difficult to think of leaving Cyril, and yet I seem to have outwardly made up my mind to do so.' As for Weidenfeld, she confessed that she was 'simply obsessed with him sexually'. Although she acknowledged that Connolly was the love of her life, she allowed herself to be divorced early in 1956. Connolly, summarising the situation in a letter to Sonia from Saint-Tropez, noted that 'It is all absolute hell. I can't say anything except I went to meet B. here & found that she had indeed promised to marry W . . . "at last I have found a man to whom I can be faithful" – on the other hand she says she loves me, feels tied to me, doesn't want to leave me, would come back at once "if he would let go his end of the rope."' Her marriage to Weidenfeld, which took place some months later, was in trouble from the honeymoon onward, when her ex-husband was discovered to be holidaying on the same Mediterranean island. Just as Weidenfeld was cited by Connolly as co-respondent in the first set of divorce proceedings, so Connolly was cited by Weidenfeld in the second.

Now in her early forties, Barbara continued to attract admirers. One of these, the painter Michael Wishart, left an arresting account of her ability to magnetise the male gaze. 'One glance explained the abundant notches in her tomahawk,' he claimed. 'The first time I saw her things swam before my eyes.' Much of her allure was associative, Wishart thought. 'She had lived with a succession of intelligent men and a dusting of their brilliance had rubbed off on her. She had an enquiring mind where the arts and sexual relationships were concerned', as well as 'the courtesan's chameleon adaptability and ruthlessness . . .' A mark of this adaptability was her decision, taken in 1959, to move to New York. Here she worked in a bookshop and as a dental assistant, and had affairs with, among others, the drama critic Kenneth Tynan, the *New Yorker* cartoonist Charles Addams and Bob Silvers, founder of the *New York Review of Books*. It was on Silvers's yacht that the young Alan Bennett, then on tour with *Beyond the Fringe*, encountered her in the summer of 1963: unsmiling and, he deduced, unapproachable. A visit to Andy Warhol's studio to watch a pornographic film being made came to an abrupt end when Barbara took offence at Warhol's suggestion that he could create a role for a grandmother.

A brief third marriage, in 1966, to Janetta's former husband Derek Jackson ('It was not for love that I married Professor Jackson') soon perished in mutual acrimony. Among its highlights was an evening in a Paris nightclub at which Jackson, exasperated by his wife's habit of talking across him to a mutual friend, seized their two heads and banged them together; Barbara then bit his thumb. On another occasion she thrust a second pet coatimundi, named Florie, in his face and urged it to bite him. Subsequently, she retreated to a Provençal farmhouse named the Mas de Colombier and embarked on a tempestuous relationship with the French writer Bernard Frank. There were trips to Antibes to visit Graham Greene, the frequent arrival of friends to stay and the destruction of a great deal of crockery. Of one meal, eaten when Connolly was a guest, she noted that 'I cannot recall the menu, but I do remember that during the dessert course a pot of cream aimed at me skimmed past Cyril's head . . .'

In her mid-seventies Barbara grew bored with France. With many of her friends dead and most of the others alienated by her two scarifying volumes of memoirs, she returned to England and very soon succumbed to an inoperable brain tumour. In her last weeks, according to Connolly's daughter Cressida, at whose Worcestershire house she was cared for, 'all her rancour, sadness and fury fell away, leaving only the best intact: her intelligence and curiosity, her elegance, her marvellously soft skin – and a loving side I had never seen before'. Barbara died in January 1996, two days before her eightieth birthday.

The end of the war found Angela still living in the West Country, making model houses which Brasco sold to souvenir shops. Subsequently, his behaviour became even more erratic and she returned to London with her two children. She was later reunited with René de Chatellus, whom she consented to marry and live with in Paris. But the sparkle had gone out of the French count, who became increasingly gloomy and prone to reflection.

Even Angela appeared to believe that her elopement with her half-sister's husband, Derek Jackson, in the summer of 1954, might possibly have been a mistake. Certainly, the passage devoted to the episode in her memoirs consists of only half-a-dozen anguished sentences:

> A new lover I was mad about joined us in Brittany, and then we lived together in France until he left me three years later. It had all caused so much pain and misery to those he had abandoned, and finally me too, that there was little happiness during those years. Many people said it served me right and I dare say it did. Others wouldn't speak to me. Only the lover went unscathed and went on to marry two or three more people. In the end I wished to God he had never wanted me or I had never given in. It makes me sick, even now, to remember and write about it.

Angela later spent time in Australia, and at the age of sixty-five married a Turk named Ali Bulent Rauf with whom she lived companionably for the last ten years of his life. Interviewed by *The Times* in her eighties, she remarked that: 'It's difficult to be monogamous. You fall in love with someone and don't look at anyone else, but the years pass and things change. I've never been married long enough to know how long monogamy is realistic. I imagine about seven years.' Now reconciled with Janetta, she spent her tenth decade at a house in the Scottish borders being cared for by the staff and students of the Beshara School of Esoteric Education, which her last husband had co-founded with the aim of helping its followers 'towards the realisation in each person of their indissoluble unity with the real being'. Angela died in 2012.

Diana had married the barrister Samuel 'Sammy' Cooke in 1945. The couple had two sons. Cooke enjoyed a distinguished legal career, was knighted and became a High Court judge, but suffered from a disease of the nervous system which caused him to take early retirement from his profession. He died in 1978. Long before this date, in fact as far back as the *Horizon* days, his widow had begun to write poetry. Her publications included *Poems* (1954) and *The Heat and the Cold* (1965). A *Collected Poems* appeared in 1973. Her subject matter included male inconstancy and unrequited love. Diana died in 2006.

Glur's marriage to the hard-drinking John Dyson Taylor was short-lived. After giving birth to two sons, she suffered a breakdown and spent a year in a convalescent home. Dyson Taylor later absconded to Kitzbühel. Sarah, Glur's daughter with Peter Quennell, was largely left to the care of her maternal grandmother. There was a brief stay at Clayton in the South Downs but, towards the end of the 1950s, Glur established herself in a small, top-floor flat in Notting Hill whose décor and furnishings remained unchanged for the next four decades. Though she retained her sense of humour and her good looks – according to one obituarist, her face in old age came to resemble a deeply etched Aztec mask – she was prey to melancholia, pining for company but sometimes prone to disparage it when it arrived. A series of lunch dates with Kingsley Amis came to an end when she discovered that he was a 'terrible bore'. Towards the end of her life, she converted to Roman Catholicism, although she once confessed to a friend: 'Darling, I believe there's something called a lapsed Catholic. I think that's what I am.' Glur died in 2000.

Joan spent the rest of her long life in the company of Patrick Leigh Fermor. Between 1949 and 1954 the couple rented a flat in Charlotte Street. Subsequently they settled in Greece and, using a providential legacy from Lady Eyres-Monsell, spent the early 1960s building a house for themselves in Kardamyli. They were married in 1968. Joan remained on friendly terms with Connolly. In 1953, for example, she accompanied Cyril and Barbara on an excursion to France. Of her preliminary stay at the 'Cot', Barbara noted that 'Cyril exaggeratedly well-mannered towards Joan in marked contrast to his attitude to me, which is worse than that of a man to his dog.' Joan died in 2003. *The Photographs of Joan Leigh Fermor: Artist and Lover* was published in 2018.

The remainder of Anna Kavan's career was seriously compromised by her addiction to heroin. She underwent another course of detoxification in 1946 at the Sanatorium Bellevue in Kreuzlingen. Of the novels that she published in the course of the next decade, *Sleep Has His House* (1948) was indifferently reviewed, while the firm she had commissioned to bring out *A Scarcity of Love* (1956) went bankrupt shortly afterwards. Two further books – *Eagles' Nest* (1957) and *A Bright Green Field* (1958) – appeared in quick succession. Thereafter her connection with their publisher, Peter Owen, lapsed for another eight years.

Meanwhile, her personal life was disintegrating. Dr Bluth, her mentor and supplier, died in 1964. Shortly afterwards she became a victim of a change in official policy towards drug users. Hitherto, hard drugs, administered intravenously, had been prescribed legally to registered addicts. Following publication of the Brain Report of 1965, it was announced that these prescriptions would require a Home Office licence. Intended to address the issue of over-prescribing, this measure effectively criminalised many long-term users. By this time, presumably by registering with several different practitioners, Kavan had managed to stockpile huge quantities of heroin. These kept her afloat throughout the rest of her life. *Ice* (1967), a metaphysical thriller advertised as a 'vision of a post-human future', was respectfully received, but over three decades of exposure to drugs had made her system dangerously tolerant of their effects. She was found dead at her flat in Hillsleigh Road, Kensington, in December 1968, fully dressed, sprawled across the bed, a syringe in her arm, her head resting on the lacquer box in which she kept her supplies. The Drugs Squad subsequently discovered 'enough heroin to kill the whole street'.

Evelyn Waugh maintained his reputation as one of the most considerable British novelists of the mid-twentieth century. His *Sword of Honour* trilogy was completed with the publication of *Unconditional Surrender* in 1961. A volume of autobiography, *A Little Learning*, appeared in 1964. Even before this date, Waugh had sunk into torpor. 'There is nowhere I want to go and nothing I want to do and I am conscious of being an utter bore', he informed a correspondent shortly before his death in April 1966.

Nancy Mitford spent the rest of her life in Paris, much of it in the fruitless pursuit of Colonel Gaston Palewski, General de Gaulle's wartime *directeur de cabinet*, whom she had met in 1942. She continued to write novels but became better known for biographical works on predominantly French subjects. These included *Madame de Pompadour* (1954), *Voltaire in Love* (1957) and *The Sun King* (1966), a study of Louis XIV, whom she described, in quintessentially Mitford-esque terms, as 'Absolute Heaven'. Nancy died in 1973.

Peter Quennell continued to thrive as an all-purpose literary man. Leaving the *Cornhill Magazine* in 1951 he became co-editor of *History Today* and remained there for the next twenty-eight years. After securing his divorce from Glur, he took a fourth wife, Sonia Leon, invariably known as 'Spider', and then, once this marriage had disintegrated, a fifth, Marilyn Peek. This union, formalised in 1967, lasted until his death. His thirty or so publications included two well-received (and highly discreet) works of autobiography, *The Marble Foot* (1977) and *The Wanton Chase* (1980). He was knighted in 1992 for services to literature. An insight into the Quennells' married life in their later years was confided by Selina Hastings to Anthony Powell. The former claimed to have witnessed Marilyn escorting her husband ('almost handcuffed to her') to a hairdresser's in Primrose Hill and leaving him in the chair with the instructions 'Will you cut its [*sic*] hair? Get rid of those whiskers and those disgusting hairs in the nostrils.' Peter Quennell died in 1993.

Feliks Topolski remained in the UK after the war, and in 1949 took British citizenship. The 3000 drawings of his celebrated *Chronicles* series appeared on a fortnightly basis from 1953 to 1979 and were exhibited around the world. In 1959 he was commissioned by the Duke of Edinburgh to design a mural commemorating the Coronation of Queen Elizabeth II. His son Daniel (1945–2015) twice represented Oxford in the University Boat Race. Topolski died in 1989.

Stephen Spender's autobiography, *World Within World*, was published in 1951. Of it Evelyn Waugh wrote, unkindly, that 'At his christening the fairy godparents showered on Mr Spender all the fashionable neuroses, but they quite forgot the gift of literary skill'. He became co-editor of the literary and political magazine *Encounter*, and taught for some years in American universities before accepting a chair in English at University College, London. His *Collected Poems* appeared in 1983. In the same year he was awarded a knighthood for services to literature. Spender died in 1995.

Kenneth Sinclair-Loutit worked for the United Nations for twenty-eight years, latterly in the World Health Organization. His long retirement was spent in Morocco, where he helped to establish RADIOCOM, a radio communications and electronic engineering company. Although he remarried and had two more children, he continued to regard Janetta as the love of his life. Sinclair-Loutit died in 2003.

Robert Kee became a highly successful writer and broadcaster. His works of popular history included *1939: The World We Left Behind* (1984) and *1945: The World We Fought For* (1985). The Partridges' lingering hopes that he and Janetta could re-establish their relationship were finally extinguished when, in 1960, he married Cynthia Judah. Cynthia's novel *A Respectable Man* (1993), published after their divorce, contains an amusing and by no means respectful portrait of life at Ham Spray in the 1950s. Robert Kee died in 2013.

Brian Howard spent most of the post-war period abroad in the company of his much younger boyfriend. Nancy Mitford, whom he visited in Paris, reported that 'Brian came here with a terrible creature called Sam. I thought I would hurt myself with laughing.' There was little amusement in Howard's subsequent career. His literary projects remained unrealised and he became addicted to synthetic morphine. Following Sam's accidental death, early in 1958, while staying in Nice, he committed suicide at the age of fifty-two.

Julian Maclaren-Ross's novel *Of Love and Hunger*, which dramatised his adventures as a vacuum-cleaner salesman on the pre-war south coast, was published in 1947. Hard-up, improvident and reduced to living in cheap hotels and furnished rooms, he described the 1950s as 'a decade I could have well done without'. His longstanding obsession with Sonia reached its high point in 1955, when he informed a friend that 'The toughest and wisest blokes in London are speculating on the outcome. The betting's on me so far – though this is the most formidable girl I've ever met'. But the relationship – if that is what it was – came to nothing. Maclaren-Ross died of a heart attack in 1964. The posthumously published *Memoirs of the Forties* (1965) offer entertaining glimpses of the life he had led in wartime literary London when the going was good.

Lucian Freud became one of the greatest artists of the post-war age. In 2008 his *Benefits Supervisor Sleeping* (1995) was sold at Sotheby's in New York for $33.6 million, the highest sum then paid for the work of a living painter. The number of his children, from a variety of liaisons, was set at fourteen, although some authorities considered this to be a substantial understatement. Lucian Freud died in 2011.

King Farouk's popularity continued to wane. The Egyptian army's poor showing in the Arab–Israeli war of 1948, which led to the creation of the state of Israel, was particularly resented by his subjects. Four years later he was deposed by the Free Officers' coup, led by Muhammad Naguib and Gamal Abdel Nasser. After a brief period in which Farouk's infant son was recognised as King Faud II, Egypt's new rulers announced the abolition of the monarchy. For a while, the royal exile, together with his second wife – he had divorced the first in 1948 – lived in Monaco. They later removed to Italy. It was here, at a table at the Ile de France restaurant in Rome, on 18 March 1965, that Farouk collapsed and died, having been poisoned by an assassin allegedly sent by Nasser.

Barbara last encountered him on a visit to Rome in 1953. At this point he was living with his Neapolitan mistress in the Grottaferrata area. The mistress, named Irma, was, according to Barbara, 'a buxom, simple, friendly girl' whose conversation turned on her dream of becoming a film star. Farouk, she reported, had become 'a lonely, sagging figure', whose ostracisation by Roman socialites was attributable not to his lax morals but to their finding him 'boring'. As

Barbara descended to her taxi on the final day of her stay, he summoned her back with the words 'You've forgotten something.' Her last glimpse was of him standing in the doorway 'with his familiar mocking smile' holding up a mislaid toothbrush.

Peter Watson died in 1956 in mysterious circumstances, drowning in the bath after his boyfriend (and legatee) Norman Fowler failed to break down the door and instead ran out into the street to summon help. In the *Sunday Times*, Cyril Connolly paid tribute to the unique place his old friend had occupied in the world of modern art. As a young man, Connolly explained, 'he stepped, gay and delightful, out of a charmed existence like a Mayfair Buddha suddenly sobered by the tragedy of his time to become the most intelligent and generous and discreet of patrons'. To Brian Howard, writing to his friend John Banting, 'he was an angel, and never did or said a mean or ignoble thing his whole life long'. Howard claimed that he could 'make a list of present-day celebrated painters and writers who owe their *all* to him. He wouldn't even tell me their names . . .'

Frances and Ralph Partridge continued to live at Ham Spray throughout the 1950s, entertaining their friends and doing their best to preserve the values of Bloomsbury in an increasingly uncertain world. Their relationship was cut short by Ralph's death in 1960, after which Frances left Wiltshire to inhabit the first in a succession of Knightsbridge flats. She was plunged into grief for a second time in 1963 when her only son Burgo died unexpectedly of an undiagnosed aortic aneurysm. In the late 1970s, beginning with *A Pacifist's War* (1978), she began to publish selections from her diaries. Nine volumes appeared in her lifetime, and she became a considerable literary celebrity. Her hundredth birthday was celebrated with a party at the Savile Club arranged by Janetta and other old friends. She died in 2004 at the age of 103.

Nicky Loutit became a successful artist. She now lives on the Suffolk coast with her third husband, the writer Jonathan Gathorne-Hardy. *New Year's Day Is Black*, a memoir of her early life, was published in 2016.

After the closure of *Horizon*, Cyril Connolly's immediate problem – aside from his relationship with Barbara – was lack of money. Stephen Spender's diary from December 1951 records an occasion on which Sonia 'provided a description of Cyril's poverty since his marriage'. His material prospects began to improve when an invitation to review books for the *Sunday Times* led, in the spring of 1951, to a summons to join its regular staff of critics. Thereafter, as one of the newspaper's lead reviewers – the other was Raymond Mortimer – Connolly became an influential voice in the dissemination of post-war taste. Never prolific, and stung by accusations of laziness, he published several books in the post-war era. These included two collections of his literary journalism, *Previous Convictions* (1963) and *The Evening Colonnade* (1973), and *The Modern Movement* (1965).

Once divorced from Barbara, Connolly showed himself anxious to marry again. 'What you want is a lovely clean old man like me', he told the novelist Elizabeth Jane Howard. In the event his third wife was a young woman named Deirdre Craig, described by one of his biographers as 'a tall, fresh-faced, whippet-thin girl in her late twenties, recently divorced and with two children'. The couple had two further offspring, a girl named Cressida, born in 1960, and, ten years later, a boy named Matthew. Barbara, hearing of Deirdre's first pregnancy, regarded it as 'the final blow'. The marriage prospered, although Deirdre occasionally complained about her husband's continued intimacy with old flames. As he remarked to Barbara sometime in the early 1960s: 'At the moment D. has whisked her [Cressida] off to Lewes after announcing that our marriage is finished as I obviously prefer you . . . she said that I was carrying your letter about in my wallet which I do because I can never remember your address. A Freudian lapse'.

At this point the Connollys were living at Bushey Lodge in Sussex. They later removed to Eastbourne, from which Connolly, clad in a pinstripe suit and every inch the elder statesman of literature, would travel up to London each Wednesday to correct the proofs of his weekly article. A year after his seventieth birthday, celebrated with a lavish dinner at the Savoy, he suffered a heart attack while staying with Barbara at the Mas du Colombier, and was flown back to England. The expenses of his last weeks at the Harley Street Clinic and St Vincent's Hospital in Ladbroke Grove were borne by his friend Sir Harry d'Avigdor Goldsmid, who remarked that 'Cyril is dying beyond my means.' The wartime world of the Lost Girls was briefly recreated around his deathbed, whose visitors included Janetta, Barbara, Sonia and Anne Dunn. Connolly died on 26 November 1974.

What was the Lost Girls' legacy? Did they, when it came to it, leave anything behind them other than the memory of a few vaguely scandalous high jinks and some doomed wartime love affairs? There were never enough of them to become a fully fledged youth movement and their influence on the cultural life of their time is largely retrospective, a matter of cameo appearances in post-war fiction and the diaries of 1940s-era literary life. Much of this was down to the highly artificial circumstances that had brought them into being. Without the war, the Blitz, Connolly and the office in Lansdowne Terrace, they lost both their animating spirit and their solidarity. The Barbara of the 1960s, working as a dental assistant in New York or hobnobbing with Warhol, is an interesting specimen of deracinated womanhood but she is not the Barbara of 1942, playing Quennell off against Topolski, turning up late at the headquarters of the Yugoslav government in exile and flitting like some malevolent wraith up and down the staircase at Bedford Square.

None of this, though, is to minimise the Lost Girls' importance to the life of their time, to the literary world of the 1940s and the landscapes that stretch out beyond it. In their spiritedness, their independence and their determination to be themselves, they offered a template for some of the female behaviour that came afterwards, and at the very least they constitute a link between the first wave of newly emancipated young women at large in the Mayfair society world of the 1920s and the much more self-conscious Dionysiac hordes of the 1960s and 1970s.

Any attempt to label them ought to be resisted, if only because most of the nets set to pinion them have a habit of tugging free. Barbara, Sonia, Lys, Janetta and the others may not have been feminists, but their sense of their own autonomy was unusual for the era in which they found themselves, and if they were regularly suborned and patronised by men then they were also capable of turning the tables on their exploiters. Their unhappiness, it might be said, was part of the price they paid for being the people they were. As for their real significance, so much of it relies on intangibles – a way of talking, a way of dressing, a way of behaving, a bat's squeak of individuality only discernible to those within their immediate circle. But every so often, in one of the great English novels of wartime life, in a Bloomsbury diary, in a letter sent back from a Cairo hotel to a Knightsbridge apartment, there comes a moment when the smoke clears for an instant and in the space suddenly revealed to view, glamorous, edgy and inimitable, a Lost Girl can be found making her presence felt.

Finale: The Last Lost Girl

April 2016

Spring has come to Knightsbridge and the property developers are hard at work furbishing up their investments. The pillared frontages of the houses in Cadogan Place gleam with coats of fresh paint, most of the upper storeys sport billowing polythene drapes, and the parking spaces are jammed up with builders' vans. At the far end, though, the atmosphere is appreciably more genteel and secluded. Real people live here, you suspect, rather than Russian oligarchs or those mysterious multinational corporates whose nameplates offer no idea of the materials in which they trade. One of them is Janetta, to whose ground-floor flat I am admitted by a polite Spanish servant. Within, all is high-end yet nicely understated opulence: elegant sofas, occasional tables on which copies of weekly magazines are neatly laid out. Here, too, are the thronged mementoes of a past life: Bloomsbury portraits; a bound set of *Horizon*; black-and-white photographs from sixty years ago; a montage of smiling grandchildren.

It is a good decade-and-a-half since I last set eyes on Janetta. Back then she was in her late seventies, spry and voluble. Now she is deep into her nineties, bent, frail and less talkative, but with a hard grey eye still glinting vigilantly away. In fact, as terrifying elderly ladies met in the course of my professional duties go, I'd put her straight into the Deborah Devonshire/Baroness Warnock class. There is an immediate difficulty when I try to hand over the caddy-full of choice Fortnum and Mason tea, purchased on the way over from Piccadilly. 'No . . .' Janetta murmurs sadly, as she turns the shiny receptacle over in her hands. 'No, I'm afraid. I really . . .' Is there a problem with the tea, I nervously enquire. It turns out that Janetta only drinks Chinese, which this variety is not, with a squeeze of lemon. Well, perhaps some of her guests might like it, I suggest. She looks doubtful, and then, anxious not to appear rude, pronounces that 'It's got a very pretty tin.'

The tea stowed away, we repair to the sofa, the tape-recorder – at which she darts several suspicious glances – between us. And here another difficulty presents itself. This is Janetta's disavowal of the thesis I intend to propound. Having attended to Peter Quennell's summary of the Lost Girls and been asked if it has any meaning to her, she instantly demurs: 'No, none at all. I think it's rather silly, really, because there weren't odd girls in and out of *Horizon*. I mean, there was always Lys there the whole time devoted to Cyril and working like mad, and there was always Sonia . . .' But did she not regard herself as part of the *Horizon* team? No indeed. 'I hardly ever went to the *Horizon* office, I mean truly hardly at all. I mean, I remember that flat and perhaps ate buns there, but I never went to one of their dinner parties or anything like that.'

Nevertheless, she consents to unpack her memories of first meeting the other members of Connolly's *ménage*: of encountering Barbara at Topolski's studio in Maida Vale; of being introduced to Sonia by Connolly at the height of an air-raid. 'I think we were in one of those buildings in Piccadilly looking out of the window at . . . searchlights and things . . . He'd just met this new person he thought was rather fascinating.' By this stage in the proceedings the thought of old scores needing to be settled has strayed into the conversation. There is, for example, talk of the portrait of Lys included in Michael Shelden's account of the *Horizon* circle: 'I mean she was not this fascinating, intelligent, wonderful person. She really was a bit of a nightmare.' In slight mitigation, as with the tin of Fortnum's bohea, Janetta concedes that 'she was a very good typist'. As for Sonia's role at *Horizon*, 'well, she practically tried to make out she was its editor by the end'.

And what about Barbara, I propose. Is it true, as has occasionally been alleged by *Horizon*'s chroniclers, that the other girls looked down on her for being insufficiently upper-middle class? 'I didn't get that impression at all,' Janetta briskly returns. 'No, I just thought her incredibly selfish . . . She didn't hesitate to do anything because she didn't care whether somebody was annoyed or cross . . . she just didn't mind at all.' Although precise details are withheld, it seems clear that some behavioural line was crossed at the time of the Connolly/Weidenfeld stand-off: 'I mean, he was very nice to me always, Weidenfeld, but my relationship with him was totally buggered up by Barbara . . . God, she was a menace.'

What does Janetta think of the relationship-buggering menace's scorching volumes of memoirs? Here aesthetic approval and loyalty to absent friends, not to mention absent husbands, uneasily commingle. 'Well, I've read those two books.' There is a pause. 'Well, I mean they're very . . . they're very clever and readable and they're funny and they're absolutely beastly about everyone. Well, one of the main people she's beastly about . . . you know she finally married someone I had been married to . . . ?' There is a split second in which the spectre of the six-times wedded Professor Derek Jackson, with his love of singing the 'Horst-Wessel-Lied' in Austrian hostelries, and of whom Ferdinand Mount so memorably remarked that 'to call his carry-on goat-like would be grossly unfair to goats', looms menacingly between us. 'And she was ghastly to him. Absolutely horrible to him.'

So she was. And yet this was a world in which being absolutely horrible to people can look like a kind of default setting. Was Evelyn Waugh at all intimidating? I wonder, with the nonchalant air of one who proposes that Mrs Thatcher might occasionally have mildly trodden down the toes of one or two of her cabinet colleagues. 'Well, he wouldn't hesitate to sort of snap back and say, "Well, you're a bit

of a bore, aren't you?" . . . And treated with such sort of respect . . .'
Janetta laments. All this raises the question of the qualities that she
admires in the members of the *Horizon* circle, what separates the
sheep from the goats and distinguishes lustre and éclat from a
straightforward ability to type. And here, it turns out that Janetta
and the man who christened her 'Mrs Bluefeet' are fighting on the
same side, for the entity that neither of them can tolerate for a
moment is a bore. Why, I ask her, are people so fascinated by
Connolly? 'Partly because he was awfully good at . . . describing
things,' Janetta assures me, 'and I mean his analysis of things was
fascinating.' Then comes the clincher: 'He wasn't a bore in any way.'
So was not being a bore important? 'I think I was awfully lucky in
knowing an awful lot of people that weren't bores . . . I mean, they
were fascinating, really, on the whole, the people I saw . . .'

And so the roll-call of the inhabitants of Cyril's world marches on:
Anthony Powell (who she 'couldn't bear'); Orwell, whose ideological
estrangement from Kenneth Sinclair-Loutit she recalls ('Orwell was
very odd, what he did . . . It was very complicated, his political
life . . . I can't really follow it'), the 'delightful' Peter Watson ('in
those days it was so awful for the poor buggers, you know, and he had
the most ghastly time: he was always being robbed or something').
All this is par for the course, but occasionally there stirs the ghost of
something else, the faint yet enticing outline of a path into a cultural
world that is nothing like our own. 'So they all knew each other,' she
remarks at one point, of the *Horizon* set. 'There was only one sort of
nucleus – there weren't all sorts of fascinating groups of people in
Hampstead and God knows where that there are now – there was just
one . . . If somebody would suddenly turn up from America, Cyril
would at once know them. And it was on its own in a way, so that if
you knew those people you met anyone that turned up . . . which was
very nice.' Outside the builders' vans jockey for position and the
polythene billows over Cadogan Place.

* * *

Janetta died in June 2018 at the age of ninety-six. Clearing out the flat, her three daughters discovered, somewhat to their surprise, that she had kept everything. From trunks and cardboard boxes spilled forth a host of photograph albums and correspondence files extending back over eighty years. Here were letters to and from her mother in the 1930s, unpublished novels from the post-war era, a cache of flimsy airmails addressed to the Partridges' lair in Wiltshire by the Cairo- and Bari-bound Kenneth. Kept apart from the main archive, and eventually run to earth in a bookcase beneath the bound volumes of *Horizon*, were a dozen or so letters from Connolly, carefully pressed between a card advertising his memorial service at St Mary le Strand, London, on 20 December 1974. Composed on *Horizon* or White's club notepaper, none of them is dated, although the subject matter – the trip to Paris, Kenneth's possible return from the Balkans – suggests that they were written in the last months of 1944 and the early part of 1945. Janetta is 'Dear Janetta'; once or twice, when the emotional thermostat is being turned up a notch or two, 'Darling Janetta'.

The remarkable thing about this 10,000 words or so of hastily scribbled correspondence is the number of different Connollys on display. Here, in quickfire succession, come a ruminative Connolly, a wistful Connolly, a despairing Connolly, a light-hearted Connolly, a vengeful Connolly, a Connolly content with the path he follows in life and a Connolly made wretched by a suspicion that he took a wrong turning many years ago and fell into a swamp from which no amount of endeavour can ever extricate him – so many Connollys, in fact, that a psychologist asked to separate out the real man from the stream of aliases would probably shake his head at the degree of emotional complexity on display. The shifts of gear can be bewildering and the endless self-examination slightly tedious – these, like everything else Connolly wrote, are essentially performances, designed to impress, to mystify and burnish up the Connolly myth along the way – but lurking beneath them, sometimes stalking their surfaces if it comes to that, is a genuine sense of concern for Janetta's wellbeing:

You must *cheer up* – if Kenneth is getting some leave – even if it is only *leave* – at least you will see him and then can put your point of view to him, and give him an ultimatum if necessary. Don't be too upset about it. You hurt H. S. [Hugh Slater] enormously without meaning to by leaving him, & now you are being hurt – all human beings hurt each other where love is concerned, except those who have found out how hurt they can get & who therefore try *not* to hurt other people. I am sure Kenneth can't *grasp* what you are feeling, because he hasn't felt all that himself. Anyhow, you have got a baby, a home and a paint-box . . . and also you know quite well that you aren't *deserted* – only *neglected* – which is quite different & not nearly so bad.

Another letter – internal evidence suggests that it was written in the first weeks of 1945 – returns to this theme, convicting Sinclair-Loutit not of callousness but defective timing: 'I think that your whole predicament is due only to a miscalculation of Kenneth's about when the war would end.' As for the immediate future:

I think it is terribly hard for you, but you have got a temporary home, which is more than most people, with substitute parents who adore you, a studio, an ability to paint & read; & the time to do so – and a baby – which I understand is held to be both a dynamo of happiness and a pledge for the future – it is really folly to undo *all this knitting* – unless you are quite certain that you don't love K. any more & never will . . .

On the other hand, Connolly's emotional generosity would always be tempered by an awareness of somebody else's pain: his own, to be exact, which pulses away beneath these reams of sound advice like a generator's hum. Janetta is there to be flattered. He has only three women friends, he tells her – herself, Elizabeth Glenconner and Joan Rayner, 'and you are so beautiful, so sympathetic, so much a part of my douceur de vivre'. But she is also there to be quietly, affectionately yet decisively reproached for not playing the central role in Connolly's life that a fairer wind and fewer emotional complications might once have allowed her. A third letter remembering long-ago days spent in the West Country develops into a paroxysm of yearning for what might have been.

> You say you always get what you want, all I can say is what a pity you didn't want me, or you would have been a painter instead of a buxom matron embowered in bourgeois bliss. At least when you were with Humphrey there was always a bracing feeling of hope. Now whenever I see you I start brooding about our might have beens, – if you had been at St Gervais when I walked round to see you, if they had given me your right address at Hammersmith instead of one in Glasgow when I sent an S.O.S. to you, if I had never met D. & we had had an affair from when we met at Patrick's party. As we should have done – or if you had never met Humphrey, or anyhow not fallen for him . . . or not married him when I asked you to marry me!

The obvious question to ask of this impassioned exercise in sub-junctive living is: how much of it is true, and how much retrospective tinkering? Did the Connolly of 1940, still married to Jean and heav-ily involved with Diana, think that he could have carried off an eighteen-year-old girl? Is he really serious? Or myth-making? And what effect is he trying to produce on Janetta? Is it really helpful, for example, to tell a twenty-three-year-old woman with a small child whose other half is somewhere in Occupied Europe that 'My Id is still in love with you and always assumes – as Ids always do – that the past is the present and that no one else exists', or that 'I would have liked to have had that baby you have got'? Or is this simply the way that Connolly's mind worked in the company of old friends and lov-ers, where anything can be said and everybody is quietly compensating for everybody else?

Certainly, several of the letters embark on Connolly's most regular emotional trick, which is to play one woman off against another. Here, somewhat unexpectedly, the villain of the piece is Diana: 'anything to do with D. always upsets me', claims a rather awful letter from sometime in 1944, 'which is why I can't bear to see her. I am emotionally incompetent, you and she were the last people whom I could have loved & married, who had the key to the ruined temple, if only you had ever made any effort in that direction'. To the web-weaver of Bedford Square, Diana is

five years of reproaches, tears, misery, doors banging, suitcases bumping, angry letters, trains, farewells, – I think she is a faithless bitch, you have no idea what an Enfer you pull me back towards & what is the good? Unless people are going to live together again they will always be disappointed again by meeting & one of them will suffer.

A little more determination, a little more insistence on bringing down the one true prize might have seen him through:

With a little more courage and ruthlessness, I could have taken the place of H. S. or even, later, of Kenneth and I know we shd have been happy. Diana and I were like two pieces in a jig-saw puzzle which one keeps fitting together because they *must* fit, they so nearly do, & yet they don't quite do, & perhaps with a little more force they would have stuck. I think she specialises in the Art of Love i.e. the art of keeping her lover perpetually in love with her through Retreat, Advance, mental titivation, books, music, uncertainties etc, while what I want is someone to go down the Dordogne from the source with me in a canoe. It doesn't matter if we never do it. They must *want* to. Now I have lost both of you & of course most of myself.

He once thought the 'community of mind' he shared with Diana was unbreakable, he concludes, 'and yet she broke it'. To which it might be pointed out that Connolly was quite happy to shatter communities of mind himself if he felt like it, and that quite a few of his emotional sulks are those of a circus ringmaster faced by a hitherto docile exhibit that has suddenly got out of hand.

And still the letter writer keeps changing shape, putting on new disguises, bewildering his correspondent with lightning about-turns and changes of tack. There is a high-spirited Connolly, in a letter that looks as if it was written towards the end of 1944, pleased by the success of *The Unquiet Grave* ('My book goes like one o'clock. The Queen sent an S.O.S. for one yesterday') and claiming to have achieved some kind of inner peace: 'I am very happy, free of remorse, regret & memory – I live in the present, I love my work, I see the war clouds drifting away & the sun of civilisation slowly rising and getting a little warmer every day.' And then there is a deeply distressed, self-pitying Connolly, who compares his wounded heart to 'a fish which has been knocked on the head & flung on the bottom of a boat & which suddenly gives a few convulsive leaps to everyone's embarrassment', for whom even the prospect of a trip to newly liberated Paris can only offer a few bittersweet intimations of a glory that has been swallowed up by time:

> My annual bid for escape having somehow failed, my heart is a cess-pool covered by a heavy iron slab, which I no longer have the strength to lift. I don't really feel I shall ever get to Paris, and even if I do I shall only find unhappy memories there. For me now Paris=Jean=youth=hope, therefore causes only pain & disillusion. Perhaps I shall find a wonderful French girl – or an American – but even then it can't ever be the same.

Jean. Diana. Janetta. Joan. Lys (whose name surfaces only twice in the entire correspondence) . . . It is tempting to see this groaning catalogue of emotional disturbance as a kind of mosaic, a swirl of dancing female figures from which a single male face stares self-aggrandisingly and, to do him justice, self-accusingly out. But perhaps a better image would be that of some far-flung galaxy, embedded deep in the rim of the cosmos, dominated by Planet Connolly, in which lesser moons and satellites oscillate back and forth. What did the correspondents make of it all? Did Connolly believe everything he had written? And did Janetta believe everything she read? Or did she assume that he was playing some complicated and well-nigh unfathomable emotional game, in which every utterance is overstated and every observation about third parties subordinate to the relationship being lived out on the page? After all, if some of the letters are sometimes there to advertise Connolly's own sense of guilt, then, equally, others are clearly intended to awaken this emotion in Janetta. And how would she have felt when she read the paragraph that runs:

> Of course, you are right about H. S. [Hugh Slater] – but who, knowing you at 17 would want to change you? As I said to him once, others, with other girls one can look on at nature – but you were nature.

Flattered? Wary? Indulgent? At this distance in time, and with both writer and recipient dead, who can tell? But now it is time to put the puppets back in the box, for our game is all played out.

Notes and Further Reading

This book makes use of a number of unpublished sources. They include the letters and diaries formerly in the possession of Barbara Skelton, hereafter [Skelton], correspondence, diaries and notebooks previously belonging to Janetta Parladé [Parladé], Lys, Sonia and Diana's letters to Connolly, now owned by the Connolly family [Connolly], Peter Watson's letters to Cecil Beaton, currently held by St John's College, Cambridge [Beaton], correspondence and a number of personal items previously owned by Sonia Orwell, now in the Orwell Archive at University College, London [Orwell Archive], Sonia's letters to William Coldstream, currently held by the Tate Gallery [Tate], Connolly's letters to Alan Pryce-Jones, now in the Beinecke Library, Yale University [Yale] and several letters sent by Barbara to Anthony and Violet Powell [Powell]. Unless otherwise stated, the place of publication is London.

Introduction: An Evening in Bedford Square

'For the undamaged survivors', see Robin Dalton, *One Leg Over: Having Fun – Mostly – in Peace and War* (Melbourne, 2017), p. 28.

1. The Wanton Chase

The first of the three letters from Peter Quennell to Barbara is undated; the second was sent on 25 October 1941 and the third on 1 January 1943 [Skelton]. For Quennell on the 'Lost Girls', see *The Wanton Chase: An Autobiography from 1939* (1980), pp. 71–2. Hilary Spurling's description of *Horizon*'s female staff is taken from *The Girl from the Fiction Department: A Portrait of Sonia Orwell* (2002), pp. 50–1.

On the beauty of individual Lost Girls, Spurling, *The Girl from the Fiction Department*, p. 27; Michael Wishart, *High Diver* (1977), p. 149. Frances Partridge, quoted in Anne Chisholm, *Frances Partridge: The Biography* (2009), p. 187. The friend who saw Sonia gambolling round Connolly was Violet Powell, Spurling, *The Girl from the Fiction Department*, p. 61. For the advice given to Angela by her mother, Angela Culme-Seymour, *Bolter's Grand-daughter* (Oxford, 2001), p. 13. 'What one did', Jonathan Gathorne-Hardy to the author. Janetta's comment on her first wedding is recorded in Frances Partridge, *A Pacifist's War* (1978), p. 90. 'I *like* things to be difficult', Quennell, *The Wanton Chase*, p. 34.

For the historical background to the rise of the Lost Girl, see Linda Simon, *Lost Girls: The Invention of the Flapper* (2017). W. N. P. Barbellion quote from *The Journal of a Disappointed Man* (new edition, 2017), p. 25. Anthony Powell remembers Vivienne Haigh-Wood in *Journals 1982–1986* (1995), p. 230. On Violet Pakenham's early life, Hilary Spurling, *Anthony Powell: Dancing to the Music of Time* (2017), pp. 180–4. For the Bright Young People, D. J. Taylor, *Bright Young People: The Rise and Fall of a Generation 1918–1940* (2007).

Julian Maclaren-Ross's description of Connolly at Lansdowne Terrace appears in *Memoirs of the Forties* (new edition, Harmondsworth, 1985), pp. 55–80. On Connolly generally, see David Pryce-Jones (ed.), *Cyril Connolly: Journal and Memoir* (1983), Michael Shelden,

Friends of Promise: Cyril Connolly and the World of Horizon (1989), Clive Fisher, *Cyril Connolly: A Nostalgic Life* (1995) and Jeremy Lewis, *Cyril Connolly: A Life* (1997). For Spender's mixed feelings, Stephen Spender, *New Selected Journals*, edited by Lara Feigel, John Sutherland and Natasha Spender (2012), pp. 740–1. 'Quick under the fat', Alan Pryce-Jones, *Devoid of Shyness: From the Journals 1926–1939* (York, 2015), p. 194.

On Connolly's relations with women, Diana Witherby's memory of his cruelty is taken from Spender, *New Selected Journals*, p. 385. Her undated letter to Janetta was probably sent in the early part of 1945 [Parladé]. 'I shall never believe in women again', quoted in Fisher, *Cyril Connolly*, p. 208. Quennell's recollections can be found in *The Wanton Chase*, p. 22. 'Most lovely company', Janetta to the author. Anna Kavan's memories are taken from two letters to her lover Ian Hamilton, dated 8 April 1943 and 2 December 1943, now in the Alexander Turnbull Library, National Library of New Zealand, Auckland. For his 'enjoyment' of romantic complications, Shelden, *Friends of Promise*, p. 147. Spender's memory of the flight to Brussels, *New Selected Journals*, p. 165.

'Is that the tug', quoted in Anthony Powell, *To Keep the Ball Rolling: The Memoirs of Anthony Powell: Volume I: Infants of the Spring* (1976), p. 120. For the conversation with Lord Jessel, Sarah Gibb to the author. On Connolly's pre-*Horizon* career, see Fisher, *Cyril Connolly*, and Lewis, *Cyril Connolly*, *passim*. 'About the only novel-reviewer in England who does not make me sick', Orwell, review of *The Rock Pool*, *New English Weekly* (23 July 1936), reprinted in George Orwell, *The Complete Works: Volume X: A Kind of Compulsion: 1903–1936*, edited by Peter Davison (1998), pp. 491–3. Auden's praise for *Enemies of Promise* is quoted in Fisher, *Cyril Connolly*, p. 171. The letter to Jean about Diana from July 1939 is quoted in Shelden, *Friends of Promise*, p. 27.

2. 'The Little Girl Who Makes Everyone's Heart Beat Faster'

For Spender's reflections on Janetta in the 1930s, see *New Selected Journals*, pp. 587–8. David Garnett's account of meeting her in 1945 is recorded in Frances Partridge, *Everything to Lose: Diaries 1945–1960* (1985), p. 14. Gerald Brenan quote taken from Jonathan Gathorne-Hardy, *Gerald Brenan: The Interior Castle* (1992), p. 297. Topolski's memories of her are included in his *Fourteen Letters* (1988), unpaginated. For Patrick Leigh Fermor's account, see Adam Sisman (ed.), *More Dashing: Further Letters of Patrick Leigh Fermor* (2018), pp. 281–2. On her appearance in old age, Sarah Gibb to the author. For Barbara's attempts to 'appear more naked', Wishart, *High Diver*, p. 149.

On the Woolley family background, Simon Courtauld, *As I Was Going to St Ives: A Life of Derek Jackson* (2007), pp. 111–12, Angela Culme-Seymour, *Bolter's Grand-daughter*, *passim*, G. H. Woolley, *Sometimes a Soldier* (1963). 'Young, good-looking and unsophisticated', Culme-Seymour, *Bolter's Grand-daughter*, p. 5. 'I knew my mother had taken out an insurance policy', Janetta to the author. For Frances and Ralph Partridge's meeting with Jan and her children in Spain, Chisholm, *Frances Partridge*, p. 167.

For the Nationalist assault on Málaga, see Gathorne-Hardy, *Gerald Brenan*, pp. 303–4; *The Times* (19, 20, 22, 25 and 27 May 1936). 'My mother was apparently a sort of relation of the Governor', Janetta to the author. On Frances's 'quasi-parental love', Chisholm, *Frances Partridge*, p. 170. Gerald Brenan quote, Gathorne-Hardy, *Gerald Brenan*, p. 317. Anne Chisholm provides a detailed account of the ski-ing trip to the French Alps, *Frances Partridge*, pp. 177–9.

Accounts of the summer 1939 excursion to France can be found in Lewis, *Cyril Connolly*, pp. 318–20, and Fisher, *Cyril Connolly*, pp. 176–7. Jean Connolly's letter is quoted in Fisher, *Cyril Connolly*, p. 176. For Waugh's view of *The Unquiet Grave*, see Evelyn Waugh, *The Diaries of Evelyn Waugh*, edited by Michael Davie (1976). Janetta's recollections are taken from an unpublished memoir [Parladé].

Quennell remembers the holiday trip with Connolly and Janetta in *The Wanton Chase*, pp. 11–12. 'An extremely nice relationship', Janetta to the author. The details of Janetta's relationship with Hugh Slater are taken from her unpublished memoir. 'I'm so glad yr with Hugh', letter from Jan Woolley, September 1939 [Parladé].

For Peter Watson, see Adrian Clark and Jeremy Dronfield, *Queer Saint: The Cultured Life of Peter Watson, Who Shook Twentieth Century Art and Shocked High Society* (2015). The Spender quote is from *New Selected Journals*, p. 224. 'Really wonderful', Janetta to the author. On the beginnings of *Horizon*, Shelden, *Friends of Promise, passim*. 'Talking for hours', Janetta to the author.

3. When the Going was Good: Lys, Connolly and *Horizon* 1939–45

'Freud' is included in Gavin Ewart, *Collected Poems* (1991), pp. 427–8. 'He still seems to be on my trail', Lys, undated letter to Connolly, probably from late 1940 [Connolly]. The ancestry of the Dunlap family can be traced via http://www.mydunlap.net. For details of Lys's early life, see Shelden, *Friends of Promise*, pp. 69–71.

On *Horizon*'s founding, Shelden, *Friends of Promise*, pp. 37–41. 'I am editing a paper', letter to Alan Pryce-Jones [Yale]. 'The blackout is really formidable', Waugh, *Diaries*, p. 446. 'This Haunted House', letter to Alan Pryce-Jones [Yale]. For the magazine's debut and reception, D. J. Taylor, *The Prose Factory: Literary Life in England Since 1918* (2016), pp. 208–9. Watson's letter about Orwell and 'Boys' Weeklies', quoted in Fisher, *Cyril Connolly*, p. 194. Waugh's letter to Connolly, dated 29 September 1961, is included in Evelyn Waugh, *The Letters of Evelyn Waugh*, edited by Mark Amory (1980), p. 578.

For Frances Partridge's 'resentment' and Julia Strachey's complaint about the 'High Priest of Smarty Literature', Partridge, *Everything to Lose*, pp. 136 and 82. Powell writes about Connolly's unsuitability for 'smart' life in *Journals 1982–1986*, p. 200. On the incident involving the dead duck, Duff Hart-Davis, *Peter Fleming: A Biography* (1974), p. 320.

The account of Diana's editorial work on *Horizon* is taken from Shelden, *Friends of Promise*, p. 51, as is Jean's letter about the cottage in the country. 'It is beginning to sink in', quoted in Fisher, *Cyril Connolly*, p. 201. 'Darling, darling heart', quoted in Shelden, *Friends of Promise*, p. 53; details of the stay at Thurlestone Sands, pp. 54–5. 'On the 16th the lease is up' and 'Our office has been bombed', undated letters from Watson to Cecil Beaton [Beaton].

For the lunch party at Lansdowne Terrace, see John Sutherland, *Stephen Spender: The Authorised Biography* (2004), p. 275. 'Ian has been shouting & screaming at me all morning', Lys, undated letter to Connolly, late 1940 [Connolly]. 'I have the Paget twins' house', letter of 11 March 1941 to Alan Pryce-Jones [Yale]. Details of the move to Drayton Gardens are taken from a letter from Lys to Michael Shelden, 8 November 1984, kindly supplied by the recipient. 'People say she is dull', quoted in Anthony Powell, *Journals 1987–1989* (1996), pp. 217–18. 'As soon as Cyril decided he wanted something', Michael Shelden, 'Broken Reel: Lys Lubbock and Cyril Connolly', *London Magazine* (June/July 1993), pp. 33–43. On the *ménage* at Drayton Gardens, Quennell, *The Wanton Chase*, p. 21; Lys, letter to Michael Shelden, 'Broken Reel'.

For Waugh on Connolly's lunch parties, see the letter to Laura Waugh of 19 September 1943, Waugh, *Letters*, p. 169, and the letter to Lady Dorothy Lygon of 23 March 1944, p. 182.

The two Quennell letters – to Barbara – are dated, respectively 4 September 1943 and 20 May 1944 [Skelton]. Diana's letter to her brother about the flat in Bedford Square is quoted in Shelden, *Friends of Promise*, p. 95. For Lys on Connolly's contentment while working on *The Unquiet Grave*, undated letter on *Horizon* notepaper, probably written towards the end of 1950 [Connolly]. Quennell's letter to Barbara about 'SECRET WEAPON WEEK' is dated 20 June 1944 [Skelton]. His description of Connolly and Lys taking refuge in their shelter was sent on 22 July 1944 [Skelton].

Waugh's comments about *The Unquiet Grave*, Waugh, *Diaries*, p. 608. For Lady Diana Cooper's remarks on Connolly's visit to Paris, Evelyn Waugh and Diana Cooper, *Mr Wu and Mrs Stitch: The Letters of Evelyn Waugh and Diana Cooper*, edited by Artemis Cooper (1991), p. 116. 'It is not the Paris we knew', quoted in Shelden, *Friends of Promise*, p. 122. Diana's comments on his letter to Lys are in an undated letter to Janetta [Parladé]. Quennell writes about Connolly's boredom in a letter to Barbara, 15 November 1944 [Skelton].

Interlude: Mapping the Forties Scene

For the responses to Virginia Woolf's WEA lecture, Adrian Wright, *John Lehmann: A Pagan Adventure* (1998), pp. 102–4. Q. D. Leavis, 'The Background of 20th Century Letters', *Scrutiny*, no. 8 (1939), pp. 72–7. Julian Symons, quoted in Martin Green, *Children of the Sun: A Narrative of 'Decadence' in England After 1918* (1976), p. 342.

4. 'Skeltie darling . . .'

Barbara's exploits in the last week of 1941 are recounted in Barbara Skelton, *Tears Before Bedtime* (1987), pp. 40–1. References from this, and its successor *Weep No More* (1989), are taken from the joint edition of 1993 with continuous pagination. For her early life, see *Tears*, pp. 1–13. 'Her attachments being multifarious and multiple', Topolski, *Fourteen Letters*. Michael Wishart remembers her 'tantalising quality' in *High Diver*, p. 149. On her pre-war trip to India, Skelton, *Tears*, pp. 14–19. For Quennell on 'the story of the young man who stowed away', *The Wanton Chase*, p. 35; 'temporary resting places', p. 38.

Barbara remembers her early wartime life in *Tears*, pp. 25–8. For her state of mind in early 1941, diary entries of 6 January, 23 January, 25 January and 14 February [Skelton]. Topolski's account of their relationship appears in *Fourteen Letters*. For Quennell's memory of their first meeting and the description of Barbara's appearance,

The Wanton Chase, p. 20. Barbara on Quennell's 'Byronic attitudes', Skelton, *Tears*, p. 31; 'What a messy existence!', p. 34. 'Gloomy gloomy', diary entry of 7 November 1941; 'ridiculous events of last night', undated letter from Quennell [Skelton]. 'What an insufferably suspicious nature!', Skelton, *Tears*, p. 38.

'It's glamorous to be left-wing these days', Skelton, *Tears*, p. 35. 'I'm sorry, I confused you with my friend', Topolski, *Fourteen Letters*. For Quennell's memory of her walking shirtless through the corn, *The Wanton Chase*, p. 38; on her knack of distinguishing her lovers' weaknesses, p. 41. Both quotations following taken from letters in the Skelton collection. 'My darling Skeltie', letter of 2 May 1942, and subsequent Quennell letters [all Skelton]; 'Found half a Hovis', Skelton, *Tears*, p. 46. Quennell letter sent on 1 January 1943 [Skelton].

'That girl he's got up there', Janetta to the author. On her meetings with Connolly on the stairs, 20 January 1943 [Skelton]. For Barbara's stay with Topolski and her decision to leave him, diary, 7 January 1943 [Skelton].For the reunion with Quennell, *The Wanton Chase*, pp. 32–3; 'Telephonings and more telephonings', p. 39. 'For the 100th time', letter dated 14 May 1943 [Skelton]. 'Is baby pleased to see Peter?', Skelton, *Tears*, p. 51.

Interlude: Glur

Most of the detail is taken from the *Daily Telegraph* obituary (20 February 2000) and a conversation with Sarah Gibb. See also Peregrine Worsthorne, *Tricks of Memory: An Autobiography* (1993). The two Quennell letters are dated 2 May 1942 and 25 January 1944 [Skelton], to the second of which the note that 'Glurky has got her Absolute' is appended.

5. Struggling to Go Beyond Herself: Sonia 1918–45

A copy of Sonia's letter to Spender about the proposed 'Young English Painters' number of *Horizon* is in the Orwell Archive. For Spender's view of Sonia, *New Selected Journals*, p. 586. 'Innate rebarbative ways', Kenneth Sinclair-Loutit, *Very Little Luggage* (privately printed, 2017), p. 144.

An account of Sonia's early life can be found in Spurling, *The Girl from the Fiction Department, passim*. The references to her 'Jesuitical' upbringing are taken from a review of Roger Peyrefitte's *Les amitiés particulières*, which appeared in the July 1946 edition of *Horizon*. 'Work was her substitute for faith', Spurling, *The Girl from the Fiction Department*, p. 15. For the Neuchatel tragedy, *The Times* (23 May 1936). The letter describing the Brownell family Christmas was sent to Janetta on 1 January 1945 [Parladé].

On her relations with Konovalov and Vinaver, Spurling, *The Girl from the Fiction Department*, pp. 21–8. For the Euston Road School, see Bruce Laughton, *The Euston Road School: A Study in Objective Painting* (Aldershot, 1986). 'Euston Road painting', Martin Gayford, *Modernists & Mavericks: Bacon, Freud, Hockney & the London Painters* (2018), p. 50. 'With a round Renoir face', Spender, *New Selected Journals*, p. 586. 'The Euston Road Venus', Spurling, *The Girl from the Fiction Department*, pp. 32–3.

'You can't think how lovely it was' and the two following quotations are taken from a letter to William Coldstream of 18 November 1939 [Tate]. 'It was lovely at Liverpool Street', letter of 9 December 1939 [Tate]. The following quotations describing her weekend with 'Stephen, Humphrey and Cuthbert', the tea-party with Spender, her concern for Coldstream's welfare, her anxieties about his life in Dover and the work of the Mobile First Aid Unit are taken from undated letters in the Tate Archive.

'Last night the big raid on London', 'I had rather a gay weekend', quotations from letters of 31 August 1940 and 17 September 1940; Connolly's possible visit to the country with Diana, letter of 20 September 1940; 'I read detective stories all day long', letter of 30

September 1940; the letters mentioning the prospect of a part-time job at *Horizon* and the account of the All Clear going off are all undated [all Tate].

For the suggestion that Sonia's life in 1942 was 'still concentrated on Coldstream', Sinclair-Loutit, *Very Little Luggage*, p. 144. On her time working for Lehmann, Wright, *John Lehmann*, p. 141. The *Horizon* helper who remembered her 'sitting at Cyril's feet' was Liza Mann, see Fisher, *Cyril Connolly*, p. 218. 'No one could enter more enthusiastically', Spender, quoted in Fisher, *Cyril Connolly*, p. 218. Both the letters describing Connolly's home life were sent to Janetta and are undated [Parladé]. Michael Shelden discusses the significance of 'Happy Deathbeds' in *Friends of Promise*, p. 77. 'A freshness of complexion and a Renoir-ish buxom mien', Sinclair-Loutit, *Very Little Luggage*, p. 144. Connolly's postcard from Cornwall is in the Orwell Archive, as is the letter dated 13 April 1944 asking Sonia to add a paragraph to *The Unquiet Grave*. Sonia's opinion of 'Palinurus' is expressed in an undated letter to Janetta [Parladé].

Interlude: Angela

The principal source for Angela's career is her autobiography, *Bolter's Grand-daughter*. James Lees-Milne quotes are from his *Fourteen Friends* (1996), pp. 112–14. 'A wonderfully beautiful girl', Courtauld, *As I Was Going to St Ives*, p. 127; 'They sleep together', p. 127. Angela's letter to Janetta, dated 18 July 1944, is in the Parladé collection, as is the letter to Janetta from her father dated 17 February 1945.

6. Blinding Impulsions: Janetta 1940–5

Kenneth Sinclair-Loutit remembers meeting Janetta for the first time in *Very Little Luggage*, pp. 129–30. 'You came to London, you lived with Sinclair-Loutit', Diana Witherby, undated letter to Janetta, early 1945 [Parladé]. Details of Janetta's relationship with Hugh Slater in the first year of the war are taken from her unpublished memoir. Orwell's *New Statesman and Nation* review of *Home Guard For Victory!* can be found in George Orwell, *The Complete Works: Volume XII: A Patriot After All: 1940–1941*, edited by Peter Davison (1998), pp. 317–19; the *Horizon* review and the Home Guard lecture notes, pp. 439–41 and 329–40.

The date of Janetta's marriage is inscribed on the inside front cover of her 1941 diary, from which each of the following quotations is taken, except 'not an easy man to talk to', which is extracted from her unpublished memoir. For Frances's account of her relationship with Hugh Slater, Partridge, *A Pacifist's War*, pp. 63, 90; on Rollo, pp. 65 and 68. 'Someone of whom I am fonder of and more closely linked', Chisholm, *Frances Partridge*, p. 187. The closing stages of Janetta's relationship with Slater are described in her unpublished memoir. 'The slight veil', Partridge, *A Pacifist's War*, p. 129; 'her new friend Kenneth', pp. 129 and 134.

For Janetta and Kenneth's life together, Sinclair-Loutit, *Very Little Luggage*, pp. 131–2, and Janetta's unpublished memoir. The trip to the Plaistow printing office is described by Janetta and in Paul Willetts, *Fear and Loathing in Fitzrovia* (revised edition, Stockport, 2005), p. 98. For Orwell's 'As I Please' column, see George Orwell, *The Complete Works Volume XVIII: Smothered Under Journalism: 1946*, edited by Peter Davison (1998), pp. 509–512. 'I went to Islington', Janetta to the author. For Frances Partridge's account of the 'lovely visit', *A Pacifist's War*, p. 149; on Jan Woolley's return to England, pp. 131, 133, 142, and Janetta's unpublished memoir.

On Rollo's death and its aftermath, Partridge, *A Pacifist's War*, pp. 155–6; on Jan's death, p. 159, and Janetta's unpublished memoir. 'Rollo you will get over', Cyril Connolly, undated letter to Janetta [Parladé]. 'Rather off-hand way', Partridge, *A Pacifist's War*, p. 164. 'A nice elegant birth certificate', Sinclair-Loutit, *Very Little Luggage*, p. 134; on their life in London 1942–3 and the encounter with Lucian Freud, pp. 132–4, 143–4 and 154–5; for Janetta's 'admirable mastery of the small things', p. 134. Janetta on Connolly's jeering attitude, unpublished memoir. The three Sinclair-Loutit quotes that follow are from *Very Little Luggage*, pp. 134–5.

'A perverse reversal of all our priorities', Sinclair-Loutit, *Very Little Luggage*, p. 138. Janetta's reaction is recorded in her unpublished memoir. 'Janetta and family are here' and following, Partridge, *A Pacifist's War*, p. 182. On the Partridges' 'pacifist anathema' and Sinclair-Loutit's arrival in Newquay, Sinclair-Loutit, *Very Little Luggage*, p. 141. The letter sent to Janetta shortly before his embarkation is undated [Parladé].

For life in Cairo, Sinclair-Loutit's relations with Topolski and his letters home, *Very Little Luggage*, pp. 165 and 173. 'I can feel your warmth + kindness', letter to Janetta, 18 August 1944 [Parladé]. On Janetta's visit to Ham Spray in early September, Partridge, *A Pacifist's War*, p. 195; 'Thought a good deal about the passing of youth', p. 199.

'I am afraid that by now', undated letter from Diana Witherby; the second letter was probably sent in early 1945; 'Oh darling Wolfers', undated letter, sent at the end of September; Sonia's letter about Arthur Calder-Marshall is undated, as are Diana's remarks about the 'old boy' finding a way [all Parladé]. For the Christmas spent at Ham Spray, Partridge, *A Pacifist's War*, p. 205. Janetta, letter to Sonia dated 10 January 1945 [Orwell Archive].

'Things have looked up quite a bit here', letter of 15 January 1945; 'Dear Wolfers . . . I am determined', letter of 1 March 1945 [both Parladé]. On Frances Partridge's opposition, Sinclair-Loutit, *Very Little Luggage*, p. 186; for the circumstances of his leave, p. 186. 'I no longer loved him', Janetta, unpublished memoir. Janetta's letter to Frances Partridge about the VE Night celebrations is quoted in Partridge, *A Pacifist's War*, p. 214. For Frances's impression of Sussex Place, Partridge, *Everything to Lose*. Evelyn Waugh's letter to Patrick Balfour is reproduced in Courtauld, *As I Was Going to St Ives*, p. 114. Janetta writes about the origin of 'Mrs Bluefeet' in her unpublished memoir. Matthew Connolly's remarks are reproduced in Shelden, *Friends of Promise*, p. 136. For Janetta's seeing 'no solution' of her difficulties and the arrival of Robert Kee, Partridge, *Everything to Lose*, pp. 19 and 20; 'Kenneth is suggesting', p. 22.

For Sinclair-Loutit's realisation that 'something is the matter', Partridge, *Everything to Lose*, pp. 27–8; on the visit to Sussex Place and the 'useless, awful letter', p. 31. The end of the relationship is described in Partridge, *Everything to Lose*, pp. 38–41, and Sinclair-Loutit, *Very Little Luggage*, pp. 216–19, from which all quotations are taken. Nancy Mitford's description of 'the final Bluefeet parting' is in Nancy Mitford and Evelyn Waugh, *The Letters of Nancy Mitford and Evelyn Waugh*, edited by Charlotte Mosley (1996), p. 23.

Interlude: Anna

For Anna's life and quotes, Jeremy Reed, *A Stranger on Earth: The Life and Work of Anna Kavan* (2006). The letter to Connolly from Torquay is in the Connolly Collection, University of Tulsa, Oklahoma.

7. Cairo Nights: Barbara 1943–4

For accounts of Barbara's trip to the Middle East, see Skelton, *Tears*, pp. 52–9, and Barbara Skelton, *A Young Girl's Touch* (1956), pp. 61–91. Quennell's letter was sent on 22 July 1943 [Skelton].

On Cairo in the autumn of 1943, Artemis Cooper, *Cairo in the War: 1939–1945* (1989), *passim*. 'Such a country', quoted in Cooper, *Cairo in the War*, p. 79; 'The war is non-existent', p. 250. PC Boot's letter is reproduced in Skelton, *Tears*, p. 61. 'Your letter – posted at Sierra Leone – has arrived', letter from Quennell dated 19 August 1943; 'Use it or not as you're inclined' and subsequent quotation, letter dated 3 September 1943 [both Skelton]. For Barbara's life in Cairo, and 'a very long time since I heard from you', letter dated 1 December 1943, Skelton, *Tears*, pp. 59–65. PC Boot's letter from

Topolski's studio, 27 November 1943 [Skelton].

'My darling Skeltie', letter from Quennell dated 29 January 1944 [Skelton]. Topolski remembers his visit in *Fourteen Letters*. 'We were told we all had to sleep', Skelton, *Tears*, p. 64. For details of Farouk's palace, Skelton, *A Young Girl's Touch*, pp. 122–3.

'Did I tell you that little Lys', letter from Quennell dated 24 May 1944; 'I was delighted', letter from Quennell dated 20 June 1944 [both Skelton]. 'Did it mean Farouk', Topolski, *Fourteen Letters*. For the 'hostile atmosphere', Skelton, *A Young Girl's Touch*, p. 172. The two Sinclair-Loutit letters to Janetta are dated 17 and 27 August 1944 [Parladé]. Barbara describes her departure from Cairo in Skelton, *Tears*, pp. 65–6. 'I was in a sensitive position,' William Stadiem, *Too Rich: The High Life and Tragic Death of King Farouk* (1991), p. 79. Interviewed by Stadiem sometime in the late 1980s, Barbara provided a frank account of her relationship with Farouk, in which she remembered that, though emphatically 'her type', he was 'really more woman than man'. Their sexual encounters, she recalled, 'gave me no pleasure whatever'. For some reason most of these reminiscences were removed from the UK edition of her book, published a year later.

Interlude: Joan

Simon Fenwick, *Joan: The Remarkable Life of Joan Leigh Fermor* (2017), for the life of Joan and quotes. For Driberg's account of the American trip of 1937, Fenwick, *Joan*, pp. 8–9. Lees-Milne quote taken from Michael Bloch, *James Lees-Milne: The Life* (2009), p. 81. 'I can't complain', Fenwick, *Joan*, pp. 138–9.

8. Ways and Means: Lost Girl Style

For Quennell on Barbara's dress styles, *The Wanton Chase*, p. 41. Topolski remembers Janetta's 'overhanging' hair in *Fourteen Letters*. Evelyn Waugh's fictional account of the *Horizon* staff can be found in his *Unconditional Surrender* (new edition, Harmondsworth, 1964), p. 40. On Lost Girl physique, Spender, *New Selected Journals*; p. 586, Woodrow Wyatt, *Confessions of an Optimist* (1985), pp. 89–90. For Barbara and the vial of 'Soir de Paris', Skelton, *Tears*, p. 53. On Janetta's 'new look', Mitford and Waugh, *Letters*, p. 97. Frances Partridge quotes, *Everything to Lose*, pp. 91 and 135.

On Barbara's 'flat, monotonous drawl', Wishart, *High Diver*, p. 149. 'Madly dangerous', Janetta, diary entry, January 1941 [Parladé]. 'Desperately depressed/dejected', Barbara, diary entries of 23 January 1941 and 26 January 1945 [Skelton]. 'A touch of commonness', Wishart, *High Diver*, p. 149. Angela remembers the evening in 1942 in *Bolter's Grand-daughter*, p. 127. 'It isn't his trying to rape me', Spurling, *The Girl from the Fiction Department*, p. 52. Sonia's letter to Theodore Roethke is quoted in Shelden, *Friends of Promise*, p. 156. 'Thank you very much for having us to stay', undated letter from Barbara to Lady Violet Powell, early 1950s [Powell].

For the atmosphere of the Jamboree, Quennell, *The Wanton Chase*, p. 25. On the Gargoyle Club during the war, Michael Luke, *David Tennant and the Gargoyle Years* (1991), *passim*; the roll-call of 'Members and Frequenters' includes Barbara, Janetta, Glur, Topolski, Anthony and Violet Powell, Ralph and Frances Partridge, Orwell, Connolly and Spender, pp. 84–5. The photograph of Glur talking to Lady Julia Mount is reproduced in Ferdinand Mount, *Cold Cream: My Early Life and Other Mistakes* (2008), p. 57. Anna Kavan's letter to Ian Hamilton describing the weekend at Tickerage was sent on 24 February 1944 (Auckland).

Barbara describes the Chelsea party in Skelton, *A Young Girl's Touch*, pp. 40–5. 'I'm sorry I haven't written', Sonia, letter to William Coldstream, 17 September 1940 [Tate]. For Penelope Fitzgerald's career during the early part of the war, see her novel *Human Voices* (1980) and Hermione Lee, *Penelope Fitzgerald: A Life* (2013), ch. 4. 'People don't realise' and 'People behaved very differently', Janetta to the author. On Mary Wesley's wartime exploits, Mary Wesley and

Eric Siepmann, *'Darling Poll': The Letters of Mary Wesley and Eric Siepmann: 1944–1967*, edited by Patrick Marnham (2017), *passim*. For Frances Partridge on Janetta's view of contemporary morality, *A Pacifist's War*, p. 196.

'Whenever things were hard', see Spurling, *The Girl from the Fiction Department*, p. 64. 'I just saw her as a man with breasts', Naim Attallah, *Of a Certain Age* (London, 1992), p. 283. Janetta's remark about Barbara and Sonia's lives going 'as they wanted them to' was made to the author. 'They felt you had to have a man', Sarah Gibb to the author. 'I absolutely agree with what you say about name & marriage', Diana Witherby, undated letter to Janetta, early 1945 [Parladé].

For Brian Howard's suggestion of marriage, see Marie-Jaqueline Lancaster, *Brian Howard: Portrait of a Failure* (2005), p. 251. Waugh remembers the *Horizon* circle in a letter to Connolly from 29 October 1961, Waugh, *Letters*, p. 578. On Sonia's fondness for using French words in conversation, Wyatt, *Confessions of an Optimist*, p. 89. 'My mother's circle', Nicky Loutit, *New Year's Day Is Black* (Norwich, 2016), unpaginated. For Waugh on Connolly and the 'Communist young ladies', Mitford and Waugh, *Letters*, p. 14. Frances Partridge quote from *A Pacifist's War*, p. 149. The account of Lys 'twittering dutifully' is taken from a letter from Quennell to Barbara, 15 November 1944 [Skelton]. 'He was very sweet with Lys', Skelton, *Tears*, p. 40. 'Lys is very pretty', Partridge, *Everything to Lose*, p. 50. Jeremy Lewis writes about Barbara's 'outsider' status in 'Battling with Barbara', *Grub Street Irregular: Scenes from Literary Life* (2008), p. 185. For the weekend with the Campbells, Frances Partridge, *Everything to Lose*, p. 191. For Barbara's account, Skelton, *Tears*, pp. 181–3.

Interlude: On Not Being Boring

Richard Pares, quoted in Richard Ollard, *A Man of Contradictions: A*

Life of A. L. Rowse (1999), p. 71. 'The only thing that concerned him', Jonathan Gathorne-Hardy, *Half an Arch: a Memoir* (2004), p. 244. Laura Waugh, quoted in Martin Stannard, *Evelyn Waugh: No Abiding City: 1939–1966* (1992), p. 478.

9. Sussex Place: Connolly, Lys, Janetta and Others 1945–9

For life at Sussex Place, see Shelden, *Friends of Promise*, Lewis, *Cyril Connolly*, Fisher, *Cyril Connolly*, *passim*. The Evelyn Waugh quote is taken from his *Diaries*, p. 681. 'I don't think we can possibly publish it as it stands', letter to Alan Pryce-Jones dated 30 September 1946 [Yale]. For Connolly on the trip to Paris, Fisher, *Cyril Connolly*, p. 257. Of the three Watson letters to Cecil Beaton quoted here, the first and third are undated; the second was sent on 13 October 1945 [Beaton].

'I really can't bear being away from you for so long', quoted in Shelden, *Friends of Promise*, p. 138; 'Did not ask you to divorce me', p. 147. Watson's letter to Beaton is dated 7 April 1946 [Beaton]. 'Have you heard about', Mitford and Waugh, *Letters*, p. 29. For Frances Partridge on Janetta and Robert Kee, *Everything to Lose*, p. 48. 'Cyril was the king' and three subsequent quotes, Loutit, *New Year's Day Is Black*. Janetta's remarks about Robert Kee no longer resenting the idea of Nicky's existence are taken from her unpublished memoir. 'Seventy years later', Nicky Loutit to the author. 'I simply couldn't bear', Loutit, *New Year's Day Is Black*. 'It is clear from her letters', Partridge, *Everything to Lose*, p. 128.

For the Ham Spray visit of July 1946, Partridge, *Everything to Lose*, p. 53, and Loutit, *New Year's Day Is Black*. 'We should have been very happy', Janetta, unpublished memoir. Topolski remembers his affair with Janetta in *Fourteen Letters*. Details of Janetta's affair with the sailor are taken from her unpublished memoir. 'It's a long time', Partridge, *Everything to Lose*, p. 70; for the Kee wedding and the subsequent descriptions of Connolly and Lys, pp. 64, 75 and 78.

'I am told he is now at work', Waugh and Cooper, *Mr Wu and Mrs Stitch*, p. 130. 'S Boots Connolly has fled the country', Mitford and Waugh, *Letters*, p. 62. 'When he travelled', letters from Lys dated 22 and 27 November 1946 [Connolly]. The following Mitford quotes are from Mitford and Waugh, *Letters*, pp. 72 and 75.

'I see Cyril's boom fading', Waugh, *Diaries*, p. 694. For Cass Canfield's report on Connolly's plans, Shelden, *Friends of Promise*, pp. 173–4. Lys's letter to the sanatorium at Tring is undated [Connolly]. 'Cyril has had an apoplectic seizure', Mitford and Waugh, *Letters*, p. 89. The letter about wishing to get Lys as a cook was sent to John Betjeman, Waugh, *Letters*, p. 270. 'Awful about Smarty's stroke', Mitford and Waugh, *Letters*, p. 91. 'But for you I would have no eyes', quoted in Shelden, *Friends of Promise*, p. 193. On the move to Bedford Square, Lys, letter to Michael Shelden, 8 November 1984, kindly supplied by the recipient. Sonia's letter about the 'sad and bedraggled sparrow', sent to Waldemar Hansen on 27 December 1948, is quoted in Shelden, *Friends of Promise*, p. 206. For Lys and the wedding ring, Fisher, *Cyril Connolly*, p. 280.

Connolly's undated letters to Sonia from the Villa Mauresque are in the Orwell Archive. For the trip to France with Joan Rayner, see Fenwick, *Joan*, pp. 166–9. Connolly's letter to his mother about his inability to leave Lys is quoted in Shelden, *Friends of Promise*, p. 201. 'I may stay at Sussex Place', quoted in Fenwick, *Joan*, p. 178. Brian Howard's letter about the visit to Sussex Place is in the Orwell Archive.

Connolly's letter accusing Lys of 'playing about' with his desertion complex is quoted in Shelden, *Friends of Promise*, p. 214. The Evelyn Waugh letter can be found in Mitford and Waugh, *Letters*, p. 131. Watson, 'A rather terrible showdown', quoted in Shelden, *Friends of Promise*, p. 216. Clive Fisher discusses the attempts to sell *Horizon* or appoint a new editor in the autumn of 1949 in *Cyril Connolly*, p. 285. Watson, 'the most dishonest series of reasons', quoted in Clark and Dronfield, *Queer Saint*, p. 278. The

Connolly quote about the closure of the *Horizon* office is taken from the introduction to Cyril Connolly, *Ideas and Places* (London, 1953). 'Please forgive me for going away', undated letter from Lys [Connolly]. For Nancy's letter of 9 June 1947 ('I love Lys'), Mitford and Waugh, *Letters*, p. 132. On Nicky Loutit's visits to Connolly's room, Shelden, *Friends of Promise*, p. 215.

Interlude: Office Life

Janetta's recollections of *Horizon* are taken from her unpublished memoir. Maclaren-Ross, 'the folder with my stories', *Memoirs of the Forties*, p. 64. For Natasha Litvin's memory of Lansdowne Terrace, see Sutherland, *Stephen Spender*, pp. 275–6. Anna Kavan, postcard to Peter Davies, 27 December 1943 (private collection). Lys Lubbock quotes taken from Shelden, 'Broken Reel'. Angus Wilson, quoted in Fisher, *Cyril Connolly*, p. 279. Anna Kavan, letter to Ian Hamilton, 24 February 1944 (Auckland). Evelyn Waugh letter to Nancy Mitford, Mitford and Waugh, *Letters*, p. 149.

10. The Man in the Hospital Bed: Sonia 1945–50

For Sinclair-Loutit's account of his last meeting with Sonia, *Very Little Luggage*, p. 144. She 'couldn't not have come across him', Celia Paget to the author. Sonia's memory of her first meeting with Orwell is quoted in Shelden, *Friends of Promise*, p. 159. Michael Sayers to the author. Tosco Fyvel remembers the domestic arrangements at Canonbury Square in *George Orwell: A Personal Memoir* (1982), pp. 147–8. 'Cabbage and unwashed nappies', quoted in Shelden, *Friends of Promise*, p. 160. Orwell's letter to Anne Popham is included in Orwell, *The Complete Works: Volume XVIII*, p. 153.

'Fuck the war', Connolly, undated letter to Janetta [Parladé]. 'I was rather sad to hear you're coming back so soon', quoted in Shelden, *Friends of Promise*, p. 161. 'Established poets would send in stuff', Francis

Wyndham to the author. The two undated Connolly letters from 1946 and 1948 are both in the Orwell Archive. 'No news from Cyril', Peter Watson, letter to Sonia, 9 February 1947, and the letters sent from Jamaica and Sicily, the second dated 21 August 1947 [all Orwell Archive]. Of the following quotations, the first is from the letter dated 21 August 1947, the second from another letter sent on the same day, and the third from a letter sent on 24 August 1947 [all Orwell Archive].

'Is your stocking size 9½?', undated letter from Peter Watson [Orwell Archive]. For Sonia and Hansen's friendship and Hansen's letter to John Myers, dated 1 July 1947, see Clark and Dronfied, *Queer Saint, passim*.

For Sonia's romantic life in the mid-1940s, Spurling, *The Girl from the Fiction Department*, p. 65; the suggestion that Lucian Freud was the father of her unborn child was made by Lys [information supplied by Michael Shelden]; on her involvement with Merleau-Ponty, pp. 73–91. The letter beginning 'Dear Sonia Brownell' is in the Orwell Archive. 'I never longed for anything', quoted in Spurling, *The Girl from the Fiction Department*, p. 84. 'I terribly want to write to you this evening' [Orwell Archive]. 'If you're madly in love', quoted in Spurling, *The Girl from the Fiction Department*, p. 81. The telegram sent on 23 December 1947 is in the Orwell Archive.

Orwell's letter of 12 April 1947 from Jura is reproduced in George Orwell, *The Complete Works: Volume XIX: It Is What I Think: 1947–1948*, edited by Peter Davison (1998), pp. 122–4. The friend who thought her an 'uneasy partner' was Sinclair-Loutit, *Very Little Luggage*, p. 144. 'As she may have told you', George Orwell, *The Complete Works: Volume XX: Our Job Is to Make Life Worth Living: 1949–50*, edited by Peter Davison (1998), pp. 116–17; letter to David Astor, pp. 147–8. 'You must learn to make dumplings', Spurling, *The Girl from the Fiction Department*, p. 96. 'Sonia lives only a few minutes away', Orwell, *The Complete Works: Volume XX* , p. 165; the *Star*'s report, pp. 169–70; letter to Richard Rees, pp. 168–9.

For the reactions of Orwell's friends to his marriage, see D. J.

Taylor, *Orwell: The Life* (2003), p. 413. Powell recalls his first meeting with Sonia in John Saumarez Smith and Jonathan Kooperstein (eds), *The Acceptance of Absurdity: Anthony Powell and Robert Vanderbilt: Letters 1952–1956* (2011), p. 45. 'Somehow she snuggled up', Wyatt, *Confessions of an Optimist*, p. 90. Copies of letters from Peter Watson to Waldemar Hansen and from Hansen to John Myers kindly supplied by Michael Shelden. Janetta's reflections are taken from her unpublished memoir. Connolly's letter to Evelyn Waugh is quoted in Fisher, *Cyril Connolly*, p. 285. 'I felt sorry for him' and 'She loved it', Janetta to the author. 'Gross mismatch', Sinclair-Loutit, *Very Little Luggage*, p. 144. Koestler's letter is reproduced in Orwell, *The Complete Works: Volume XX*, p. 329.

Most of the quotations relating to the last months of Orwell's life, his marriage to Sonia and his death are taken from Taylor, *Orwell*, pp. 414–18. Janetta's memories of the wedding ceremony are taken from her unpublished memoir [Parladé]. For Frances Partridge's comments, *Everything to Lose*, pp. 96 and 98. 'Poor George has had a relapse', Lys, letter to Connolly dated 10 November 1949 [Connolly]. Peter Watson's letter of condolence, dated 29 January 1950 [Orwell Archive].

Interlude: Sonia's Things

All the artefacts referred to here are in the Orwell Archive.

11. The Destructive Element: Barbara, Connolly and Others 1944–51

Topolski reflects on his relationship with Barbara in Luke, *David Tennant*, pp. 184–6. For Barbara's travels in 1944–5, Skelton, *Tears*, pp. 69–74. 'Turned out', diary, 2 July 1945 [Skelton]. Topolski's letter c/o John Davenport is dated 9 January 1946; 'Your Sydney St abode', letter from Gerda Treat, dated 24 February 1946 [both Skelton].

'Went to the cottage alone', diary, 26 January 1945; the quotations that follow are taken from diary entries of 7 February, 30 April, 3 May, 4 May, 2 November and 25 February 1946 [all Skelton]. Letter from Poppet John, 15 September 1947 [Skelton]

The two letters from John Sutro are dated 18 July 1949 and September 1948; Gerda Treat refers to Barbara's illness in a letter of 8 August 1948; for the remark about her doctor 'professing sterility', diary entry of 4 May 1945 [all Skelton]. On her relationship with Pierre Savaigo and his eviction from Queen Street, Skelton, *Tears*, pp. 77–80. Robin Dalton recalls her encounter with Barbara in *One Leg Over*, p. 80. For the North African trip, diary entries, May 1949 [Skelton].

'Cyril was bored with Lys', Skelton, *Tears*, p. 81. For the visit to Sussex Place, the 'deflating quips' and the allotting of marks to Connolly's women friends, Skelton, *Tears*, pp. 82–3. For the weekends in Kent, and 'Talk of our living together', Skelton, *Tears*, pp. 84–5 and 88. 'B. is certainly unhappy', letter to Hamish Hamilton of 24 November 1950, quoted in Fisher, *Cyril Connolly*, p. 296. Barbara's account of the journey to France to visit Farouk, Skelton, *Tears*, 90–3. 'Don't do anything in a hurry', Lys, undated letter, late 1950 [Connolly]. For the wedding, Skelton, *Tears*, pp. 94–5. Evelyn Waugh's letter to Nancy Mitford, dated December 1950, is reproduced in Mitford and Waugh, *Letters*, p. 207. On the aftermath, Skelton, *Tears*, pp. 95–6.

'What you don't realise', Skelton, *Tears*, p. 97. 'I feel very badly', quoted in Fisher, *Cyril Connolly*, p. 296. For the Christmas and New Year of 1950–1, Skelton, *Tears*, pp. 98–9. 'I cheer myself up', Lys, undated letter, late 1950 [Connolly]. Joan's letter is quoted in Fenwick, *Joan*, p. 203. 'Had a sleepless night', Skelton, *Tears*, p. 103. 'He is in great trouble', Evelyn Waugh to Nancy Mitford, 8 April 1951, Mitford and Waugh, *Letters*, p. 221.

Interlude: Parents and Daughters

Geoffrey Woolley's letters to Janetta are in the Parladé collection. On the inscribed copy of *Winnie the Pooh*, Nicky Loutit to the author. For Jeremy Lewis's memory of meeting Barbara's sister, see 'Battling with Barbara' in *Grub Street Irregular*, pp. 182–5.

12. The Invisible Worm: Cyril and the Women

'They are grateful for the gifts', undated letter from Diana, early 1940s; 'Thank you again, dearest Cyril', undated letter from Sonia on *Horizon* notepaper, probably written in 1946–7; 'I am very glad you liked the review', undated letter from Diana, early 1940s [all Connolly].

'Have a lovely wonderful time', Sonia; 'I suggest we have a kind of upstairs sit-down buffet', Lys, postcard dated 14 January 1947; 'Harris has just had your message', Lys, letter dated 11 January 1944; 'Why don't you try Mr Neal for fibrositis?', undated letter sent from 9 Paultons Square, early 1951(?) [all Connolly]. Further quotes in the remainder of the chapter from Lys and Diana's letters are from undated correspondence in the Connolly collection.

'It is quite understandable that you should prefer Jean's assets', undated letter from Diana, early 1940s; 'It is unreasonable', undated letter sent from 18 Percy Street, sometime in 1950; 'I now see that I set myself an impossible task', undated letter from Lys, 1950; 'It is wrong of you', undated letter from Lys sent from Paultons Square [all Connolly].

'I do think it's very important whom you marry', undated letter on *Horizon* notepaper, 1950; 'I will always fall short', undated letter from Diana, early 1940s; 'You must not forget that I tried really hard', undated letter sent from Orthez, probably in April 1950; 'I know I shall never find anybody else like you again', letter sent from 18 Percy Street; 'I have no wish for revenge'; 'It is because I am convinced'; 'You are the only person', undated letter from Orthez [all Connolly].

13. Projections: The Lost Girls in Fiction

Barbara Skelton, undated letters to Anthony Powell [Powell]. Powell writes about the identification of Barbara with Pamela Flitton in *Journals 1987–1989* (1996), pp. 44 and 50, and *Journals 1990–1992* (1997), p. 219. For details of the writing of *A Room in Chelsea Square*, see Gregory Woods, introduction to the 2014 reissue. The letter of 29 October 1961 in which Evelyn Waugh claims to be 'greatly annoyed' about comparisons between *Horizon* and *Survival* is reproduced in Waugh, *Letters*, p. 578.

For Waugh's comments on *The Ruthless Innocent*, see Mitford and Waugh, *Letters*, pp. 94 and 196.

On Barbara's conviction that she 'is' Pamela, Powell, *Journals 1987–1989*, p. 50.

Hilary Spurling writes about Sonia's influence on Julia in *Nineteen Eighty-Four* in *The Girl from the Fiction Department*, *passim*; for her comments on Orwell's determination to 'take her as his model', p. 67; on the *Horizon* review of Peyrefitte's *Les amitiés particulières*, pp. 67–9. Orwell's letter to George Woodcock can be found in Orwell, *The Complete Works: Volume XVIII*, p. 373. The review of Harold Laski's *Faith, Reason and Civilisation*, rejected by the *Manchester Evenings News*, is included in George Orwell, *The Complete Works: Volume XVI: I Have Tried to Tell the Truth: 1943–1944*, edited by Peter Davison (1998), pp. 122–4.

Interlude: Barbara's Style

'As with so many female writers', Powell, *Journals 1987–1989*, p. 216. For the libel proceedings against *A Love Match*, *Daily Mail* (29 October 1971). Waugh's comments were made in a *Sunday Telegraph* review of Nancy Mitford's *The Water Beetle* (1962), reprinted in Evelyn Waugh, *The Essays, Articles and Reviews of Evelyn Waugh*, edited by Donat Gallagher (Harmondsworth, 1986), pp. 600–1.

14. Afterwards

Peter Watson, letter to Lys, 26 April 1950, kindly supplied to the author by Michael Shelden. Lys's letter to Sonia, dated 2 April 1950 is in the Orwell Archive, as is Peter's letter, 'Cyril asked me', his letter to Sonia dated 4 May 1950 ('she will spend so much money'). 'Lys has been adopted', Evelyn Waugh to Nancy Mitford, 10 April 1951, Mitford and Waugh, *Letters*, p. 221. The Connolly letter from 1953 is quoted in Shelden, 'Broken Reel'.

Waugh writes about the 'very happy day in London' to Nancy Mitford, Mitford and Waugh, *Letters*, p. 336. For Spender on the Kochs' visit to London, *New Selected Journals*, pp. 296–7. Michael Shelden's visit to Lys in 1984 and their subsequent contacts, 'Broken Reel', *passim*.

Frances Partridge's account of the Kees' visit to Ham Spray can be found in *Everything to Lose*, p. 115. For Derek Jackson, Courtauld, *As I Was Going to St Ives*. See also 'Derek Jackson: Off the Radar', Ferdinand Mount's *London Review of Books* review, reprinted in his *English Voices: Lives, Landscapes, Laments* (2016), pp. 70–8. On Jackson's near-lynching, David Pryce-Jones to the author. 'She hoped never to return to married life', Partridge, *Everything to Lose*, p. 124; subsequent quotations, pp. 133, 135, 136. For Janetta's desertion by Jackson, Courtauld, *As I Was Going to St Ives*, pp. 130–1.

Janetta's affair with Koestler is described in Michael Scammell, *Koestler: The Indispensable Intellectual* (2009), pp. 421–3. For Nicky's re-encounter with Jackson, Loutit, *New Year's Day Is Black*. Frances Partridge on her first meetings with Jaime Parladé, *Everything to Lose*, pp. 272 and 275. On Janetta's marriage and her later life, see Paul Levy's *Independent* obituary (4 July 2018). James Lees-Milne records his impressions of Alcuzcuz in *Ceaseless Turmoil, Diaries 1988–1992* (2004), pp. 192–3.

For Orwell's funeral, Taylor, *Orwell*, pp. 7–9. On Sonia's later life and Ivy Compton-Burnett's comment, Spurling, *The Girl from the*

Fiction Department, passim. Frances Partridge's account of the evening in 1965 is in *Other People: Diaries 1963–1966* (1993), p. 186. Sonia's letter to Janetta outlining her financial and other problems is dated 2 November 1979; Janetta's reflections on Sonia's death are taken from a diary entry of 12 December 1980 [both Parladé].

'His Animal has been sacked from the zoo', Evelyn Waugh to Nancy Mitford, Mitford and Waugh, *Letters*, p. 336. 'People literally hiding in cupboards in hotels', Janetta to the author. 'The situation is getting more insoluble', Skelton, *Tears*, p. 213. Connolly's letter from Saint-Tropez is in the Orwell Archive. 'One glance' and subsequent quotations, Wishart, *High Diver*, pp. 149–50. For the encounter on Bob Silvers's yacht, Alan Bennett to the author. On the visit to Warhol's studio, Skelton, *Tears*, p. 325; 'It was not for love', p. 328; 'I cannot recall the menu', p. 360. For Barbara's later years, Lewis, 'Battling with Barbara', in *Grub Street Irregular*, pp. 164–99.

Angela describes her later life in *Bolter's Grand-daughter, passim.* See also Courtauld, *As I Was Going to St Ives.* For Glur, Sarah Gibb to the author and *Daily Telegraph* obituary (20 February 2000). For Joan Leigh Fermor, see Fenwick, *Joan.* 'Cyril exaggeratedly well-mannered', Skelton, *Tears*, pp. 126–7. On Anna Kavan, Reed, *A Stranger on Earth.* Evelyn Waugh's letter to Diana Mosley, Waugh, *Letters*, p. 639.

For Quennell at the hairdresser's, Anthony Powell, *Journals 1990–1992* (1997), p. 133. Topolski's later career is described in *Fourteen Letters.* Evelyn Waugh's *Tablet* review of Spender's autobiography can be found in Waugh, *The Essays*, pp. 394–8. For Spender's later life, see Sutherland, *Stephen Spender.* On Sinclair-Loutit, *Very Little Luggage, passim.* For Brian Howard, Lancaster, *Brian Howard.* Julian Maclaren-Ross, Willetts, *Fear and Loathing in Fitzrovia.* Barbara describes her final meeting with Farouk in Skelton, *Tears*, pp. 203–6. On Peter Watson's last years, Clark and Dronfield, *Queer Saint.* Connolly's tribute is reproduced in Skelton, *Tears*, p. 218. The extract from Howard's letter is in Lancaster, *Brian Howard*, p. 546.

Spender's diary for December 1951, quoted in Fisher, *Cyril Connolly*, p. 299. The quotations following are from Lewis, *Cyril Connolly*, pp. 487, 492, 495 and 500.

Finale: The Last Lost Girl

All Connolly quotes taken from undated letters, probably written between 1944 and 1945, (private collection).

A Selection of Lost Girl Literature

Patrick Balfour, *Ruthless Innocent* (1950).
Elizabeth Bowen, *The Death of the Heart* (1938).
Gavin Ewart, 'Freud', in *Collected Poems* (1991).
Julian Maclaren-Ross, 'Five Finger Exercise', in Julian Maclaren-Ross, *Selected Short Stories*, edited by Paul Willetts (Stockport, 2004).
Nancy Mitford, *The Blessing* (1951).
Michael Nelson, *A Room in Chelsea Square* (1958).
George Orwell, *Nineteen Eighty-Four* (1949).
Anthony Powell, *The Military Philosophers* (1968).
Anthony Powell, *Books Do Furnish a Room* (1971).
Anthony Powell, *Temporary Kings* (1973).
Barbara Skelton, *A Young Girl's Touch* (1956).
Barbara Skelton, *Born Losers* (1965).
Barbara Skelton, *A Love Match* (1969).
Barbara Skelton, *Tears Before Bedtime* (1987).
Barbara Skelton, *Weep No More* (1989).
Evelyn Waugh, *Men at Arms* (1952).
Evelyn Waugh, *Officers and Gentlemen* (1955).
Evelyn Waugh, *Unconditional Surrender* (1961).
Diana Witherby, *Collected Poems* (1973).

Acknowledgements

I owe a particular debt of gratitude to the various copyright holders who allowed me to reproduce previously unpublished material. Cyril Connolly's letters are reproduced with the kind permission of Rogers, Coleridge & White and Mrs Deirdre Levi. I should like to thank Nicky Loutit, who kindly allowed me to print extracts from letters sent by her father, the late Kenneth Sinclair-Loutit; Georgie Kee, who allowed me to print extracts from the diaries and letters of her mother, the late Janetta Parladé, and her grandfather, the late G. H. Woolley; the Orwell Estate, in the person of Bill Hamilton of A. M. Heath Ltd, who performed a similar service with regard to material held in the Orwell Archive at University College London and at the Tate; Mrs Sarah Gibb, who generously permitted me to quote from letters written by her father, the late Peter Quennell; Cressida Connolly for allowing me to examine Barbara's diaries and Professor Michael Shelden for allowing me to make use of letters from the late Waldemar Hansen. Peter Watson's letters are reproduced with the kind permission of his family. For permission to reproduce part of a letter from Angela Culme-Seymour to Janetta, I am grateful to Jonny Culme-Seymour. Extracts from Anna Kavan's letters are reproduced with the kind permission of David Higham Associates.

I should also like to thank several professional colleagues with specialist knowledge of the period for their unstinting help. Pride of place must go to Barbara Skelton's hospitable biographer Graham Page, who generously supplied me with copies of Barbara's letters from Peter Quennell, Feliks Topolski and other friends. Professor Michael Shelden was a mine of information and supplied me with several valuable pieces of material to which I would not otherwise have had access. I should also like to thank Dr Victoria Walker for sharing details of her research into the life of Anna Kavan.

Among those directly connected to the Lost Girls or their circle, I should like to thank Janetta's daughters, Nicky Loutit and Georgie Kee, for allowing me to consult their mother's papers and contributing recollections of her, and Sarah Gibb for supplying details about her mother, Glur Dyson Taylor. Cressida Connolly was an indefatigable source of information and encouragement.

Among the institutions where I undertook research, I should like to thank Gill Furlong and her successor Sarah Aitchison of the Special Collections department at University College London, the staff of Tate Archive and Kathryn McKee of the Special Collections Archive, St John's College Cambridge.

Part of Chapter 4 originally appeared in a centenary tribute to Barbara printed in the *Guardian Saturday Review*. I should like to thank the editors for permission to reprint this material.

Warm thanks are also extended to Mark Amory, Ariane Bankes, Anne Chisholm, Matthew Connolly, Artemis Cooper, Simon Courtauld, Jonny Culme-Seymour, Mark Everett, Jonny Gathorne-Hardy, Geordie Greig, Henry Layte, Imogen Lees, Petra Lewis, Alasdair Nagle, the late Janetta Parladé, John Powell, David Sinclair-Loutit, Alexander Waugh and Paul Willetts. I am, as usual, indebted to the superlative editorial advice of Andreas Campomar, Claire Chesser and Howard Watson. Love and thanks, as ever, to Rachel Felix, Benjy and Leo.

The late Jeremy Lewis took an unflagging interest in the early stages of the project and supplied innumerable pieces of good advice. I hope that he might have approved the end result.

Index